VB-MAPP

*Verbal Behavior Milestones
Assessment and Placement Program*

Second Edition

GUIDE

A Language and Social Skills Assessment Program
for Children with Autism or Other Intellectual Disabilities

Mark L. Sundberg, Ph.D., BCBA-D

2014

AVB Press
Advancements in Verbal Behavior

www.avbpress.com

VB-MAPP, Verbal Behavior Milestones Assessment and Placement Program: Guide - 2nd ed.
Copyright 2007-2018, Mark L. Sundberg, Ph.D., BCBA-D

EESA, Early Echoic Skills Assessment
Copyright 2007-2018, Barbara E. Esch, Ph.D., BCBA-D, CCC-SLP

Library of Congress Control Number: 2010549765

ISBN #978-0-9818356-6-2
10 9 8 7 6 5 4 3

AVB Press
Advancements in Verbal Behavior

www.avbpress.com

TABLE OF CONTENTS

ACKNOWLEDGEMENTS

B. F. Skinner's groundbreaking analysis of human behavior (1953) and language (1957) has stood the test of time. Of the many theories of human learning and language, Skinner's has led to the most effective methods for the assessment and treatment of children and adults with autism or other intellectual disabilities. The application of Skinner's analysis of verbal behavior (1957) to language assessment contained in the VB-MAPP represents the efforts of many people over the past 50 years. Dr. Jack Michael has led the way as the consummate teacher of Skinner's analysis, and as the visionary for its many applications. I thank Jack for being my teacher and mentor.

Dr. Joseph Spradlin was the first to apply Skinner's analysis of verbal behavior to language assessment for the intellectually disabled. He created the Parsons Language Sample (Spradlin, 1963) and inspired others to join him in his effort to use Skinner's analysis for language assessment. The current program is firmly rooted in Dr. Spradlin's pioneering work.

The VB-MAPP spans a 40-year history of research and development. My first version of a verbal behavior assessment program was developed at The Kalamazoo Valley Multihandicap Center (KVMC) during the 1970s, while I was one of Jack Michael's graduate students at Western Michigan University. I would like to acknowledge the many staff members of KVMC who participated in the over 50 verbal behavior research projects conducted at KVMC during that period. I would especially like to acknowledge my co-authors on the 1979 version of the verbal behavior assessment and intervention program, David A. Ray, Dr. Steven J. Braam, Mark W. Stafford, Thomas M. Rueber, and Dr. Cassandra Braam. I thank Dr. Jerry Shook, the former Director of KVMC, for his help and support; Dr. Louise Kent for teaching me about language from a Speech Pathologist's point of view; and Dr. Norm Peterson and Dr. Scott Wood who always left me with more to think about. I would also like to acknowledge Dr. A. Charles Catania and Dr. Ernie Vargas for editing various versions of this material, and Dr. James W. Partington and Dr. Mary Ann Powers for their contributions to the 1998 ABLLS version of the assessment program. Also, I would like to acknowledge the staff members of the former STARS School for their research assistance and feedback through the years, and thank the children and parents who have taught me many valuable lessons.

The VB-MAPP has benefited from the input of behavior analysts, speech pathologists, occupational therapists, special education teachers, psychologists, and parents of children with special needs. I have appreciated their many suggestions for improvement and hope they will be pleased with this content that they have helped to shape. I'd like to especially thank those who have worked with me in public school classrooms during the last few years; Dr. Mary Ann Powers, Rikki Roden, Kaisa Weathers, Shannon Rosenhan, Shannon Montano, and Eileen Cristobal-Rodriguez.

The VB-MAPP is conceptually a better learning, language, and social skills assessment program because of the valuable field-testing and feedback from several groups in the United States and Canada. I'd like to thank Dr. Carl Sundberg, Michael Miklos, Dr. William Galbraith, Dr. Anne Cummings, Dr. Rebecca Godfrey, and Brenda Terzich for sharing their time, resources, and expertise. Also, I'd like to thank Lisa Hale, Cindy Sundberg, and Dr. Carl Sundberg for their field-testing with a wide range of typically developing children. The results of this field-testing have provided important new information about various aspects of language acquisition and social behavior.

I'd like to offer a special thanks to Dr. Barbara E. Esch, CCC-SLP, for her willingness to include her Early Echoic Skills Assessment (EESA) as a subtest of the VB-MAPP, and for her many suggestions for the program as both a Speech and Language Pathologist and a Behavior Analyst trained under Dr. Jack Michael.

The fields of behavior analysis, linguistics, and developmental psychology are filled with giants, many whose work is cited throughout this guide. I would like to particularly acknowledge Dr. Douglas Greer for moving the application of verbal behavior forward through his extensive research program at Columbia University Teachers College. I'd also like to acknowledge Dr. Vince Carbone and Dr. Patrick McGreevy for the growth and interest in verbal behavior that has been generated by their work.

I thank Steve Payne and Patricia E. Young for skillfully and artistically transforming my VB-MAPP beta versions to the current color-coded typeset version. I also want to thank my sons John and Dan for their help with the VB-MAPP. And last, but never least, I thank my wife Cindy for her unwavering support and for her many contributions to the VB-MAPP, and editing countless versions of this material over the past 30 years.

The second edition of the VB-MAPP Guide contains a number of updates and improvements. Several changes have been made to improve the tool by clarifying the targeted skills, elaborating on the instructions, scoring process, and placement content, adding new references, and making other adjustments designed to increase scorer reliability. Additionally, efforts have been made to help the assessor gain a better understanding of some of the conceptual and applied issues regarding the use of Skinner's (1957) analysis of verbal behavior as a guide for language assessment and intervention. There have been several changes in the milestones since the publication of the original VB-MAPP in 2008. Specifically, there are two new milestones (Social Behavior and Social Play 1-M and LRFFC 9-M) and changes in 13 other milestones. A listing of the milestone changes can be found at **www.avbpress.com/downloads**. Some of these milestone changes have already been included in previous re-printings of the Protocol and Guide. In addition, 61 changes have been made in the 1 and ½ point scoring criteria for the milestones. Also, the instructions for the Task Analysis section include a clearer distinction between tasks that are earlier steps toward a milestone, and those that are independent of the specific milestone, but are "supporting skills." The changes and improvements in the VB-MAPP are the result of feedback from the users of the system, along with a variety of field-testing activities. I thank all of those who have provided me with feedback and edits over the years, especially Dr. Rebecca Godfrey and Cindy Sundberg.

Mark L. Sundberg
May, 2016

CHAPTER 1

A Behavioral Approach to Language Assessment

The Verbal Behavior Milestones Assessment and Placement Program (VB-MAPP) presented in this Guide and the accompanying Protocol is based on B.F. Skinner's *Verbal Behavior* (1957), a landmark analysis in the study of language. Skinner's book provides a comprehensible and sensible approach to language that is derived from the solid empirical foundation of learning principles, and has stood the test of time (Andresen, 1990; Schlinger, 2008). In addition to Skinner's study of language, his groundbreaking work in behavioral psychology and learning led to the professional field known as applied behavior analysis (Cooper, Heron, & Heward, 2007; Morris, Smith, & Altus, 2005; Skinner, 1953).

Applied behavior analysis (ABA) has provided many successful applications to the learning and language problems faced by children with autism or other intellectual disabilities (e.g., Guess & Baer, 1973; Halle, Marshall, & Spradlin, 1979; Koegel & Koegel, 1995; Krantz & McClannahan, 1993; Leaf & McEachin, 1998; Lovaas, 1977, 2003; Maurice, Green, & Luce, 1996; Wolf, Risley, & Mees, 1964). The VB-MAPP brings together the procedures and teaching methodology of ABA and Skinner's analysis of verbal behavior in an effort to provide a behaviorally based language assessment program for all children[1] with language delays.

About the VB-MAPP

There are five components of the VB-MAPP presented in this Guide. The first is the **VB-MAPP Milestones Assessment,** which is designed to provide a representative sample of a child's existing verbal and related skills. The assessment contains 170 measurable learning and language milestones that are sequenced and balanced across three language development age levels (0-18 months, 18-30 months, and 30-48 months). The skills assessed include mand, tact, echoic, intraverbal, listener, motor imitation, independent play, social and social play, visual perceptual and matching-to-sample, linguistic structure, group and classroom skills, and early academics. Included in the Milestones Assessment is the Early Echoic Skills Assessment (EESA) subtest developed by Barbara E. Esch, Ph.D., CCC-SLP, BCBA-D.

The second component is the **VB-MAPP Barriers Assessment,** which provides an assessment of 24 common learning and language acquisition barriers faced by children with autism or other developmental disabilities. The barriers include behavior problems, instructional control, impaired mands, impaired tacts, impaired echoic, impaired imitation, impaired visual perception and matching-to-sample, impaired listener skills, impaired intraverbal, impaired social skills, prompt dependency, scrolling, impaired scanning, impaired conditional discriminations, failure to generalize, weak

---

[1] The VB-MAPP can be used for any individual with significant language delays regardless of age. Several items need to be modified or dropped for older persons (e.g., some of the early skills in the play area, such as cause and effect play), but the core language and social skills remain the same. For ease of reading, "child" and "children" will be used throughout the manual.

motivators, response requirement weakens the motivators, reinforcer dependency, self-stimulation, impaired articulation, obsessive-compulsive behavior, hyperactive behavior, failure to make eye contact, and sensory defensiveness. By identifying these barriers, the clinician can develop specific intervention strategies to help overcome these problems, which can lead to more effective learning.

The third component is the **VB-MAPP Transition Assessment**, which contains 18 assessment areas and can help to identify whether a child is making meaningful progress and has acquired the skills necessary for learning in a less restrictive educational environment. This assessment tool can provide a measurable way for a child's individualized education program (IEP) team to make decisions and set priorities in order to meet the child's educational needs. The assessment is comprised of several summary measures from other parts of the VB-MAPP, as well as a variety of other skills that can affect transition. The assessment includes measures of the overall score on the VB-MAPP Milestones Assessment, the overall score on the VB-MAPP Barriers Assessment, negative behaviors, classroom routines and group skills, social skills, academic independence, generalization, variation of reinforcers, rate of skill acquisition, retention, natural environment learning, transfer skills, adaptability to change, spontaneity, independent play, general self-help, toileting skills, and eating skills.

The fourth component is the **VB-MAPP Task Analysis and Supporting Skills**, which provides a further breakdown of the skills, and serves as a more complete and ongoing learning and language skills curriculum guide. There are approximately 750 skills presented covering 14 domains of the VB-MAPP. Once the milestones have been assessed and the general skill level has been established, the task analysis and supporting skills can provide further direction for a particular child. There are two types of skills included in this section of the VB-MAPP. The task analysis skills can be identified as those that are directly related to the target milestone and represent earlier steps in reaching that milestone. The supporting skills contains a large number of language, learning, and social skills that a child needs to acquire in addition to the specific milestones. These skills may not be significant enough to identify as milestones or IEP goals, but each of them play an important role in moving a child's repertoire closer to that of a typically developing child. They also provide parents and teachers with a variety of activities that can facilitate generalization, maintenance, spontaneity, retention, expansion, and the functional use of skills in a variety of educational and social contexts.

The task analysis of the learning and language skills contained in the VB-MAPP presents an updated sequence of the verbal behavior curriculum that is developmentally balanced. Collectively, these four components of the VB-MAPP represent over 40 years of research, clinical work, field-testing, and revisions by the author and colleagues (Partington & Sundberg, 1998; Sundberg, 1980, 1983, 1987, 1990; Sundberg & Michael, 2001; Sundberg & Partington, 1998; Sundberg, Ray, Braam, Stafford, Rueber, & Braam, 1979).

The fifth and final component is the **VB-MAPP Placement and IEP Goals**, which correspond with the four assessments above. The placement guide provides specific direction for each of the 170 milestones in the Milestones Assessment as well as suggestions for IEP goals. The placement recommendations can help the program designer balance out an intervention program, and ensure that all the relevant parts of the necessary intervention are included.

Research Using the VB-MAPP

The VB-MAPP is designed to be an empirical measure of a child's language and social skills, and has been used for that purpose in several different published research studies (e.g., Grannan, & Rehfeldt, 2012; Gunby, Carr, & LeBlanc, 2010; Kaitlin et al., 2013; Lepper, Petursdottir, & Esch, 2013; Lorah et al., 2013; Vandbakk et al., 2012; Watts et al., 2013). It also can be used for purposes of providing outcome data on participants' progress with any type of language intervention program (e.g., Dipuglia & Miklos, 2014, May; Sundberg, Hall, & Elia, 2014, May). Additional studies that have used the VB-MAPP in research can be found on the FAQs page at www.avbpress.com.

The Importance of Assessment

The primary purpose of an assessment is to identify the baseline level of a child's skills, and to compare it to those of his[2] typically developing peers. If an intervention program is warranted, the data from the assessment should provide the essential information for determining the basic elements of an IEP and a language curriculum. The assessment should provide guidance in terms of (1) what skills need to be the focus of the intervention (2), what level of the skill should the intervention program begin with, (3) what barriers to learning and language acquisition need to be addressed (e.g., non-compliant behaviors, echolalia, failure to generalize), (4) what type of augmentative communication, if any, might be best for a child, (5) what specific teaching strategies might be the most effective for the child (e.g., discrete trial training, natural environment training), and (6) what type of educational setting might best meet the child's needs (e.g., in-home, 1:1 classroom, small group, or full inclusion).

In order to obtain the maximum benefit from the VB-MAPP, it is essential that the assessor have a basic understanding of the principles of behavior analysis and Skinner's analysis of verbal behavior. It is beyond the scope of the current Guide to provide an overview of behavior analysis and the reader is referred to the many texts on this topic (e.g., Cooper, Heron, & Heward, 2007; Malott & Trojan, 2008; Martin & Pear, 2003; Miltenberger, 2004; Vargas, 2009). However, this chapter will provide a brief overview of Skinner's analysis of verbal behavior and how to use it to assess a child's language and related skills (for more detail on Skinner's analysis and its applications to education and special education, the reader is referred to Sundberg, 2007 and Vargas, 2009).

Skinner's Analysis of Verbal Behavior

Skinner (1957) proposed that language is learned behavior, and that the same basic principles of behavior that constitute the foundation of applied behavior analysis apply to verbal behavior. According to Skinner (1957), humans acquire their ability to talk and understand language much in the same way that they learn other behaviors such as reaching, grasping, crawling, and walking. The motor behavior involved in vocal cord movement gets shaped by the effects those movements produce on others (including the infant himself). A baby cries and adults attend to (i.e., reinforce) the child in various ways. Crying thus gradually becomes a form of social communication (for a more complete analysis see Bijou & Baer, 1965). Language has special properties in that it involves a social interaction between speakers (those doing the talking) and listeners (those responding to the speaker).

The Term "Verbal Behavior"

In searching for a name for his analysis of language, Skinner chose the term "verbal behavior" because he found the term "speech" too limiting (e.g., gestures can be communicative), and the term "language" too general (e.g., the practices of a whole community of speakers as in the "English langauge"). Thus, he chose "verbal behavior" and his usage of this term includes all forms of communication such as sign langauge, icon exchange (e.g., PECS), written language, gestures, or any other form that communicative responses might take. And, the focus is on individual speakers and listeners rather than the practice of a whole language community (e.g., speakers of English rather than the linguistic rules of English).

---

[2] For ease of reading, the male gender is used as a pronoun for the child being assessed throughout the VB-MAPP.

The Distinction Between the Speaker and Listener

A major theme in *Verbal Behavior* is Skinner's clear distinction between the behavior of the speaker and the behavior of the listener. In contrast with most traditional approaches, Skinner is primarily concerned with the behavior of the speaker (the person doing the talking), but does not neglect the listener. He recommends against the use of the terms "expressive language" and "receptive language," as a way to distinguish between the speaker and listener, because of the implication that these two types of "language" are merely different manifestations of the same underlying cognitive processes (Skinner, 1957, pp. 2-7). It is important to teach a child to both react to a speaker, and to behave verbally as a speaker himself, but these are different skills. In most cases, learning one type of behavior facilitates learning another, but this is not always the case, especially for children with language delays.

Form and Function

Perhaps one of the most commonly misunderstood aspects of Skinner's analysis of verbal behavior is the view that he completely rejects traditional structural linguistics, and the classification system of nouns, verbs, prepositions, adjectives, etc. This is not the case. His position is that in addition to identifying the topography or structure of emitted words and phrases, there must be an accounting of what causes the emission of those words. This is where the contention lies. The causes of language are typically attributed to an assumed cognitive processing system (e.g., metaphors of coding, decoding, storage), or genetically inherited biological structures, rather than to environmental variables. However, the description of language, as it occurs in structural linguistics, is still an essential part of measuring and studying language. These two aspects of language are often described as the formal and functional properties of language (Catania, 1972, 1998; Skinner, 1957). The formal properties involve the structure or topography of the verbal response (i.e., the specific words and phrases emitted), while the functional properties involve the causes of the verbal response (i.e., why those specific words were emitted). A complete account of language must consider both of these separate elements. Skinner (1957) states that:

> Our first responsibility is simple *description*: what is the topography of this subdivision of human behavior? Once that question has been answered in at least a preliminary fashion we may advance to the stage called *explanation*: what conditions are relevant to the occurrences of the behavior—what are the variables of which it is a function? (p. 10)

The field of structural linguistics specializes in the description of language (the formal properties). The topography of what is said can be measured by (1) phonemes: the individual speech sounds that comprise a word, (2) morphemes: the units "with an individual piece of meaning," (3) lexicon: the total collection of words that make up a given language, (4) syntax: the organization of words, phrases, or clauses into sentences, (5) grammar: adherence to established conventions of a given language, and (6) semantics: what words "mean."

The formal description of a language also involves classifying words as nouns (persons, places, or things), verbs (actions), prepositions (spatial relations between things), adjectives (properties of objects), adverbs (properties of verbs or adjectives), pronouns (words that stand for nouns), conjunctions (words that join noun or verb phrases), and articles (modifiers of nouns). There are many other aspects of a formal description of language, such as prepositional phrases, clauses, gerunds, tense markers, particles, predicates, as well as articulation, prosody, intonation, pitch, and emphasis (e.g., Barry, 1998). Sentences are then made up of the syntactical arrangement of the lexical categories of speech with adherence to the grammatical conventions of a given verbal community.

Most commonly used language assessments for children with autism or other intellectual disabilities assess only the formal properties of language (Esch, LaLonde, & Esch, 2010), while neglecting the functional properties, despite recommendations from within the field of Speech-Language Pathology to include function along with form (Hegde, 2010).

A Functional Analysis of Verbal Behavior

Skinner's (1957) main premise in *Verbal Behavior* is that language is learned behavior with the primary cause being the same types of environmental variables that cause non-language behavior (i.e., stimulus control (S^D), motivating operations (MOs), reinforcement, extinction, etc.). In Chapter 1 of *Verbal Behavior*, Skinner presents what he identifies as a "functional analysis of verbal behavior." The functional analysis is quite similar to a descriptive and/or functional analysis commonly used in the treatment of behavior problems (e.g., Iwata, Dorsey, Slifer, Bauman, & Richman, 1994; Neef & Peterson, 2007). The first eight chapters of Skinner's book define a functional analysis of verbal behavior and what he calls the "basic elementary verbal operants" (see below). The remainder of the book contains detailed analyses of how these elementary operants constitute the components of more complex language, such as thinking, problem solving, memory, syntax, grammar, literature, self-editing, composition, and scientific verbal behavior.

The Unit of Analysis

The question of how to measure language is an important issue when assessing a child's language skills, as well as developing intervention programs. The traditional method of measuring language consists of recording the formal properties of language as described above (e.g., nouns, verbs, sentence length, vocabulary size, etc.). The unit of analysis in a behavioral analysis of language is both the formal and the functional properties of an utterance, that is, the basic antecedent-behavior-consequence framework (Table 1-1). Skinner refers to this unit as a "verbal operant," and he refers to a set of operants in a particular individual as a "verbal repertoire" (1957, pp. 19-22).

Table 1-1
The traditional and the behavioral unit of analysis.

Traditional Unit of Analysis
The formal properties of the response:
Words, phrases, sentences, mean length of utterances (MLU)

Behavioral Unit of Analysis
The formal properties of the response in the context of the functional properties
(the antecedents and consequences)
Antecedent ⟶ Response ⟶ Consequence
The Elementary Verbal Operants

The Elementary Verbal Operants

Skinner suggests that a complete language repertoire is composed of several different types of speaker and listener behavior. At the core of Skinner's functional analysis of speaker behavior is the distinction between the **mand**, **tact**, and **intraverbal**. These three types of verbal behavior are traditionally all classified as "expressive language." Skinner suggests that this practice masks important distinctions between these functionally independent types of language. In addition to these three elementary verbal operants, Skinner (1957) also presents the **echoic**, **textual**, **transcriptive**, and **copying-a-text** relations. See Table 1-2 for a general description of each verbal operant (including the listener), and the material below for a more detailed treatment of each language skill.

Table 1-2
General descriptions of the elementary verbal operants.

Mand	Asking for reinforcers that you want. Asking for shoes because you want your shoes to go outside. Mands can also be emitted to remove undesireable items or activities (e.g., "Stop it!").
Tact	Naming or identifying objects, actions, events, etc. Saying "shoes" because you see your shoes.
Intraverbal	Answering questions or having conversations where your words are controlled by other words. Saying, "shoes" because someone else says, "What do you wear on your feet?"
Listener	Following instructions or complying with the mands of others. Getting one's shoes when told, "Get your shoes."
Echoic	Repeating what is heard. Saying "shoes" after someone else says "shoes."
Imitation	Copying someone's motor movements (as they relate to sign language). Tapping your fists together after someone else taps their fists together (the sign for "shoes").
Textual	Reading written words. Saying "shoes" because you see the written word "shoes."
Copying-a-text	Writing the word "shoes" because someone else wrote the word "shoes."
Transcription	Spelling words spoken to you. Writing "shoes" because you hear "shoes" spoken.

An Overview of the Sixteen Milestone Domains

Mand

The mand is a type of language whereby a speaker asks for (or states, demands, implies, etc.) what he needs or wants. For example, when a hungry child asks for something to eat, this type of verbal behavior would be classified as a mand. A mand can also be emitted to remove undersirable items or activities. Skinner (1957) selected the term mand because it is conveniently brief and is similar to the common English words "com**mand**," "de**mand**," "repri**mand**," and "**mand**atory." In technical terms (Skinner, 1957, pp. 35-51; Michael, 1984, 1988), the mand occurs when the form of the verbal response (i.e., what a person says) is under the functional control of MOs (i.e., what a person wants) and specific reinforcement (i.e., what a person gets). For example, food deprivation will (a) make food effective as reinforcement and (b) evoke behavior such as the mand "cookie," if this manding behavior produced cookies in the past. It is important to keep in mind that motivation can be strong or weak, learned or unlearned, to get desirable items or activities, or to get rid of undesirable items or activities. Michael (2007) used the umbrella term "motivating operations (MO)" to include all of these effects (as well as some others). For example, when motivation is strong to get or remove something this is termed an "establishing operation (EO), when the MO is weakened this is termed an "abolishing operation" (AO) (e.g., satiation). The current text will use the term MO respecting that there are varying degrees of reinforcement value (for more detail on Michael's analysis of motivation see Miguel, 2013).

The specific reinforcement that strengthens a mand is directly related to the relevant MO. For example, if a child has strong MO for being pushed on a swing, the specific reinforcement is a push by someone. The response form may occur in several topographical variations, such as gesturing, crying, pushing someone out of the way, reaching, or saying "push." All of these behaviors could be mands for being pushed on a swing if there is a functional relation between the MO, the response, and the specific reinforcement history. An important point here is that "communication" is not restricted to only words. In fact, much of the problem behaviors of children who have weak, delayed, or impaired verbal repertoires may be technically "mands" (e.g., Carr & Durand, 1985).

Mands are very important for the early development of language, and for the day-to-day verbal interactions between children and others. Mands are the first type of communication acquired by a child (Bijou & Baer, 1965; Novak, 1996). These early mands usually occur in the form of eye contact or differential crying when a child is hungry, tired, in pain, cold, afraid, or wants social attention. As a child grows, crying and eye contact can also occur as a mand for toys, help, movement of objects and people, or for the removal of aversive stimuli. Typically developing children soon learn to replace crying with words, or other standard forms of communication. Manding lets children control not only some of the delivery of reinforcers, but it begins to establish the speaker and listener roles that are essential for further verbal development.

Skinner (1957, p. 36) points out that the mand is the only type of verbal behavior that directly benefits the speaker, meaning the mand (often) gets the speaker what he wants such as edibles, toys, activities, attention, or the removal of aversive stimuli. As a result, mands can become strong forms of verbal behavior because they satisfy an immediate need experienced by the child. Young children often engage in a very high rate of manding because of these special effects. Eventually, a child learns to mand for many different reinforcers, including mands for verbal information with words like "what," "who," and "where," and the child's acquisition of new verbal behavior accelerates rapidly (Brown, Cazden, & Bellugi, 1969). Ultimately, mands become quite complex and play a critical role in social interaction, conversations, academic behavior, employment, and virtually every aspect of human behavior.

Perhaps one of the most valuable pieces of initial information about a child is the nature of his existing mand repertoire. Given the role of the mand in typical development, especially the development of language and possible negative behavior, many issues can be revealed by an analysis of a child's existing ability to mand. The assessor's task is to determine the exact nature of the child's manding skills. The most difficult part of a mand assessment is that the motivating variables that evoke the mands may not be easily accessible. For example, a child may cry when he wants attention, but it may be difficult to identify and quantify "wanting attention." Some motivators are more obvious, such as a child wanting and reaching for a certain toy. This may confirm that the motivation for the toy is strong, at least at that moment.

Mands may also be multiply controlled in that other antecedent variables might be present, such as the desired item (making the response part tact), some related verbal stimulus such as, "What do you want to eat?" (making the response part intraverbal), an echoic prompt like "say cookie" (making the response possibly more echoic than mand), or a combination of these variables. It is important that the person assessing a child's mand repertoire be able to identify and discriminate among these various sources of antecedent control. All children have basic needs that must be met, and the child must in some way communicate those needs to others. The goal of a mand assessment is to determine if the child uses words, gestures, signs, or icons to let those needs be known. The primary question is: How does the child make his needs and wants known to others? Additional questions to consider are: Does the child emit negative behaviors to get those needs met? Are the responses dependent on prompts such as echoic prompts, or yes/no answer type prompts (e.g., "Do you want a drink?")? Is there only a small number of mands that the child emits, despite him having a large number of motivators? Does it appear that the child really wants what he mands for? The answers to these questions will help establish priorities for an individualized mand intervention program.

Tact

The tact is a type of language whereby a speaker names things, actions, attributes, etc. in the immediate physical environment. The speaker has direct contact with these "nonverbal" stimuli through any of the sense modes. For example, if a child says "dog" because he sees a dog, this type of verbal behavior would be classified as a tact. Or, if a child hears a dog barking and says "dog," this too would be classified as a tact because the antecedent stimulus was nonverbal. Skinner (1957) selected the term tact because it suggests that a speaker is making contact with the physical environment. Technically, the tact is a verbal operant under the functional control of a nonverbal discriminative stimulus (S^D), and it produces generalized conditioned reinforcement. The tact relation is closely synonymous with what is commonly identified as "expressive labeling" in many language training programs for children with language delays (e.g., Lovaas, 2003).

There are many nonverbal stimuli in a child's world that he eventually must learn to tact. Caretaker's names, toys, common household objects, and children's items often make up some of the first tacts that children acquire (e.g., mama, dada, chair, table, book, shoe, car, spoon, ball, or bed). Nonverbal stimuli come in many forms. They can be, for example, static (nouns), transitory (verbs), relations between objects (prepositions), properties of objects (adjectives), or properties of actions (adverbs), and so on. Nonverbal stimuli can be as simple as a shoe or as complex as a cancerous cell. A stimulus configuration may have multiple nonverbal properties, and a response may be under the control of those multiple properties, as in the tact: "The red fire truck is under the little table." Nonverbal stimuli may be observable (e.g., a car) or unobservable (e.g., pain), subtle (e.g., a wink) or salient (e.g., neon lights), properties common to many nonverbal stimuli (e.g., size, color), and so on. Given the variation and ubiquity of nonverbal stimuli in the physical world, it is no surprise that the tact is a primary topic in the study of language (Skinner, 1957).

The tact repertoire is so significant to language development that it is often treated as the only element that needs direct training. However, a substantial body of research now exists that shows that mand and intraverbal responses may not emerge from tact-only training in early language intervention for children with language delays (for a review of the research see Sautter & LeBlanc, 2006). The goal in teaching tacting is to bring a verbal response under nonverbal stimulus control (i.e., making nonverbal stimuli S^Ds for specific words). If a child has a strong echoic repertoire, then tact training can be much easier (or a strong motor imitation repertoire for a child learning sign language). A language trainer can present a new target nonverbal stimulus (e.g., a tree) along with an echoic prompt (e.g., "say tree"), differentially reinforce a correct response, and then fade the echoic prompt. However, for some children tact training is more difficult and special procedures may be required. Once tacts are acquired, control can be transferred to a mand (e.g., asking to go climb a tree) or intraverbal (e.g., talking about climbing a tree when one is no longer present), although in some circumstances mands or intraverbals may be acquired first, and then later transferred to tact relations.

Assessing the strength of a child's tact repertoire is relatively straightforward. When presented with an item, action, property, etc., can the child provide the name of that stimulus or not? If he can, then in behavioral terminology it would be said that the particular stimulus exerts stimulus control (it is an "S^D") over the responses emitted by the child. As the stimuli become more complex (e.g., those relevant to verbs, adjectives, prepositions, conjunctions, or multiple stimuli) it is common to see stimulus control weaken at various levels of language development. The goal of this part of the assessment is to identify where nonverbal stimulus control of tacting is strong and where it begins to weaken. Once these boundaries are identified, priorities for language instruction on the tact repertoire can be established.

Intraverbal

The intraverbal is a type of language whereby a speaker verbally responds to the words of others (he also can intraverbally respond to his own words). In general, intraverbal behavior involves "talking about" things and activities that are not present. For example, saying "bus" as a result of hearing someone say "the wheels on the..." is intraverbal behavior. Answering questions like, "What did you do yesterday?" is also intraverbal behavior. Typically developing children emit a high frequency of intraverbal responses in the form of singing songs, telling stories, describing activities, explaining problems, and so on. Intraverbal responses are also important components of many normal intellectual repertoires (e.g., when asked, "What does a plant need to grow?" saying "water, soil, and sunshine," or, saying "ten" as a result of hearing "five plus five equals..."). The intraverbal repertoire is seemingly endless, exemplified by the fact that typical adults have hundreds of thousands of intraverbal connections in their language repertoires, and they may emit thousands of them every day (however many may be covert as in "thinking").

In technical terms, an intraverbal occurs when a verbal S^D evokes a verbal response that does not have point-to-point correspondence with the verbal stimulus (Skinner, 1957, pp. 71-78). No point-to-point correspondence means the verbal stimulus and the verbal response do not match each other, as they do in the echoic and textual relations (see below). Like all verbal operants (except the mand), the intraverbal produces generalized conditioned reinforcement. For example, in an educational context, the reinforcement for correct answers usually involves some form of generalized conditioned reinforcement such as hearing "right" from a teacher, receiving good grades, or the opportunity to move to the next problem or level.

An intraverbal repertoire facilitates the acquisition of other verbal and nonverbal behavior. Intraverbal behavior prepares a speaker to respond rapidly and accurately with respect to words and sentences, and plays an important role in continuing a conversation. For example, a child hears an adult say "beach" in some context. If the word "beach" evokes several other words for the child, such as "swim," "water," "sand," and "bucket," then he is better able to "understand" what the adult is talking about. One might say that the child is now "thinking" about the beach and now has relevant verbal responses at strength to talk about going to the beach.

A high percentage of children with language delays fail to acquire a functioning intraverbal repertoire. There are many causes of this, but one preventable cause is that the intraverbal relation is not typically identified or assessed as a separate verbal skill. It is often assumed that intraverbal skills, like manding, will simply develop from training on tact and listener skills. Often, by the time a child's conversational, social, and verbal skills are identified as weak or impaired, a long history of rote responding, negative behavior, failing to verbally respond to verbal stimuli, and social isolation may make it hard to develop a functional intraverbal repertoire. Typical children begin to acquire intraverbal behavior following the acquisition of solid mand, tact, and listener repertoires. For many children, the emergence of intraverbal behavior can be observed at around the age of two years old. However, many of the early intraverbal relations are quite simple, such as songs, animal sounds, and one- and two-word intraverbal associations and relations. More complex intraverbal responses such as answering multiple component questions (e.g., "Where do you live?") may not occur until around age three or four years old. It is extremely critical to identify the current nature of the child's existing intraverbal repertoire in order to design an individualized intervention program.

Differences Between the Mand, Tact, and Intraverbal

There are several important differences between the mand, tact, and intraverbal. First, the reader should note that the same word can occur as a mand, tact, or intraverbal (see Table 1-2). For example, a child can say "mommy" when he sees his mother (a tact), or say "mommy" when he wants his mother (a mand), or say "mommy" when someone says "daddy and..." (an intraverbal). Skinner's distinction between the mand, tact, and intraverbal is that the same word (response topography) can be controlled by different antecedent and consequent variables, and because a response is acquired under one type of antecedent control doesn't mean it will occur under another type of control (for a review of the empirical research supporting this independence of the verbal operants see Oah & Dickinson, 1988; Sautter & LeBlanc, 2006).

The implications of this distinction are that these three repertoires need to be individually assessed, and training may need to occur for each verbal skill as well. That is, it is a mistake to assume that if a child can tact, for example, Sponge Bob when he sees Sponge Bob, that the same child can mand for the Sponge Bob show on television when the motivational variable is present, but he does not see Sponge Bob, or intraverbally answer the question, "Who lives in a pineapple under the sea?" when Sponge Bob is not visually present. While the response "Sponge Bob" is topographically the same in all three examples, the three repertoires are functionally separate behaviors (Skinner, 1957).

People talk for a variety of reasons, but much of what people talk about is evoked by one (or more) of three major environmental variables: personal motivation (mands), elements of the physical environment (tacts), and verbal stimuli they encounter (intraverbal, echoic, textual). A conversation, for example, can involve a mix of mands, tacts, and intraverbals in the following ways: (1) a mand repertoire allows a speaker to ask questions, (2) a tact repertoire allows a speaker to talk about items or events that are physically present, and (3) an intraverbal repertoire allows a speaker to answer questions and talk about (and think about) objects and events that are not physically present. The functional analysis of these three major sources of control can be of significant value for assessment and intervention programs designed to develop language skills (there are also other skills involved in a conversation such as listener, echoic, and imitation skills). However, it is critical that a parent or professional be able to distinguish between motivating variables (that control manding) and S^Ds (that control all other language skills). In addition, it is important to be able to distinguish between nonverbal S^Ds (that control tacts) and verbal S^Ds (that control intraverbal, textual, echoic, transcription, and copying-a-text). For more information on these distinctions see Michael (2007) and Sundberg (2007).

Echoic

The echoic is a type of language whereby a speaker repeats the sounds, words, and phrases of another speaker (or himself). For example, a child who says "kitty" after hearing "kitty" spoken by his mother is demonstrating echoic behavior. Repeating the words, phrases, and other auditory verbal stimuli is common for all speakers in day-to-day discourse. Technically speaking, the echoic is controlled by a verbal S^D that matches (has point-to-point correspondence with) the response. Echoic behavior produces generalized conditioned reinforcement such as praise and attention

(Skinner, 1957, p. 56). The ability to echo the phonemes and words of others is essential for language development. A parent might say, "That's a bear! Can you say bear?" If the child can respond "bear," then the parent says "Right!" Eventually, the child learns to name (tact) a bear without the echoic prompt. This often occurs within a few trials. The echoic repertoire is very important for teaching language to children with language delays, and it serves a critical role in the process of teaching more complex verbal skills (e.g., Lovaas, 1977, 2003).

The assessment of the echoic repertoire for the VB-MAPP is accomplished with the Early Echoic Skills Assessment (EESA) subtest developed by Barbara E. Esch, Ph.D., CCC-SLP, BCBA-D. The EESA also contains a guideline for the progression of speech sounds, blends, words, and phrases acquired by typically developing children. However, for children with speech delays and articulation problems it is suggested that the services of a speech and language pathologist be obtained.

Motor Imitation

Motor imitation can have the same verbal properties as echoic behavior, as demonstrated by its role in the acquisition of sign language by children who are deaf. For example, a child may learn to imitate the sign for cracker first, and then mand for a cracker without an imitative prompt. Imitation is also critical for teaching sign language to children who can hear, but are nonvocal (Sundberg, 1980). Many children do not have an adequate echoic repertoire for vocal language instruction, and extensive time is spent on attempting to teach echoic behavior rather than more useful types of verbal behavior such as manding and tacting. A strong imitative repertoire permits a teacher to immediately use sign language to teach advanced forms of language (e.g., mands, tacts, and intraverbals). Sign language can allow a child to quickly learn to communicate with others without using inappropriate behavior (e.g., tantrums) to get what is wanted. A child's ability to imitate the motor actions of others also plays an important role in the acquisition of other behaviors such as self-care skills (see the VB-MAPP self-care checklist at www.avbpress.com/downloads), attending, classroom routines, and even echoic skills. In addition, imitation helps in the development of play and social behavior, and other types of group activities (e.g., arts and crafts, music).

The primary goal of this part of the assessment is to determine if the child can copy the motor movements of others when asked to do so. For example, if an adult claps her hands, will the child clap his hands? The child may require a verbal prompt, such as "do this," to respond, but during the assessment he should not receive any physical prompts or specific verbal prompts such as saying "clap." (Note that the presence of the specific verbal prompt makes the response actually part listener behavior; if the word is spoken, it may be difficult to then determine the relevant antecedent that evokes the response.) One outcome of this part of the assessment, along with the results of the echoic and matching-to-sample assessment, can be important information that may help determine if augmentative communication (AC) is necessary, and which form might be most appropriate for an individual child.

Textual (Reading)

Textual behavior (Skinner, 1957) is the actual skill of being able to identify what a word says, but not necessarily reading "with understanding" what is being read. Understanding what is read usually involves other verbal and nonverbal skills such as intraverbal behavior (e.g., comprehension) and listener discriminations (e.g., following instructions or compliance). For example, saying the word "book" upon seeing the written word "book" is textual behavior. Understanding that books are things to look at and read is not textual behavior, it is intraverbal behavior. Understanding is typically identified as reading comprehension. Skinner chose the term "textual" for this part of the skill because the term "reading" refers to many processes at the same time. Technically, textual behavior involves a verbal S^D and a verbal response that have point-to-point correspondence to each other, but **do not** have "formal similarity" (i.e., an exact match like that of echoic, imitation, and copying-a-text). In a sense, in textual behavior there is a "code" between the written word and corresponding spoken word that a child must learn in order to read (Michael, 1982b).

Many children with language delays acquire reading skills with instruction. A small percentage of the children diagnosed with autism are identified as "hyperlexic," and often acquire whole word and phonetic reading and spelling with very little instruction, but comprehension is typically absent or weak. The VB-MAPP Milestones Assessment contains early measures of textual skills and reading comprehension. These include showing interest in books and being read stories, the ability to identify letters and read one's own name, and finally, matching a few written words to pictures, and vice versa. Other areas of the VB-MAPP (intraverbal) assess intraverbal comprehension of stories read to a child. Also, the VB-MAPP Reading Task Analysis provides a number of additional supporting activities for a beginning textual and reading comprehension repertoire. The goal of this part of the assessment is to determine if pre-reading and beginning reading skills are emerging as they do for typically developing three- to four-year-old children.

Transcription (Spelling) and Copying-a-Text

Transcription consists of spelling words that are spoken (Skinner, 1957). Skinner also refers to this behavior as "taking dictation," with the key repertoires involving not only the manual production of letters, but also accurate spelling of the spoken word. In technical terms, transcription is a type of verbal behavior where a spoken verbal S^D controls a written, typed, or finger spelled response. Like the textual operant, there is point-to-point correspondence between the stimulus and the response product, but **no** formal similarity. For example, when asked to spell the spoken word, "hat" a response, "h-a-t" is a transcription. The stimulus and the response product have point-to-point correspondence, but they are not in the same sense mode or physically resemble each other (i.e., formal similarity). Spelling English words is a difficult repertoire to acquire. Many words in the English language are not spelled like they sound; hence, it is often difficult to shape an appropriate discriminative repertoire, and even many adults struggle with this repertoire.

Copying-a-text is in the same class of skills as echoic and imitation (Michael, 1982b). Copying letters and words is a form of imitation without any implications of understanding. Technically, copying-a-text is a verbal response controlled by a verbal S^D that has point-to-point correspondence and formal similarity (a perfect match). The eventual ability to write, type, or fingerspell letters and words is an essential component of spelling and composition.

Children usually begin the process of learning to write by scribbling, coloring, and engaging in cause-and-effect interactions between a writing instrument and a writing surface. Several of these behaviors are assessed in the task analysis section of the Visual Perceptual and Matching-to-Sample area of the VB-MAPP. Writing with control usually does not occur until after three years of age. The assessment of controlled writing occurs in Level 3 of the VB-MAPP (e.g., tracing shapes, staying within boundaries, copying letters, and writing his own name). The goal of this part of the assessment is to determine if the child is able to demonstrate some early writing skills and determine if they are commensurate with those of a typically developing three- to four-year-old child.

Listener Responding

There are many different behaviors that fall under the rubric of listener skills. In addition to paying attention to people when they are speaking, serving as an audience for those speakers, and responding to a speaker's behavior, there is "understanding" of what a speaker says. This understanding can be measured by both verbal and nonverbal responses. If the child's response was verbal, then it would be classified as intraverbal, and assessed in the intraverbal section; but if the response was nonverbal it would be classified as listener behavior (or often termed receptive language or receptive labeling).

The most common way to assess listener behavior is to determine if a speaker's verbal behavior evokes a specific nonverbal response from the child, such as performing a target action (e.g., "Clap your hands."), or following an instruction (e.g., "Go to the bathroom and get a Kleenex."), or selecting a certain item from an array of other items (e.g., "Can you find the brown animal?"). The verbal tasks of the assessment gradually become more complex to include verbs, adjectives, prepositions, adverbs, and multiple combinations of several of these parts of speech. The goal of this part of the assessment is to identify a child's ability to understand the words of others as measured by the child's nonverbal behavior in relation to those words.

Listener Responding by Function, Feature, and Class (LRFFC)

A major milestone in advancing a child's language skills is the ability to understand more complex and abstract words, phrases, and sentences spoken by others. One aspect of the words spoken by others is that people often talk about things and activities without specifically naming them. For example, a person may talk about a baseball game with words like "bats," "gloves," "balls," "bases," "Yankees," and "home runs," but may never say the words "baseball game." Many aspects of day-to-day verbal interactions involve describing things and activities by their function (e.g., "What do you do with a bat?"), their features (e.g., "What is long and made out of wood?"), or its class (e.g., "What things do you need to play a baseball game?"). Part of a child's listener skills includes the ability to correctly respond nonverbally when objects and activities are described or talked about, but not specifically named.

The assessment of LRFFC skills requires both a list of increasingly complex verbal stimuli along with an increasingly complex visual array. The objective is to determine at what point do the questions become too hard, and/or the array too complex. For example, the assessment begins with simple verbal stimuli like "you eat..." while showing the child an array of three or four items, one of which is a food item. The task is to see if the child can select the food item when given only the words "you eat." Gradually, the verbal stimuli become more complex and the array becomes larger and begins to contain items that all look similar in some way (e.g., same color, shape, function). For example, asking a child to, "Find something you use to eat soup," when shown a messy silverware drawer in a kitchen is a harder task then picking a spoon out of a neat array containing a shoe, horse, and spoon.

Visual Perceptual Skills and Matching-to-Sample (VP-MTS)

Many intelligence tests contain sections on various visual discrimination tasks such as part-to-whole puzzles, block designs, patterns, sequences, and matching-to-sample. Some of these are timed to determine how quickly an individual can make the critical discrimination and respond appropriately. A number of skills are directly or indirectly related to visual discrimination skills. For example, listener discriminations common to much of standard receptive language requires that the child observe and discriminate among visual stimuli. The goal of this part of the assessment is to identify the strength of the child's visual perceptual skills as they relate to a variety of tasks, most notably, matching-to-sample tasks.

Independent Play

For purposes of this assessment a distinction will be made between two types of play: independent play and social play. Independent play involves spontaneously engaging in behavior that is automatically reinforcing (Vaughan & Michael, 1982). In lay terms, the behavior is entertaining in and of itself. It seems pleasurable and enjoyable to the child and does not require outside reinforcers to maintain it. That is, the activity itself has self-sustaining reinforcing properties (i.e., it is automatically reinforced behavior). For example, a child may sit alone in a play area and move cars through a toy garage without adult prompts or adult delivered reinforcers, or an older child may construct a building with Lego blocks. Independent play shapes a number of important skills (e.g., eye-hand coordination, production of cause-and-effect, visual discriminations) and allows the child to have productive free time. This may help to avoid negative behaviors often caused by attention seeking boredom, and may reduce self-stimulatory behaviors. In addition, the development of appropriate play skills are important for teaching a child to stay on task, and provide a basis for social behavior, which often involves joint play skills. Arming a child with an arsenal of play skills may make him more valuable to peers and bring him positive attention.

Social Behavior and Social Play

A significant component of the diagnosis of autism involves deficits in social development. There are several elements of what is called "social behavior." Much of social behavior involves language, such as mands for information from others, tacts of current stimuli in the environment, intraverbal responding to a peer's questions, and listening to peers talk. For example, one child might ask, "What are you drawing?" (a mand for information); the second child responds "A spaceship." (a tact and an intraverbal). "Do you want to draw one too?" the first child asks (a mand); the second child says, "I don't have any paper." (a tact, but possibly also a mand), and so on. Social play involves interactions with others (adults and peers) and the reinforcement is socially mediated through those other individuals. More advanced social play behavior, such as role-playing, pretend play, and board games, also involves verbal behavior. These aspects are assessed in Level 2 and Level 3. The goal of Level 1 is to target specific behaviors that might help to determine if the child's social behavior matches that of a Level 1 typically developing child. Young children tend to be very social in that they want adult attention and interaction. They will often seek this attention in a variety of ways. However, if a child exhibits behavior that suggests physical contact is aversive and people in general are not reinforcing to him, he may socially isolate, or engage in negative behaviors to terminate social interaction.

Spontaneous Vocal Behavior

Vocal play and vocal babbling are extremely important for language development. Babbling strengthens the vocal muscles, making it possible for a child to control those muscles and emit specific sounds that eventually develop into words. This control allows for vocal responses to eventually become echoic, mand, tact, and intraverbal responses. The absence of vocal babbling and vocal play with sounds decreases the needed practice, but efforts to increase vocal productions can often be quite successful. Auditory testing should be conducted for a child who does not babble, in order to determine if there are any physical abnormalities involved with the child's auditory system.

Classroom Routines and Group Skills

Classroom routines can help to establish a number of important skills, such as imitating peers (e.g., lining up when other children line up), following group instructions (e.g., "everybody line up"), self-help skills (e.g., using a napkin), reducing prompt dependency, and promoting independence and self-direction. Once a child is able to follow the basic classroom routines and move from one activity to another without much adult prompting, the focus can shift to learning specific skills in a group teaching format. Since much of the instructional format in a less restrictive setting involves group instruction, it is important that a child be able to learn and make meaningful gains in a group setting.

While many children benefit significantly from a 1:1 teacher-to-student ratio, this instructional format throughout the whole day may not be in the best interest of the child. Perhaps the most obvious problem is that the adult acquires strong stimulus control over behavior due to a long history of careful stimulus presentation and reinforcement delivery. The child's success within a 1:1 format may make it difficult to respond in more typical adult-to-child social and educational ratios. These more typical situations and group teaching formats may not involve, for example, prompts, errorless teaching, or careful reinforcement delivery. However, there are a number of important social and learning opportunities that are available for the child in such arrangements, and at a certain point in an educational program, group instruction can be very valuable.

Linguistic Structure

An important measure of language development is a child's acquisition of more sophisticated words, phrases, and sentence structure. There are several ways to measure the emergence of these skills, such as articulation, vocabulary size, mean length of utterances (MLU), appropriate syntax, the use of various modifiers for nouns and verbs (e.g., adjectives, prepositions, adverbs), types of inflections (e.g., affixes for plurals and tense markers), and so on. The goal of this aspect of the assessment is to determine the nature of the child's verbal output and the degree to which it matches various linguistic developmental milestones.

Math

There are a wide variety of different skills that make up what is usually identified as math skills. For example, early math skills can involve measuring, counting, identifying specific numbers as a listener, tacting numbers, matching quantities of items to written numbers, etc. The assessment of these early math skills occurs in Level 3 of the VB-MAPP. The goal of this part of the assessment is to determine if the child is able to demonstrate some of these early math skills and if they are commensurate with those of typically developing three- to four-year-old children.

Summary

Behavior analysis has made several contributions to the treatment of children with autism or other developmental disabilities over the past 50 years. Most notably, the use of behavioral teaching procedures derived from applied behavior analysis has helped established an effective approach to instructional methodology (e.g., Lovaas, 1977; Maurice, Green, & Mace, 1996; Wolf, Risley, & Mees, 1964). This chapter described how Skinner's analysis of verbal behavior adds to these gains by providing a behavioral analysis of language as the foundation of the language assessment and intervention program (Sundberg & Michael, 2001). This chapter also presented the five components of the VB-MAPP, a brief overview of Skinner's analysis of language (for more detail see Sundberg, 2007), and a description of each area assessed on the VB-MAPP Milestones Assessment. The next chapter contains the general instructions for administering the VB-MAPP Milestones Assessment and basic information regarding the Task Analysis and Supporting Skills program in the accompanying VB-MAPP Protocol.

CHAPTER 2

General Administration Guidelines

for the Milestones Assessment and for the Task Analysis and Supporting Skills

The VB-MAPP Milestones Assessment is designed to identify the existing language and related skills for children with autism or other intellectual disabilities (although it can be valuable for teens and adults with limited language skills as well). The results of this assessment, along with the results of the VB-MAPP Barriers Assessment and the Transition Assessment, will suggest the short and long term priorities and focus of an intervention program. The current chapter contains the general instructions for conducting the VB-MAPP Milestones Assessment as well as instructions for using the Task Analysis and Supporting Skills lists.

Learning and Language Milestones

Milestones mark a significant point along the way to a greater destination. The common goal for a child with language delays is to achieve a level of linguistic competence commensurate with his typically developing peers. By identifying milestones, the focus of the intervention program can be sharper and the direction clearer. The IEP goals can match these milestones and help to avoid placing too much emphasis on minor skills, or steps that are not developmentally appropriate. The complete task analysis of each verbal operant and related skill is still relevant and valuable, but for measuring progress and setting goals, milestones are more meaningful and manageable, and provide a better overall curriculum guide.

The suggested milestones in the VB-MAPP Milestones Assessment were selected and sequenced by averaging the milestones from over fifty developmental charts obtained from a variety of sources. The milestones were then reclassified in terms of Skinner's analysis of verbal behavior (none of the existing developmental charts had mand or intraverbal sequences, although there were many examples of these skills). A variety of child development books were also consulted as guides, such as Bijou and Bear (1961, 1965, 1967), Brazelton and Sparrow (2006), Novak (1996), and Schlinger (1995). In addition, guidance was provided by the author's own experience in teaching college-level child development courses, supervising child development labs, conducting language research, and conducting language assessments for a wide variety of children over the past 35 years. The milestones were also frequently adjusted based on field-testing data and feedback from behavior analysts, speech pathologists, psychologists, occupational therapists, special education teachers, and parents of children with language delays.

Conducting the Assessment

This assessment tool contains 16 separate measurements of language and language-related skills. Most of the scales correspond with Skinner's classification of verbal operants (i.e., echoic, mand, tact, intraverbal). Standard linguistic measures such as mean length of utterance (MLU), vocabulary size, and the use of various syntactical and grammatical conventions (autoclitics) are also assessed, as well as a variety of listener skills and visual perception skills. In addition, there are measures of vocal output, play, and socialization skills. These 16 domains are presented in a developmental sequence that is presented in three linguistic levels. Level 1 contains 9 measures that are designed to approximately correspond with the learning and language skills demonstrated by a typically developing child between 0 and 18 months of age. Level 2 contains 12 measures that are designed to approximately correspond with the learning and language skills demonstrated by a typically developing child between 18 and 30 months of age. Level 3 contains 13 measures that are designed to approximately correspond with the learning and language skills demonstrated by a typically developing child between 30 and 48 months of age. Some measures are present in all three levels, such as the mand, tact, and listener repertoires, while others are contained in only the relevant levels, such as vocal babbling for Level 1, intraverbal and listener responding by function, feature, and class (LRFFC) for Levels 2 and 3, and reading, writing, and math for Level 3.

The scores for the individual areas at each level are approximately balanced. That is, a score of 5 on the Level 1 mand is developmentally about the same as a score of 5 on the Level 1 tact, echoic, listener, etc. For example, a typically developing 18-month-old child is likely to emit about 10 different mands, be able to tact about 10 nonverbal stimuli, and understand about 20 words as a listener. This pattern is held throughout the VB-MAPP except for very early development (0-6 months) where play, social, and visual perceptual skills develop well before echoic, imitation, and tact skills. Thus, these early scales may seem a little out of balance. The attempt to match these scales to typical development should be viewed as an approximation, since all children develop at different rates and there is significant variation in language development, especially in intraverbal, social, and academic skills.

Once a child meets a specific milestone it is extremely important to not assume that training on that skill is finished. Rather, that skill should be moved on to a more advanced level. For example, if a child meets the Tact Milestone 2-7 ("Tacts 10 actions"), he still needs to learn more tacts of actions, generalize those tacts, incorporate them into natural environment activities, learn to use them with nouns, use them with peers, use them as mands and intraverbals, and eventually be able to read those words and act on what was read. The VB-MAPP Placement and IEP Goals (Chapters 8, 9, and 10) further describes the milestones and provides general curriculum direction upon meeting each of the milestones.

Age and Diagnosis of the Individual Tested

The VB-MAPP can be conducted with any language-delayed individual, regardless of age or specific diagnosis. While the focus of the program is clearly on younger children and children with autism or other developmental disabilities, the program can be modified to accommodate teenagers and adults, as well as those with other forms of language delays such as expressive and receptive language disorder, or those produced by traumatic brain injury (Sundberg, San Juan, Dawdy, & Arguelles, 1990). The examples, materials used, and specific test items should be adjusted to account for age-appropriateness (e.g., many of the play milestones can be dropped), but this does not change the general progression of language acquisition, or the need to assess all the verbal operants and related skill areas.

Who Can Conduct a VB-MAPP Assessment?

Language assessment is not an easy process. The VB-MAPP has been designed to be as user friendly as possible, however, there are still several necessary prerequisite skills for an adult to conduct the assessment. Here are five skills sets that an assessor should have: 1) It is essential that the tester have a basic understanding of Skinner's (1957) analysis of verbal behavior. For example, in order to assess a child's mand repertoire, the tester must understand what a mand is, and how the mand is related to motivating operations (MOs); 2) knowledge of basic behavior analysis, for example, being aware of the subtleties of the various types of prompts, and being able to determine if a response is controlled by inadvertent prompting, is essential for determining exactly what skills a child has truly mastered; 3) it is also important that the assessor be familiar with basic linguistic structure; 4) be familiar with the linguistic development of typically developing children; and 5) have a good understanding of autism and other types of developmental disabilities. Finally, as with any language assessment tool, one must read and study the manual, and practice administering the tool. In fact, it has been demonstrated that a "behavioral skills training package" involving, for example, modeling, hands on practice, and feedback, can help to improve a person's accuracy in conducting a VB-MAPP assessment (Barnes, Mellor, & Rehfeldt, 2014). The more skilled a person is in all of these areas the more s/he will get out of the assessment.

In order to capitalize on individual expertise, multiple people can be involved in the assessment of the individual skills (e.g., linguistic structure and the echoic may be best assessed by a speech and language pathologist). Also, some children may be more comfortable with their parent or caretaker present or assisting in the assessment process. The assessment may also be completed quicker if those individuals who know the child are available to provide relevant information (as long as it is accurate). Assessing for generalization also requires that additional people be involved.

Determining the "Operant Level"

The goal of assessment is to determine the specific skills that are present or absent in a child's language and related repertoires (e.g., tacting verbs, manding for information, social interaction with peers). The baseline level of a skill (what the child currently knows) is called the "operant level" in behavioral terminology, and this assessment attempts to determine each child's operant level across the various skills. Many of the items on the VB-MAPP Milestones Assessment may be well below the operant level of a specific child (e.g., Level 1 tacting for a child who can tact 100s of items), and these items can be completed without formal testing if the assessor is familiar with the child, has data on his learning history, or has reliable sources of information (e.g., parents, in-home therapists, teachers). Therefore, in the specific scoring instructions contained in the next three chapters, the tester should quickly score a task if it is clearly below the child's operant level and move on to later items. As the assessment tasks reach a child's operant level of a skill (e.g., tacting relative adjectives), more formal testing will be necessary to determine the operant level of the skill. If a child misses three milestones in a row, it is reasonable to stop the assessment (a ceiling). However, some children may demonstrate splinter skills and be successful at a task that is developmentally out of sequence (e.g., reading, math), and should be given credit for having those skills.

Methods of Measurement

The degree to which one empirically measures each milestone during the assessment depends on the purpose of the assessment for any given child. If the VB-MAPP is to be used for a formal research study or outcome study, then the assessment should be conducted in a more rigid manner, including careful recording and measurement of each skill and reliability measures taken by a second individual. However, the more common use of the tool is for clinical or educational purposes, where the goal is to as efficiently and effectively as possible set up an intervention program that is appropriate for the child being tested. For this type of use, information regarding a specific child can be gathered in a variety of ways, including interviews with parents and others who know the child well. If these individuals can provide reliable information regarding certain skills (e.g., independent play) it will speed up the assessment process. However, the assessment of some skills requires the careful eye of a trained professional (e.g., a mand without prompts, intraverbal skills, or linguistic structure). This is especially the case with the VB-MAPP Barriers

Assessment. Each situation is different, and those involved with the child must decide on the best way to determine a child's skill level, and priorities for an intervention program.

Many skills can be assessed simply by observing if they occur or not in a natural setting. For example, by observing a child in a play setting one can assess many play and social skills. Does the child interact with others, mand to others, or imitate his peers? Some skills need to be assessed within a specific time frame, such as the number of minutes spent sitting in a group activity. Some skills are best assessed with specific testing, such as being able to tact "long" and "short," or "big" and "little." Many skills can be assessed by either observation or testing, such as manding for missing items. The specific method of measurement is identified for each milestone on the VB-MAPP Milestones scoring forms, and for all the skills on the Task Analysis and Skills Tracking scoring forms. More specific information about the four methods of measurement is presented below.

Formal testing (T): A formal test consists of specifically presenting the child with a task and recording his response. For example, Tact Milestone 1-5 states that the child will "Tact any 10 items." A formal test would involve presenting the child with each item along with the verbal prompt, "What's that?" and recording the child's response as correct or incorrect. The goal is to directly determine if the child can emit the target skill or not.

Observation (O): An observation consists of watching for the skill to occur in any number of environmental situations, without any formal stimulus presentation on the part of the assessor (there are no time limits for this measurement). For example, Tact Milestone 1-4 states that the child will "Spontaneously tact (no verbal prompts) 2 different items." An observation would simply consist of noting on a data sheet that a spontaneous tact occurred. The goal here is to determine if any tacts are free from verbal prompts.

Either formal testing or observation (E): The assessor can acquire the relevant data by formal testing or direct observation of the child. For example, Mand Milestone 1-6 states that the child will "Mand for 20 different missing items without prompts (except, e.g., "What do you need?")" Observations of manding in the natural environment could provide the necessary information for scoring (e.g., while playing with a doll the child says "Where's the bottle?"). Or, the skill could be tested directly by giving the child part of a desired item (e.g., the doll), but not another part (e.g., the doll's bottle).

Timed observation (TO): The target response must occur is a time-limited period. For example, Social Behavior and Social Play Milestone 1-5 states that the child will "Spontaneously follow peers or imitate their motor behavior 2 times in a 30-minute period." In order to receive the point for this measure, the child needs to emit the behavior within the fixed time, without adult prompts. However, this time period can be broken up into separate observations, such as two 15-minute recess periods.

Reinforcement and Scoring

Correct responses should be reinforced using a reinforcement schedule appropriate for each individual child. Approximations may be scored as correct in many circumstances, and should be noted in the Comments/notes section of the forms. For example, in testing the tact repertoire when a child is presented with a book, the child reliably says "ook." The tact is functionally correct, but poor in form. This response should be counted as a known tact. If the child calls many things "ook," then the response in not functionally correct. Tasks that are clearly beyond a child's skill levels, such as tacting pronouns for a child who can only tact a few nouns need not be tested at this time.

Testing Environment and Administration Time

Formal testing and observations can be conducted in a classroom, home, or community, and with no time limits for completing the whole assessment (except for the timed observations). The total administration time depends on the child's general level, his cooperation, the assembly of materials, etc., but the use of milestones rather than a whole task analysis significantly speeds up the assessment process. Some children may be more comfortable in one setting or another (e.g., home versus school). Young children may do better on a floor, while older children who have been in a school program may work better at a table. However, some settings may be more conducive to determining a child's skill level. For example, a playroom may be too distracting for testing matching-to-sample, but perfect for testing independent play and social play.

Testing Sequence

The skills should be tested in the sequence presented in the skill areas, but an assessor could conduct a few tests on the echoic, then one on the mand, then a couple on the tact, etc. While order is essentially irrelevant, some higher numbered tasks are clearly based upon success at earlier levels (e.g., number of tacts). The objective is to determine if the child can emit the targeted skill, and a mixed format may be more conducive to maintaining the child's attention. Also, some skills involve the same material and can be assessed together such as tact, listener discriminations, and matching-to-sample. A variety of additional suggestions for conducting the assessment are presented in Table 2-1.

Identifying the Barriers

The assessment of potential barriers should be conducted simultaneously with the assessment of the milestones (see Chapter 6). Some problems may be clearly obvious and reported by parents and others who know the child (e.g., behavior problems, self-stimulation, hyperactivity). However, some of the more subtle problems (e.g., an impaired mand, prompt dependency, scrolling, failing to generalize) may require a trained professional in order to spot the specific problems. This part of the VB-MAPP assessment tool is only to determine quickly if a barrier exists and if it is in need of a further analysis.

Table 2-1
Tips for the tester.

- **Before beginning the assessment have the child's family complete a reinforcer survey.** Utilize the information from the survey to familiarize yourself with the child's interests, such as favorite and familiar activities, songs, movies, snacks, family pets, and family members. This information can also be valuable for identifying potential items to be used for the mand, tact, and listener assessments.

- **Establish rapport with the child.** Allow time for the child to be at ease with you by pairing yourself with fun activities and reinforcement delivery. Also, keep the initial demands at a minimum and progress cautiously.

- **Maintain control of the test items and reinforcers.**

- **Reinforce correct responses.** Use a reinforcement schedule that is appropriate for the child.

- **Reinforce desirable behavior.** Intermittently reinforce and provide natural sounding social reinforcement for attending, good sitting, making eye contact, and smiling. Use descriptive praise such as, "Nice looking," "You're a cool guy."

- **Use both preferred items and novel items that might interest the child.** Self-stimulatory objects can be used, if necessary.

- **Smile when you praise.** Give the child a reason to look at you.

- **Choose reinforcing activities and items for testing that are strong and typical for the child's age group.** Although the child's abilities might not be commensurate with the child's chronological age, most children learn some type of age-appropriate skills regardless of their developmental functioning level. If, for example, you are testing a 14-year-old who is demonstrating early intraverbal skills, you might not want to use "twinkle twinkle little…" as an intraverbal fill-in, but maybe choose a familiar rap song, or the theme song from the child's favorite TV show.

- **When testing an early mand repertoire follow the child's motivation (MOs).** For example, if a child wants to play on the swing go to the swing and determine if he will mand "swing" or "push." This will probably require some contriving like holding the swing and not pushing him right away, rather say, "What do you want?" and use a delay to see if this situation evokes the mand "swing" or "push."

- **Use materials that are either gender neutral or specific to the child's gender.** When assessing and teaching mands and play and social skills, your best results may come from using activities that are gender specific. A little girl may be reinforced by having her nails painted, or by pretending to put on make-up like mommy. A little boy may prefer rough-and-tumble play. Using activities that the child is interested in can often evoke otherwise undetected mands, tacts, intraverbals, listener behavior, motor imitation, and play and social skills.

- **Use an appropriate level of enthusiasm.** Use a more enthusiastic tone of voice for unprompted correct responses, without being too over dramatic.

- **Allow time for mini-breaks.** You might break the assessment into sections by testing parts of each skill and take short breaks. This especially applies to times when testing is at a table, as in matching-to-sample. Take your time conducting the assessment. The objective is to learn what the child can do; there is no time limit.

- **When giving mini-breaks don't allow the child to play with your most powerful reinforcers.** Give him a reason to come back when you are ready to start again.

- **Acknowledge and respond to appropriate spontaneous vocalizations and gestures.** Laugh at the child's humor, smile, nod, and encourage the child to continue responding.

- **Keep the process interesting and pair yourself with reinforcers by delivering them in fun and engaging ways.** For example, fly the reinforcer in like an airplane to the child, drive the reinforcer in a toy car across the table, or act like a magician and pretend to pull the reinforcer out of the child's ear.

- **Intersperse known tasks with more challenging tasks.**

- **Occasionally provide free (non-contingent) reinforcers.**

- **Avoid excessive cueing or prompting when conducting the assessment.** This masks the child's true operant level.

- **Give the child 3-5 seconds to respond, if necessary.**

- **Repeat the question or task presentation 2 or 3 times, if necessary.**

- **Use least-to-most prompting procedures to assess the child's skill level.** This helps to determine what the child can do independently or with minimal prompts.

- **Always end a testing period or session with a correct response and on a positive note.**

Testing Materials

The use of milestones greatly reduces the number of materials necessary to conduct the assessment. Many of the necessary items can be found in a classroom or in the home, and some of the assessment can be conducted in natural environment settings such as a playroom, playground, yard, park, etc. A list of suggested materials for each level is presented in Table 2-2. Additional suggestions for materials can be found in the specific instructions for each of the 170 milestones (Chapters 3, 4, and 5).

Table 2-2
Materials list.

All Levels

- Stop watch, timer, or watch with second hand for timing responses
- Pencil and data sheets for taking notes and tallying responses
- Reinforcers appropriate to the child (e.g., bubbles, snacks, drinks, wind-up toys, pop-up toys, games, iPad).

Level 1

- Pictures of family members, people, pets, and everyday items that are familiar to the child
- Common objects: items the child comes in contact with on a daily basis (e.g., toothbrush, cup, spoon, ball, stuffed animal)
- Inset puzzles: two or three for ages 1-3 years old
- Blocks: four, standard-size blocks, any color
- Picture books: three books that are developmentally age appropriate
- Peg and peg board set
- Puzzle box for ages 1-3 years old

Level 2

- Items to encourage the child to mand for missing items (e.g., a juice box without a straw, track without a train, Mr. Potato Head without the body parts, bubbles without the wand, balloon without air)
- Picture books, picture cards or snapshots for tacting (items, actions, and activities seen in everyday life), matching-to-sample (items that are similar, e.g., three pictures of flowers in an array with a house, a bell, and a horse), LRFFC (animals that make specific sounds, e.g., cow, duck, dog, cat, pig) pictures of items that have similar functions or are in the same class (e.g., clothing, silverware, dishes, furniture, food, vehicles, musical instruments, toys, school supplies), and pictures with items of the same color or shape (e.g., red apple, red car, red barn and round ball, round balloon, round orange)
- Identical items: 25 for matching-to-sample (e.g., spoons, toy cars, shoes, pictures of cartoon characters the child enjoys)
- Sets of similar colored items: three for sorting similar colors (e.g., red toy car, red hat, red toy fire truck, yellow banana, yellow balloon, yellow toy truck)
- Sets of similar shapes, but different colors for sorting, (e.g., red squares, blue squares, red circles, blue circles)
- Sets of similar but non-identical objects (e.g., a basketball and a soccer ball)
- Objects that are similar for matching-to-sample in an array: 25 (e.g., 3 or 4 spoons in an array with a butter knife and a fork)

- Children's scissors, glue stick, crayons, and paper
- Items (or recordings) that make environmental sounds (e.g., phone ringing, bell, baby crying, dog barking, car horn)
- Inset puzzles: four or five for ages 1-3 years old
- Stacking ring
- Toys for independent play (e.g., Duplo blocks, train, dollhouse, and dolls)
- Props for pretend and social play (e.g., tea set, pretend food, dolls, fire hat, a princess veil, cardboard boxes)

Level 3

- Cards with shapes and colors: five each for tacting and matching to sample
- Picture books, picture cards, and/or photos similar to those needed for Level 2
- Inset puzzles for ages 2-5 years old
- Block design cards: 25 pattern options
- Colored blocks for sequencing
- Alphabet letter cards
- Number cards from 1 to 5
- Step and short-story seriation cards
- Size seriation cards
- Items that are samples of relative adjectives and measurement (e.g., light and heavy, clean and dirty, hot and cold, wet and dry, big and little, long and short)
- Ten small items to assess counting and more and less (e.g., beans, M&Ms)
- Beginning sight words with pictures (three or four letters, such as "dog" and "cat")
- Lined paper and a pencil
- Arts and crafts supplies (e.g., crayons, construction paper, coloring book, lined paper, scissors, glue, beads for stringing, items for sorting)
- Pictures or a book with community helpers (e.g., police, nurse, doctor, firefighter, teacher, mail carrier, construction worker, bus driver, ambulance driver)
- Toys for independent play (e.g., puzzles, Duplo blocks, Tinker Toys, train and tracks, dollhouse, doll and furniture, arts and crafts)
- Child's clothing or a dressing doll with a zipper, snap, button, buckle, tie, Velcro
- Three developmentally appropriate activity books (e.g., dot-to-dot, mazes, picture search)

Scoring the VB-MAPP Milestones Assessment Forms

There is space on the forms for four separate administrations of the VB-MAPP Milestones Assessment (Figure 2-1), but additional administrations can be conducted if needed. In general, the VB-MAPP should be administered once per year, or school year. The Master Scoring Form should be used to create a student profile across all the domains and levels. The order of the domains presented on the Master Form does not reflect an order for acquisition, but was determined more by an attempt to line up similar skills at all three levels. For example, manding occurs in the first column for all three levels. However, the seventh column contains imitation for Levels 1 and 2 and reading for Level 3, because imitation is no longer a key assessment target for

Figure 2-1

A filled-out sample of the Milestones Master Scoring Form.

VB-MAPP Milestones Master Scoring Form

Child's name:	Elizabeth
Date of birth:	6/30/05
Age at testing:	**1** 3 yrs. **2** **3** **4**

Key:	Score	Date	Color	Tester
1ST TEST:	52	6/1/08		MS
2ND TEST:				
3RD TEST:				
4TH TEST:				

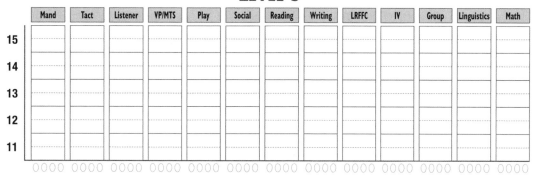

LEVEL 3

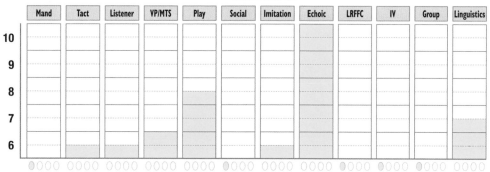

LEVEL 2

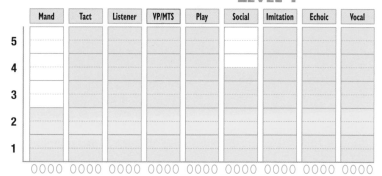

LEVEL 1

children that have mastered the earlier skills. Imitation is still important, but the skills at that level should be moved into the natural environment as part of daily living and other functional activities (e.g., imitating play, games, sports, self-help, academic activities, and other forms of social behavior). Reading, writing, and math appear in Level 3, but not in Levels 1 and 2, because they are not key assessment skills at those earlier levels.

It is extremely important only to score a skill as correct if the adult can reliably evoke the behavior on demand, or an adult specifically observes it. Alternatively, if the goal is spontaneity, the relevant variables should be present (e.g., an MO) without inadvertent prompts. These prompts relate to, in part, what is known in behavioral psychology as stimulus control, and many important decisions are based on the presence or absence of stimulus control in both language assessment and language training. For example, a presumed "spontaneous mand" may be controlled by discriminative stimuli such as an eye prompt rather than a motivative variable such as wanting to draw with a marker. It is better for the assessor to err on the conservative side. Assuming a child has a skill when actually the skill is absent, prompted, rote, or in some way defective will affect the development of other skills that might be based on that targeted skill.

There are four boxes for each individual item (see Figure 2-2). The boxes are for each administration of the assessment (i.e., put scores in the first box for the baseline assessment). There are three options for scoring each skill: 0, ½, or 1. Score a response based on the criteria identified in each section of the specific milestone scoring instructions (Chapters 3, 4, and 5). If a child receives a score of 0, place a 0 in the individual item scoring form. If the item is not tested (such as reading for an early learner), place a 0 in the box. There are two steps in transferring the data to other sections of the assessment. First, total up all the points acquired for one skill area, such as a "4½" for the tact (Figure 2-1). Place this score in the appropriate box marked "total score" at the top of

Figure 2-2
A sample of a filled-out assessment form for Level 1 tacting.

each skill area. Then, total up all of these scores for each area at each level and transfer this total score to the appropriate scoring section on the Milestones Master Scoring Form.

The next task is to fill in the Milestones Form using a different color for each administration of the VB-MAPP Milestones Assessment (see Figure 2-1). The data from each individual item should be transferred to the Milestones Form by coloring in the appropriate box with the color designated for that administration of the VB-MAPP (e.g., all boxes for the first administration might be filled in with yellow). If the score is 1, fill in the whole box. If the score is ½ fill in the bottom half of the box and leave the top half of the scoring box blank. If the score is 0 leave the whole box blank. Note that some earlier skills might be scored as 0 or ½ while later skills are scored as a 1 (splinter skills). Thus, the scoring is individually completed for each box, that is, it is **not** a cumulative score. There is a circle below each section for each administration that can be used to indicate that the skill was tested, even though the child did not obtain any points for that section.

The VB-MAPP Task Analysis and Supporting Skills

The VB-MAPP Protocol contains 35 pages of Task Analysis and Supporting Skills for 14 of the 16 domains of the Milestones Assessment (there is no task analysis and supporting skills list provided for the echoic or spontaneous vocal behavior domains). The task analysis skills can be identified as those that are directly related to the target milestone and represent earlier steps in reaching that milestone. The supporting skills supplement the milestones with a number of important language, learning, and social skills that should be developed along with the milestones. The supporting skills are not necessarily prerequisites for a specific milestone, or need to be worked on in the exact order that they are presented (like the task analysis skills require). Nonetheless, the supporting skills contained in this section of the Protocol are an essential part of any intervention program.

The Task Analysis and Supporting Skills are combined together in the Protocol grids for each milestone. For example, Mand Milestone 5-M states that the child "Emits 10 different mands without prompts (except, *What do you want?*) — the desired item can be present (e.g., *apple, swing, car, juice*)." The Task Analysis and Supporting Skills contain five additional skills (5-a to 5-e) in that section of the VB-MAPP Protocol. An example of a task analysis skill that is an "earlier step" of the relevant milestone is task 5-b that states, "Emits 3 different mands without verbal prompts — can be with an object prompt." On the other hand, an example of a supporting skill that is not directly related to the relevant milestone is skill 5-e that states, "Continues to emit a mand 2 times if the reinforcer is not delivered (persistence)." These supporting skills are important and should be developed. They may or may not warrant a specific IEP goal, but may be important to include them in the program when a child is ready for them.

There are approximately 750 skills identified in this section of the VB-MAPP. While these skills are important for the reasons described above, they are not provided to be used as an assessment in the same manner that the Milestones Assessment is used. An assessment should be a sample of skills. The Milestones Assessment is designed to target the major linguistic, learning, and social skills that correspond with those of typically developing children in their early years of language acquisition, without being encumbered with the breakdown of those skills. For those who found value in using the whole task analysis contained in the Assessment of Basic Learning and Language Skills: The ABLLS (Partington & Sundberg, 1998) for assessment, they will find the content in the Task Analysis and Supporting Skills section of the VB-MAPP familiar, although significantly expanded, re-sequenced, and developmentally matched to the acquisition of language and social skill experienced by typically developing children (e.g., Sundberg & Sundberg, 2011).

The Task Analysis and Supporting Skills are presented in the same three developmental levels as the Milestones Assessment, and are color coded to match that assessment. These two sets of skills are framed by each milestone, which is presented in a bold lettering with a shaded background that matches the color code for that particular level. The individual tasks correspond with a milestone and level, and are identified by the milestone number and a letter for that task. For example, Mand Level "1-a" is "Makes eye contact (gaze shift) as a mand for attention or for other reinforcers 2 times." The milestone at the end of this section (Mand 1) is identified as a bolded **1-M** and is the same Mand Level 1-1 Milestone that appears throughout the different sections of the VB-MAPP.

The measurement system for the Task Analysis and Supporting Skills is the same as described previously for the Milestones Assessment. The four methods of assessing a specific skill are: (1) formal testing (**T**), (2) observation (**O**), (3) either observation or testing (**E**), and (4) a timed observation (**TO**). On the right side of the form is a column to mark that the task has been "Met" by either a check system or by placing the date in that column. Many of the skills may require a further breakdown, and teaching the skills will require data sheets to track progress more efficiently, and assess performance. Once a task has been met the box in the skills tracking chart that corresponds with the skill (e.g., 1-a) can be filled in. Some may prefer to fill in the boxes at the same time that the Milestones Assessment is repeated (e.g., for an IEP), rather than after each skill is acquired.

Some skills appear in multiple sections in the Task Analysis and Supporting Skills, and may seem similar or even the same throughout the various skills and levels. This is in an effort to help spot specific skills that may be strong in one context, but weak in another context. For example, the task in Mand 1-a, "Makes eye contact (gaze shift) as a mand for attention or for other reinforcers 2 times," and the task in Social Skills 1-c, "Orients towards or makes eye contact with familiar people 5 times" may seem like the same goal, but they are different in that they look at the same behavior under two different sources of control.

When a child mands because a strong MO for attention is present, he may be more likely to make eye contact to get his needs met; however, when an MO for attention is low, he may have little interest in others and may not make eye contact, but it is still important to identify if he looks at people under these circumstances as well. These subtle differences are important and can provide information about how the target skill is developing, and if it has the components that would be expected for a typically developing child. This same "eye contact" skill is also assessed at a later level involving eye contact with peers when talking, and appears in a few other configurations of the VB-MAPP (including in the Barriers Assessment).

Summary

A language and social skills assessment is only a sample of a child's existing skills. Common language and social skills milestones, within a Skinnerian (1957) framework of language, can provide a convenient and comprehensive tool for conducting an assessment. Also, by identifying milestones, the focus of the intervention program can be sharper and the direction clearer, making it easier to write IEP goals. This chapter presented a variety of general instructions for conducting the VB-MAPP Milestones Assessment and the Task Analysis and Supporting Skills, as well as a suggested list of materials and a list of "tips for the tester." The following three chapters will describe the specific scoring instructions and criteria for each of the 170 milestones, beginning with Level 1 in Chapter 3.

Milestones Scoring Instructions: Level 1

This chapter contains the specific instructions for administering Level 1 of the VB-MAPP Milestones Assessment. These instructions contain the objective for each milestone, suggested materials, examples, and the scoring criteria. The task for the person conducting the assessment is to identify the "operant level" of each skill (i.e., the current level of performance or "baseline" level), in order to determine where to start an intervention program. If a test item is clearly below the child's skill level (which means it is too easy), score that milestone as a 1, and move on to the next milestone. If the child is reaching his operant level in a skill area, more careful and thorough testing is warranted. If the child misses three milestones in a row, it is reasonable to stop testing him (however, some children may demonstrate splinter skills such as reading and math and should be given credit for what they know).

Level 1 manding includes three types of response forms: speech, sign language, and icons such as PECS (Frost & Bondy, 2002). These three different response forms can work in a similar manner at the early mand level. However, as language becomes more complex, especially with tact and intraverbal behavior, icon selection becomes less effective and requires some special considerations that will be described in the Level 1 Placement and IEP Goals (Chapter 8). In order to make the presentation of the following content easier to read, only vocal responses are used in the milestones and examples, with the exception of this first section on manding. However, sign language is implied in all cases, and in some cases an icon system can also be similarly used (e.g., manding, matching-to-sample, LD, LRFFC).

It is important that the examiner be familiar with the basic elements of Skinner's analysis of verbal behavior as presented in Chapter 1 (and in Sundberg, 2007), and with the general instructions presented in Chapter 2. As a reminder, the four methods of assessing a specific skill are: (1) formal testing (T), (2) observation (O), (3) either observation or testing (E), and (4) a timed observation (TO). For more detail on each type of measurement see Chapter 2.

MAND – LEVEL 1

MAND 1-M	Emits 2 words, signs, or icon selections, but may require echoic, imitative, or other prompts, but no physical prompts (e.g., *cracker, book*). (E)
Objective:	To determine if a child mands with echoic prompts. For a child using sign language or a child selecting icons, can the child mand with imitative or pointing prompts? If early manding is weak, limited, or typically requires physical prompting, a more careful assessment of the child's exact level will be necessary.
Materials:	Gather items or plan actions that function as reinforcement for the child.
Examples:	A child says "cookie" when he wants a cookie, but he needs an echoic prompt in order to respond. For a signing child, he signs "cookie" when he wants and sees a cookie, but he needs an imitative prompt and perhaps needs to hear the word in order to respond. For a child using icons, he selects an icon of "cookie" when he

wants and sees a cookie, but he needs a pointing prompt in order to respond. A mand for a push on a swing would be an example of a mand for action.

1 point score: Give the child 1 point if he responds when an adult provides an echoic prompt, such as "say cookie" when a cookie is present, for 2 desired items or activities. For a child using sign language, give him 1 point if he responds when the adult provides an imitative prompt, or speaks the word (intraverbal prompt). For a child using an icon system, the adult may point to the target picture and verbally prompt the child to pick it up. Do not give the child any points if physical prompts are required for signing or selecting a picture or icon.

½ point score: Give the child ½ point if he only emits 1 mand.

MAND 2-M	Emits 4 different mands without prompts (except, *What do you want?*) the desired item can be present (e.g., *music, Slinky, ball*). (E)

Objective: To determine if a child mands without echoic prompts, and for a child using signs or selecting icons, mands without imitative or pointing prompts, respectively.

Materials: Gather items or plan actions that function as reinforcement for the child.

Example: A child says or signs "swing" when he is on a swing and wants to be pushed, and he does so without an echoic or imitative prompt.

1 point score: Give the child 1 point if he mands for 4 different reinforcers without the adult saying the target word (echoic prompt), giving an imitative or pointing prompt, or for a child using signs, speaking the word (intraverbal prompt). The desired item or activity can be present, as well as the verbal prompt, "What do you want?" (or something similar).

½ point score: Give the child ½ point if he emits 3 of these types of mands.

MAND 3-M	Generalizes 6 mands across 2 people, 2 settings, and 2 different examples of a reinforcer (e.g., mands *bubbles* from mom and dad, inside and outside, a red bottle and a blue bottle). (E)

Objective: To determine if the mand repertoire is generalizing to different people, settings, and materials. The objective is to make sure that in the very early aspects of language training the child is learning to emit the same response under slightly different conditions. A common problem for many children with language delays is that verbal responses become rote and fail to occur under novel or varied conditions, and generalization training can help prevent that learning barrier.

Materials: Use several different examples of items or activities that function as reinforcement such as several different types of cookies, crackers, cars, balls, or books; or playgrounds that have swings. Also, assess the mand in different settings and with different people.

Examples: Once a child mands for one type of car, for example, a green Matchbox car, does he mand for cars that are a different color, size, or type? The child mands "spin" in one office chair, does he mand "spin" in other chairs that spin? The child mands "bubbles" for one staff member, will he mand for "bubbles" for another staff member? The child mands "jump" in the motor room, will he mand "jump" in the classroom?

1 point score: Give the child 1 point if he generalizes 6 mands across 2 people, 2 settings, and 2 examples of the reinforcer.

½ point score: Give the child ½ point if he generalizes to 3 mands across 2 people, 2 settings, and 2 examples of the reinforcer.

MAND 4-M	Spontaneously emits (no verbal prompts) 5 mands — the desired item can be present. (TO: 60 min.)

Objective: To determine if manding is occurring without adults initiating the manding response (i.e., prompted manding). The primary source of control for the mand must be the motivating operation (MO), not an adult prompt.

Materials: Reinforcers that occur in a child's natural environment.

Examples: The child sees another child playing with a Slinky and mands "Slinky." The child wants to go outside and mands "out."

1 point score: Give the child 1 point if he spontaneously mands 5 times (using at least 2 different mands) during a 1-hour observation (without, "What do you want?" or similar prompts).

½ point score: Give the child ½ point if he spontaneously mands 5 times during a 1-hour observation, but it is always the same word.

MAND 5-M	Emits 10 different mands without prompts (except, *What do you want?*) — the desired item can be present (e.g., *apple, swing, car, juice*). (E)

Objective: To determine if a child mands for 10 different reinforcers without echoic prompts, and for a child using signs or selecting pictures, mands without imitative or pointing prompts, respectively.

Materials: Gather items or plan actions that may function as reinforcement for the child.

Examples: A child mands for "book," "bubbles," "car," "candy," "up," "iPad," "music," and "spin," without prompts.

1 point score: Give the child 1 point if he mands for 10 different reinforcers without the adult saying the target word, giving an imitative or pointing prompt, or for a child using signs, speaking the word (intraverbal prompt). The desired item can be present, as well as the verbal prompt, "What do you want?" (or something similar). Mands to remove aversives such as saying "no" or "mine" can also be counted.

½ point score: Give the child ½ point if he emits 8 different mands.

Tact – Level 1

Tact 1-M	Tacts 2 items with echoic or imitative prompts (e.g., people, pets, characters, or favorite objects). (T)
Objective:	To determine if a particular nonverbal stimulus (e.g., a child's mother) evokes the word "mama" (or an approximation). A child's first tacts may also be part mand in that young children tend to tact things that are reinforcing to them, such as their parents, siblings, pets, favorite characters, toys, etc. It may be hard to tell if the response "mama" is a mand or a tact, but that's okay because at this early stage the goal is to determine if the child discriminates between the nonverbal stimulus of his mother versus, for example, his father. If he calls everybody "mama" do not give him credit for this skill.
Materials:	Use natural reinforcers and items that occur in the child's daily environment.
Examples:	"Doggie," "mama," "dada," "Elmo," "Sponge Bob," "Dora," etc.
1 point score:	Give the child 1 point if he names 2 items with or without echoic prompts when tested (e.g., "Who's that?" or "What's that?").
½ point score:	Give the child ½ point if he names 1 item with or without echoic prompts when tested, but do not give him ½ point if he calls everything by the same name.

Tact 2-M	Tacts any 4 items without echoic or imitative prompts (e.g., people, pets, characters, or other objects). (T)
Objective:	To determine if the tact repertoire is growing, and if an adult can evoke tacts during testing without echoic or imitative (for signers) prompts. These tacts may also still be part mand at this point.
Materials:	Use common items and reinforcers in the child's natural environment.
Examples:	"Spiderman," "Nemo," "car," "doll," "juice," "book," etc.
1 point score:	Give the child 1 point if he names 4 items without echoic prompts when tested.
½ point score:	Give the child ½ point if he names 3 items without echoic prompts when tested.

Tact 3-M	Tacts 6 non-reinforcing items (e.g., *shoe, hat, spoon, car, cup, bed*). (T)
Objective:	To determine if the tacts are breaking free from motivation as a source of control, and that the tact repertoire is growing.
Materials:	Use common items in the child's natural environment.
Examples:	"Table," "chair," "book," "shirt," "door," "cat," "dog," "bowl," etc.
1 point score:	Give the child 1 point if he tacts 6 items without echoic prompts when tested. Do not give the child credit for responses that are also part mand (e.g., he says "book" because he sees and wants the book).
½ point score:	Give the child ½ point if he tacts 5 items.

Tact 4-M	Spontaneously tacts (no verbal prompts) 2 different items. (TO: 60 min.)
Objective:	To determine if tacting is occurring without adult prompts to tact. Typically, children begin to tact items without prompts or contrived reinforcers, because tacting the item correctly becomes automatically reinforcing for the child (e.g., "Dora!").
Materials:	Use common items in the child's natural environment.
Example:	The child sees a picture of Spiderman and says "Spiderman," not as a mand, but because he likes seeing and saying "Spiderman" (automatic reinforcement).
1 point score:	Give the child 1 point if he spontaneously tacts (no verbal or nonverbal prompts) 2 different items during a 60 minute observation.
½ point score:	Give the child ½ point if he spontaneously tacts 1 item during a 60 minute observation.

Tact 5-M	Tacts 10 items (e.g., common objects, people, body parts, or pictures). (T)
Objective:	To determine if the tact repertoire is growing.
Materials:	Use common items (including pictures) in the child's natural environment.
Examples:	"Nose," "eyes," "truck," "tree," "sock," "spoon," "ball," "crayon," "scissors," etc.
1 point score:	Give the child 1 point if he tacts 10 items without echoic prompts when tested.
½ point score:	Give the child ½ point if he tacts 8 items.

LISTENER RESPONDING – LEVEL 1

Listener 1-M	Attends to a speaker's voice by making eye contact with the speaker 5 times. (TO: 30 minutes)
Objective:	To determine if speech sounds are discriminative stimuli (S^{D}s) for attending to and making eye contact with people. Also, to determine if the child discriminates between speech sounds and other sounds in his environment.
Materials:	None.
Example:	When an adult is playing with the child and the adult sings a song or talks to the child, does the child look at the adult's eyes, and in some way seem interested in the speech sounds (e.g., smiles)? There is no implication that the child understands what the person is saying, just that the child reacts to linguistic auditory stimuli.
1 point score:	Give the child 1 point if he makes eye contact when others talk 5 times in 30 minutes.
½ point score:	Give the child ½ point if he makes eye contact when others talk 2 times in 30 minutes.

LISTENER 2-M	**Responds to hearing his own name 5 times (e.g., looks at the speaker). (T)**
Objective:	To determine if a child discriminates between his own name and other verbal stimuli that he hears throughout the day. This is one of the most common forms of early listener understanding for a child, and occurs because of the frequent pairing of a child's name with adult attention, physical contact, and delivery of other reinforcers.
Materials:	None.
Example:	When the child is looking away and an adult says his name, he turns his head and looks at the adult.
1 point score:	Give the child 1 point if he attends to adults by making eye contact when his name is called on 5 separate trials within one day.
½ point score:	There is no ½ point score for this skill.

LISTENER 3-M	**Looks at, touches, or points to the correct family member, pet, or other reinforcer when presented in an array of 2, for 5 different reinforcers (e.g., *Where's Elmo? Where's mommy?*). (E)**
Objective:	To determine if the child discriminates as a listener among verbal stimuli and associates those verbal stimuli with the matching nonverbal stimuli. Children learn to distinguish between their parents and strangers quite early in development, and the related verbal stimuli (i.e., "mama" and "dada") are often in the first group of words that acquire differential stimulus control over listener behavior. Other reinforcing items such as a favorite pet, stuffed animal, a cartoon character, or toy may also help to establish early listener skills.
Materials:	Use reinforcers in the child's natural environment.
Example:	A Dora doll may be on a chair, and the adult says "Where's Dora!" and the child looks right at Dora.
1 point score:	Give the child 1 point if he correctly identifies 5 different family members, pets, or other reinforcers when individually named by an adult. Make sure that there is at least one other item in the array.
½ point score:	Give the child ½ point if he correctly identifies 2 different reinforcing stimuli.

LISTENER 4-M	**Performs 4 different motor actions on command without a visual prompt (e.g., *Can you jump? Show me clapping*). (T)**
Objective:	To determine if a child's motor behavior is under an adult's verbal stimulus control (no imitative prompts).
Materials:	A list of actions.
Examples:	When an adult says "jump," the child will jump. When an adult says "clap," the child will clap. When an adult says "arms up," the child will raise his arms.

1 point score:	Give the child 1 point if he emits the correct motor behavior to any verbal stimulus that requires a specific motor action 2 times during testing for 4 different actions without scrolling. It is important to only score this response as correct if the verbal stimulus alone evokes the correct response. For example, the word "kiss" might evoke kissing behavior, but if the adult sticks out her chin, puckers her lips, point to her lips, or prompts in any visual way, these stimuli are more likely the source of stimulus control rather than the spoken word.
½ point score:	Give the child ½ point if he emits the correct motor behavior 2 times during testing for 2 different actions.

LISTENER 5-M	**Selects the correct item from an array of 4, for 20 different objects or pictures (e.g., Show me cat. Touch shoe). (T)**
Objective:	To determine if spoken words evoke 1) scanning of an array of choices, and 2) a selection response for the correct item. The array for these early discriminations can be in the natural environment, but should also be in a more formal teaching situation (i.e., on the floor or at a table).
Materials:	Use common items in the child's natural environment such as an array with a hat, book, spoon, and ball, or a shoe, sock, doll, and cup.
Examples:	When there are several toys on the table and the adult says, "Give me the hat," the child can successfully select the hat from the array. Or, when several people are in a room and an adult says, "Where is Uncle Joe?" the child looks directly at, or goes to, Uncle Joe.
1 point score:	Give the child 1 point if he correctly identifies 20 different items in an array of 4 on the first two trials during testing. When giving credit for differentially looking at items to demonstrate listener skills, make sure there is an array from which to discriminate, and that the response is clearly directed to the target stimulus.
½ point score:	Give the child ½ point if he correctly identifies 15 different items in an array of 4 on the first two trials during testing.

VISUAL PERCEPTUAL SKILLS AND MATCHING-TO-SAMPLE (VP-MTS) – LEVEL 1

VP-MTS 1-M	**Visually tracks moving stimuli for 2 seconds, 5 times. (TO: 30 min.)**
Objective:	To determine if the child watches and visually follows moving stimuli.
Materials:	Common stimuli in the child's natural environment.
Example:	If a favorite pet enters the room, the child will look at the pet and watch it move across the room.
1 point score:	Give the child 1 point if he visually tracks moving stimuli for 2 seconds, 5 times during the 30-minute observation.

½ point score: Give the child ½ point if tracks moving stimuli for 2 seconds, 2 times during the 30-minute observation.

VP-MTS 2-M	Grasps small objects with thumb and index finger (pincer grasp) 5 times. (O)

Objective: To determine if the child has effective eye-hand coordination, and is successful in reaching for and grabbing small items with his thumb and index finger.

Materials: Age-appropriate toys, and common objects found in the natural environment.

Example: The child sees a crayon and reaches for it and picks it up with his thumb and index finger.

I point score: Give the child 1 point if he is successful with small motor eye-hand coordination activities, such as reaching for and grabbing small toys and other objects, 5 times during observation.

½ point score: Give the child ½ point if he usually requires 2 or more attempts to successfully obtain small items in front of him.

VP-MTS 3-M	Visually attends to a toy or book for 30 seconds (not a self-stim item). (O)

Objective: To determine if the child maintains visual attention to toys, objects, or activities for sustained periods of time without prompts.

Materials: Age-appropriate toys and books.

Example: When presented with a pop-up toy the child will attend to the toy for 30 seconds without prompts.

I point score: Give the child 1 point if he demonstrates sustained attention to a specific, and possibly reinforcing, visual stimulus for 30 seconds. Do not give the child a point if it is always the same item, or other items that might be classified as self-stimulation for the child (e.g., a stick that the child stims with).

½ point score: Give the child ½ point if he attends to visual stimuli for 15 seconds.

VP-MTS 4-M	Places 3 items in a container, stacks 3 blocks, or places 3 rings on a peg for 2 of these or similar activities. (E)

Objective: To determine if the child has the eye-hand coordination, fine motor control, visual discrimination, and the motivation to independently complete these activities.

Materials: Blocks, form and shape balls, pegs and rings, and containers.

Examples: Placing blocks or shapes in an open container or in formed holes, stacking blocks, putting rings on pegs, or putting items in a container.

1 point score:	Give the child 1 point if he successfully and independently places 3 items in a container, stacks 3 blocks, places 3 rings on a peg, etc., for any 2 activities during observation or testing.
½ point score:	Give the child ½ point if he places 2 items in a container, stacks 2 blocks, places 2 rings on a peg, etc., for any single activity during observation or testing.

VP-MTS 5-M	Matches any 10 identical items (e.g., inset puzzles, toys, objects, or pictures). (E)
Objective:	To determine if the child visually matches items that are alike, and if the child has the fine motor skills to independently complete the task. This behavior may require some verbal prompting and contrived reinforcers.
Materials:	Matching inset puzzles; form balls; matching toys such as cars, figurines, characters, animals, blocks, pictures, etc.
Examples:	A child is shown a Sponge Bob figurine and selects a second matching Sponge Bob figurine from a small group of figurines. A child places a puzzle piece of a blue ball in the form puzzle that has a background picture in the frame that matches the blue ball on the puzzle piece.
1 point score:	Give the child 1 point if he successfully matches 10 items in an array of 3.
½ point score:	Give the child ½ point if he matches 5 items in an array of 3.

INDEPENDENT PLAY – LEVEL 1

PLAY 1-M	Manipulates and explores objects for 1 minute (e.g., looks at a toy, turns it over, presses buttons). (TO: 30 min.)
Objective:	To determine if the child is interested in objects (i.e., reinforced by them) and independently manipulates them as a form of entertainment. In short, the "play" or exploring behavior is "fun" for the child, and occurs without adult mediated consequences (thus, the reinforcers are "automatic," not contrived).
Materials:	Items that function as reinforcement for the child, and common items found in the child's natural environment.
Examples:	Holding and looking at toys, objects, clothing, etc., and turning them over, moving them from hand to hand, shaking them, exploring them visually, banging them against things, placing them in specific positions, etc.
1 point score:	Give the child 1 point if he independently manipulates and explores objects for a total of at least 1 minute during a 30-minute observation.
½ point score:	Give the child ½ point if he independently manipulates and explores objects for a total of at least 30 seconds during a 30-minute observation.

PLAY 2-M	**Shows variation in play by independently interacting with 5 different items (e.g., plays with rings, then a ball, then a block). (TO: 30 min.)**

Objective: To determine if the child plays with a variety of items and toys.

Materials: Common toys and objects found in a child's home or school environment.

Examples: The child plays with a toy school bus for about 1 minute, then moves to a fishing games for about 30 seconds, then sits and plays with plastic tools for 2 minutes, then later picks up a Koosh ball.

1 point score: Give the child 1 point if he independently plays with 5 different items for a total of at least 5 minutes during a 30-minute observation.

½ point score: Give the child ½ point if he independently plays with 3 different items for a total of at least 5 minutes during a 30-minute observation.

PLAY 3-M	**Demonstrates generalization by engaging in exploratory movement and playing with the toys in a novel environment for 2 minutes (e.g., in a new playroom). (TO: 30 min.)**

Objective: To determine if a child will look around, check out the toys, and play with them in a novel environment. This is a form of generalization.

Materials: Items available in novel environments (not necessarily just children's toys).

Example: When a child enters a children's play area at a store for the first time, he will look around at what is there and select something to play with, often briefly, but then will select other things to play with.

1 point score: Give the child 1 point if he independently engages in exploratory movement and touching in a new or novel play area for 2 minutes during a 30-minute observation.

½ point score: Give the child ½ point if he independently engages in exploratory movement and touching in a new or novel play area for 1 minute during a 30-minute observation.

PLAY 4-M	**Independently engages in movement play for 2 minutes (e.g., swinging, dancing, rocking, jumping, climbing). (TO: 30 min.)**

Objective: To determine if the child spontaneously and independently engages in motor behaviors that are maintained by automatic consequences. Does the child enjoy dancing, running, climbing, etc., and do these behaviors occur without adult prompts or reinforcers? In short, the reinforcement for these behaviors is automatically provided by the physical activity itself.

Materials: Parks, playgrounds, playhouses, trampolines, etc.

Examples: The child goes down slides, likes swinging on a swing, rides a merry-go-round, likes to be chased, etc.

1 point score: Give the child 1 point if he engages in movement play for 2 minutes during a 30-minute observation.

½ point score: Give the child ½ point if he engages in movement play for 1 minute during a 30-minute observation.

PLAY 5-M	**Independently engages in cause-and-effect play for 2 minutes (e.g., dumping containers, playing with pop-up toys, pulling toys, etc.). (TO: 30 min.)**

Objective: To determine if the child is reinforced by cause-and-effect activities, and will engage in these activities without adult prompts or reinforcers.

Materials: Common toys and items found in a child's home or school environment.

Examples: Placing items in and out of containers, dropping things, pulling things out of cupboards, pushing buttons to makes sounds on toys, playing with pop-up toys, stacking and knocking over blocks, pushing things to watch them move, pulling toys, throwing things, etc.

1 point score: Give the child 1 point if he independently engages in cause-and-effect play for 2 minutes during a 30-minute observation.

½ point score: Give the child ½ point if he independently engages in cause-and-effect play for 1 minute during a 30-minute observation.

SOCIAL BEHAVIOR AND SOCIAL PLAY – LEVEL 1

SOCIAL 1-M	**Makes eye contact as a type of mand 5 times. (TO: 30 min.)**

Objective: To determine if the child uses eye contact as a mand for social interaction.

Materials: None.

Examples: A parent enters a room and the child makes eye contact with the parent and smiles as the parent approaches.

1 point score: Give the child 1 point if he makes eye contact as a mand at least 5 times during a 30-minute observation.

½ point score: Give the child ½ point if he makes eye contact as a mand at least 2 times during a 30-minute observation.

SOCIAL 2-M	**Indicates that he wants to be held or physically played with 2 times (e.g., climbs up on his mom's lap). (TO: 60 min.)**

Objective: To determine if physical contact with familiar adults is a form of reinforcement for the child, and if he will seek out this reinforcement.

Materials: None.

Examples: The child will approach an adult and reach out his arms for tickles, or to be lifted up. When on the floor the child will climb up on an adult's lap, back, or shoulders and seem to enjoy the physical interaction. The number of people that are reinforcing might be limited, but with familiar people he clearly enjoys physical attention, demonstrated by smiling, laughing, and continuing to seek this type of interaction.

1 point score: Give the child 1 point if he indicates that he wants to be held or physically played with 2 times during a 1-hour observation.

½ point score: Give the child ½ point if he indicates that he wants to be held or physically played with 1 time during a 1-hour observation.

SOCIAL 3-M	Spontaneously makes eye contact with other children 5 times. (TO: 30 min.)

Objective: To determine if a child makes eye contact with peers. Are peers discriminative stimuli (S^Ds) for attending to them?

Materials: Peers.

Example: When another child comes in the room the target child looks at him and makes eye contact.

1 point score: Give the child 1 point if he spontaneously makes eye contact with other children 5 times during a 30-minute observation.

½ point score: Give the child ½ point if he spontaneously makes eye contact with other children 2 times during a 30-minute observation.

SOCIAL 4-M	Spontaneously engages in parallel play near other children for a total of 2 minutes (e.g., sits in the sandbox near other children). (TO: 30 min.)

Objective: To determine if a child will stand or sit by other children without adult prompts to do so.

Materials: Peers and common group items found in a child's home or school (e.g., sandbox, water table, rice bins, play tables, etc.).

Examples: The target child will sit in the play area by other children, but may not interact with the children. The target child will stand next to other children at a bin containing beans, play with the beans, but may not interact with the other children.

1 point score: Give the child 1 point if he spontaneously engages in parallel play (without adult prompting) by other children for a total of 2 minutes during a 30-minute observation in a free play setting.

½ point score: Give the child ½ point if he spontaneously engages in parallel play (without adult prompting) by other children for a total of 1 minute during a 30-minute observation in a free play setting.

SOCIAL 5-M	Spontaneously follows peers or imitates their motor behavior 2 times (e.g., follows a peer into a playhouse). (TO: 30 min.)
Objective:	To determine if a child will imitate the behavior of peers without prompts from adults.
Materials:	Peers.
Examples:	A peer stands up and walks over to a toy and the target child looks at the peer and also stands up and follows the peer to the other location without being told to do so. When playing with a train set, one child pulls the train in circles, and the target child imitates the peer's behavior with his train.
1 point score:	Give the child 1 point if he spontaneously follows peers or imitates their motor behavior 2 times during a 30-minute observation.
½ point score:	Give the child ½ point if he spontaneously follows peers or imitates their motor behavior 1 time during a 30-minute observation.

MOTOR IMITATION – LEVEL 1

IMITATION 1-M	Imitates 2 gross motor movements when prompted with, *Do this* (e.g., clapping, raising arms). (T)
Objective:	To determine if the child imitates the gross motor behaviors of others when asked to do so with a verbal prompt such as, "Do this."
Materials:	A list of possible age-appropriate imitative behaviors.
Examples:	Clapping, stomping feet, raising arms up, tapping a table, and jumping.
1 point score:	Give the child 1 point if he imitates 2 gross motor movements presented by an adult. Even if the responses are approximations, score them as correct.
½ point score:	Give the child ½ point if he imitates only one motor action. Don't give any points if the child always emits the same behavior, such as clapping (this may be obvious when the child claps before the adult claps).

IMITATION 2-M	Imitates 4 gross motor movements when prompted with, *Do this.* (T)
Objective:	To determine if the child imitates the gross motor behaviors of others when asked to do so with a verbal prompt such as, "Do this."
Materials:	A list of possible age-appropriate imitative behaviors.
Examples:	Clapping, stomping feet, raising arms up, tapping a table, and jumping.
1 point score:	Give the child 1 point if he imitates 4 motor movements presented by an adult. Even if the responses are approximations, score them as correct.
½ point score:	Give the child ½ point if he imitates 3 motor movements.

IMITATION 3-M	Imitates 8 motor movements, 2 of which involve objects (e.g., shaking a maraca, tapping sticks together). (T)
Objective:	To determine if the child's imitative repertoire is growing, and if he is able to imitate the behaviors of others when a specific object is involved.
Materials:	A list of possible imitative behaviors, and a collection of matching objects that can be used for specific actions to imitate.
Example:	An adult picks up a maraca and shakes it, and the child imitates the shaking behavior with the maraca without physical prompts.
1 point score:	Give the child 1 point if he imitates 6 motor movements presented by an adult, and can imitate 2 adult motor behaviors involving objects (a total of 8 imitations). Even if the responses are approximations, score them as correct.
½ point score:	Give the child ½ point if he imitates 6 behaviors of any type. (Make a note in the "Comments/notes" section of the VB-MAPP Milestones Form if the child fails to imitate any actions with objects or if all imitation must involve objects.)

IMITATION 4-M	Spontaneously imitates the motor behaviors of others on 5 occasions. (O)
Objective:	To determine if the child's imitative repertoire is breaking free from verbal prompts. A major goal in imitation training is the development of spontaneous imitation because it can be of great value to a child in a variety of situations (e.g., social behavior, arts and crafts, classroom routines).
Materials:	No specific materials are required.
Example:	An adult pulls a wind-up car backwards and it shoots forward fast, and the child spontaneously attempts to imitate that behavior with his car.
1 point score:	Give the child 1 point if he spontaneously imitates at least 2 different motor behaviors of others on 5 occasions.
½ point score:	Give the child ½ point if he spontaneously imitates any motor behavior of others on 2 occasions.

IMITATION 5-M	Imitates 20 motor movements of any type (e.g., fine motor, gross motor, imitation with objects). (T)
Objective:	To determine if the child's imitative behavior is becoming stronger and generalized.
Materials:	A list of possible imitative behaviors, and a collection of matching objects that can be used for specific actions to imitate.
Examples:	Wiggle fingers, tap shoulders, touch toes, close fist, spin a top, etc.
1 point score:	Give the child 1 point if he imitates 20 motor movements of any type.
½ point score:	Give the child ½ point if he imitates 15 motor movements of any type.

EARLY ECHOIC SKILLS ASSESSMENT (EESA) SUBTEST
BY BARBARA E. ESCH, PH.D., BCBA-D, CCC-SLP

PURPOSE

Early speech skills can vary widely. When asked to vocally imitate sounds or words (e.g., say "mama"), some children may have difficulty echoing these models accurately, if at all. The ability to repeat what one hears is essential in learning how to talk and in acquiring more complex forms of language. Thus, even if children are beginning to make some sounds on their own or to produce beginning words, it may be important to evaluate their ability to make sounds in response to hearing these models from someone else.

The Early Echoic Skills Assessment (EESA) evaluates a child's ability to repeat a speech model. The EESA samples this echoic repertoire through speech phonemes, syllable combinations (words and phrases), and intonation patterns that are typically acquired between birth and 30 months of age (the EESA protocol is contained in the VB-MAPP Protocol). As the echoic subtest of the VB-MAPP, EESA assesses echoic skills at VB-MAPP Level 1 (0-18 months) and Level 2 (18-30 months). There is no echoic subtest for VB-MAPP Level 3.

SPEECH SKILLS, BIRTH TO 30 MONTHS

Early speech often contains many articulation errors. Some of these errors do not greatly interfere with intelligibility ("goggy" for "doggy"), whereas other errors may render words nearly unrecognizable ("pah kaw," for "hot dog"). Even in early speech learners, though, most vowels are usually accurate whereas consonants may be mispronounced for months before accuracy is achieved.

As a general guide, children between birth and 30 months of age follow this progression of skill acquisition:

- Vowels and diphthongs are acquired first
- Echoic skills emerge by about 11 months
- Prosodic features of intonation, duration, and loudness are evident by 6 months and all are noted by 23 months (but accuracy may be inconsistent)
- Consonants appear first at the beginning of syllables (several by 18 months)
- Typical early consonants are p, b, m, n, h, and w; these are followed by k, g, t, d, f, ng, and y
- 1- and 2-syllable words and phrases begin to appear between 6-18 months; those that are 2-syllables are often reduplicated ("ma-ma," "da-da")
- Many 2- and 3-syllable words and phrases are acquired by about 18-30 months

EESA COMPONENTS

There are 100 total points in five groups of EESA test items. Targets in the first three groups are arranged in a developmental progression. Group 1 (25 points) samples vowels and diphthongs and some early consonants, all of which represent speech skills that are typically acquired up to 18 months of age. Groups 2 and 3 (30 points each) present all early consonants in 2- and 3-syllable combinations, respectively. Groups 4 and 5 have a total of 15 items. They assess a child's ability to imitate prosodic features of speech such as pitch, loudness, and vowel duration. Together, items in these groups represent speech skills that are common in children at ages 18-30 months.

Who can Give the EESA?

Anyone can administer the EESA although optimal results may be obtained by speech pathologists due to their specific training in listening to speech production and identifying articulatory and prosodic differences.

What Speech Components are Scored?

Since EESA is a test of a speaker's echoic skill, examiners should listen for speech components that differ from the model. Components tested on EESA include vowels, consonants, number of sounds or syllables, and prosodic features of intonation, duration, and loudness (see below for the scoring criteria for EESA).

How is EESA Administered?

General instructions

- Ensure cooperation by having important reinforcers available.
- Administer test item(s) followed by a reinforcer as appropriate for the child.
- If desired, EESA can be given over multiple sessions, a few items at a time.

Specific directions

- Ask the child to repeat each test item (say "hop"). Omit "say" if child repeats it.
- Enter the appropriate point score (see below) in the box next to each item.
- Give up to 3 trials, scoring the best response, if the initial response is inaccurate or absent.

Scoring the EESA

Scoring criteria for all groups are listed on the Milestones Assessment EESA Protocol. In addition, examples for scoring items in Groups 1-3 are listed below.

Score 1 point for each response in which all sounds are correct.

Score ½ point if the echoic response is recognizable but identifies:
- Incorrect consonants ("poo-ey," for "foo-ey")
- Missing consonants ("-itty," for "kitty")
- Extra syllables ("moo moo moo," for "moo")

Score 0 points for:
- No response
  OR if the echoic response identifies:
- Incorrect vowels ("oo," for "ah")
- Deleted syllables ("ma," for "mama")

ECHOIC (EESA) SUBTEST – LEVEL 1

ECHOIC 1-M	Scores at least 2 on the EESA subtest.
Objective:	To determine if the child emits some echoic behavior.
Materials:	The EESA subtest.
Examples:	The child emits "moo" and "ah" when tested.
1 point score:	Give the child 1 point if he scores 2 or more on the EESA subtest
½ point score:	Give the child ½ point if he scores 1 on the EESA subtest.

ECHOIC 2-M	Scores at least 5 on the EESA subtest.
Objective:	To determine if the child's echoic repertoire is growing.
Materials:	The EESA subtest.
Examples:	The child emits "boy," "pipe," or "wow," when tested.
1 point score:	Give the child 1 point if he scores 5 or more on the EESA subtest.
½ point score:	Give the child ½ point if he scores 3 on the EESA subtest.

ECHOIC 3-M	Scores at least 10 on the EESA subtest.
Objective:	To determine if the child's echoic repertoire is growing.
Materials:	The EESA subtest.
Examples:	The child emits "baby," "papa," or "bye bye," when tested.
1 point score:	Give the child 1 point if he scores 10 or more on the EESA subtest.
½ point score:	Give the child ½ point if he scores 7 on the EESA.

ECHOIC 4-M	Scores at least 15 on the EESA subtest.
Objective:	To determine if the child echoic repertoire is growing.
Materials:	The EESA subtest.
Examples:	The child emits "uh-oh," "puppy," and "oh boy," when tested.
1 point score:	Give the child 1 point if he scores 15 or more on the EESA subtest.
½ point score:	Give the child ½ point if he scores 12 on the EESA subtest.

ECHOIC 5-M	Scores at least 25 on the EESA subtest (at least 20 from group I).
Objective:	To determine if the child is beginning to echo whole words.
Materials:	The EESA subtest.
Example:	The child echoes "open," "cookie," and "meow," when tested.
I point score:	Give the child 1 point if he scores 25 or more on the EESA subtest, with at least 20 from group 1.
½ point score:	Give the child ½ point if he scores 20 on the EESA subtest with at least 15 from group 1.

SPONTANEOUS VOCAL BEHAVIOR – LEVEL I

VOCAL I-M	Spontaneously emits an average of 5 sounds each hour. (TO: 60 min.)
Objective:	To determine if a child will emit speech sounds without prompts.
Materials:	None.
Example:	The child emits "ah" a few times an hour.
I point score:	Give the child 1 point if he spontaneously emits an average of 5 speech sounds each hour. A time-sample type of data recording can be used to measure this behavior (do not give the child credit if the sounds are a type of self-stimulation).
½ point score:	Give the child ½ point if he spontaneously emits an average of 2 speech sounds each hour.

VOCAL 2-M	Spontaneously emits 5 different sounds, averaging 10 total sounds each hour. (TO: 60 min.)
Objective:	To determine if the child is beginning to emit different speech sounds, and the frequency is increasing.
Materials:	None.
Examples:	The child emits "ah," "ba," "ma," "oh," and "ga," a few times an hour.
I point score:	Give the child 1 point if he spontaneously emits 5 different sounds, averaging 10 total sounds each hour (not including self-stim sounds).
½ point score:	Give the child ½ point if he spontaneously emits 3 different sounds, averaging 10 total sounds each hour (not including self-stim sounds).

VOCAL 3-M	**Spontaneously emits 10 different sounds with varying intonations, averaging 25 total sounds each hour. (TO: 60 min.)**

Objective: To determine if the number and frequency of vocal sounds is increasing.

Materials: None.

Examples: The child emits "ee," "ba," "da," "ih," "pa," and "ta," several times each hour with different intonations.

1 point score: Give the child 1 point if he spontaneously emits 10 different sounds with varying intonations, averaging 25 total sounds each hour.

½ point score: Give the child ½ point if he spontaneously emits 5 different sounds with varying intonations, averaging 25 total sounds each hour.

VOCAL 4-M	**Spontaneously emits 5 different whole word approximations. (TO: 60 min.)**

Objective: To determine if the rate of vocal play is increasing, and if whole words are beginning to occur.

Materials: None.

Examples: The child emits "mama," "dada," "og," (for dog) "eat," "uh oh," but not necessarily in the appropriate context.

1 point score: Give the child 1 point if he spontaneously emits 5 word approximations during the 60 minute observation.

½ point score: Give the child ½ point if he spontaneously emits 2 word approximations during the 60 minute observation.

VOCAL 5-M	**Spontaneously vocalizes 15 whole words or phrases with appropriate intonation and rhythm. (TO: 60 min.)**

Objective: To determine if the child is beginning to emit more whole words in vocal play, and with the appropriate intonation and rhythm.

Materials: None.

Examples: The child emits "shoe," "get it," "there it is," and "bye-bye." It also appears like the child is "talking," but it may be hard or impossible to understand all the words.

1 point score: Give the child 1 point if he spontaneously emits 15 different identifiable word approximations during a 1-hour observation.

½ point score: Give the child ½ point if he spontaneously emits 8 different identifiable word approximations during a 1-hour observation.

CHAPTER 4

Milestones Scoring Instructions: Level 2

This chapter contains the specific instructions for administering Level 2 of the VB-MAPP Milestones Assessment. There are four new domains added to Level 2: Listener Responding by Function, Feature, and Class (LRFFC), Intraverbal, Classroom Routines and Group Skills, and Linguistic Structure. These areas were not included in Level 1 because most typically developing 18 month old children have not acquired them yet. In addition, these domains should be avoided as part of the curriculum for a child with language delays whose scores fall primarily in Level 1. It is hoped that by presenting these skills in Level 2 it makes it clearer what skills to focus on for a child scoring in each of the levels. One domain, Spontaneous Vocal Behavior, is not included in Level 2 because it is less of a target area for a child who has acquired echoic behavior. As a reminder, the four methods of assessing a specific skill are: (1) formal testing (**T**), (2) observation (**O**), (3) either observation or testing (**E**), and (4) a timed observation (**TO**).

MAND – LEVEL 2

MAND 6-M	Mands for 20 different missing items without prompts (except, e.g., *What do you need?*) (e.g., mands for paper when given a crayon). (E)
Objective:	To determine if a child mands for items when a part of a desired item is missing from a toy or desired activity, or simply not present, but desired.
Materials:	Gather items that are reinforcing for a child that have multiple parts, such as a Play Doh set. The removal of one part of a toy can create motivation (MOs) for that part.
Examples:	A child is playing with Play Doh and wants to make star shapes, but the star form has been removed. When asked, "What's missing?" does the child ask for the missing star form? If the child likes juice and drinks it with a straw, give him a juice box without a straw and test if he mands for a straw.
1 point score:	Give the child 1 point if he mands for 20 different missing items without prompts (other than verbal prompts such as, "What's missing?" or "What do you need?"). It is important that the item that is missing be valuable to the child at that moment, (i.e., there must be a current MO at strength for that item).
½ point score:	Give the child ½ point if he mands for 10 different missing items without prompts.

LEVEL 2

MAND 7-M	Mands for others to emit 5 different actions needed to enjoy a desired activity (e.g., *open* to get outside, *push* when on a swing). (E)

Objective: To determine if a child mands for actions that are necessary to enjoy a desired action or activity.

Materials: Develop a list of actions that are of value to the child, or activities that involve specific actions.

Examples: A child who is sitting on a swing and wants to be pushed mands "push me." A child who wants to go outside is standing at the door and mands "open." A child who likes to see a spinning top mands "spin." A child who wants to be chased by an adult or peer mands "get me."

1 point score: Give the child 1 point if he mands for 5 different actions or missing actions needed to enjoy a desired activity during observation or testing without prompts (other than verbal prompts such as, "What do you want me to do?"). It is important that the activity that is missing be valuable to the child, (i.e., there must be a current MO at strength for the activity).

½ point score: Give the child ½ point if he mands for 2 different actions or missing actions needed to enjoy a desired activity during observation or testing without prompts (other than verbal prompts such as, "What do you want me to do?").

MAND 8-M	Emits 5 different mands that contain 2 or more words (not including *I want*) (e.g., *Go fast. My turn. Pour juice.*). (TO: 60 min.)

Objective: To determine if the mand repertoire is showing variation, and if the mand's mean length of utterance (MLU) is increasing.

Materials: A data sheet that allows for the tracking of the different mands emitted by the child over time.

Examples: The child says "open door," "no shoe," or "go night night."

1 point score: Give the child 1 point if he emits 5 different mands that contain 2 or more words (not including "I want") during a 1-hour observation. A list of the different mands emitted by the child should be kept and used as the data base for meeting this milestone.

½ point score: Give the child ½ point if he emits 2 different mands that contain 2 or more words (not including "I want") during a 1-hour observation.

MAND 9-M	Spontaneously emits 15 different mands (e.g., *Let's play. Open. I want book.*). (TO: 30 min.)

Objective: To determine if mands are occurring at a frequent rate, are related to a variety of MOs, and are initiated by the child (free from adult prompting).

Materials: Reinforcing items and activities found in the child's natural environment.

Examples: A child initiates these mands without any prompts from adults: "Where's Spiderman?" "I want up." "It's my turn." "More juice."

1 point score: Give the child 1 point if he spontaneously emits 15 different mands (no adult delivered prompts) during a 30-minute observation. The mands should be controlled by different MOs.

½ point score: Give the child ½ point if he spontaneously mands (no adult delivered prompts) 8 times during a 30-minute observation. Also, give the child ½ point if his mands contain different response topographies, but are for the same MO (i.e., he asks for the same thing with different words).

MAND 10-M	Emits 10 new mands without specific mand training (e.g., spontaneously says *Where kitty go?* without formal mand training). (O)

Objective: To determine if new mands are acquired through the natural transfer of control from existing verbal skills such as tact and echoic.

Materials: Reinforcing items and activities found in the child's natural environment.

Example: When another child picks up a pinwheel and blows on it, the target child says, "I want to spin" without ever having a training trial on manding for spinning a pinwheel. The child probably could tact and LD spin, but prior to this situation, had never manded for spinning a pinwheel.

1 point score: Give the child 1 point if he learns 10 new mands without formal mand training on those words. Record each new mand on a daily data sheet.

½ point score: Give the child ½ point if he learns 5 new mands without formal mand training on those words.

TACT – LEVEL 2

TACT 6-M	**Tacts 25 items when asked, *What's that?* (e.g., *book, shoe, car, dog, hat*). (T)**
Objective:	To determine if the child is learning to tact more things in his physical environment.
Materials:	Use common items (including pictures) in the child's natural environment.
Examples:	Upon holding up a toy car and asking a child, "What's this?" he says "car" on the first trial. When pointing to a shoe and asking a child, "What's that?" he says "shoe" on the first trial.
1 point score:	Give the child 1 point if he tacts 25 items when tested.
½ point score:	Give the child ½ point if he tacts 20 items when tested.

TACT 7-M	**Generalizes tacts across 3 examples of 50 items, tested or from a list of known generalizations (e.g., tacts 3 different cars). (T)**
Objective:	To determine if the child has learned to generalize across static stimuli (nouns).
Materials:	Assemble a collection of 3 variations of known items.
Example:	After a child learns to tact a small yellow plastic bus, test to see if the response has generalized to other items that would be called a bus, but look different in some way (i.e., different sizes, shapes, colors, pictures, etc.).
1 point score:	Give the child 1 point if his tacts have generalized across 3 examples of 50 items when tested. A list of mastered (known) generalizations can be used if it is available and the scoring has been reliable (e.g., the 300 common nouns list from www.avbpress.com/downloads contains generalization columns).
½ point score:	Give the child ½ point if his tacts have generalized across 3 examples of 25 items when tested.

TACT 8-M	**Tacts 10 actions when asked, for example, *What am I doing?* (e.g., *jumping, sleeping, eating*). (T)**
Objective:	To determine if the child is able to tact physical movement when asked to do so.
Materials:	Use common moving stimuli in the child's natural environment, or contrive them in a testing situation.
Examples:	When jumping up and down and asking, "What am I doing?" the child says "jumping." While rolling a ball and asking, "What am I doing?" the child says "rolling." Other verbal prompts can be used such as, "What is he doing?" or, "What's happening?"
1 point score:	Give the child 1 point if he tacts 10 actions when tested.
½ point score:	Give the child ½ point if he tacts 5 actions when tested.

TACT 9-M	Tacts 50 two-component verb-noun or noun-verb combinations tested or from a list of known two-component tacts (e.g., *washing face, Joe swinging, baby sleeping*). (T)

Objective: To determine if the child attends to and correctly names a static stimulus and a moving stimulus in one task (a two-component stimulus and a two-component response).

Materials: Use known nouns and verbs.

Examples: When presented with a jumping stuffed monkey and a verbal stimulus such as, "What do you see?" the child says "jumping monkey" or "The monkey is jumping." When another child is pulling a wagon and the assessor presents the verbal stimulus, "What's Joey doing?" The target child responds "Pulling the wagon." When a child sees his father laughing and asked, "What's he doing?" the child says "Daddy's laughing."

1 point score: Give the child 1 point if he tacts 50 two-component noun-verb (or verb-noun) relations when tested. A list of mastered (known) noun-verb or verb-noun combinations can be used if it is available and reliable (for a list of noun-verb combinations, see www.abvpress.com/downloads).

½ point score: Give the child ½ point if he tacts 25 two-component noun-verb (or verb-noun) relations.

TACT 10-M	Tacts a total of 200 nouns and/or verbs (or other parts of speech) tested or from an accumulated list of known tacts. (T)

Objective: To determine if the child continues to learn and retain new tacts.

Materials: Use books, scenes, picture cards, and common environmental objects and actions.

Examples: When holding up a sandwich and asking a child, "What's that?" he says "sandwich" on the first trial. When a baby is crawling on the floor and the target child is asked, "What's he doing?" the child says "crawling."

1 point score: Give the child 1 point if he tacts 200 items and/or actions when tested. An accummulated list of the child's known nouns and verbs can be used for this measure (e.g., the 300 common nouns list from www.avbpress.com/downloads). Also, many children's books, such as a picture dicitonary, are great resources because they contain pictures of hundreds of items, and can easily be used to assess a tact repertoire without needing to find individual pictures.

½ point score: Give the child ½ point if he provides the name of 150 items and/or actions.

LISTENER RESPONDING – LEVEL 2

LISTENER 6-M	Selects the correct item from a messy array of 6, for 40 different objects or pictures (e.g., *Find cat. Touch ball.*). (T)
Objective:	To determine if the child can find an increasingly larger variety of different items in a larger array on command.
Materials:	Use pictures and/or common items in the child's natural environment.
Example:	When presented with a randomly positioned collection of 6 pictures, one of which is a chair, and given the verbal stimulus, "Can you find the chair?" the child is able to select the chair.
1 point score:	Give the child 1 point if he identifies 40 items in a messy array of 6 (i.e., not lined up) when tested.
½ point score:	Give the child ½ point if he identifies 25 items in a messy array of 6 when tested.

LISTENER 7-M	Generalizes listener discriminations (LDs) in a messy array of 8, for 3 different examples of 50 items (e.g., the child can find 3 examples of a train). (T)
Objective:	To determine if the child has learned to generalize LD tasks across several variations of the same item.
Materials:	Assemble a collection of 3 variations of known items (picture books can be used as long as the target item is in an array of at least 8 other items).
Example:	The child is able to select 3 different cars (i.e., different size, shape, color, make, etc.) when each is independently presented in an array containing 7 other items.
1 point score:	Give the child 1 point if he generalizes LDs across 3 examples of 50 items.
½ point score:	Give the child ½ point if he generalizes LDs across 3 examples of 30 items.

LISTENER 8-M	Performs 10 specific motor actions on command (e. g., *Show me clapping. Can you hop?*). (T)
Objective:	To determine if the child is able to perform several different motor actions on command, without imitative prompts.
Materials:	A list of common actions.
Examples:	When an adult says "run," the child will run. When an adult says "show me crying," the child will rub his eyes and pretend to cry. When an adult says, "Can you stomp your feet?" the child will stomp his feet.
1 point score:	Give the child 1 point if he demonstrates 10 actions on command. Approximations should be scored as correct.
½ point score:	Give the child ½ point if he demonstrates 5 actions on command.

LISTENER 9-M	Follows 50 two-component noun-verb and/or verb-noun instructions (e.g., *Show me the baby sleeping. Push the swing.*). (T)
Objective:	To determine if the child correctly follows instructions that contain both a noun and a verb. It is important that the instruction be given as one task, and that the response contains two parts but occurs as one response unit (i.e., a two-component stimulus and a two-component response).
Materials:	Use known nouns and verbs.
Example:	When presented with an array of objects on the table (e.g., car, straw, crayon) and the verbal stimulus, "Show me spinning the crayon," the child is able to spin the crayon without any additional prompts.
1 point score:	Give the child 1 point if he follows (LDs) 50 two-component noun-verb and/or verb-noun instructions.
½ point score:	Give the child ½ point if he follows (LDs) 30 two-component noun-verb and/or verb-noun instructions.

LISTENER 10-M	Selects the correct item in a book, picture scene, or natural environment when named, for 250 items (tested or from an accumulated list of known words). (T)
Objective:	To determine if the child's listener vocabulary is growing and becoming more complex. Additionally, a goal is to determine if the child is learning to scan larger and more complex visual arrays (e.g., scenes and books that contain similar stimuli).
Materials:	Use scenes, books, and common environmental settings.
Example:	When looking at the *Goodnight Moon* book an adult says, "Good night light. Can you find the light?" and the child successfully points to the light in the book.
1 point score:	Give the child 1 point if he selects 250 different items in a book, picture scene, or natural environment when named. An accumulated list of known LDs with nouns can be used for this measure (e.g., the 300 common nouns list from www.avbpress.com/downloads), and children's picture books.
½ point score:	Give the child ½ point if he selects 150 items in a book, picture scene, or natural environment when asked.

VISUAL PERCEPTUAL SKILLS AND MATCHING-TO-SAMPLE (VP-MTS) – LEVEL 2

VP-MTS 6-M	Matches identical objects or pictures in a messy array of 6, for 25 items. (T)
Objective:	To determine if the child's ability to match identical items is growing, and that he can find the matching items in an increasingly complex visual array.
Materials:	Common items found in the child's natural environment, and pictures of items relevant to or of interest to the child.
Example:	When an adult shows a child a figurine of Tigger, the child finds Tigger from an array of 6 items randomly placed on a table.
1 point score:	Give the child 1 point if he successfully matches 25 identical objects or pictures in a messy array of 6 (the items are not lined up on the table).
½ point score:	Give the child ½ point if he successfully matches 15 identical objects or pictures in a messy array of 4.

VP-MTS 7-M	Matches similar colors and shapes for 10 different colors or shapes given models (e.g., given red, blue, and green bowls and a pile of red, blue, and green bears the child matches the items by color). (T)
Objective:	To determine if the child can match colors and shapes that are identical.
Materials:	Different colored objects and shapes.
Examples:	When given a pegboard with the four basic colors and a collection of four different colored rings, the child matches each colored ring with the peg of the same color. When given a shape board and a collection of shapes the child can match the shapes.
1 point score:	Give the child 1 point if he matches similar colors and/or shapes for 10 different colors or shapes given models, but no other prompts (other than a verbal prompts such as "match the colors," or "match the shapes").
½ point score:	Give the child ½ point if he matches similar colors and/or shapes for 5 different colors or shapes given models, but no other prompts (other than verbal prompts).

VP-MTS 8-M	Matches identical objects or pictures in a messy array of 8 containing 3 similar stimuli, for 25 items (e.g., matches a dog to a dog in an array that also contains a cat, pig, and pony). (T)
Objective:	To determine if the child can find matching items in a visual array that contains comparison items that look similar to the sample item.
Materials:	Common items and pictures of items found in the child's natural environment, and comparison items that look similar to the sample item.

Example: When presented with a sample of a spoon, the adult places a knife, fork, spoon, and straw in a messy comparison array that includes 4 additional items.

1 point score: Give the child 1 point if he successfully matches identical objects or pictures in a messy array of 8 containing 3 similar stimuli, for 25 items.

½ point score: Give the child ½ point if he successfully matches identical objects or pictures in a messy array of 8 containing 3 similar stimuli, for 10 items.

VP-MTS 9-M	Matches non-identical objects or non-identical pictures in a messy array of 10, for 25 items (e.g., matches a Ford truck to a Toyota truck). (T)

Objective: To determine if the child matches non-identical items that are in a large array that contains at least 3 comparison items that look similar to the sample item. This task requires a more effective scanning and discrimination repertoire then the prior matching tasks.

Materials: A collection of common items and pictures of items found in the child's natural environment, and comparison items that look similar to the sample item.

Example: After randomly placing at least 10 pictures on the table (or on a computer screen) that include a cement truck, a red bus, a fire truck, and a white Honda Accord, and giving the child a picture of a red 1957 Chevy and a verbal prompt such as, "Can you match this?" the child selects the white Honda Accord from the comparison array.

1 point score: Give the child 1 point if he matches non-identical objects or non-identical pictures in a messy array of 10 containing 3 similar stimuli, for 25 items.

½ point score: Give the child ½ point if he matches non-identical objects or non-identical pictures in a messy array of 10 containing 3 similar stimuli, for 10 items.

VP-MTS 10-M	Matches non-identical objects (3D) to pictures (2D) and/or vice versa, in a messy array of 10 containing 3 similar stimuli, for 25 items. (T)

Objective: To determine if the child matches items across dimensions.

Materials: A collection of common items and non-identical pictures of those items, and comparison items that look similar to the sample item.

Example: After randomly placing at least 10 pictures on a table (or on a computer screen), 3 of which are round and red (e.g., a red ball, a red tomato, and a red apple), and giving the child a plastic red apple and saying, "Can you match this?" the child selects the picture of the apple from the comparison array.

1 point score: Give the child 1 point if he matches non-identical objects (3D) to pictures (2D) and/or vice versa in a messy array of 10 containing 3 similar stimuli, for 25 items.

½ point score: Give the child ½ point if he matches non-identical objects (3D) to pictures (2D) and/or vice versa in a messy array of 10 containing 3 similar stimuli, for 10 items.

INDEPENDENT PLAY – LEVEL 2

PLAY 6-M	Searches for a missing or corresponding toy or part of a set for 5 items or sets (e.g., a puzzle piece, a ball for a drop-in toy, a bottle for a baby doll). (E)

Objective: To determine if the child demonstrates motivation (has a strong MO) for missing items, and acts on that motivation during object play.

Materials: Common toys and items that have a variety of parts, and the child has shown interest in these items in the past.

Examples: When given a toy that the child enjoys like Mr. Potato Head without some of the parts, does the child look around for the parts? Or, when given a desired bottle of bubbles without a wand, does the child look around for a wand?

1 point score: Give the child 1 point if he actively and independently searches for a missing or corresponding toy or part of a set for 5 items or sets when items are removed or naturally missing.

½ point score: Give the child ½ point if he actively and independently searches for a missing or corresponding toy or part of a set 2 items or sets when items are removed or naturally missing.

PLAY 7-M	Independently demonstrates the use of toys or objects according to their function for 5 items (e.g., placing a train on a track, pulling a wagon, holding a telephone to the ear). (O)

Objective: To determine if the child has learned that particular toys and objects have particular functions or uses.

Materials: Familiar toys and items found in a child's home or school environment.

Examples: When given a hairbrush does the child attempt to brush his hair? When given a car does the child attempt to push it? When given a hat does the child attempt to put it on?

1 point score: Give the child 1 point if he independently demonstrates the use of toys or objects according to their function for 5 items.

½ point score: Give the child ½ point if he independently demonstrates the use of toys or objects according to their function for 2 items.

PLAY 8-M	Plays with everyday items in creative ways 2 times (e.g., uses a bowl as a drum or a box as an imaginary car). (O)
Objective:	To determine if the child is generalizing his play skills by demonstrating creative and imaginative play activities with different objects.
Materials:	Toys and items found in a child's home or school environment.
Examples:	The child places leaves and sticks in a toy shopping cart. The child places farm animals in a cup.
1 point score:	Give the child 1 point if he plays with 2 different everyday items in creative ways (except for stimming on a toy).
½ point score:	Give the child ½ point if he plays with 1 item in a creative way.

PLAY 9-M	Independently engages in play on structures and playground equipment for a total of 5 minutes (e.g., going down a slide, swinging). (TO: 30 min.)
Objective:	To determine if the child likes to engage in physical activities involving age appropriate play structures and playground equipment.
Materials:	Playgrounds, play structures, and other related equipment.
Examples:	The child gets on a merry-go-round, goes down a slide, climbs through tunnels, swings on monkey bars, jumps on rope bridges, etc.
1 point score:	Give the child 1 point if he engages in play on play structures and playground equipment without prompts for a total of 5 minutes during a 30-minute observation.
½ point score:	Give the child ½ point if he engages in play on play structures and playground equipment without prompts for a total of 2 minutes during a 30-minute observation.

PLAY 10-M	Assembles toys that have multiple parts for 5 different sets of materials (e.g., Mr. Potato Head, Little People sets, Cooties bugs, Kid K'Nex). (O)
Objective:	To determine if the child plays with items that have multiple parts and can appropriately assemble those parts.
Materials:	Common toys and items found in a child's home or school environment.
Examples:	Duplos, train sets, blocks, vehicles and car garages, Little People sets, Winnie the Pooh party set, dolls and dollhouses, tea sets, farm animals, etc.
1 point score:	Give the child 1 point if he independently constructs, assembles, or sets up toys or other play items and does so for 5 different sets of materials.
½ point score:	Give the child ½ point if he independently constructs, assembles, or sets up toys or other play items and does so for 2 different sets of materials.

SOCIAL BEHAVIOR AND SOCIAL PLAY – LEVEL 2

SOCIAL 6-M	**Initiates a physical interaction with a peer 2 times (e.g., a push in a wagon, hand holding, Ring Around the Rosy). (TO: 30 min.)**

Objective: To determine if a child will initiate an interaction with other children without prompts from an adult. This interaction can be nonverbal or verbal.

Materials: Peers and age-appropriate items and activities.

Examples: On the playground the target child spontaneously tags a peer shortly after playing a prompted game of tag with staff and peers. The target child joins a peer at a water table and splashes the water, which makes the peer laugh, and the child repeats the same behavior later. The target child approaches a peer, grabs his arm, and pulls him towards the water table.

1 point score: Give the child 1 point if he initiates an interaction with a peer 2 times during a 30-minute observation. Note that unprompted initiations may occur with negative events first, such as the child pushing another child off a bike in order to obtain the bike; however, do not count negative types of initiations.

½ point score: Give the child ½ point if he initiates an interaction with a peer 1 time during a 30-minute observation.

SOCIAL 7-M	**Spontaneously mands to peers 5 times (e.g., *My turn. Push me. Look! Come on.*). (TO: 60 min.)**

Objective: To determine if a child will mand to a peer without adult prompts. The mand can be of any type.

Materials: Peers and age-appropriate items found in a child's home or school.

Examples: When the target child is sitting in a wagon he mands to a peer "pull me" without adult prompts. When sitting at an art table, the target child mands to a peer "look" and shows him his project. When a peer is eating Gummy Bears the target child mands to the peer, "I want gummy." On the playground the target child spontaneously mands to a peer "come on," when the child wants the peer to join him in an activity. Manding to peers also includes mands to remove undesirable things or activities, such as manding a peer to stop an activity or behavior.

1 point score: Give the child 1 point if he spontaneously mands with at least 2 different mands to peers 5 times during a 1-hour observation.

½ point score: Give the child ½ point if he spontaneously mands to peers 2 times during a 1-hour observation.

SOCIAL 8-M	**Engages in sustained social play with peers for 3 minutes without adult prompts or reinforcement (e.g., cooperatively setting up a play set, water play). (TO: 30 min.)**

Objective: To determine if a child will independently play with peers for a sustained period in any one of a variety of activities that involve specific verbal and/or nonverbal interaction between the children.

Materials: Peers and age appropriate items found in a child's home or school.

Examples: The target child and a peer are throwing water balloons at each other and filling up new ones at a faucet. The target child and a peer are playing in a log cabin playhouse and are pretending to have dinner. The target child and the peer are working on building a Lego structure together.

1 point score: Give the child 1 point if he engages in sustained social play with peers for 3 minutes without prompts during a 30-minute observation. There must be specific verbal or nonverbal interaction in order to receive credit. Do not give points at this level for simply participating in an activity (e.g., watching a video) when peers are close by; this would be more like parallel play.

½ point score: Give the child ½ point if he engages in sustained social play with peers for 2 minutes without prompts during a 30-minute observation.

SOCIAL 9-M	Spontaneously responds to the mands from peers 5 times (e.g., *Pull me in the wagon. I want the train.*). (E)

Objective: To determine if a child is learning to attend to the content of the verbal behavior of peers. One early demonstration of this skill is the child's ability to correctly respond to the mands of peers without prompts from adults.

Materials: Peers and age-appropriate items found in a child's home or school.

Examples: A peer asks the target child for the scissors during an art project, and the target child gives the peer the scissors without an adult prompting. A peer says, "Give me the fire truck," and the target child gives the fire truck to the peer. A peer asks the target child to pull him in the wagon, and the target child pulls the peer. The peer asks the target child to open a door because the peer's hands are full and he wants to get outside, and the target child complies with the peer's mand.

1 point score: Give the child 1 point if he spontaneously responds to at least 2 different mands from peers 5 times during observation or testing. Do not give the child any points if an adult must prompt the behavior in any way.

½ point score: Give the child ½ point if he spontaneously responds to the mands from peers 2 times during observation or testing.

SOCIAL 10-M	Spontaneously mands to peers to participate in games, social play, etc., 2 times (e.g., *Come on you guys. Let's dig a hole.*). (TO: 60 min.)

Objective: To determine if a child asks another child to join him in an activity.

Materials: Peers and age-appropriate items found in a child's home or school.

Examples: The target child says to a peer, "Come play with me." "Do you want go in the playhouse?" "Let's be monsters."

1 point score: Give the child 1 point if he spontaneously mands to peers to participate in games, social play, or other social activities 2 times during a 1-hour observation.

½ point score: Give the child ½ point if he spontaneously mands to peers to participate in games, social play, or other social activities 1 time during a 1-hour observation.

LEVEL 2

MOTOR IMITATION – LEVEL 2

IMITATION 6-M	Imitates 10 actions that require selecting a specific object from an array (e.g., selects a drumstick from an array also containing a horn and a bell, and imitates an adult's drumming). (T)
Objective:	To determine if the child imitates a particular modeled motor behavior with a particular object. Thus, there are two tasks involved both of which require attending, discriminating, and imitating. The goal is to build the basic repertoires necessary for imitating other people (especially other children) during play, social interactions, and academic activities. This type of imitation also begins to build the motor skills necessary for noun-verb listener behaviors (i.e., performing motor actions with objects on verbal command, for example, "spin the wheel").
Materials:	A list of possible actions and a collection of objects from the child's natural environment.
Examples:	Drinking, kissing, hugging, rolling, squeezing, eating, blowing, hiding, spinning, pushing, dressing, climbing, flying, and waving.
1 point score:	Give the child 1 point if he imitates 10 different actions with an object that matches the adult's object selected from an array of 3 when prompted, "Do this."
½ point score:	Give the child ½ point if he imitates 5 different actions with an object that matches the adult's object selected from an array of 3 when prompted, "Do this."

IMITATION 7-M	Imitates 20 different fine motor actions when prompted, *Do this* (e.g., wiggling fingers, pinching, making a fist, making a butterfly). (T)
Objective:	To determine if the child's fine motor imitative behavior is becoming stronger and generalized.
Materials:	A list of possible fine motor imitative behaviors.
Examples:	Claw fingers, pointing at items, wiggle index finger, clasp hands, touch fingertips, hold up the number 2, pretend walking on two fingers, wiggle rabbit ears, making letters from fingerspelling, making signs from sign language.
1 point score:	Give the child 1 point if he imitates 20 different fine motor actions when prompted, "Do this."
½ point score:	Give the child ½ point if he imitates 10 different fine motor actions when prompted, "Do this."

IMITATION 8-M	Imitates 10 different three-component sequences of actions when prompted, *Do this* (e.g., clapping, jumping, touching toes; pick up a doll, place her in a crib, and rock the crib). (T)
Objective:	To determine if the child can imitate multiple behaviors in a contrived or natural context.
Materials:	No special materials.

Examples:
An adult taps his knees, shoulders, and tummy, and the child copies all three behaviors as one sequence of responding. An adult picks up a remote control and points it at the TV and pushes the buttons, and the child copies this behavior with another remote that is sitting on the table.

1 point score:
Give the child 1 point if he imitates 10 three-component actions in contrived or natural settings modeled by a peer or an adult.

½ point score:
Give the child ½ point if he imitates 5 two-component actions in contrived or natural settings modeled by a peer or an adult.

IMITATION 9-M	Spontaneously imitates 5 functional skills in the natural environment (e.g., eating with a spoon, putting on a coat, removing shoes). (O)

Objective:
To determine if the child imitates functional behaviors in a natural context without any prompts from others.

Materials:
No specific materials are required.

Examples:
After watching another child get a bowl to pour a snack into, the target child copies the behavior by getting a bowl himself. When an adult pulls a blanket up over herself, the target child pulls his blanket up also.

1 point score:
Give the child 1 point if he spontaneously imitates 5 functional skills in the natural environment.

½ point score:
Give the child ½ point if he spontaneously imitates 2 functional skills in the natural environment.

IMITATION 10-M	Imitates (or attempts to with approximations) any novel motor action modeled by an adult with and without objects (i.e., a "generalized imitative repertoire"). (T)

Objective:
To determine if the child has acquired the ability to successfully imitate (or approximate) new movements or activities without specific training on each of them. This ability is quite valuable and is identified as a "generalized imitative repertoire" in the behavioral literature.

Materials:
No special materials.

Examples:
An adult and a child both have croquet mallets, and the adult models how to hit the ball and the child attempts to imitate the adult's hitting the ball on the first trial. A peer puts his feet up on a table and the target child copies the behavior.

1 point score:
Give the child 1 point if he imitates (or approximates) many novel motor actions with and without objects modeled by an adult when prompted with, "Do this."

½ point score: None.

ECHOIC (EESA) SUBTEST – LEVEL 2

ECHOIC 6-M	Scores at least 50 on the EESA subtest (at least 20 from Group 2). (T)
Objective:	To determine if the child is able to echo more whole words, some of which contain two syllables.
Materials:	The EESA subtest.
Examples:	The child echoes "monkey," "window," and "open," when tested.
1 point score:	Give the child 1 point if he scores 50 on the EESA subtest (20 from Group 2).
½ point score:	Give the child ½ point if he scores 40 on the EESA subtest (15 from Group 2).

ECHOIC 7-M	Scores at least 60 on the EESA subtest.
Objective:	To determine if the child continues to demonstrate a more complex echoic repertoire.
Materials:	The EESA subtest.
Examples:	The child echoes "banana," "yucky," and "go bye bye" when tested.
1 point score:	Give the child 1 point if he scores 60 on the EESA subtest.
½ point score:	Give the child ½ point if he scores 55 on the EESA subtest.

ECHOIC 8-M	Scores at least 70 on the EESA subtest.
Objective:	To determine if the child continues to demonstrate a more complex echoic repertoire.
Materials:	The EESA subtest.
Examples:	The child echoes "hey me too," "teddy bear," and "do high five" when tested.
1 point score:	Give the child 1 point if he scores 70 on the EESA subtest.
½ point score:	Give the child ½ point if he scores 65 on the EESA subtest.

ECHOIC 9-M	Scores at least 80 on the EESA subtest.
Objective:	To determine if the child is beginning to demonstrate the ability to echo words with 3 syllables. Also, to determine if the child is able to echoic the dynamic properties of speech such as volume, pitch, and prosody.
Materials:	The EESA subtest.

Examples: The child echoes "win a toy," "funny king," and "one cookie," when tested.

I point score: Give the child 1 point if he scores 80 on the EESA subtest.

½ point score: Give the child ½ point if he scores 75 on the EESA subtest.

ECHOIC 10-M	Scores at least 90 on the EESA subtest (at least 10 from Groups 4 and 5).

Objective: To determine if the child is reaching the acquisition of a generalized echoic repertoire where he can echo, or approximate most novel words or short phrases. Also, to determine if the child is becoming proficient at echoing the dynamic properties of speech, such as volume, pitch, and prosody.

Materials: The EESA subtest.

Examples: The child echoes whispering, and echoes a continuous warble when tested.

I point score: Give the child 1 point if he scores 90 on the EESA subtest (at least 10 from Groups 4 and 5).

½ point score: Give the child ½ point if he scores 85 on the EESA subtest (at least 10 from Groups 4 and 5).

LISTENER RESPONDING BY FUNCTION, FEATURE, AND CLASS (LRFFC) – LEVEL 2

LRFFC 6-M	Selects 5 different foods or drinks when each are presented in an array of 5 (along with 4 non-food or non-drink items) and asked the verbal fill-ins *you eat...* and *you drink...* (T)

Objective: To determine if a child identifies a food or drink without saying the name of the food or drink, but rather by verbally stating the class that the item belongs to. "Eat" and "drink" are used at this early level of LRFFC only because of the strong motivation associated with them. Otherwise, classes tend to be more difficult and are not included in the program until later aspects of LRFFC development.

Materials: Use the foods and drinks that the child likes. Pictures of these items may work for many children. Also, distracter items that are not foods or drinks should be assembled for placement in the array.

Example: Given an array of 5 items, one of which is a food item and the others are common household items, an adult says "you eat..." and the child selects a cookie (or sandwich, crackers, cheese, banana, etc.).

I point score: Give the child 1 point if he correctly selects without prompts 5 different food or drink items when each are presented an array of 5 items, and an adult gives the verbal statement "you eat..." and "you drink..."

½ point score: Give the child ½ point if he correctly selects without prompts 2 different food or drink items when each are presented an array of 5 items, and an adult gives the verbal statement "you eat..." and "you drink..."

LRFFC 7-M	Selects the correct item from an array of 8, for 25 different LRFFC fill-in statements of any type (e.g., *You sit on a...*). (T)

Objective: To determine if a child can identify items without the adult saying the name of the item, but by describing the item in some way. The current task focuses on the child's ability to identify a specific item by verbally stating the action (verb) associated with the item in a fill-in-the-blank format. Often, the action constitutes an example of the function of an item (e.g., a chair is for sitting).

Materials: Use known objects or pictures (i.e., items that the child can already tact and LD) that correspond with the target LRFFC statements, and a collection of distracter items for the array. Pictures tend to be much easier to manage in LRFFC tasks, and it is easier to find multiple examples of items.

Examples: "You sleep in a"... bed; "you climb a"... ladder; "you bounce a"... ball; "you swim in a"...pool; "you ride in a"...wagon; "you spin a"...top; "you blow up a" ...balloon; "you jump on a"...trampoline.

1 point score: Give the child 1 point if he correctly selects the item from an array of 8, for 25 different LRFFC fill-in-the-blank statements.

½ point score: Give the child ½ point if he correctly selects 12 items in this type of LRFFC task.

LRFFC 8-M	Selects the correct item from an array of 10 (or from a book), for 25 different verb-noun LRFFC *what, which,* or *who* questions (e.g., *What do you ride? Which one barks? Who can hop?*). (T)

Objective: To determine if a child can identify a specific item without the adult naming the item, but by verbally stating a function, feature, or class of the item in a "what," "which," or "who" question (WH) format.

Materials: A collection of known objects or pictures (items that the child can already tact and LD) that correspond with the target LRFFC statements, and a list of known and corresponding verbs.

Examples: "What do you wear?"...shirt; "Who takes you to school?"...mom; "Which one can fly?"...bird; "Who is Patrick's friend?"...Sponge Bob; "Which one do you pull?"...wagon.

1 point score: Give the child 1 point if he correctly selects the item from an array of 10 or from a book for 25 different LRFFC WH questions.

½ point score: Give the child ½ point if he correctly selects 12 items in this type of LRFFC task.

LRFFC 9-M	Selects an item given 3 different verbal statements about each item when independently presented (e.g., *Find an animal. What barks? What has paws?*) for 25 items. (T)

Objective: To determine if a child can demonstrate stimulus generalization by selecting the same target item when given different verbal statements about that item. This is also referred to as the establishment of verbal stimulus classes. It is important that this skill is tested across a variety of items (e.g., animals, clothing, food, vehicles, etc.) to ensure that stimulus generalization is occurring.

| Materials: | A collection of known objects or pictures (items that the child can already tact and LD) that correspond with at least three different LRFFC target statements. |

| Examples: | "What can fly?"...airplane; "What has wings?"...airplane; "How did you get to your grandmothers?"...airplane. |

| 1 point score: | Give the child 1 point if he correctly selects the item from an array of 10 or from a book, for 3 different LRFFC verbal statements for 25 items. |

| ½ point score: | Give the child 1/2 point if he correctly selects the item from an array of 10 or from a book, for 3 different LRFFC verbal statements for 12 items. |

| LRFFC 10-M | **Spontaneously tacts the item on 50% of the LRFFC trials (e.g., says *dog* given the verbal statement *find an animal,* and a visual array containing a picture of a dog). (O)** |

| Objective: | To determine if the verbal question along with the object in the array will evoke a response without an adult prompting the child to tact the item. This is an important step in the progression to intraverbal behavior. If a child begins to spontaneously tact the item in the array in an LRFFC format, this is a good indicator that he is ready for more intensive intraverbal training. |

| Materials: | No new materials are required to assess this skill. |

| Example: | Says "lunchbox" when asked, "Where is your sandwich?" in the presence of the lunchbox in the array of 10 items. |

| 1 point score: | Give the child 1 point if he spontaneously tacts the target item on 50% of the LRFFC trials. Some children will quickly begin to tact the items given a couple of verbal prompts. Give the child credit if he continues to tact the items after prompts have been removed and does so at least 50% of the time on future trials. |

| ½ point score: | Give the child ½ point if he spontaneously tacts the target item on 25% of the LRFFC trials, or if he tacts on 50% of the trials, but always requires one prompt at the beginning of an LRFFC session. |

INTRAVERBAL – LEVEL 2

| INTRAVERBAL 6-M | **Completes 10 different fill-in-the-blank phrases of any type (e.g., song fill-ins, social games and fun fill-ins, animal or object sounds). (T)** |

| Objective: | To determine if specific words evoke related words without the presence of any objects or echoic prompts. In short, intraverbal behavior consists of words controlled by other words, not words controlled by objects or actions (tacts), or words controlled by motivation (mands). However, in the early assessment of intraverbal development it is common to see motivation share control with verbal stimuli. For example, the response "go" to, "ready, set..." may also be part mand (e.g., the child wants to be chased), but this is okay at this point in intraverbal development, and the child should be given credit for this type of intraverbal response. |

Materials:	A list of potential songs, common or fun phrases, animal sounds, common object sounds, and other verbal associations relevant to the child.
Examples:	"Head, shoulders, knees, and..." "Old McDonald had a..." "A sheep says..." "A fire truck goes..." "Ready, set..." "Peek-a-..." "Up and..." "Mommy and...."
I point score:	Give the child 1 point if he fills in the missing words for 10 different songs, fun activities, animal sounds, toys or object sounds, or any other verbal associations.
½ point score:	Give the child ½ point if he fills in 5 phrases.

INTRAVERBAL 7-M	**Provides first name when asked, *What is your name?* (T)**
Objective:	To determine if the child can provide his own name when asked to do so.
Materials:	None.
Example:	None.
I point score:	Give the child 1 point if he can say his name when asked without echoic prompts. Do not give any points if he identifies everybody by his name.
½ point score:	None.

INTRAVERBAL 8-M	**Completes 25 different fill-in-the-blank phrases (not including songs) (e.g., *You eat... You sleep in a... Shoes and...*). (T)**
Objective:	To determine if specific words evoke related words without the presence of any objects, echoic prompts, or motivational variables (other than general attention).
Materials:	A list of potential fill-in-the-blank phrases relevant to the child.
Examples:	"You sleep in a..." "You put on your..." "You open the..." "You sit at the..." "Shoes and..." "Wash your..." "Lay your head on the..." "Turn on the..." "Blow the..." "Push the..." "Sweep the..." "See you later alligator...."
I point score:	Give the child 1 point if he fills in the missing words from 25 different phrases, associations, common sayings, or out-of-context daily activities.
½ point score:	Give the child ½ point if he fills in 12 phrases.

INTRAVERBAL 9-M	**Answers 25 different *what* questions (e.g., *What do you like to eat?*). (T)**
Objective:	To determine if the child can answer common "what" questions when they are presented out of a visual context, and without a specific motivational variable related to the response.
Materials:	A list of potential "what" questions.
Examples:	"What do you drink?" "What do you bounce?" "What do you play in?" "What do you spin?" "What animals do you like?"

1 point score: Give the child 1 point if he answers 25 different "what" questions without echoic prompts, and without the presence of the relevant object.

½ point score: Give the child ½ point if he answers 12 "what" questions.

INTRAVERBAL 10-M	Answers 25 different *who* or *where* questions (e.g., *Who is your friend? Where is your pillow?*). (T)

Objective: To determine if the child can answer questions asking for the name of a person or character, or for the location of items without an echoic prompt.

Materials: A list of potential "who" and "where" questions.

Examples: "Who helps you at school?" "Who is your pet?" "Who is Dora's friend?" "Who helps you when you are sick?" "Where are the spoons?" "Where is a hammer?" "Where is your dad's car?" "Where is your pillow?" "Where is your toothbrush?" "Where are the cookies?" "Where is a paintbrush?" "Where are the sparkles?"

1 point score: Give the child 1 point if he answers 25 different "who" or "where" questions without echoic prompts, or the presence of the object (must have at least 8 of each).

½ point score: Give the child ½ point if he answers 12 different "who" or "where" questions (note if all are either "who" or "where").

CLASSROOM ROUTINES AND GROUP SKILLS – LEVEL 2

GROUP 6-M	Sits at a group snack or lunch table without negative behavior for 3 minutes. (O)

Objective: To determine if the child will comply with instructions to sit at a table with a group of other children, and stay at the table for a defined period of time.

Materials: Standard classroom chairs and tables and snack or lunch items.

Example: When told to sit at the table, while pointing to the table, the child will sit down and remain there for 3 minutes without any additional adult prompts to remain seated.

1 point score: Give the child 1 point if he sits at a group snack or lunch table with gestural and verbal prompts without negative behavior for 3 minutes. He can be prompted to sit down, but must remain seated for 3 minutes without an adult prompt to sit back down.

½ point score: Give the child ½ point if he sits at a group snack or lunch table with gestural and verbal prompts without negative behavior for 1 minute.

GROUP 7-M	Puts away personal items, lines up, and comes to a table with only 1 verbal prompt. (O)

Objective: To determine if the child will comply with general classroom instructions without excessive prompting.

Materials: Standard classroom materials such as chairs and tables, coat racks, cubbys, etc.

Examples:	When told to line up the child will get in line with the other children. When told, "put your lunch in your cubby" he will do so.
1 point score:	Give the child 1 point if 80% of the time he puts away a backpack, coat or lunch, and lines up and comes to a table when verbally prompted only once by an adult.
½ point score:	Give the child ½ point if 80% of the time he puts away a backpack, coat or lunch, and lines up and comes to a table, but it requires 2 or more prompts.

GROUP 8-M	Transitions between classroom activities with no more than 1 gestural or verbal prompt. (O)
Objective:	To determine if the child will move from one activity to another without excessive prompting or emitting negative behavior.
Materials:	Standard classroom material.
Example:	When told to go to the circle group, the child will go.
1 point score:	Give the child 1 point if he transitions at least 80% of the time between classroom activities with only 1 gestural and/or 1 verbal prompt and no negative behavior.
½ point score:	Give the child ½ point if he transitions between classroom activities, but requires 2 or more prompts of any type (except physical).

GROUP 9-M	Sits in a small group for 5 minutes without disruptive behavior or attempting to leave the group. (O)
Objective:	To determine if the child will at least passively participate in a group circle for a brief period of time.
Materials:	Standard classroom material.
Examples:	When in a circle group the child sits in the group without standing up, pushing his chair out of the group, falling on the floor, or running away.
1 point score:	Give the child 1 point if 80% of the time he sits in a circle group of 3 or more children for 5 minutes without disruptive behavior or attempting to leave the group.
½ point score:	Give the child ½ point if 80% of the time he sits in a circle group of 3 or more children for 2 minutes without disruptive behavior or attempting to leave the group.

GROUP 10-M	Sits in a small group for 10 minutes, attends to the teacher or material for 50% of the period, and responds to 5 of a teacher's S^{D}s. (O)
Objective:	To determine if the child will attend to the ongoing activities in a group instruction setting and respond to the S^{D}s presented by the teacher to the individual child or the whole group.
Materials:	Standard classroom material.

Example: When in a circle group the child makes eye contact with the teacher or the material that she is presenting, and when the teacher says "Sarah pick a song," Sarah will come up to the front of the group and select a song card from an array of cards, without additional prompts.

1 point score: Give the child 1 point if 80% of the time he sits in a group activity (e.g., circle, arts and crafts, stations) with 3 or more children for 10 minutes and attends to the teacher or presented material for 50% of the period (using a time sample recording system), and responds to 5 teacher questions or instructions.

½ point score: Give the child ½ point if 80% of the time he sits in a group activity (e.g., circle, arts and crafts, stations) with 3 or more children for 10 minutes and attends to the teacher or presented material for 33% of the period, and responds to 2 teacher questions or instructions.

LINGUISTIC STRUCTURE – LEVEL 2

LINGUISTICS 6-M	The child's articulation of 10 tacts can be understood by familiar adults who cannot see the item tacted. (T)

Objective: To determine if adults can understand the child's spoken words when the adult cannot see the items that the child is tacting.

Materials: Items that the child can tact.

Example: When one adult holds up a picture card and asks the child to tact the item, a second adult, without seeing the picture, can understand the word emitted by the child.

1 point score: Give the child 1 point if familiar adults who cannot see the item tacted can understand his articulation for 10 tacts.

½ point score: Give the child ½ point if familiar adults who cannot see the item tacted can understand his articulation for 5 tacts.

LINGUISTICS 7-M	Has a total listener vocabulary of 100 words (e.g., *Touch nose. Jump. Find keys.*). (T)

Objective: To determine if the child's listener vocabulary is growing.

Materials: Common and age appropriate items and activities.

Example: When an adult asks the child, "Can you find a fire truck?" the child touches a fire truck in a picture scene containing several vehicles.

1 point score: Give the child 1 point if he has a total listener vocabulary of 100 words demonstrated by selecting an item from an array of 5, or performing a specific action.

½ point score: Give the child ½ point if he has a total listener vocabulary of 50 words demonstrated by selecting an item from an array of 5, or performing a specific action.

LINGUISTICS 8-M	**Emits 10 different 2-word utterances per day of any type except echoic (e.g., mand, tact). (O)**

Objective: To determine if the child is putting 2 or more words together in a single phrase or sentence.

Materials: No particular materials.

Examples: The child tacts "bye mommy" or mands "big cookie."

1 point score: Give the child 1 point if he emits 10 different 2-word utterances per day of any type except echoic (e.g., mand, tact). These responses can include verbal prompts to respond such as, "What is that?" or "What do you want?"

½ point score: Give the child ½ point if he emits 5 different 2-word utterances per day of any type except echoic (e.g., mand, tact).

LINGUISTICS 9-M	**Emits functional prosody (i.e., rhythm, stress, intonation) on 5 occasions in one day (e.g., puts emphasis or stress on certain words such as It's MINE!). (O)**

Objective: To determine if the child is demonstrating variation is his vocal production and that this variation has a verbal function. Specifically, will the addition of a certain variation affect a listener in a special way, such as showing the listener the child's current emotional state.

Materials: No particular materials.

Examples: The child says, "I don't want to go" in a whiney voice.

1 point score: Give the child 1 point if he emits functional prosody (i.e., rhythm, stress, intonation) on 5 occasions in one day.

½ point score: Give the child ½ point if he emits functional prosody (i.e., rhythm, stress, intonation) on 2 occasions in one day.

LINGUISTICS 10-M	**Has a total speaker vocabulary of 300 words (all verbal operants, except echoic). (E)**

Objective: To determine if the child's speaking vocabulary is growing.

Materials: Common and age-appropriate items and activities.

Example: When an adult asks the child to name a variety of pictures in a children's picture book, the child is able to do so.

1 point score: Give the child 1 point if he has a total speaker vocabulary size of 300 words.

½ point score: Give the child ½ point if he has a total speaker vocabulary size of 200 words.

CHAPTER 5

Milestones Scoring Instructions: Level 3

This chapter contains the specific instructions for administering Level 3 of the VB-MAPP Milestones Assessment. There are three new domains added to Level 3: reading, writing, and math. These domains were not included in the earlier levels because most typically developing children at those levels have not acquired these basic academic skills (although some children do). In addition, these academic skills should be avoided as part of the curriculum for a child with language delays whose scores fall primarily in Level 1 or 2. By presenting these advanced skills in Level 3, it is hoped that it will be clearer as to what skills to focus on in the earlier levels. It is usually the case that the Level 1 and 2 skills need to be firmly established before moving to the more complex areas, such as beginning academics. Two domains, echoic and imitation, are not included in Level 3 because they are less of a target area for a child who has reached this Level. As a reminder, the four methods of assessing a specific skill are: (1) formal testing (**T**), (2) observation (**O**), (3) either observation or testing (**E**), and (4) a timed observation (**TO**).

MAND – LEVEL 3

MAND 11-M	Spontaneously mands for different verbal information using a WH question or question word 5 times (e.g., *What's your name? Where do I go?*). (TO: 60 min.)
Objective:	To determine if the child spontaneously asks questions, and for what reason. Specifically, is there a strong MO for the answer to the question (information), and does the answer function as reinforcement for the child? Does he really want to know the answer or does the question occur for some other reason, such as attention?
Materials:	Reinforcing items and activities found in the child's natural environment.
Examples:	"What's that?" "What are you doing?" "Where are we going?" "Can I go?" "Do you have it?" "Who's coming?" "When can we go?"
1 point score:	Give the child 1 point if he spontaneously mands for different verbal information using at least 2 different WH questions or other question words 5 times during a 1-hour observation.
½ point score:	Give the child ½ point if he spontaneously mands for different verbal information using a WH question or other question words 2 times during a 1-hour observation.

MAND 12-M	Politely mands to stop an undesirable activity, or remove any aversive MO under 5 different circumstances (e.g., *Please stop pushing me. No thank you. Excuse me, can you move?*). (E)
Objective:	To determine if the child can politely and appropriately mand to remove aversive items and events with words, and not with negative behavior.
Materials:	Aversive items and activities found in the child's natural environment.
Examples:	"Please don't do that." "Can I take a break?" "Can you leave me alone?" "No thanks. I don't want to play." "Maybe later." "Can I go now?"
1 point score:	Give the child 1 point if he appropriately (i.e., without negative behavior) mands without prompts to stop an undesirable activity, not participate in an activity, or to otherwise remove an aversive under 5 different circumstances.
½ point score:	Give the child ½ point if he appropriately (i.e., without negative behavior) mands without prompts to stop an undesirable activity, not participate in an activity, or to otherwise remove an aversive under 2 different circumstances.

MAND 13-M	Mands with 10 different adjectives, prepositions, or adverbs (e.g., *My crayon is broken. Don't take it out. Go fast.*). (TO: 60 min.)
Objective:	To determine if the child's mand repertoire contains multiple components, and is moving beyond just nouns and verbs to include different parts of speech.
Materials:	Reinforcing items and activities found in the child's natural environment.
Examples:	"I want the red heart." "Put it in the house." "You hide under the table." "Go quietly." "That's my piece of paper." "I want a big chip."
1 point score:	Give the child 1 point if he mands with 10 different adjectives, prepositions, or adverbs during a 1-hour observation or testing. There should be at least 2 from each group (i.e., adjectives, prepositions, or adverbs) in order to get full credit.
½ point score:	Give the child ½ point if he mands with 5 different adjectives, prepositions, or adverbs during a 1-hour observation.

MAND 14-M	Gives directions, instructions, or explanations as to how to do something or how to participate in an activity 5 times (e.g., *You put the glue on first, then stick it. You sit here while I get a book*). (O)
Objective:	To determine if the child's mand repertoire is functional in daily activities with other people, especially other children.
Materials:	Reinforcing items and activities found in the child's natural environment.
Examples:	"First I'll go, and then you go next." "Don't put glue in your mouth." "Come sit down." "It's your turn now." "You go hide, and I'll count."
1 point score:	Give the child 1 point if he gives directions, instructions, or explanations as to how to do something or participate in an activity 5 times as measured by a daily tracking sheet.

½ point score: Give the child ½ point if he gives directions, instructions, or explanations as to how to do something or participate in an activity 2 times as measured by a daily tracking sheet.

MAND 15-M	Mands for others to attend to his own intraverbal behavior 5 times (e.g., *Listen to me... I'll tell you... Here's what happened... I'm telling the story...*). (O)

Objective: To determine if the child mands for an audience to attend to his on-going verbal behavior.

Materials: Reinforcing items and activities found in the child's natural environment.

Examples: "I'm going to talk." "Here is what she said." "I'm talking." "It's my turn." "I was telling her." "Do you know what she said?"

1 point score: Give the child 1 point if he mands for others to attend to his own intraverbal behavior 5 times during any number of observations. Generally, this can be measured by a mand that precedes or is imbedded in some intraverbal sequence (e.g., a child's description of how to make pancakes).

½ point score: Give the child ½ point if he mands for others to attend to his own intraverbal behavior 2 times during observation periods.

TACT – LEVEL 3

TACT 11-M	Tacts the color, shape, and function of 5 objects (15 trials) when each object and question is presented in a mixed order (e.g., *What color is the refrigerator? What shape is the valentine? What do you do with the ball?*) (This is part tact and part intraverbal). (T)

Objective: To determine if the child can tact any one of three different features or functions of a single object when asked to do so. It is important to mix the questions and the objects, since many children can be successful if all color questions are asked, then all shape questions are asked, etc. This is a prompt of sorts. Mixing up the three questions and the different objects is a harder task and reveals whether the child really has this skill or not.

Materials: Common items found in the child's natural environment that he can easily tact, and a list of possible features and functions of those items.

Examples: Using pictures of a round green apple, a square brown wastebasket, and a rectangular white refrigerator, the child is shown one picture at a time and asked, "What do you do with this?" then shown another picture and asked, "What color is this?" then shown a third picture and asked, "What shape is this?" and so on (i.e., mix up the questions and the pictures).

1 point score: Give the child 1 point if he tacts the color, shape, and function of 5 different objects (15 trials) when each is asked during a mixed order of testing.

½ point score: Give the child ½ point if he tacts 2 features or functions of 5 different objects (10 trials) when each is asked during a mixed order of testing.

TACT 12-M	**Tacts 4 different prepositions (e.g., *in, out, on, under*) and 4 pronouns (e.g., *I, you, me, mine*). (E)**

Objective: To determine if the child can tact the spatial relations between objects in the environment, and if the child can tact by using pronouns.

Materials: Common items found in the child's natural environment that he easily can tact and select (LD), and a list of possible prepositions and pronouns.

Examples: When asked, "Where is the dog?" and the child correctly says "under the chair," and later when the dog is on the chair the same question is presented the child says "on the chair." When asked, "Whose turn is it?" and the child correctly responds "It's his turn" and later when asked the same question, "Whose turn is it?" and the child says, "It's my turn."

1 point score: Give the child 1 point if he tacts 4 different prepositions and 4 different pronouns when tested.

½ point score: Give the child ½ point if he tacts a total of 4 prepositions or pronouns, but has some from each category. Give the child ½ point if he tacts 4 different prepositions, but not 4 pronouns, or vice versa. Identify what he was able to do, and not do, in the "Comments/notes" section of the VB-MAPP Milestones Form.

TACT 13-M	**Tacts 4 different adjectives, excluding colors and shapes (e.g., *big, little, long, short*) and 4 adverbs (e.g., *fast, slow, quietly, gently*). (E)**

Objective: To determine if the child can tact the properties of objects (e.g., size, length, weight, texture) and the properties of actions (e.g., speed, consistency, intensity) and can tact the comparison of those properties of one object or action to the properties of another object (e.g., long and short, light and heavy, old and new) or action (e.g., faster, slower).

Materials: Common items found in the child's natural environment that he can easily tact and LD, and a list of possible adjectives and adverbs.

Examples: When presented with 2 straws of different length and the question, "Can you tell me about the length of this one?" the child says, "It's longer than then that one." Later, when shown the same straw first shown, but the comparison is a longer straw, the same question evokes, "It is shorter than that one." When testing adverbs, show a video of two cars racing and present the question, "Can you tell me about the speed of this one?" The child says, "It's going slower than that one." Later, when shown the same car, but the comparison array contains slower cars, the same question evokes, "It's going faster than that one." (Note that a correct response in both examples is part intraverbal and part tact, and the intraverbal part affects what is tacted, thus a type of conditional discrimination).

1 point score: Give the child 1 point if he tacts 4 different adjectives (excluding color and shape) and 4 different adverbs when tested.

½ point score: Give the child ½ point if he tacts a total of 4 adjectives or adverbs, but has some from each category. Give the child ½ point if he tacts 4 different adjectives, but not 4 adverbs, or vice versa. Identify what he was able to do, and not do, in the "Comments/notes" section of the VB-MAPP Milestones Form.

TACT 14-M	**Tacts with complete sentences containing 4 or more words, 20 times. (E)**

Objective: To determine if the child is emitting full sentences, and that those sentences contain at least 4 words.

Materials: Common items and actions from the child's natural environment.

Examples: "That is a big ice cream cone!" "There is my mom." "That's his lunch box?" "He put a star on it."

1 point score: Give the child 1 point if he tacts with complete sentences containing 4 or more words 20 times.

½ point score: Give the child ½ point if he tacts with complete sentences containing 3 or more words 20 times.

TACT 15-M	**Has a tact vocabulary of 1000 words (nouns, verbs, adjectives, etc.), tested or from an accumulated list of known tacts. (T)**

Objective: To determine the size of the child's tact repertoire.

Materials: Use books (e.g., a picture dictionary), scenes, picture cards, and common environmental objects, actions, properties, etc.

Examples: Easily tacts many items on each page in a children's picture book.

1 point score: Give the child 1 point if he tacts 1000 nonverbal stimuli (nouns, verbs, adjectives, adverbs, pronouns, etc.). An accumulated list of the child's known words can be used for this measure. Note that this may seem like a lot of words, but a typically developing 4 year old has a 1500 to 2000 word speaking vocabulary or even more. There are many children's books that contain over 1000 pictures. This measure can occur over longer periods of time if necessary (i.e., an accumulated list) or by sampling the repertoire. If a child can easily tact hundreds of items, actions, properties, etc., it is unlikely that he will need tacting IEP goals.

½ point score: Give the child ½ point if he tacts 750 nonverbal stimuli (nouns, verbs, adjectives, adverbs, pronouns, etc.). An accumulated list of the child's known words can be used for this measure.

LISTENER RESPONDING – LEVEL 3

LISTENER 11-M	**Selects items by color and shape from an array of 6 similar stimuli, for 4 colors and 4 shapes (e.g., *Find the red car. Find the square cracker.*). (T)**

Objective: To determine if the child responds to a complex instruction that requires him to attend to a specific item and a property of that item (either color or shape).

Materials: A list of colors and shapes, and a collection of different colored shapes.

Example: When an adult says, "Where is the blue cup?" the child selects the blue cup from an array that also contains a blue hat, a red cup, a blue plate, etc.

1 point score: Give the child 1 point if he selects items by color and shape from an array of 6 similar stimuli for 4 colors and 4 shapes when tested.

½ point score: Give the child ½ point if he selects items by color and shape from an array of 6 similar stimuli for 2 colors and 2 shapes.

LISTENER 12-M	**Follows 2 instructions involving 6 different prepositions (e.g., *Stand behind the chair.*) and 4 different pronouns (e.g., *Touch my ear.*). (T)**

Objective: To determine if the child can discriminate as a listener among the spatial relations between objects in the environment, and if the child can follow instructions containing pronouns, when asked to do so.

Materials: Common items found in the child's natural environment that he can easily tact and LD, and a list of possible prepositions and pronouns.

Examples: When instructed to place a toy "in" the box versus "under" the box the child is successful across a variety of items (e.g., cup, bowl, Lego). Alternatively, when asked to, "Give the toy to him" (without looking or pointing), the child is successful in discriminating between a male and a female hearing only the pronoun "him" or "her."

1 point score: Give the child 1 point if he follows 2 instructions for each of 6 different prepositions and 4 different pronouns when tested.

½ point score: Give the child ½ point if he follows 2 instructions for each of 3 different prepositions and 2 different pronouns. Give the child ½ point if he follows 2 instructions for each of 6 different prepositions, but not 4 pronouns, or vice versa. Identify what he was able to do, and not do, in the "Comments/notes" section of the VB-MAPP Milestones Form.

LISTENER 13-M	**Selects items from an array of similar stimuli based on 4 pairs of relative adjectives (e.g., *big-little, long-short*) and demonstrates actions based on 4 pairs of relative adverbs (e.g., *quiet-loud, fast-slow*). (T)**

Objective: To determine if the child can discriminate as a listener among the relative properties of objects (e.g., size, length, weight, texture), and follow instructions involving the relative properties of actions (e.g., speed, consistency, intensity).

Materials: Common items found in the child's natural environment that he can easily tact and LD, and a list of possible adjectives and adverbs.

Examples: Given an array of three different size items and the question "Which one is bigger?" the child selects the biggest item. Given a demonstration of two different words spoken at different volumes and the question, "Which word was louder?" the child correctly identifies the louder word.

1 point score: Give the child 1 point if he selects items from an array of similar stimuli based on 4 pairs of relative adjectives, and follows instructions involving 4 pairs of relative adverbs when tested.

½ point score: Give the child ½ point if he selects items from an array of similar stimuli based on 2 pairs of relative adjectives and follows 2 instructions involving 2 different adverbs, but has some from each category. Give the child ½ point if he LDs 4 different adjectives, but not 4 adverbs, or vice versa. Identify what he was able to do, and not do, in the "Comments/notes" section of the VB-MAPP Milestones Form.

LISTENER 14-M	Follows 3-step directions for 10 different directions (e.g., *Get your coat, hang it up, and sit down.*). (T)

Objective: To determine if the child can follow instructions that have multiple components.

Materials: Common items found in the child's natural environment that he can easily tact and LD, and a list of possible 3-step instructions.

Examples: "Touch the dog, cow, and pig." "Get the feather, put glue on it, and paste it on the hat." "Take you cup to the sink and wash and dry your hands." "Touch the big red truck." "Take this book to mommy and come back." "Get a tissue, blow your nose, and throw the tissue in the garbage."

1 point score: Give the child 1 point if he follows ten 3-step directions.

½ point score: Give the child ½ point if he follows five 3-step directions.

LISTENER 15-M	Has a total listener repertoire of 1200 words (nouns, verbs, adjectives, etc.), tested or from an accumulated list of known words. (T)

Objective: To determine the size of the child's listener repertoire.

Materials: Use books, scenes, picture cards, and common environmental objects, actions, and properties.

Example: Identifies as a listener many items on each page in a picture book when asked, for example, "Do you see any watermelons?"

1 point score: Give the child 1 point if he identifies 1200 nonverbal stimuli (nouns, verbs, adjectives, adverbs, pronouns, etc.). An accumulated list of the child's known words can be used for this measure, if it is reliable. (Note: see the comments regarding this measure in Tact Level 3-15.)

½ point score: Give the child ½ point if he identifies 800 nonverbal stimuli (nouns, verbs, adjectives, adverbs, pronouns, etc.). An accumulated list of the child's known words can be used for this measure, if it is reliable.

VISUAL PERCEPTUAL SKILLS AND MATCHING-TO-SAMPLE (VP-MTS) – LEVEL 3

VP-MTS 11-M	Spontaneously matches any part of an arts and crafts activity to another person's sample 2 times (e.g., a peer colors a balloon red and the child copies the peer's red color for his balloon). (O)

Objective: To determine if the child matches in a functional way in the natural environment and under the control of a peer's sample.

Materials: Standard arts and crafts materials.

Example: A peer cuts out a square and uses it as a hat for his art project, and the target child cuts out a similar square and also uses it as a hat.

1 point score: Give the child 1 point if he spontaneously matches any part of an arts and crafts activity to an adult or peer's sample 2 times.

½ point score: Give the child ½ point if he spontaneously matches any part of an arts and crafts activity to an adult or peer's sample once.

VP-MTS 12-M	Demonstrates generalized non-identical matching in a messy array of 10 with 3 similar stimuli, for 25 items (i.e., matches new items on the first trial). (T)

Objective: To determine if the child has acquired the ability to find the closest match of any sample item. This is usually referred to as a "generalized matching repertoire."

Materials: A collection of common items and matching pictures (e.g., a plastic banana and a picture of a banana) and comparison items (several other fruits).

Example: When shown a plastic pineapple for the first time, and then shown a comparison array containing a pineapple along with several fruits and vegetables, the child is able to find the pineapple on the first trial without any training on pineapple.

1 point score: Give the child 1 point if he demonstrates generalized non-identical matching with a novel item in a messy array of 10 with 3 similar stimuli, for 25 items.

½ point score: Give the child ½ point if he demonstrates generalized non-identical matching with a novel item in a messy array of 10 with 3 similar stimuli, for 15 items.

VP-MTS 13-M	Completes 20 different block designs, parquetry, shape puzzles, or similar tasks with at least 8 different pieces. (T)

Objective: To determine if the child can complete tasks that involve the assembly of three-dimensional items into specific patterns demonstrated on two-dimensional cards.

Materials: Block design kits and other similar shape puzzles and accompanying pattern cards. These and similar items are available at many educational stores and websites.

Example:	When shown a block pattern of 8 blocks with different colors, the child is able to match the design exactly with real blocks.

1 point score:	Give the child 1 point if he completes 20 different block designs, shape puzzles, or similar tasks with at least 8 different parts.

½ point score:	Give the child ½ point if he completes 20 different block designs, shape puzzles, or similar tasks with at least 4 different parts.

VP-MTS 14-M	**Sorts 5 items from 5 different categories without a model (e.g., animals, clothing, furniture). (T)**
Objective:	To determine if the child can sort items by categories, without being told the name of the category or given the first member of the category.
Materials:	Pictures of several different known items from a variety of categories.
Example:	When given a mixture of 15 pictures of foods, clothing, and vehicles, the child is able to separate the items into the 3 related groups.
1 point score:	Give the child 1 point if sorts at least 5 items from 5 different categories without a model or given the first member of the category (but the adult can use a starter prompt such as, "Can you sort these?").
½ point score:	Give the child ½ point if he sorts at least 3 items from 3 different categories without a model (other than verbal prompts) or the first member of the category.

VP-MTS 15-M	**Continues 20 three-step patterns, sequences, or seriation tasks (e.g., star, triangle, heart, star, triangle...). (T)**
Objective:	To determine if the child can identify a pattern or sequence of stimuli demonstrated by matching that pattern without prompts (other than a starter prompt such as, "Can you continue this?").
Materials:	Many common materials can be used to create a pattern (e.g., pumpkins, witches, and ghosts). Seriation sets, part-to-whole sets, and similar materials can be found at many educational stores and websites.
Example:	When given a sequence of colored connecting cubes such as red, white, blue, red, white, blue, the child is able to repeat the sequence without prompts by selecting the correct colors from an array of colored cubes.
1 point score:	Give the child 1 point if he continues 20 three-step patterns, sequences, or seriation tasks.
½ point score:	Give the child ½ point if he continues 20 two-step patterns, sequences, or seriation tasks.

INDEPENDENT PLAY – LEVEL 3

PLAY 11-M	Spontaneously engages in pretend or imaginary play on 5 occasions (e.g., dressing up, a pretend party with stuffed animals, pretends to cook). (O)

Objective: To determine if the child can go beyond concrete play with objects to pretend play that involves novel and creative components, role-playing, and symbolic play.

Materials: Toys and items found in a child's home or school environment that might be used for pretend play (e.g., costumes, pretend food, tea set).

Examples: The child acts out a character like a princess or a fireman. The child pretends to cook and serve dinner.

1 point score: Give the child 1 point if he spontaneously engages in different pretend or imaginary play on 5 occasions.

½ point score: Give the child ½ point if he spontaneously engages in different pretend or imaginary play on 2 occasions.

PLAY 12-M	Repeats a gross motor play behavior to obtain a better effect for 2 activities (e.g., throwing a ball in a basket, swinging a bat at a T-ball, foot stomping to launch a rocket, pumping a swing). (O)

Objective: To determine if the child is persistent and motivated by accomplishing improved outcome for physical play activities such as sports.

Materials: Common play and sports equipment.

Examples: The child continues to try and hit a golf ball on a putting green until it goes into the hole, or kicks at a ball until he makes contact.

1 point score: Give the child 1 point if he will repeat a gross motor play behavior in an attempt to obtain a desired effect for 2 different activities.

½ point score: Give the child ½ point if he will repeat a gross motor play behavior in an attempt to obtain a desired effect for 1 activity.

PLAY 13-M	Independently engages in arts and crafts type activities for 5 minutes (e.g., drawing, coloring, painting, cutting, pasting). (O)

Objective: To determine if the child can stay on task and use common arts and crafts items such as scissors, glue, paper, crayons, buttons, pipe cleaners, etc., to create projects, and seems to enjoy these activities.

Materials: Arts and crafts supplies.

Example: The child draws a face then cuts out a nose and glues it to the face.

1 point score: Give the child 1 point if he independently (no adult prompts or reinforcers) engages in arts and crafts type activities for 5 minutes.

½ point score: Give the child ½ point if he independently (no adult prompts or reinforcers) engages in arts and crafts type activities for 2 minutes.

PLAY 14-M	Independently engages in sustained play activities for 10 minutes without adult prompts or reinforcement (e.g., playing with an Etch-a-sketch, playing dress-up). (O)

Objective: To determine if the child engages in play activities for a sustained period of time without adult involvement.

Materials: Common toys and items found in a child's home or school environment.

Examples: The child plays with car garages and cars for a 10-minute period. The child plays with Legos for a few minutes, then plays with a dump truck, then plays with a kitchen set, totaling 10 minutes of continuous play, all without adult interaction.

1 point score: Give the child 1 point if he independently engages in sustained play activities spontaneously for 10 minutes without adult prompts or reinforcement.

½ point score: Give the child ½ point if he independently engages in sustained play activities spontaneously for 5 minutes without adult prompts or reinforcement.

PLAY 15-M	Independently draws or writes in pre-academic activity books for 5 minutes (e.g., dot-to-dot, matching games, mazes, tracing letters and numbers). (O)

Objective: To determine if the child will work independently in age-appropriate workbooks, and is reinforced by that type of activity.

Materials: Children's pre-academic workbooks.

Example: The child will complete dot-to-dot games without adult reinforcement.

1 point score: Give the child 1 point if he independently draws or writes in activity books for 5 minutes.

½ point score: Give the child ½ point if he independently draws or writes in activity books for 2 minutes.

SOCIAL BEHAVIOR AND SOCIAL PLAY – LEVEL 3

SOCIAL 11-M	Spontaneously cooperates with a peer to accomplish a specific outcome 5 times (e.g., one child holds a bucket while the other pours in water). (E)

Objective: To determine if a child has the skills to engage in cooperative behavior with a peer in order to achieve a specific goal, without adult prompting or reinforcement.

Materials: Peers and toys or items found in a child's home or school.

Examples: The target child and a peer both cooperate to use a teeter-totter or a wagon. The child and peer cooperatively build a tower of blocks. The child and a peer throw a ball back and forth.

1 point score: Give the child 1 point if he spontaneously cooperates with a peer to accomplish a specific outcome 5 times during observation or testing (the peer can be prompted to engage the target child in a cooperative activity such as helping to carry a box).

½ point score: Give the child ½ point if he spontaneously cooperates with a peer to accomplish a specific outcome 2 times during observation or testing.

SOCIAL 12-M	Spontaneously mands to peers with a WH question 5 times (e.g., *Where are you going? What's that? Who are you being?*). (TO: 60 min.)

Objective: To determine if a child will mand to peers for verbal information without adult prompts or reinforcement.

Materials: Peers and items found in a child's home or school.

Examples: The target child mands to the peer, "Where is the red crayon?" (when working on an art project), or "What are you building?" (when the peer is playing with Legos).

1 point score: Give the child 1 point if he emits 5 different spontaneous mands in a 1-hour period that involves asking peers questions, or for other mands seeking information.

½ point score: Give the child ½ point if he emits 2 different spontaneous mands in a 1-hour period that involves asking peers questions, or for other mands seeking information.

SOCIAL 13-M	Intraverbally responds to 5 different questions or statements from peers (e.g., verbally responds to *What do you want to play?*). (E)

Objective: To determine if a child will intraverbally respond to a peer's verbal behavior without adult prompting or reinforcement.

Materials: Peers and items and activities in the natural environment.

Examples: A peer mands to the target child, "What are you building?" and the target child answers his question with "A space ship." A peer mands to the target child, "What do you have for lunch?" and the target child answers his question with "A peanut butter sandwich."

1 point score: Give the child 1 point if he intraverbally responds to 5 different questions or statements from peers without adult prompting or reinforcement during a 1-hour observation or testing period.

½ point score: Give the child ½ point if he intraverbally responds to 2 different questions or statements from peers without adult prompting or reinforcement, during a 1-hour observation or testing period.

SOCIAL 14-M	Engages in pretend social play activities with peers for 5 minutes without adult prompts (e.g., dress up play, acting out videos, playing house). (O)

Objective: To determine if a child will engage in unprompted pretend and/or social play with peers for sustained periods of time.

Materials: Peers and items and activities in the natural environment.

Examples: When out on the playground several children are going in and out of a log cabin playhouse. The target child is participating in the activity, following other children, sitting in the chairs in the cabin with the others, having a pretend drink, taking a pretend nap, laughing when others laugh, manding to the peers, imitating the peers, and intraverbally responding to the peer's verbal behavior.

1 point score: Give the child 1 point if he engages with peers in a pretend or social play activity for 5 minutes.

½ point score: Give the child ½ point if he engages with peers in a pretend or social play activity for 2 minutes.

SOCIAL 15-M	Engages in 4 verbal exchanges on 1 topic with peers for 5 topics (e.g., the children go back and forth talking about making a creek in a sandbox). (O)

Objective: To determine if a child will have a "conversation" with peers that consists of exchanges back and forth on a single topic.

Materials: Peers and items and events in the natural environment.

Example: During an art activity, a peer says, "I need some glue," and the target child says, "Here it is," and gives the glue to the peer. After the peer uses the glue the target child says to the peer, "I want the glue," and the peer delivers the glue. Then, the peer says, "Look, you spilled some glue," and the target child says, "I need a paper towel." The peer gets a towel and says, "Here's a towel." The target child says, "Thank you."

1 point score: Give the child 1 point if he initiates a verbal interaction, or spontaneously responds to the verbal behavior of a peer with additional and relevant verbal behavior, and has a reciprocal verbal interaction that lasts for 4 exchanges during an observation period (note that any type of verbal behavior counts—mands, tacts, or intraverbals).

½ point score: Give the child ½ point if he initiates a verbal interaction, or spontaneously responds to the verbal behavior of a peer with additional and relevant verbal behavior, and has a reciprocal verbal interaction that lasts for 2 exchanges during an observation period.

READING – LEVEL 3

READING 11-M	Attends to a book when a story is being read to him for 75% of the time. (TO: 3 min.)
Objective:	To determine if the child shows an interest in books and having adults read to him.
Materials:	Children's books.
Example:	The child will sit with an adult while she reads a book and looks at the pages in the book while a story is being read, with no prompts to attend to the book.
1 point score:	Give the child 1 point if he attends to a book when a story is being read to him for 75% of the time in a 3 minute period, without any prompts to attend to the book.
½ point score:	Give the child ½ point if he attends to a book when a story is being read to him for 50% of the time in a 3-minute period, without any prompts to attend to the book.

READING 12-M	Selects (LDs) the correct uppercase letter from an array of 5 letters, for 10 different letters. (T)
Objective:	To determine if the child discriminates as a listener among uppercase letters.
Materials:	A collection of uppercase letters.
Example:	When presented with an array of at least 5 different letters and asked to "touch the letter R," the child touches the letter R.
1 point score:	Give the child 1 point if he selects the correct uppercase letter from an array of 5 letters for 10 different letters.
½ point score:	Give the child ½ point if he selects the correct uppercase letter from an array of 5 letters for 5 different letters.

READING 13-M	Tacts 10 uppercase letters on command. (T)
Objective:	To determine if the child tacts some uppercase letters.
Materials:	A collection of uppercase letters.
Example:	When presented with an "R" and the verbal prompt, "What letter is this?" the child says "R."
1 point score:	Give the child 1 point if he tacts 10 uppercase letters.
½ point score:	Give the child ½ point if he tacts 5 uppercase letters.

READING 14-M	Reads his own name. (T)
Objective:	To determine if the child reads his name.

Materials: The child's name written on a card or piece of paper, as well as a few written distracter words.

Example: When presented with the written word "RYAN" the child says "Ryan," but does not say "Ryan" when shown a few distracter words.

1 point score: Give the child 1 point if he reads his own name when shown his name and given the verbal prompt, "What does this say?" Be careful not to say something like, "Whose name is this?" as this verbal stimulus alone may intraverbally evoke the child's name (unless several names are used). Also, be sure other words don't evoke his own name, or that it is not just his personal name card that evokes the response (certain colors, patterns, etc., may be the source of control).

½ point score: None

READING 15-M	**Matches 5 words to the corresponding pictures or items in an array of 5, and vice versa (e.g., matches the written word *bird* to a picture of a bird). (T)**

Objective: To determine if the child matches written words to the corresponding pictures or items, and vice versa (this is one example of reading comprehension).

Materials: A collection of simple written words and the related pictures or objects (e.g., dog, cat, baby, ball).

Example: When presented with the written word "car," the child can match the word to a picture of a car contained in an array of at least 4 other items.

1 point score: Give the child 1 point if he matches 5 words to the corresponding pictures or items in an array of 5, and vice versa.

½ point score: Give the child ½ point if he matches 3 words to the corresponding pictures or items in an array of 3, and vice versa.

WRITING – LEVEL 3

WRITING 11-M	**Imitates 5 different writing actions modeled by an adult using a writing instrument and writing surface. (T)**

Objective: To determine if the child can hold a writing instrument and copy simple drawing movements of an adult.

Materials: Any type of writing instrument (e.g., crayon, marker, chalk, pencil) and related surface (e.g., paper, white board, or Magna Doodle).

Examples: The child will imitate drawing back and forth, up and down, in circles, and curved lines.

1 point score: Give the child 1 point if he imitates 5 different writing actions modeled by an adult.

½ point score: Give the child ½ point if he imitates 3 different writing actions modeled by an adult.

WRITING 12-M	**Independently traces within ¼ inch of the lines of 5 different geometrical shapes (e.g., circle, square, triangle, rectangle, star). (T)**
Objective:	To determine if the child can control the writing instrument enough to trace specific geometric shapes within a defined boundary.
Materials:	Any type of writing instrument (e.g., crayon, marker, chalk, pencil), and related surface (e.g., paper, white board, or Magna Doodle).
Example:	The child will trace a 3-inch circle and stay within ¼ inch of the sample.
1 point score:	Give the child 1 point if he independently traces at least 80% of the figure within ¼ inch of 5 different geometrical shapes. Shapes with several angles (e.g., a star) may be difficult but give the child full credit if he is close.
½ point score:	Give the child ½ point if he independently traces at least 80% of the figure within 1/2 inch of 5 different geometrical shapes.

WRITING 13-M	**Copies 10 letters or numbers legibly. (T)**
Objective:	To determine if the child can copy specific letters and numbers.
Materials:	Any type of writing instrument (e.g., crayon, marker, chalk, pencil), and related surface (e.g., paper, white board, or Magna Doodle).
Examples:	The child will copy the letters A, B, and C, and the numbers 1 and 2.
1 point score:	Give the child 1 point if he copies 10 letters or numbers of any size legibly (i.e., an observer can identify the letter or number without seeing the model).
½ point score:	Give the child ½ point if he copies 5 letters or numbers of any size legibly.

WRITING 14-M	**Legibly spells and writes his own name without copying. (T)**
Objective:	To determine if the child can write his own name, and that it is legible by a second party.
Materials:	Any type of writing instrument (e.g., crayon, marker, chalk, pencil), and related surface (e.g., paper, white board, or Magna Doodle).
Example:	The child will write his name on a lined piece of paper.
1 point score:	Give the child 1 point if he independently and legibly writes and correctly spells his own name ("legible" does not need to be neat, this will come with practice).
½ point score:	Give the child ½ point if he approximates the letters in his name, but they are not clear enough to read, and/or he misspells his name.

WRITING 15-M	Copies all 26 uppercase and lowercase letters legibly. (T)

Objective: To determine the child's ability to copy specific letters.

Materials: Any type of writing instrument (e.g., crayon, marker, chalk, pencil), and related surface (e.g., paper, white board, or Magna Doodle).

Examples: The child will copy any letter when given a sample.

1 point score: Give the child 1 point if he independently copies all 26 uppercase and lowercase letters with legible facsimiles.

½ point score: Give the child ½ point if he approximates the letters, but they are not clear enough to read.

LISTENER RESPONDING BY FUNCTION, FEATURE, AND CLASS (LRFFC) – LEVEL 3

LRFFC 11-M	Selects the correct item from an array of 10 that contains 3 similar stimuli (e.g., similar color, shape, or class, but they are the wrong choices), for 25 different WH-question LRFFC tasks. (T)

Objective: To determine if a child discriminates among items that look very similar in the array given an LRFFC task.

Materials: A set of known objects or pictures (the child is able to tact and LD) that correspond with the target LRFFC statements, and three additional stimuli that look similar to the target stimulus in some way (e.g., if the target stimulus is a straw and the question is, "Which one do you sip juice with?" there should be three additional items in the array that look a like a straw, such as a pencil, stick, and knife).

Example: If the target LRFFC verbal stimulus is, "What do you wash with?" and the target item is a bar of soap, the array of 10 or so pictures should contain three pictures that look very much like a small box, a mini book, and a small brick of clay.

1 point score: Give the child 1 point if he correctly selects the item from an array of 10 or from a book that contains 3 or more similar stimuli, for 25 different LRFFC tasks.

½ point score: Give the child ½ point if he correctly selects 15 items given this type of LRFFC task.

LRFFC 12-M	Selects items from a book based on 2 verbal components: either a feature (e.g., color), function (e.g., draw with) or class (e.g., clothing) for 25 LRFFC tasks (e.g., *Do you see a brown animal? Can you find some clothing with buttons?*). (T)

Objective: To determine if a child can respond to more complex verbal stimuli in an LRFFC format. The verbal stimuli become more complex by involving two or more words that containing a function, feature, or class.

Materials: A set of known objects or pictures (the child is able to tact and LD) that correspond with the target LRFFC statements, and a list of corresponding functions, features, and classes that the child can correctly respond to when presented individually.

Examples: When in the child's living room, ask the child to, "Find a brown piece of furniture." When looking at a book, such as *Goodnight Moon*, ask the child to, "Find something round in the sky." When looking at picture of the Simpsons, ask the child, "Who has blue hair?"

1 point score: Give the child 1 point if he correctly selects 25 items from a scene or the natural environment given this type of LRFFC task.

½ point score: Give the child ½ point if he correctly selects 15 items from a scene or the natural environment given this type of LRFFC task.

LRFFC 13-M	Selects items from a page in a book or in the natural environment based on 3 verbal components (e.g., verb, adjective, preposition, pronoun), for 25 WH-question LRFFC tasks (e.g., *Which fruit grows on trees?*). (T)

Objective: To determine if the child can respond to even more complex verbal stimuli (a mix of verbs, nouns, prepositions, adjectives, or adverbs) embedded in a WH-question format, and can respond to nonverbal arrays that contain multiple stimuli (e.g., a scene) and stimuli that look similar to the target stimulus.

Materials: Use items in the natural environment, and/or pictures scenes and books (the child is able to tact and LD) that correspond with the target LRFFC statements. Also, compile a list of adjectives (e.g., colors, shapes, sizes, textures), verbs (e.g., spin, twist, pull, run), prepositions (e.g., in, on, under, above), and adverbs (e.g., slow, fast, quiet, loud) that the child knows at least as a listener. Also, compile a list of various combinations of the different parts of speech. Note, it is usually easiest to find the materials first, and then arrange the questions about the materials.

Examples: When in the child's living room, ask the child, "What is something pretty on the table?" (e.g., flowers). When looking at a picture from a birthday party, ask the child, "Where is something brown and cold that you eat?" (e.g., chocolate ice cream).

1 point score: Give the child 1 point if he correctly selects 25 items from a scene or the natural environment given this type of LRFFC task.

½ point score: Give the child ½ point if he correctly selects 15 items from a scene or the natural environment given this type of LRFFC task.

LRFFC 14-M	Selects the correct items from a book or the natural environment given 4 different rotating LRFFC questions about a single topic (*Where does the cow live? What does the cow eat? Who milks the cow?*) for 25 different topics. (T)

Objective: To determine if the child can respond to several different rotating WH questions about a single topic when presented in succession. Each question will change what will be the correct response. This task will require that the child carefully attend to the changing and multiple verbal stimuli.

Materials: A set of pictures scenes or books (the child is able to tact and LD) that correspond with the target LRFFC statements. Also, compile a list of potential WH questions about each item in the scene or book.

Example: When in the child's play area and the child is playing with a train set, ask the child, "Where is your train going?" (the child points to a bridge). "What pulls the train?" (the child points to the engine). "Who drives the train?" (the child points to the engineer). "What's on your train?" (the child points to the logs on a car).

1 point score: Give the child 1 point if he correctly selects 4 items from a scene or the natural environment for 25 different topics presented in this type of LRFFC task. Note that the child may also verbalize the correct answer instead of pointing to it, which would make it part intraverbal and part tact (if he looked at the nonverbal item), if this occurs give him credit for this LRFFC milestone because the intraverbal-tact skill is more advanced than the LRFFC skill (unless it is rote).

½ point score: Give the child ½ point if he correctly selects 4 items from a scene or the natural environment for 15 different topics presented in this type of LRFFC task.

LRFFC 15-M	Demonstrates 1000 different LRFFC responses, tested or obtained from an accumulated list of known responses. (T)

Objective: To determine if the child responds to a large variation of LRFFC tasks. Usually by this time the child should be able to respond to thousands of different combinations of words presented in an LRFFC format.

Materials: Use materials from books, scenes, and the natural environment.

Examples: When looking at a picture dictionary ask the child several LRFFC questions for each page, such as, "Where's something to drive?" "What's she cleaning the car with?" "What's he building?"

1 point score: Give the child 1 point if he correctly demonstrates 1000 different LRFFC responses, tested or obtained from an accumulated list of known responses. (Note: see the comments about vocabulary size in Tact Level 3-15.)

½ point score: Give the child ½ point if he correctly demonstrates 750 different LRFFC responses, tested or obtained from an accumulated list of known responses.

INTRAVERBAL – LEVEL 3

INTRAVERBAL 11-M	**Spontaneously emits 20 intraverbal comments (can be part mand) (e.g., Dad says *I'm going to the car*, and the child spontaneously says *I want to go for a ride!*). (O)**

Objective: To determine if the child attends to, and verbally responds to, the content of the verbal stimuli that he encounters in his day-to-day contact with other people, without prompts. The spontaneous component of this milestone is critical. The verbal stimuli should occur naturally and not contain elements that might prompt the child's response, such as a "discrete trial tone of voice," or stating the child's name. This verbal response can also be part mand in that a verbal stimulus might create an MO, and the MO and verbal stimulus combine to evoke the response. This effect is very common for young children.

Materials: A data sheet. No other specific materials are necessary.

Examples: The child hears, "We're going to grandma's house today," and this spontaneously evokes from the child, "Grandma has a lot of toys." The child hears, "Spiderman is trapped in the giant web," and this spontaneously evokes from the child, "Someone needs to help Spiderman." The child hears a peer say, "I'm building a castle," and this spontaneously evokes from the child, "I'm building a boat." The child, sitting in a large group of children, hears, "Who can tell me the name of a fruit?" and the child says "banana." The verbal stimulus, "Who wants ice cream?" may immediately increase the value of ice cream and at the same time intraverbally strengthen, "I want chocolate." The response, "I want chocolate" is controlled in part by an MO for chocolate, but also by the verbal stimulus "ice cream" and is thus part mand and part intraverbal.

1 point score: Give the child 1 point if he spontaneously emits 20 intraverbal responses in the natural environment in the course of a single day.

½ point score: Give the child ½ point if he spontaneously emits 10 intraverbal comments in a day.

INTRAVERBAL 12-M	**Demonstrates 300 different intraverbal responses, tested or obtained from an accumulated list of known intraverbals. (T)**

Objective: To determine if the size of the intraverbal repertoire is growing. This measure is just a sample of the repertoire, since it may be nearly impossible to measure all of the intraverbal relations that a child may be able to emit. The number of intraverbal relations should grow to several thousand as the child progresses to the next couple of intraverbal milestones.

Materials: A data sheet. A list of potential intraverbal questions and tasks.

Examples: "What's your favorite animal?" "Do you know some colors?" "Where does a fish live?" "Who takes you to school?" "What do you like to drink?"

1 point score: Give the child 1 point if he demonstrates at least 300 different intraverbal responses when asked to do so. Many programs maintain data sheets containing known intraverbal responses. This list can be used if it is reliable.

½ point score: Give the child ½ point if he demonstrates at least 200 different intraverbal responses when asked to do so.

INTRAVERBAL 13-M	**Answers 2 questions after being read short passages (15+ words) from books, for 25 passages (e.g., *Who blew the house down?*). (T)**

Objective: To determine if the child attends to a story being read to him, and if it strengthens relevant intraverbal behavior that the child is able to emit after hearing the story. This skill is an important milestone because it involves several linguistic activities such as comprehension, recall, and expansion of novel verbal content. It also constitutes a major teaching format for many elementary education classrooms, in that reading stories and discussing those stories can establish more complex verbal behavior for children. Thus, it is important to teach this repertoire to children. The most significant part of the measurement components of this milestone is that the child is able to intraverbally respond to the questions after hearing the story. Avoid questions that are leading, contain prompts (e.g., echoic, intraverbal), or require just yes/no answers.

Materials: A variety of children's books.

Examples: After reading the following passage from *Winnie the Pooh*, "Piglet turns his head very slowly—and he sees that Pooh is snoring! 'Oh Pooh Bear!' Piglet says." The adult asks, "What was Pooh doing?" And the child responds, "He was snoring!" After reading the *Three Little Pigs*, the adult asks questions like, "What did the big bad wolf do?" "Where did all the pigs go?" "What were the pig's houses made out of?"

1 point score: Give the child 1 point if he answers 2 questions for each of 25 short passages (15+ words) from books, or other written materials.

½ point score: Give the child ½ point if he answers 1 question for each of 25 short passages of at least 10 words.

INTRAVERBAL 14-M	**Describes 25 different events, videos, stories, etc. with 8+ words (e.g., *Tell me what happened... The big monster scared everybody and they all ran into the house*). (E)**

Objective: To determine if the child can talk about things that are not physically present, and describe them in a manner coherent enough that a listener can understand what occurred. This activity exemplifies one of the significant values of intraverbal skills, in that a speaker is able to talk about things and events, even though those things or events may have occurred in the past, or are not physically present. Note that the events should be fairly recent and relevant or interesting to the child.

Materials: No specific materials are required.

Examples: After a child is asked about an event such as, "What did you do at Grandma's house?" The child says, "Grandma and I made cookies and we ate them." Or, after watching a segment from the Lion King and the adult asks, "What have you been watching?" and the child says, "Scar was a mean lion and made Mufasa fall off the mountain."

1 point score: Give the child a score of 1 if he describes 25 different events, videos, stories, etc. with at least 8 words. The responses should only be scored as correct if they occur without echoic prompts. Also, the verbal descriptions should be evoked by other words, not the visual events themselves (that would make the response part tact).

½ point score: Give the child ½ point if he describes at least 12 different events, videos, stories, etc., with at least 5 words.

INTRAVERBAL 15-M	**Answers 4 different rotating WH questions about a single topic for 10 topics (e.g., *Who takes you to school? Where do you go to school? What do you take to school?*). (T)**

Objective: To determine if the child can successfully respond to rotating WH questions where the content that follows the WH word is similar, or about the same topic. These types of questions are hard for many children because they involve complex verbal conditional discriminations where one word alters the effects ("meanings") of the other words in a sentence, and they start with similar sounds, but have quite different meanings. A child must carefully attend to each word in the sentence to give the right answer. Usually, children are around 4 years of age before they can successfully respond to these types of questions, and errors remain common for a year or two depending on the topic and components of the question. Note that "when" questions involve time concepts and many typically developing 4-year-olds do not get them right.

Materials: A list of potential topics and questions.

Examples: "Where did you go for your birthday party?" "What presents did you get at your birthday party?" "Who came to your birthday party?" "Which cake did you eat at your birthday party?"

1 point score: Give the child 1 point if he answers 4 different WH questions about a single topic for 10 topics. The questions should be asked one right after another in a natural (non discrete trial) manner, with variation and expression.

½ point score: Give the child ½ point if he answers 3 different WH questions about a single topic for 5 topics.

CLASSROOM ROUTINES AND GROUP SKILLS – LEVEL 3

GROUP 11-M	Uses the toilet and washes hands with only verbal prompts. (O)
Objective:	To determine if the child can successfully use a toilet and wash his hands when told to do so, and does not require physical prompts.
Materials:	A toilet, sink, soap, a towel, and a step stool for the sink.
Example:	When told to use the toilet, the child will sit or stand to use the toilet without any physical prompts.
1 point score:	Give the child 1 point if he uses the toilet and washes his hands with verbal prompts.
½ point score:	Give the child ½ point if he uses the toilet and washes his hands, but requires physical assistance.

GROUP 12-M	Responds to 5 different group instructions or questions without direct prompts in a group of 3 or more children (e.g., *Everybody stand up. Does anyone have a red shirt on?*). (O)
Objective:	To determine if the child can successfully respond to verbal instructions that do not include the child's name, or any direct verbal prompt for the individual child to respond. These types of general verbal instructions are often referred to as "group instructions" and are common to small and large group classroom activities.
Materials:	No specific materials.
Examples:	When the teacher says, "All the boys line up with the other boys," and the target child does so. Or, when the teacher says, "Who knows what tastes sour?" the target child responds "a lemon."
1 point score:	Give the child 1 point if he responds to 5 different group instructions or questions without prompts in a group of 3 or more children.
½ point score:	Give the child ½ point if he responds to 2 different group instructions or questions without prompts in a group of 3 or more children.

GROUP 13-M	Works independently for 5 minutes in a group, and stays on task for 50% of the period. (O)
Objective:	To determine if the child can work on an assigned task in a group setting for a sustained period of time without adult prompts to stay focused on that task.
Materials:	A data sheet and standard classroom materials.
Example:	The child completes two pages from a set of programmed math material with only an initial adult prompt to complete the task.

1 point score: Give the child 1 point if he works independently for 5 minutes in a group activity/session involving 3 or more children, and stays on task for 50% of the period.

½ point score: Give the child ½ point if he works independently for 2 minutes in a group activity/session involving 3 or more children, and stays on task for 50% of the period.

GROUP 14-M	Acquires 2 new behaviors during a 15-minute group-teaching format involving 5 or more children. (T)

Objective: To determine if the child can learn new skills in a group-teaching format.

Materials: A data sheet and standard classroom materials.

Example: Following a group session containing a discussion on fire safety, the child is able to answer a question about what to do if there is a fire.

1 point score: Give the child 1 point if he acquires 2 new behaviors in a 15-minute group-teaching format involving 5 or more children as measured by an individual post-test given 5 minutes after the session.

½ point score: Give the child ½ point if he acquires 1 new behavior in a 15-minute group-teaching format involving 5 or more children as measured by an individual post-test given 5 minutes after the session.

GROUP 15-M	Sits in a 20-minute group session involving 5 children without disruptive behaviors, and answers 5 intraverbal questions. (T)

Objective: To determine if the child can emit appropriate group skills consisting of appropriate behavior and attending, and participation in the verbal activities during an academic group-teaching activity.

Materials: A data sheet and standard classroom materials.

Example: During a discussion about plants the teacher asks, "Who knows what plants must have to grow?" And the target child, who is sitting appropriately, raises his hand, and after being called upon responds, "Sunshine and water."

1 point score: Give the child 1 point if he sits appropriately, and answers 5 intraverbal questions presented in a 20-minute group-teaching format involving 5 or more children.

½ point score: Give the child ½ point if he sits appropriately, and answers 2 intraverbal questions presented in a 20-minute group-teaching format involving 5 or more children.

LEVEL 3

LINGUISTIC STRUCTURE – LEVEL 3

LINGUISTICS 11-M	Emits noun inflections by combining 10 root nouns with suffixes for plurals (e.g., *dog vs. dogs*) and 10 root nouns with suffixes for possessions (e.g., *dog's collar vs. cat's collar*). (E)
Objective:	To determine if the child can appropriately emit singular and plural nouns, and tag nouns with an "s" for possession.
Materials:	Common household or classroom items.
Examples:	For noun-plurals; "Where are my books?" "For noun-possession: " That's Joey's bike."
1 point score:	Give the child 1 point if he emits noun inflections in any of the verbal operants but echoic (i.e., mand, tact, or intraverbal) by combining 10 root nouns with suffixes for plurals and 10 root nouns with suffixes for possessions.
½ point score:	Give the child ½ point if he emits noun inflections for 10 noun-plural combinations, but not for 10 noun-possession combinations, or vice versa.

LINGUISTICS 12-M	Emits verb inflections by combining 10 root verbs with affixes for regular past tense (e.g., *played*) and 10 root verbs with affixes for future tense (e.g., *will play*). (E)
Objective:	To determine if the child can appropriately emit past and future tense regular verbs.
Materials:	Common household or classroom items.
Examples:	For past tense verbs: "I rolled the ball down the hill." For future tense verbs: "We're going to get ice cream."
1 point score:	Give the child 1 point if he emits verb inflections in any of the verbal operants but echoic (i.e., mand, tact, or intraverbal) by combining 10 root verbs with suffixes for past tense and 10 root verbs with affixes for future tense.
½ point score:	Give the child ½ point if he emits verb inflections in any of the verbal operants but echoic (i.e., mand, tact, or intraverbal) for 10 past tense verbs, but not for 10 future tense verbs or vice versa.

LINGUISTICS 13-M	Emits 10 different noun phrases containing at least 3 words with 2 modifiers (e.g., adjectives, prepositions, pronouns) (e.g., *He's my puppet. I want chocolate ice cream.*). (E)
Objective:	To determine if the child modifies common nouns with adjectives (e.g., color, size, shape, flavors), prepositions (e.g., location in space or in relation to other items), or pronouns (e.g., possession, replacement of a noun phrase).
Materials:	Common household or classroom items.

Examples: "I want the blue Cubs hat." "Put the train in the tunnel." "The dog chewed my shoe."

1 point score: Give the child 1 point if he emits 10 different 3-word noun phrases in any of the verbal operants except echoic (mand, tact, or intraverbal) with 2 modifiers.

½ point score: Give the child ½ point if he emits 5 different 3-word noun phrases in any of the verbal operants except echoic (mand, tact, or intraverbal) with 2 modifiers.

LINGUISTICS 14-M	Emits 10 different verb phrases containing at least 3 words with 2 modifiers (e.g., adverbs, prepositions, pronouns) (e.g., *Push me hard. Go up the steps.*). (E)

Objective: To determine if the child modifies common verbs with adverbs (e.g., where, when, and how actions are carried out), prepositions (e.g., location in space or in relation to other items or actions), or pronouns (e.g., possession, replacement of a verb phrase).

Materials: Common household or classroom items.

Examples: "Make it go slow." "I kicked the ball hard." "You are being really silly."

1 point score: Give the child 1 point if he emits 10 different 3-word verb phrases in any of the verbal operants except echoic (mand, tact, or intraverbal) with 2 modifiers.

½ point score: Give the child ½ point if he emits 5 different 3-word verb phrases in any of the verbal operants except echoic (mand, tact, or intraverbal) with 2 modifiers.

LINGUISTICS 15-M	Combines noun and verb phrases to produce 10 different syntactically correct clauses or sentences containing at least 5 words (e.g., *The dog licked my face.*). (E)

Objective: To determine if the child connects noun and verb phrases to form more complete sentences with a longer mean length of utterance.

Materials: Common household or classroom items.

Examples: Engage the child in a discussion about a topic of interest to him, such as a movie or specific event. Then ask questions such as, "What happen to the witch in the Wizard of Oz? "She melted when Dorothy threw water on her." Or, "Why did you stop playing outside?" "My red ball rolled out in the street."

1 point score: Give the child 1 point if he combines noun and verb phrases in any of the verbal operants except echoic (mand, tact, or intraverbal) to produce 10 different syntactically correct clauses or sentences.

½ point score: Give the child ½ point if he combines noun and verb phrases in any of the verbal operants except echoic (mand, tact, or intraverbal) to produce 5 different syntactically correct clauses or sentences.

MATH – LEVEL 3

MATH 11-M	Identifies as a listener the numbers 1-5 in an array of 5 different numbers. (T)

Objective: To determine if the child discriminates as a listener (LD) between the numbers 1 and 5 when they are presented in a mixed-up array of 5 numbers.

Materials: The written numbers 1-5 on cards, or in any other form.

Example: The child selects the number 3 from an array of 5 numbers when asked, "Can you find the number 3?"

1 point score: Give the child 1 point if he discriminates as a listener among the numbers 1-5 in an array of 5 different numbers.

½ point score: Give the child ½ point if he discriminates as a listener among the numbers 1-3 in an array of 3 different numbers.

MATH 12-M	Tacts the numbers 1-5. (T)

Objective: To determine if the child can tact the numbers 1 to 5 when they are presented in a mixed up order, one at a time.

Materials: The written numbers 1-5 on cards, or in any other form.

Example: The child tacts the number 4 when presented with the number 4 and asked, "What number is this?"

1 point score: Give the child 1 point if he tacts the numbers 1 to 5 when they are presented in a mixed up order, one at a time.

½ point score: Give the child ½ point if he tacts any 3 numbers.

MATH 13-M	Counts out 1-5 items from a larger set of items with 1 to 1 correspondence (e.g., *Give me 4 cars. Now give me 2 cars*). (T)

Objective: To determine if the child demonstrates 1:1 correspondence between his vocal counting and his pointing to (or in some way indicating) individual items for up to 5 items when given a larger group of items and asked to count out a certain amount.

Materials: Common household or classroom items.

Example: The child is able to count out 3 spoons from a utensil tray when asked, "Can you get me 3 spoons." The child picks up each spoon as he counts and correctly stops at the number 3 without any adult prompts and perhaps even demonstrates enumeration (emphasis on the last number).

1 point score: Give the child 1 point if he counts out 1-5 items from a larger set of items with 1 to 1 correspondence when verbally asked.

½ point score: Give the child ½ point if he counts out 1-3 items from a larger set of items with 1 to 1 correspondence when verbally asked.

MATH 14-M	Identifies as a listener 8 different comparisons involving measurement (e.g., *show me more or less, big or little, long or short, full or empty, loud or quiet*). (T)

Objective: To determine if the child can discriminate as a listener among math concepts involving comparisons of size, length, height, width, volume, and auditory intensity.

Materials: Common household or classroom items.

Example: For example, when presented with two piles of blocks that differ by several blocks (e.g., 5 vs. 10), and asked which pile has more blocks and which pile has less blocks, the child consistently selects the correct pile. This would constitute two comparisons.

1 point score: Give the child 1 point if he identifies as a listener 8 different comparisons involving measurement.

½ point score: Give the child ½ point if he identifies as a listener 6 different comparisons involving measurement.

MATH 15-M	Correctly matches a written number to a quantity and a quantity to a written number for the numbers 1-5 (e.g., matches the number 3 to a picture of 3 trucks). (T)

Objective: To determine if the child can match a visual number (not a vocal number) to the correct quantity and match a specific quantity to the correct visual number.

Materials: Numbers, and common household or classroom items, or pictures of 1-5 items from card sets or math workbooks.

Example: When presented with the visual number 3 the child matches the 3 to a picture of 3 items or counts out 3 items (without any prompts). Also, when presented with 3 items or a picture of 3 items, the child matches the picture or items with the number 3 (by selecting the 3 from an array of different numbers).

1 point score: Give the child 1 point if he correctly matches a written number to a quantity and a quantity to a written number for the numbers 1-5 presented in random order.

½ point score: Give the child ½ point if he correctly matches a written number to a quantity and a quantity to a written number for the numbers 1-3 presented in random order.

CHAPTER 6

The Barriers Assessment Scoring Instructions

The VB-MAPP Barriers Assessment is a tool that is designed to identify and score twenty-four learning and language acquisition barriers that might impede a child's progress (Table 6-1). The purpose of this assessment is to determine if a barrier exists. Once a specific barrier has been identified, a more detailed descriptive and/or functional analysis of that problem is required. For example, there are many ways that a mand repertoire can become impaired, and an individualized analysis will always be necessary to determine what the nature of the problem is for a specific child, and what intervention program might be most appropriate.

There are several general categories of barriers that can affect learning. First, many children with autism or other developmental disabilities exhibit strong and persistent negative behaviors that impede teaching and learning (e.g., tantrums, aggression, self-injurious behaviors). Second, any one or more of the verbal operants or related skills may be absent, weak, or in some way impaired (e.g., echolalia, rote intraverbals). Third, social behavior can also become impaired for a variety of reasons (e.g., limited motivation for social interaction or impaired mands). Fourth, there are several fundamental barriers to learning that must be analyzed and ameliorated to achieve significant gains (e.g., the failure to generalize, weak motivators, or prompt dependency). Fifth, there are a variety of specific behaviors that can compete with learning (e.g., self-stimulation, hyperactive behavior, or sensory defensiveness). And, finally, some problems may be related to physical or medical barriers that must be overcome, accommodated, or accounted for in some way (e.g., seizures, illnesses, sleep disorders, cerebral palsy, visual impairments).

An intervention program for a child with autism or other developmental disabilities should include both skills that need to be increased (e.g., mands, tacts, play and social skills), and behaviors or barriers that need to be decreased (tantrums, rote responding). Often, it is the case that the absence of skills and the presence of barriers are closely related, and a comparison of a child's scores on both the Milestones Assessment and the Barriers Assessment can provide direction for a more focused intervention program. For example, the Milestones Assessment may show that a child needs to learn to mand (see Figure 2-1), and this skill should be targeted for intervention with a focus on increasing the number of different mands that the child emits. However, the barriers assessment might reveal that a child is excessively prompt bound and scrolls (i.e., guesses) through words when learning new vocabulary (see Figure 6-1). These two barriers must be removed in order for the mand repertoire to grow and become functional for the child. Thus, the intervention program should contain a careful focus on freeing the existing mands from prompts and other unwanted sources of control and eliminate scrolling when manding. These problems must be fixed before new mands are added, because until they are, the mands will be of little true functional value to the child. In order to make the relation between Milestones and Barriers easier to assess, the two summary forms can be viewed side-by-side in the VB-MAPP Protocol (pages 4 and 5).

Table 6-1
Twenty-four learning and language acquisition barriers.

Negative behaviors

Instructional control (escape and avoidance behaviors)

Absent, weak, or impaired mand

Absent, weak, or impaired tact

Absent, weak, or impaired motor imitation

Absent, weak, or impaired echoic

Absent, weak, or impaired matching-to-sample

Absent, weak, or impaired listener repertoires

Absent, weak, or impaired intraverbal

Absent, weak, or impaired social behavior

Prompt dependent

Scrolling responses

Impaired scanning skills

Failure to make conditional discriminations (C^{D}s)

Failure to generalize

Weak or atypical motivators

Response requirement weakens motivation

Reinforcement dependent

Self-stimulation

Articulation problems

Obsessive-compulsive behavior

Hyperactivity

Failure to make eye contact, or attend to people

Sensory defensiveness

Some of the barriers presented in this assessment appear in different configurations in other components of the VB-MAPP. For example, the Barriers Assessment contains an item identified as "Failure to generalize," and the Transition Assessment (Chapter 7) contains a measure on "Generalization of skills across time, settings, behaviors, materials, and people." While the measurements are similar (but not exactly the same), each fit within the context of the two separate assessments. Rather than referring the reader back and forth between the instruments, they appear in both of them.

Figure 6-1
A sample Barriers Scoring Form.

VB-MAPP Barriers Scoring Form

Child's name:	Donny
Date of birth:	1-22-03
Age at testing:	**1** 4½ yrs. **2** **3** **4**

Key:	Score	Date	Color	Tester
1ST TEST:	49	7-03-07		MS
2ND TEST:				
3RD TEST:				
4TH TEST:				

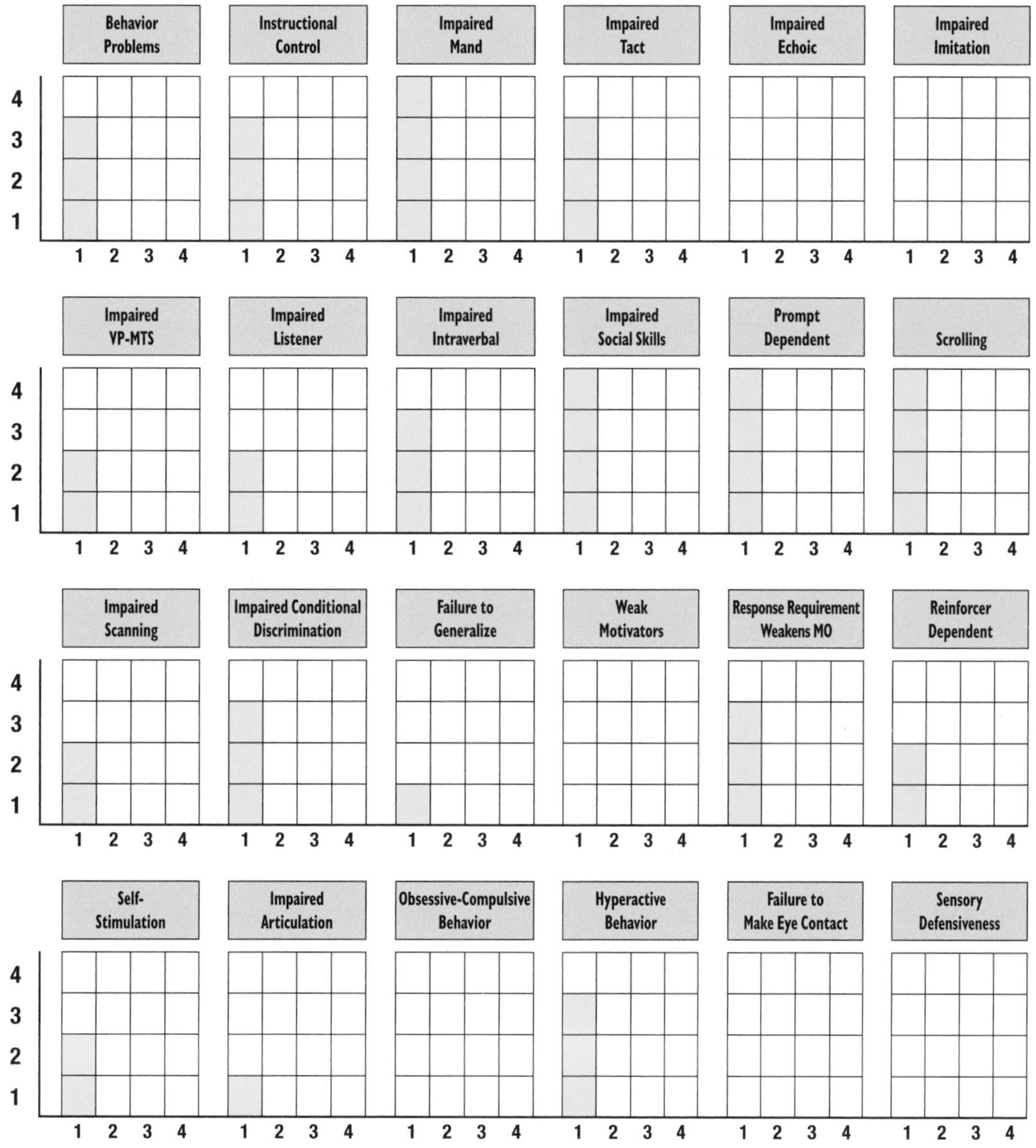

Scoring the VB-MAPP Barriers Assessment

The Barriers Assessment differs in several ways from the Milestones Assessment. First, the primary focus is on undesirable behaviors that must be reduced (i.e., barriers to learning), rather than skills that need to be developed (i.e., milestones to acquire). Second, given there are a wide range of barriers, it is not the case that a child will receive a score in all of the 24 barriers (a score of 0 indicates "no barrier is present"). Third, new barriers may emerge as a child progress. For example, a child may not demonstrate "rote intraverbal" behavior when his milestones scores are primarily in Level 1, but he may develop rote intraverbals later when more skills are acquired and his milestones scores begin to move to Level 2. And fourth, the total barriers scores cannot be used in the same manner as the total milestones scores (the numbers may increase, although the child has improved in many other areas). Thus, the barriers scores should primarily be used to identify priorities for the intervention program (e.g., repair an impaired mand repertoire). The actual data on barrier reduction should be the daily data on the relevant target behaviors (e.g., the frequency and variability of effective manding).

The scoring criteria and the scoring forms for the Barriers Assessment can be found in the VB-MAPP Protocol. Rate the child on the VB-MAPP Barriers Assessment (Protocol pages 25-29) using a Likert-type scale of 0 to 4, based on the criteria identified for each barrier, and transfer the score to the Barriers Assessment Scoring Form (Protocol page 5, see Figure 6-1). Note that the examples of behaviors presented at each score level in the Protocol do not constitute an exhaustive list, nor is it required that a child exhibit all the behaviors identified to receive a score at that level. The examples are simply provided to give the assessor a sample of the types of behaviors that might qualify for a specific score. A low score is a good score in that barriers must be reduced or removed. A score of 0 indicates that there are no significant barriers in the targeted area, and no intervention is necessary. Give the child a 0 on the score area of the Barriers Assessment, but do not write a score on the VB-MAPP Barriers Scoring Form (only fill in the form for scores of 1-4, which show that a barrier exists). A score of 1 suggests that an occasional problem exists and it should be monitored, but it may not warrant a formal intervention. A score of 2 indicates that a moderate problem exists and a further analysis and possibly an intervention program should be considered before the problem becomes worse. A score of 3 indicates that a persistent problem exists and is in need of a behavioral analysis and formal intervention program. A score of 4 indicates a severe problem exists and is also in need of an analysis and formal intervention program.

It may be the case that for some children the immediate intervention program should be more focused on removing a particular barrier, than on language or academic instruction. Once a particular barrier is reduced or removed (e.g., aggression, non-compliance, or self-injurious behavior), efforts to teach language, social behavior, or academics may be more effective. On the other hand, some form of language intervention, such as mand training, may be an important component of the program for reducing a barrier. That is why it may be necessary to have a trained professional analyze the nature of the specific problem experienced by an individual child, and design an individualized intervention program. An overview of each barrier will be provided below, along with more detail about the scoring criteria.

Scoring Guidelines for the Barriers Assessment

1. Negative Behavior

Most children exhibit some form of negative behavior during their early development (e.g., whining, crying, tantruming, aggression). Usually, these behaviors subside in frequency and are replaced with other more acceptable behaviors (e.g., language and socialization). However, for some children with autism or other developmental disabilities the negative behaviors do not subside, and may become worse as the child grows. The causes of these behaviors can vary tremendously (e.g., attention, demands, removal of reinforcers), and it always requires an analysis of the individual child to determine the specific cause of any given behavior problem. Help from a qualified professional that includes training for a child's teachers and caretakers will be a key component of the intervention program.

There is a substantial amount of research on the causes of negative behavior, as well as on effective intervention strategies (e.g., Foxx, 1982; Neef & Peterson, 2007). Most negative behaviors are due to various types of reinforcement consisting of inadvertent or accidental reinforcement provided by adults in one way or another (e.g., accidental attention provided for negative behaviors, promise of reinforcers if the behavior stops, or unintentional or unavoidable removal of demands). For example, a child may want a candy bar at a store and may begin to whine and tantrum to get the candy bar. The caretaker may begrudgingly give the child the candy bar to stop him from making a scene, and may even reprimand the child, but still the child gets the candy bar, and the behavior will likely occur again in the future. Or at school, a child may not be receiving the amount of adult attention that he would like to receive, and he has learned that when he hits other children the teacher or other adults are quick to attend to him. For this child, despite adult reprimands, the child gets attention, which may function as reinforcement. The reinforcement effects of negative attention may become more apparent in the future when the child again is not receiving enough adult attention, and hits another child.

Scoring Criteria

Use the criteria provided in the Barriers Assessment scales located in the VB-MAPP Protocol (pp. 22-29) and the information below to determine the degree of negative behaviors exhibited by the target child. Give the child a score of 0 (no problem) if he typically does not demonstrate behavior problems that impede his learning or cause difficulty to those working with him. Give him a score of 1 (occasional problem) if he has some minor behavior problems (e.g., occasional crying or whining), but they are brief and recovery back to his typical disposition is quick, despite the child not getting what may have caused him to tantrum in the first place. Give the child a score of 2 (moderate problem) if he emits a variety of minor negative behaviors every day (e.g., crying, verbal refusal, falling to the floor). Some behaviors may be persistent and long lasting, and in general the behaviors are becoming more severe.

Give the child a score of 3 (persistent problem) if he emits more severe and frequent negative behavior (e.g., tantrums, throwing things, property destruction). These behaviors may be quite difficult for adults to manage and may result in the child controlling the daily activities. Give the child a score of 4 (severe problem) if negative behaviors occur several times a day and present a danger to himself or others (e.g., aggression, property destruction, or self-injurious behavior). If the child's score on the assessment is a 1, the behavior should be monitored. If the occurrences are infrequent or go down for other reasons (e.g., sleeping better), no additional analysis may be necessary. However, this may not always be the case and some immediate intervention may be necessary to prevent the problems from becoming worse. If the child scores a 2 to 4, a further analysis of the barrier is certainly required in order to determine what type of intervention program is necessary (e.g., Neef & Peterson, 2007).

2. Poor Instructional Control (escape and avoidance of demands placed upon a child)

A significant component of working with children with special needs is the establishment of what can be identified as instructional control (or "compliance"). Basically, instructional control is when a teacher (or parent, aide, OT, etc.) asks a child to do something and he complies. Often, each teacher and individual working with a child must earn instructional control, especially with more difficult children. Some of these children have learned to emit a variety of behaviors to avoid or terminate demands placed upon them. These behaviors range from mild behaviors, such as simply looking away and not responding, to severe aggressive and self-injurious behaviors. However, the function of the behavior is often the same: escape from undesirable activities (e.g., putting on shoes, being put in car seats, or academic demands), or to avoid the onset of any stimuli that indicate unwanted activities are about to happen (e.g., signs that it's bedtime, an adult picking up a remote control to turn off the TV, or being told to come to the table for academic tasks).

Escape and avoidance behaviors are common in typically developing children, but can become quite severe for a child with autism or other developmental disabilities for a variety of reasons (e.g., weak language skills, strong obsessions with particular reinforcers). Instructional control problems can be considered a subset of behavior problems, but because of their ubiquitous nature and consistent source of control (see below), they will be treated as a separate barrier. It is also the case that some children only engage in negative behavior when it is related to instructional control. That is, when no demands are placed on the child there are no negative behaviors. In effect, the child shapes the adult's behavior by emitting negative behavior when demands are placed on him, thus reducing an adult's tendency to put demands on the child.

Technically, demands often serve as aversive motivators or what Michael (2007) identifies as "conditioned motivating operations-reflexive" (CMO-R). These types of motivators constitute some type of aversive event affecting a child (e.g., sitting in a group), and the child learns to emit behavior that will delay or remove the aversive event (e.g., running from the teacher). The negative behaviors related to CMO-Rs often get reinforced by delays or even removal of the undesired activity, and usually become stronger in the future (Sundberg, 1993a, 2004). There are a variety of strategies that can be effective in reducing avoidance and escape behaviors such as extinction of the behavior (e.g., don't allow the child to get out of tasks by falling on the floor) along with reinforcement for compliance. Carbone, Morgenstern, Zecchin-Tirri, and Kolberg (2008) provide an overview of these types of behavioral problems for children with special needs, along with a number of intervention strategies.

Scoring Criteria

Give the child a score of 0 on the Barriers Assessment if he is typically cooperative with adult instructions and demands. Give the child a score of 1 if some demands evoke minor noncompliant behavior, but usually the child is cooperative with adult instructions and recovers quickly from the situation even though he does not get what he wants. Give the child a score of 2 if he emits noncompliant behavior a few times a day with minor tantrums or other behaviors, and it is often difficult to get him to stop engaging in these behaviors when he does not get what he wants.

Give the child a score of 3 if he is showing a progression towards more persistent and severe instructional control problems as measured by an increase in the frequency of noncompliance, a wider range of situations that evoke noncompliance, and an increase in the severity of the behavior emitted in an attempt to avoid or escape the demand (instruction). Give the child a score of 4 if the noncompliant behavior is a major issue everyday and the child is quick to emit strong and severe behaviors, such as aggression or property destruction if demands are not removed. If the child's score on the assessment is a 1, monitor the behavior and handle it accordingly for each situation. However, if the child scores a 2 to 4, a further analysis of the noncompliant behavior is required.

3. Absent, Weak, or Impaired Mand Repertoire

A substantial number of children with autism or other developmental disabilities have difficulty acquiring an effective mand repertoire. Many of these same children may have extensive tact and listener skills, as well as elevated scores on other areas of the VB-MAPP Milestones Assessment. An absent, weak, or impaired mand repertoire is a significant barrier because manding serves several important functions for a child. Successful manding allows a child to inform the adult of important motivators that are immediately affecting him such as hunger, thirst, or a desire for comfort or physical contact. For example, when a child is thirsty and wants a drink, a mand can produce that specific reinforcer from an adult when it is most desired. In addition, manding allows a child to remove what he does not want (e.g., fear, pain, heat, fatigue). For example, if a child is frightened by an approaching dog and emits a mand for help, the adult can immediately remove the aversive stimulus by picking up the child.

An important effect of this verbal interaction is that the adult is paired with the delivery of reinforcement or removal of aversive events for the child. This pairing process can be of significant value to all children (Bijou & Baer, 1965), especially those with language delays. Manding allows the adult to provide the relevant consequence (delivery or removal) at a point in time when that consequence is the most valuable, thus increasing the adult's status as a conditioned reinforcer for the child. This interaction contributes to the bonding process, and begins to establish a foundation for social relationships. An absent, weak, or impaired mand repertoire may disrupt this process.

The distinction between the mand and the other types of verbal behavior (e.g., tact or intraverbal) is supported by decades of conceptual and empirical research (for reviews see Oah & Dickenson, 1989; Sautter & LeBlanc, 2006). The functional difference between the types of verbal behavior is based on the distinction, first suggested by Skinner (1938), between discriminative stimulus control (S^D) and motivational control (MO). For example, a word acquired under S^D control, such as the tact "garage," may not automatically transfer to a mand (MO control). That is, the child may be able to say "garage" when he sees a toy car garage (the S^D), but later when he wants to play with that same toy garage and it is not present (now an MO is strong, but not the S^D), he may not be able to emit the word "garage." Often, under these circumstances it is not uncommon to see the child engage in a tantrum or some other negative behavior (e.g., Hall & Sundberg, 1987). This effect is captured in the common adage "out of sight, out of mind." A behavioral translation of this saying is that S^D control does not guarantee MO control (for more detail on this distinction see Carbone, et al., 2008; Michael, 1982a, 2007; Sundberg, 2004).

Scoring Criteria

There are many possible reasons why a child might fail to acquire mands, or have learned some type of impaired mand (e.g., Drash & Tutor, 2004). If a child has an elevated score on the VB-

MAPP Barriers Assessment, the next step involves an analysis of that child's existing mand repertoire and the potential barriers that need to be removed. Give the child a score of 0 on the Barriers Assessment if he has an appropriate mand repertoire that is proportionate with his other skills on the Milestones Assessment (i.e., the mand is developmentally in balance with his other skills). Give the child a score of 1 if he does mand, but his LD and tact VB-MAPP Milestones Assessment scores are higher than his mand scores. This is an early "red flag" that indicates that the child's manding is trailing behind his other language skills. Give the child a score of 2 if his mands are few in number and limited to a small set of consumable or tangible reinforcers, despite strong tacts, LDs, and echoic skills.

Give the child a score of 3 if for example, his mands are prompt bound, rote, scrolling occurs, responses do not match the MOs, negative behaviors function as mands, excessive or inappropriate mands occur, or the child rarely mands spontaneously. Give the child a score of 4 if he does not have any functional mands, or demonstrates many of the problems listed in number 3, but does not have many other verbal skills either. It is likely that this child engages in frequent negative behaviors that have a mand function. Establishing a mand repertoire is at the top of this child's language training priorities. If the score on this Barriers Assessment is a 1, his progress should be closely monitored, and a stronger focus should be placed on mand training. If the child scores a 2 to 4, a further analysis of the specific barriers affecting the child's development of manding is required.

4. Absent, Weak, or Impaired Tact Repertoire

The tact repertoire is less susceptible to becoming impaired than the mand or intraverbal, due in part, to the nature of the controlling variables for the tact. Nonverbal stimulus control is more measurable and accessible, and in general, much clearer than motivational control (mand) and verbal stimulus control (intraverbal). However, there are still a number of problems that can become barriers along the road to establishing a tact repertoire for a child with language delays. It is often the case that the wrong nonverbal stimulus acquires control of the tact. For example, when teaching tacts related to verbs, the goal is that the specific moving nonverbal stimulus controls a specific response, not the object related to the movement. Some children learn to emit a word that is a verb in form, but not in function, as in the response "drinking juice," when the child is shown a cup, or "throwing ball," when just shown a ball.

Some children with language delays do not have problems with nouns and verbs, but do have difficulty with more complex tacts such as those involving adjectives, prepositions, adverbs, pronouns, and identifying emotional states. For these children, the same problems identified above may be occurring (there are many other possibilities as well). For example, after working on teaching the tacts "above," and "below," by placing items above and below other items such as a toy car above and below a table, a child is later shown just the car and asked, "What is this?" The child responds "above table." Gone unchecked, these rote tacting errors can be difficult to change and may become the source of other verbal problems experienced later in training, such as rote intraverbal responding. There are a variety of ways that tacting can become impaired, and an individual analysis is required to determine the problem for a specific child.

Scoring Criteria

Give the child a score of 0 on the Barriers Assessment if he has an appropriate tact repertoire that is in proportion with his other skills on the Milestones Assessment (i.e., the tact is developmentally in balance with his other skills). Give the child a score of 1 if he can tact some items and has good echoic skills (indicating that he has the most important prerequisite skill—echoic—for tact training), but his listener vocabulary markedly outnumbers his tact vocabulary. This is a common problem for many children with language delays, but for a child with a strong echoic repertoire, it can be amended with a tact training intervention program. Give the child a score of 2 and if tacting errors occur frequently, the child scrolls, or the tacts are in some way prompt bound (e.g., lip prompts), and require frequent maintenance trials to keep them in the child's repertoire.

Give the child a score of 3 if his tact repertoire is significantly out of balance with his other skills. Also give him a score of 3 if his tacts are clearly impaired as indicated by failing to generalize, lack of spontaneity, limited functional use of the skill, rote tacts, escape and avoidance behaviors during tact training, or failing to move beyond single word tacts. Give the child a score of 4 if his tact repertoire is nonexistent or limited to a few tacts, despite a strong echoic and LD repertoire. He may also demonstrate many of the problems in number 3, and have a long history of failing to acquire a tact repertoire. If the child's score on this Barriers Assessment is a 1, his progress should be monitored, and there should be an increased focus on tact training. If the child scores a 2 to 4, a further analysis of the specific barriers affecting the child's tact repertoire is required.

5. Absent, Weak, or Impaired Motor Imitation

Imitating the motor behavior of others plays an important role in many aspects of human development, especially in early play, social development, and learning self-help skills. Some children with autism or other developmental disabilities easily acquire this repertoire with formal training; however, for other children it can be difficult to establish. There are a variety of ways that imitation can become impaired, such as becoming prompt bound, or learning skills that are not functional for the child. Imitation can also become problematic in other ways as well. For example, some children become dependent on subtle imitative prompts for other skills (e.g., self-help or when learning sign language as a response form), and often adults do not notice the presence of these prompts. Another problem involves imitation of negative or inappropriate behaviors by some children.

Scoring Criteria

Give the child a score of 0 on the Barriers Assessment if his motor imitation skills are consistently growing, are age appropriate, and are in proportion with the other skills on the VB-MAPP Milestones Assessment. Give the child a score of 1 if he does imitate, but his VB-MAPP imitation scores are lower than those on the other milestones skills. Some children may easily acquire a few gross motor imitative responses or imitation with objects, but they may have difficulty progressing much beyond that (e.g., to fine motor imitation, two step imitation, functional imitation). One possibility is that imitation requires muscle control and coordination, and some children may have weak muscle control, which makes motor imitation difficult (especially fine motor imitation). Give the child a score of 2 if he demonstrates difficulty in generalizing imitation skills to different conditions, is dependent on imitative prompts in other areas of instruction, or copies the inappropriate behaviors of others (e.g., nose picking or throwing things).

Give the child a score of 3 if his imitation is prompt bound physically or verbally. That is, despite skills in other areas, the child must be prompted by either physically moving his body (even to start an imitative behavior), or verbally prompted with, for example, "do this." If these prompts are not provided, imitative behavior will not occur. The child may also demonstrate a weak MO for imitation. If a child shows very little interest in the behavior of others, it may be difficult to get him to attend to the motor behavior of others, let alone copy that behavior. Give the child a score of 4 if he has no imitation skills and previous attempts to teach imitation have repeatedly failed. Alternatively, give him a score of 4 if he can imitate, but never does so spontaneously or in any functional way, he rarely imitates peers, and demonstrates some of the problems from the earlier measures (e.g., prompt bound). If the child's score on this Barriers Assessment is a 1, his progress should be monitored and imitation encouraged, but there probably is not a major cause for concern. If the child scores a 2 to 4, a further analysis of the specific barriers affecting the child's motor imitation skills is required.

6. Absent, Weak, or Impaired Echoic Repertoire

A child's ability to echo words on command is one of the most important early measures of his potential for language development. This is because it is often easy to transfer the control of a spoken word from echoic control to mand, tact, or intraverbal sources of control using transfer of stimulus control procedures (Sundberg, 1980; Touchette, 1971). However, the inability to echo words presents a major barrier to future language development, and thus is often a key component of language intervention programs (e.g., Guess, Sailor, & Baer, 1976; Kent, 1974; Leaf & McEachin, 1998; Lovaas, 1977, 2003; Sundberg & Partington, 1998). However, echoic behavior can become too strong (echolalia) and also become a barrier to language development. Delayed echolalia (or "palilalia") and scripting (i.e., excessive out-of-context repeating of previously heard words) is another common problem related to echoic behavior. These behaviors may actually be a form of self-stimulation involving verbal behavior that is automatically reinforcing. There are a variety of potential causes of these problems such as reinforcement and impaired intraverbal skills.

Scoring Criteria

Give the child a score of 0 on the Barriers Assessment if his echoic skills are consistently growing, are age appropriate, and are in proportion with the other skills on the VB-MAPP Milestones Assessment. Give the child a score of 1 if he does echo, but his VB-MAPP echoic scores are lower than those on the other Milestones skills. Give the child a score of 2 if he becomes echoically prompt bound, and the transfer of control to new verbal operants is difficult due to a dependence on echoic prompts. Also give him a 2 if echoic acquisition is falling further behind imitation, LDs, and matching-to-sample, or if there are limited indicators of acquiring a generalized echoic repertoire.

Give the child a score of 3 if his echoic repertoire becomes too strong, as demonstrated by the emergence of echolalia or delayed echolalia. Alternatively, also score the child with a 3 if the repertoire is relatively weak and acquisition of new echoic skills is slow, requires extensive teaching and maintenance, and there are no occurrences of spontaneous echoic behavior. Give the child a score of 4 if he fails to acquire any echoic behavior, despite having learned imitation, matching, and listener skills. Attempts to teach echoic behavior may also evoke negative behavior (i.e., escape and avoidance behaviors). This child may be using sign language, PECS, or some other form of augmentative communication. If the child's score on this Barriers Assessment is a 1, his progress should be monitored and echoic behavior encouraged. If the child scores a 2 to 4, a further analysis of the specific barriers affecting the child's echoic development is required.

7. Absent, Weak, or Impaired Visual Perceptual Skills and Matching-to-Sample (VP-MTS)

The ability to attend to and discriminate among visual stimuli is often a component of IQ tests. It is quite common for some children with language delays to do well on these tasks, especially matching-to-sample. However, there are some children who have extreme difficulty with visual tasks. One of the inherent complexities of these tasks is that they require careful visual attending where the child must attend to one visual stimulus (the "sample stimulus"), scan an array of other visual stimuli (the "comparison stimuli"), and select a matching item based on some specific criteria (i.e., identical or non-identical item, color, or associated item). Technically, this is a type of multiple stimulus control (two things to look at) that involves multiple responding (looking and selecting), and is termed a "conditional discrimination" (see the conditional discrimination barrier for more detail). Many individuals with various types of disorders have difficulty with these tasks, which is why they are frequently on IQ tests.

Visual perceptual and matching errors need to be identified and corrected as soon as possible for young learners. For example, some children fail to attend to the sample stimulus or scan the array of choices and simply guess. If the array is small, they may have a reasonable chance of being correct without emitting a discrimination. They may also develop certain patterns of responding, such as always picking the comparison stimulus on the left, or the one that is in the same position as the last reinforced item. Scrolling also occurs in this task where a child might continue to select several different choices until reinforcement is delivered, or, if a selection response is not reinforced, the child keeps on guessing. There are a variety of additional causes for problems with visual tasks, such as poor instructional control, the child's tendency to stim on the presented material, or a poorly sequenced curriculum.

Scoring Criteria

Give the child a score of 0 on the Barriers Assessment if his visual perception and matching-to-sample skills are growing consistently, are age appropriate, and are in proportion with the other skills on the VB-MAPP Milestones Assessment. Give the child a score of 1 if he demonstrates some matching, but his VP-MTS scores are lower than those on the other Milestones skills, especially LD scores. This is because some children can successfully scan an array given a verbal stimulus (LD), but not a visual stimulus. This may be due to the difficulty of visually attending twice in a single task. Give the child a score of 2 if he is showing any one of a number of missing elements of the task, such as failing to scan the array or attend to the sample stimulus, or responding before the sample is presented. Also, give a score of 2 if his selection behavior is affected by a side or position bias (or other prompts), rote patterns of responding, scrolling, or is limited to small arrays.

Give the child a score of 3 if he has acquired some MTS skills, but they are not progressing in proportion to his other skills, and he exhibits negative behaviors (escape and avoidance) during attempts to further develop MTS. Also, give the child a score of 3 if the repertoire is limited to small arrays, similar stimuli cause major problems, or there is a failure to generalize MTS discriminations to the natural environment. Give the child a score of 4 if he fails to acquire any significant MTS skills despite having other skills and repeated attempts to teach MTS. Alternatively, give him a score of 4 if he has acquired the skills, but they are rote, defective in the ways previously mentioned, or never occur in any functional way in his day-to-day environment (e.g., choosing two of the same shoes, matching socks, arts and crafts, or leisure activities). If the child's score on this Barriers Assessment is a 1, his progress should be monitored and MTS activities should be encouraged. If the child scores a 2 to 4, a further analysis of the specific barriers affecting the child's visual perceptual and matching skills is required.

8. Absent, Weak, or Impaired Listener Repertoires (LD and LRFFC)

There are many skills that can be classified as listener behavior, and any or all of them can be absent, weak, or impaired for a given child. The three major skills in a listener repertoire involve (1) attending to someone who is speaking, and serving as an audience for that person, (2) reinforcing a person who is speaking, and (3) demonstrating understanding as to what a speaker says. These repertoires can become quite complicated and difficult for some children to acquire, and barriers can occur at several levels. Attending to others when they talk may require eye contact, focus on the person, and what the person is saying. Reinforcing a speaker also requires behavior on the part of the listener such as nods, agreement, and remaining in close proximity. Demonstrating understanding of what is said is obviously the most complex and usually the biggest source of difficulty for many individuals. This understanding is commonly referred to as "receptive language," or what is called listener discriminations (LDs) in the current text. Understanding can also involve verbal responses, but that would be classified as intraverbal behavior and will be discussed in the next section.

Many of the same problems presented previously for MTS can occur in LDs and LRFFCs, because both of these tasks involve selecting items from an array, or from the natural environment. These problems include failing to scan the array, position and side biases, scrolling, inadvertent prompts, difficulty with larger arrays, or having similar stimuli in the array. Other potential barriers may be that single stimulus and single response training has been over conditioned. Thus, moving beyond verbal stimuli consisting of single nouns and verbs may be difficult (e.g., "Touch book," "Show me jump") and skills involving multiple verbal stimuli (e.g., "Show me jumping monkey.") and LRFFC tasks (e.g., "Can you find a food that's hot?") are never established. Generalization may be limited, conditional discriminations may be weak, and escape and avoidance behavior may occur to terminate listener tasks. Several of these problems are assessed in other sections of this chapter as separate barriers.

Scoring Criteria

Give the child a score of 0 on the Barriers Assessment if his listener skills are growing consistently, are age appropriate, and are in proportion with the other skills on the VB-MAPP Milestones Assessment. Give the child a score of 1 if he demonstrates some listener skills, but his listener scores are lower than those on the other milestones skills, especially his tact scores. This may be due to the fact that some children have difficulty with conditional discriminations that cross modalities (i.e., these tasks involve both an auditory and visual stimuli). Give the child a score of 2 if he does not typically attend to speakers or reinforce their verbal behavior, or is showing any one of a number of missing elements from an LD task (e.g., failing to scan the array or attend to the sample stimulus), or responding before the sample is even presented. Also, give him a score of 2 if he demonstrates a side or position bias (or other prompts), rote patterns of responding, scrolling, or limitations to small arrays.

Give the child a score of 3 if he has acquired some LD skills, but they are not progressing in proportion to his other skills, and he exhibits negative behaviors (escape and avoidance) during attempts to further develop LDs or rarely attends to speakers or reinforces their verbal behavior. Also, give the child a score of 3 if the repertoire is limited to small arrays, similar stimuli cause major problems, complex verbal stimuli cause problems (e.g., adjective-noun combinations), or there is a failure to generalize MTS discriminations to the natural environment. Give the child a score of 4 if he fails to acquire any significant LD skills despite other skills and repeated attempts to teach LD. Alternatively, give him a score of 4 if he has acquired the skills, but they are rote, impaired in the ways previously mentioned, or never occur in any functional way in his day-to-day environment (e.g., following instructions in a functional skill, attending to and listening to peers, or getting specific items from a specific location when asked). If the child's score on this Barriers Assessment is a 1, his progress should be monitored and LD activities should be encouraged. If the child scores a 2 to 4, a further analysis of the specific barriers affecting the child's listener repertoires is required.

9. Absent, Weak, or Impaired Intraverbal Repertoire

Intraverbal behavior is the most complex type of verbal behavior to teach, and it is the most prone to becoming impaired for children with autism or other developmental disabilities. Despite having learned hundreds of tacts, some children fail to acquire even simple intraverbal relations, such as providing their name when asked, "What's your name?" Other problems include rote responding to questions, failing to maintain a conversation, or irrelevant and out-of-context verbal responses. There are many reasons why intraverbal behavior is harder to teach than the other language skills. Perhaps the main difficulty is that words and sentences as antecedent stimuli typically contain many parts and change frequently, unlike objects, pictures, numbers, and letters, which tend to be quite constant in terms of both the stimulus and the response. A spoon is always a spoon, and the number 2 is always a 2. There generally is a consistent relation between the stimulus and the response with the echoic, tact, and LD repertoires. Intraverbal relations, by their very nature, are for the most part constantly changing, and that includes both the stimulus and the response. For example, a tree is always a tree for echoic, tacting, matching, and LD, but an intraverbal discussion about trees can be comprised of hundreds, if not thousands, of different intraverbal relations. Furthermore, the discussion about trees may never occur exactly the same way each time.

The task of directly teaching intraverbal behavior is endless. A typically developing 3- to 4-year-old child usually has acquired thousands of different intraverbal relations, and that number continues to multiply as a child grows. Most adults have hundreds of thousands of different intraverbal relations as a part of their verbal repertoires. The mand and the tact, while certainly always capable of growing, are relatively limited by an individual's MOs, and the nonverbal stimuli in the immediate environment. Consider, for example, all the books in a public library or verbal stimuli on the Internet. Each standard-size book contains thousands of intraverbal relations in the form of facts, descriptions, metaphors, stories, historical events, predictions, fantasy, and so on. Contact with these verbal stimuli can evoke endless intraverbal responses, such as opinions, reactions, or discussions of the facts. Given the complexities of intraverbal behavior, it is important for adults to carefully monitor a child's early intraverbal development. Potential barriers are plentiful, many of which are the same barriers that affect all children (e.g., rote responding or forgetting the answers to questions), but they may be exacerbated for children with language delays (Sundberg & Sundberg, 2011).

Scoring Criteria

Give the child a score of 0 on the Barriers Assessment if his intraverbal repertoire is growing consistently and is in proportion with the other skills on the VB-MAPP Milestones Assessment. Give the child a score of 1 if he does demonstrate some intraverbal responses, but his intraverbal scores are markedly lower than those on the other Level 2 Milestones skills, especially his tact, LD, and LRFFC scores. Give the child a score of 2 if intraverbal errors occur frequently, or if the child has become prompt bound in some way such as partial echoic prompts or tact prompts. Also, give him a score of 2 if scrolling through other responses occurs, or echolalia occurs, spontaneous intraverbal behavior never occurs, or if certain words automatically evoke rote intraverbal responses despite the context. For example, the word "dog" always evokes "barks" despite the question being, "What does a dog eat?"

Give the child a score of 3 if rote responding is frequent and becoming a more obvious problem, responses are quickly forgotten, no generalization occurs, responses are prompt bound, or the child never engages in intraverbal behavior spontaneously, or with peers, despite strong mand, tact, LD, and LRFFC skills. Also, score him at this level if these problems occur somewhat, but overall progress in the intraverbal is markedly slower than observed in the other skills. Give the child a score of 4 if he fails to acquire any significant or functional intraverbal behavior despite strong mand, tact, and LRFFC skills, or if he shows the problems identified in number 3, but does not demonstrate these problems in other skills (e.g., scrolling does not occur with tact and listener skills, but does occur with intraverbals). If the child's score on this Barriers Assessment is a 1, his progress should be monitored and intraverbal training activities increased. If the child scores a 2 to 4, a further analysis of the specific barriers affecting the child intraverbal repertoire is required.

10. Absent, Weak, or Impaired Social Skills

Children are generally quite social, and children diagnosed with developmental disabilities are no exception, especially children with certain disabilities like Down's Syndrome. Many children with autism are reinforced by social interactions as well. But like many individuals, including typically developing children, they may struggle with learning appropriate social behavior, and suffer from a variety of social deficits. There are several reasons why social skills may become impaired. Social behavior is complex and comprised of many different skills, and "social rules" are vague and constantly changing. What's accepted or expected in one setting or with one group is not accepted or expected in another setting or with another group. Further complicating the problem is that any one of the 23 other barriers identified on this assessment can affect the development of social behavior (e.g., behavior problems, impaired mands, self-stimulation, hyperactivity, sensory defensiveness). Thus, it's important that these barriers be identified and ameliorated as soon as possible.

Some barriers are more common or problematic for social development than others, and these will be used as the major components of the social skills Barriers Assessment. Perhaps the most significant cause of social problems involves weak motivators (MOs) for social interaction or aversive motivators (e.g., other children might take a child's toy) that make it difficult to get a child to socially interact with others. Also, a significant component of social behavior involves verbal behavior, and if a child cannot mand, respond with intraverbal answers to the mands of others, or serve as a listener, social interactions will be limited. Behavior problems such as aggression, property destruction (especially a peer's property), and self-injurious behaviors can also affect a child's social interaction with others. Other general barriers like prompt dependency, dependence on reinforcers, failing to generalize, and response requirements that weaken motivators are all salient barriers. Some children may not demonstrate these problems with adults, but only with peers. There are a variety of reasons for this discrepancy (e.g., a strong reinforcement history with adults and much less success with peers, minimal competition for reinforcers, or high prompt level). Therefore, the main focus for this assessment should be on age-appropriate social interaction with peers. It should be noted that typical children are often relatively more interested in adults than peers until about 2 ½ to 3 years old.

Scoring Criteria

Give the child a score of 0 on the Barriers Assessment if his social skills are growing consistently and are in proportion with the other skills on the VB-MAPP Milestones Assessment. Give the child a score of 1 if social behavior occurs, but his social skills scores are falling behind the other milestones scores. For example, if a child is showing strong imitation and mand skills, but does not imitate peers or mand to peers, then that is a red flag for social development. Give the child a score of 2 if he rarely initiates a social interaction with a peer (however, he may initiate interactions with an adult), or if he emits socially negative behavior, such as grabbing toys from others, pushing, or other forms of aggression. Also, give him a score of 2 if he rarely spontaneously imitates, plays with, or mands to peers.

Give the child a score of 3 if he stays by himself during play periods, does not take turns or share items with other children, does not respond to peer's mands, or does not show signs of verbally engaging with peers. However, the child may demonstrate verbal interaction with adults. Give the child a score of 4 if he has language skills, but actively avoids other children. He may also emit negative or inappropriate behaviors when forced into a social situation. Also, he may almost never respond to the mands from peers to participate in activities. If the child's score on this Barriers Assessment is a 1, his progress should be monitored and social skills training should be included as part of the child's intervention program. If the child scores a 2 to 4, a further analysis of the specific barriers affecting the child is required.

11. Prompt Dependent

A prompt is like a hint, it helps someone come up with the correct answer, or perform a particular behavior when that behavior might be weak for some reason. Prompts can be positive or negative (aversive) and are usually beneficial in the day-to-day functioning of most individuals. For example, a bill sent in the mail from the utility company (aversive) prompts the homeowner for payment, a secretary from a doctor's office calls to "remind" the patient of an appointment, a Post-It on the refrigerator has the time of an evening parent meeting, and planning calendars remind the user of social and professional commitments. A busy person may function much better by taking advantages of prompts. However, problems occur when the prompts are not available, such as if the Post-It falls off the refrigerator and is swept away, or the calendar is misplaced. Some people become prompt bound in that the desired behavior will not occur in the absence of the prompt. Doctor's appointments and meetings are missed, calls are not returned, and payments are late because the person "forgot."

Prompts are also a valuable tool for teaching all children. However, a common problem faced by some children is that they become "prompt bound." That is, if the prompt is not provided, the answer does not occur. For example, when asked to select a picture of a cup from an array of pictures, a child may select the correct picture because of the adult's eye gaze, or head nod toward the correct picture, rather than what is on the picture. If subtle prompts such as these are not identified early in training and appropriately faded out, the child may become prompt bound and this will affect future skill acquisition. Typically, prompt dependency is not restricted to a specific task, but often permeates many different elements of a child's linguistic, educational, social, and daily living skills. Many children who do not initiate or are identified as failing to emit spontaneous language are actually prompt bound in one way or another.

Prompt dependency can take many forms, and it often requires a trained observer to carefully analyze the true source of control of the child's responses. In language instruction, a major goal is to develop verbal independence where responses are free from unwanted sources of control such as echoic, imitative, nonverbal, or other prompts, and controlled exclusively by the correct antecedent variable. However, many children experience difficulty moving beyond a reliance on these additional "hints" that result in seemingly "correct" responses. The primary cause of prompt dependency is that the prompt has not been properly faded from the teaching arrangement; hence the target stimulus fails to acquire the necessary stimulus control required to demonstrate learning.

Scoring Criteria

Give the child a score of 0 on the Barriers Assessment if he is consistently learning new skills and does not show any signs of prompt dependency. Give the child a score of 1 if he usually needs several trials of prompting and prompt fading to learn new skills, but the transfer of stimulus control process is typically successful. Give the child a score of 2 if it is often hard to fade prompts, especially with more difficult skills (e.g., intraverbal or social interactions). Give the child a score of 3 if it is hard to eliminate prompts, his verbal skills are limited skills, and prompts may be subtle. Give the child a score of 4 if prompts are very difficult to fade, and most skills are prompt bound by echoic, imitative, or verbal prompts. The child may also emit negative behaviors when prompts are not provided. If the child's score on this Barriers Assessment is a 1, his progress should be monitored, but there probably is no cause for concern at this point. If the child scores a 2 to 4, a further analysis of the specific prompts and why they cannot be faded is required.

12. Scrolling Responses

A common barrier faced by many early language learners is the tendency to "guess" at the correct answer by emitting several words (or signs or icon selections) that have been reinforced in previous sessions. For example, when shown a book and asked, "What is that?" the child may say "car," "hat," "book." This behavior can be termed "scrolling." Usually, the words that are scrolled are not random, they are the words that have been worked on in the same session, or in previous sessions, or words from the same verbal operant class (i.e., mand scrollers may go through several of their mand words). Some children who are using sign language as a response form may even give one sign with one hand and another sign with the other hand. Others will blend two signs together, such as signing "bubbles" with fingers while signing "cracker" with arms.

Scrolling can occur with all language skills and at any level of verbal behavior. For example, intraverbal scrolling occurs when a child is asked a question like, "What's in a kitchen?" and the child responds "tub," "bed," "stove." Scrolling in listener tasks occurs when a child touches several pictures, and will often continue to touch different pictures until an adult says "right!" The primary cause of scrolling is that the response is never thoroughly brought under the correct S^D control. That is, stimulus control is not established before moving on to a new word (i.e., the response is possibly prompt bound in some way). Then, unsuspecting adults who don't see the wrong responses, or consider the responses as "self-correcting," intermittently and inadvertently reinforce scrolling behavior.

Scoring Criteria

Give the child a score of 0 on the Barriers Assessment if he does not scroll responses. Give the child a score of 1 if he occasionally scrolls when new words are added, but after a small number of discrimination training trials he stops scrolling, and usually demonstrates solid acquisition and generalization of the word. Give the child a score of 2 if scrolling is frequently a problem, and usually occurs when new words are introduced. It may take several discrimination trials between new and old words, but eventually the child acquires the new word and will rarely continue to scroll that word.

Give the child a score of 3 if scrolling continues to resurface with previously "acquired" words, meaning he may have never "known" the words to begin with (they were prompted in some way). Scrolling may only occur with the harder skills (i.e., mand, tact, LD, and intraverbal), but not with easier skills (echoic or imitation). Give the child a score of 4 if scrolling occurs during almost every trial. If prompts are not quickly provided, attempts at fixing the scrolling problem may have a long history of failure, and only a few words occur without scrolling. If the child's score on this Barriers Assessment is a 1, his progress should be monitored, but there probably is no cause for concern at this point. If the child scores a 2 to 4, a further analysis of the specific causes of his scrolling is required.

13. Impaired Scanning Skills

There are three major repertoires that require a child to scan a visual array (i.e., carefully look at stimuli): (1) MTS, (2) LD, and (3) LRFFC. The ability to select the correct items from an array of choices cannot occur without first scanning the array. For example, when asked to find a picture of a ball from an array of items (e.g., the array contains a car, dog, book, and ball), the child must first look at the array in order to find the target item. Many children fail to adequately scan an array and learn side or position biases, or become prompt bound by eye movements, facial expressions, hand positions, placement order, or other very subtle prompts inadvertently given by the adult. Watch the child's eyes and if he immediately focuses on the array and demonstrates scanning behavior, this is desirable. If the child looks at the adult's face or hands, there may be problems. If these problems are not corrected in the early phases of training, they can become quite difficult to eliminate later on.

Scoring Criteria

Give the child a score of 0 on the Barriers Assessment if he typically scans a visual array on tasks that requires scanning behavior. Give the child a score of 1 if he does scan arrays with 6 to 8 items in them without prompts to scan, but begins to have difficulty with arrays larger than 10, or arrays that have similar stimuli in them. Give the child a score of 2 if he must be frequently prompted to attend to the array, and usually cannot select the correct item from an array larger than 5, or from a scene in a book or from a picture. Give the child a score of 3 if scanning is limited to an array of 2 or 3, and when he does select the correct item it is often by chance or prompted in some way. As a result, his VB-MAPP scores on VP-MTS, LD, and LRFFC will be quite low. Give the child a score of 4 if he does not scan arrays, responds before scanning, or when required to scan he emits negative behavior (escape and avoidance behaviors). If the child's score on this Barriers Assessment is a 1, his progress should be monitored, but there probably is no cause for concern at this point. If the child scores a 2 to 4, a further analysis of his failure to scan is required.

14. A Failure to Make Conditional Discriminations

Despite the common impression of a behavioral approach as "discrete trial training" with a clearly presented antecedent, a defined response, a programmed consequence, and an intertrial interval, rarely is it the case that human behavior involves only a single stimuli-response-consequence relation. Rather, most behavior involves multiply controlled responses containing interlocking contingencies, non-programmed consequences, a variety of relevant historical and biological variables, private events, and often interwoven respondent contingencies (Michael, 2003; Michael, Palmer, & Sundberg, 2011; Skinner, 1953). In order to accurately analyze an individual's behavior, it is essential to account for all these variables. One such variable that permeates almost all aspects of verbal and nonverbal behavior is the interlocking contingences that make up what is identified in behavior analysis as a "conditional discrimination" (e.g., Catania, 1998; Michael, 2003; Sidman & Tailby, 1982; Spradlin, Cotter, & Baxley, 1973).

A conditional discrimination (C^D) involves at least two interlocking three-term contingencies (i.e., two antecedent-behavior-consequence relations), where the effectiveness of one three-term contingency is dependent on the other. More specifically, one stimulus changes the significance of another stimulus. For example, in a matching-to-sample task, the presentation of the sample stimulus (e.g., a picture of a ball) changes what functions as an S^D in the comparison array (the ball versus a boat). If a boat is shown as the sample, the picture of a boat in the array becomes an S^D for selection, and is now the response that will be reinforced. Thus, the child must attend to two stimuli (the sample ball and the comparison ball), where the effectiveness of one is dependent on the other. This is a complicated task for many children with autism or other developmental disabilities, especially those who have difficulty attending to even one stimulus.

Conditional discriminations involve not only multiple nonverbal relations (e.g., MTS), but also interactions between verbal and nonverbal stimuli as in LD and LRFFC tasks, MOs and S^{D}s as in some mands, and verbal stimuli as in intraverbal relations. For example, in an LD task the verbal stimulus "ball" establishes the nonverbal stimulus of a ball in an array of choices as an S^D for nonverbal selection. In LRFFC, the verbal stimulus "you bounce a..." establishes the ball as an S^D for nonverbal selection. In a mand relation, an MO may alter the value of a specific nonverbal stimulus, such as a dark room that establishes a light switch as an S^D for switch flipping behavior. In an intraverbal relation, one part of a verbal antecedent may alter a second part of a verbal stimulus, such as the different effects of the words "first" and "current" on the word "president," as in the two verbal S^{D}s "Who was the **first** president?" "Who is the **current** president?" A correct response is dependent on a conditional discrimination. Many children have a difficult time learning to make conditional discriminations, especially when the antecedent stimuli are verbal, multiple, and complex (Sundberg & Sundberg, 2011).

Defective conditional discriminations can be caused by a variety of variables, and a functional analysis of those relevant to a particular child can provide insight to the problems, and a more effective intervention strategy. It is not uncommon to overlook these problems with simple tasks and not identify them as a barrier until a child is presented with more complex tasks, such as a multiple component LRFFC like, "Can you find a big animal?" Often, by that time a child has been over-conditioned with single stimulus-response-consequence tasks, and rote responding has been firmly established. A return to basic conditional discrimination training is required.

Scoring Criteria

Give the child a score of 0 on the Barriers Assessment if he makes conditional discriminations at a level that is in balance with his other milestones scores. Give the child a score of 1 if he has trouble when the C^D requires more effort or attending, which is usually the case when the arrays get bigger, contain stimuli that are similar, or are in the context of a natural environment setting. Give the child a score of 2 if he has difficulty when the stimulus involves multiple verbal components (e.g., "What animal has a tail?"), but he can correctly respond to each stimulus independently, and in other verbal operants, but not in a combination in a verbal conditional discrimination.

Give the child a score of 3 if he fails at most tasks that involve C^Ds, except matching-to-sample. He may frequently emit negative behavior (escape and avoidance) during tasks that require conditional discriminations (i.e., they are hard for him), and there may have been several failed attempts to establish these skills. Give the child a score of 4 if he does not make C^Ds, despite having some (or even many) simple discrimination skills, such as those in single mands, echoic, tacts, or imitative behaviors. If the child's score on this Barriers Assessment is a 1, his progress should be monitored, but there probably is no cause for concern at this point. If the child scores a 2 to 4, a further analysis of why the child cannot make conditional discriminations is required.

15. Failure to Generalize

A common problem faced by many children with language delays, especially those with autism, is that they acquire exactly what is taught and fail to generalize to new conditions or they fail to provide any variation in their responses. Generalization should occur across all of the 16 skill areas identified in the VB-MAPP Milestones Assessment, thus all areas should be checked for possible generalization problems. It is not uncommon to find out that generalization does occur with some skills (e.g., imitation), but not with others (e.g., tacting). Alternatively, certain types of generalization might be more problematic than others for some children (e.g., a child might have extreme difficulty generalizing to new people). It is important to identify generalization problems early in learning when they are easier to correct.

There are two major types of generalization; stimulus generalization and response generalization (e.g., Cooper, et al., 2007; Stokes & Bear, 1977). In stimulus generalization a child may learn a response under the control of one stimulus condition (e.g., the child will tact "ball" when his mother shows him a ball), and then without further training emits the response under different stimulus conditions. There are several different situations where stimulus generalization should occur for an early learner. These include performing the behavior at different times (e.g., tacting "ball" later in the day when he sees a ball), in different settings (e.g., tacting "ball" in his bedroom), for different people (e.g., tacting "ball" for his father), with different types of verbal prompts to tact (e.g., "What is that?" What do you see?"), and with different material (e.g., tacting a picture of a ball). If a child shows difficulty with any of these types of generalizations, a formal intervention program may be warranted.

The second type of generalization is response generalization. Here, a child may learn one response under the control of one stimulus (e.g., saying "cat" when asked to name an animal), but fail to provide any other responses that would be considered appropriate under that same stimulus (e.g., the response "rabbit" would also be considered a correct response to the question). The failure to demonstrate response generalization is often part of what is often identified as "rote verbal responding." A child always gives the same answer to questions, despite the fact that there could be many variations to what would be considered a correct answer. The failure to demonstrate these two types of generalization can constitute a significant learning barrier because generalization allows for more opportunities to practice skills in a natural and functional way and can accelerate learning.

Scoring Criteria

Give the child a score of 0 on the Barriers Assessment if he typically demonstrates both stimulus and response generalization at a level commensurate with his other skills. For example, if the child's milestones scores fall primarily in Level 1, he should be demonstrating some generalization of his imitative, mand, tact, echoic, listener and matching skills at a rate that might be observed with a typically developing child. It would not be expected, for example, that a child at this level would demonstrate intraverbal response generalization. Give the child a score of 1 if he shows some kind of difficulty with any type of stimulus generalization (e.g., generalization to new materials is relatively slow) or with any skill (e.g., echoic generalization is falling behind). Give the child a score of 2 if he requires formal generalization training on most skills. For example when learning a new tact such as "phone" he needs multiple exemplar training consisting of 5 different examples of phones before he gets one untrained, but he usually gets and retains the skill.

Give the child a score of 3 if generalization training is laborious and often not very successful in that the child frequently looses skills that were once thought to be generalized. Give the child a score of 4 if he does not demonstrate any generalization to untrained stimuli, despite extensive efforts to provide formal generalization training. This child is likely to have a limited amount of skills given the presence of this particular barrier. If the child's score on this Barriers Assessment is a 1, his progress should be monitored and frequent opportunities to generalize new skills should be provided. If the child scores a 2 to 4, a further analysis as to why generalization is not occurring for this child is required.

16. Weak or Atypical Motivating Operations (MOs)

One variable that makes every human different from one another is motivation. All humans are born with a similar collection of unlearned motivators (e.g., hunger, thirst, oxygen, warmth, or removal of pain), but soon learn a much broader and varied collection of learned motivators that are unique to each individual (Michael, 2007). For a young child these learned motivators usually begin with wanting attention, a parent's presence and voice, and other things that are initially associated with the unlearned motivators. But soon motivation develops for other visual and auditory stimuli (e.g., colorful items, entertaining sounds, textures, toys, games, and activities). As a child grows these motivators change constantly, as parents quickly find out. However, some children with developmental disabilities may demonstrate a limited range of MOs, or a collection of odd or atypical motivators, some of which may become quite strong.

In the unlearned category of motivators hunger and physical contact may not always be strong motivators for some children, or may be impaired in some way (e.g., Bijou & Ghezzi, 1999). Also, some children may seem to be less affected by painful stimuli. In the learned category of motivators, toys, manipulatives, cause-and-effect items, games, and the hundreds of other items and actions that a typically developing child might want to experience at one time or another, may not be of any value to some children with special needs. On the other hand, for some of these children, especially those with autism, odd forms of motivators may become particularly strong, such as repeated motions (self-stims), patterns, colors, shapes, sounds, peculiar items, or particular behaviors. Motivation is an important teaching tool because of its relation to reinforcement (e.g., the value of food as a reinforcer is directly related to the degree of hunger). If a child has a limited range of motivators, both unlearned and learned, teaching and learning become more difficult and special efforts are necessary to create, contrive, and capture motivation for teaching purposes (Hall & Sundberg, 1987; Sundberg, 1993a, 2004)

Scoring Criteria

Give the child a score of 0 on the Barriers Assessment if he demonstrates a wide range of age-appropriate MOs, and they are predictably strong or weak and show variation. Give the child a score of 1 if others begin to notice that the motivators are slightly different from those of typically developing children (e.g., the child does not seem interested in what other children are playing with or doing). Give the child a score of 2 if he demonstrates strong MOs for odd behavior patterns, such as repetitive play with a specific item or odd body, arm, leg, or finger postures. Or, give him a score of 2 if he seems to have weak MOs for age-appropriate reinforcers, and social reinforcement from others.

Give the child a score of 3 if he demonstrates aberrant MOs for unlearned reinforcers such as sleep, food, or the removal of pain. Or, give him a score of 3 if MOs quickly weaken after a short contact with a "desired" item (e.g., often he seems to really want to play with an item, but drops it or walks away after a few seconds). This child may also be demonstrating high rates of stereotypy and little interest in social reinforcement. Give the child a score of 4, if he has a very limited range of MOs, perhaps just 2 or 3, and they may be odd MOs (such as strings, twirling in circles, or mouthing items) that are very strong, and negative behavior may occur if he is not allowed to engage in the behaviors. If the child's score on this Barriers Assessment is a 1, there should be an increased effort to develop social and other types of motivators. If the child scores a 2 to 4, a further analysis of the specific motivation barrier that is affecting the child is required.

17. Response Requirement Weakens the MO

A common problem faced by many teachers and parents is a child's quick loss of interest in something as a reinforcer when he must work in order to obtain it. That is, the child will eagerly take an item if it is free, but when a demand is placed on the child, he may not want the item. This is a common behavioral effect that is well known in the experimental literature. Response effort is correlated with reinforcement value. For example, blowing bubbles may be a fun and reinforcing activity, but the response requirement of sitting in a chair and responding to instructional tasks may be too high and the value of bubbles as a form of reinforcement quickly weakens. It simply is not worth it from the child's point of view.

Many examples of this effect can be observed in day-to-day interactions involving adults. One might ask is $20 a reinforcer? It, of course, depends on the response requirement. If there is no response requirement it will likely strengthen any behavior that precedes the delivery of the $20 (thus functioning as reinforcement). If the behavior is minimal or commensurate with the $20 (e.g., helping a stranger jump start his car) it may increase the behavior. However, the $20 could function as punishment if the response requirement is too high. For example, spending all day working on repairing a carburetor for a stranger, then receiving $20, may decrease the future probability of your helping strangers with car problems.

In behavioral terms this effect is called an abolishing operation (AO) by Michael (2007). Another example of the AO effect is satiation. After a big lunch, food may not function as reinforcement for a child. Add a high response requirement to the situation and one might predict negative behavior or some form of escape or avoidance is likely, if food is the consequence being used and demands are high. Some children are very prone to this problem due to a conditioning history where behavior that indicates lack of interest in a potential reinforcer results in the removal of the demand, or the delivery of a higher amount of reinforcement.

Scoring Criteria

Give the child a score of 0 on the Barriers Assessment if the child does not typically lose interest in reinforcers when reasonable demands are placed on him. If the demands far outpace the reinforcer, he may lose interest in the reinforcer. Give the child a score of 1 if he demonstrates some lack of interest if the demands become too high, or if signs are showing that the demand is about to be increased (e.g., a new box of materials brought up to the table). Give the child a score of 2 if he is strongly motivated by a wide variety of items and activities, but quick to walk away from them or looses interest in them if the demands exceed a small set or are not in a predicted routine.

Give the child a score of 3 if he is quick to show a lack of interest after a few responses are required. Give the child a score of 4 if he will walk away for what are considered his strongest reinforcers (e.g., food, Thomas the Tank Engine) if even the slightest demand is placed on him. If the child's score on this Barriers Assessment is a 1, his progress should be monitored, but there probably is no cause for concern at this point. If the child scores a 2 to 4, a further analysis of the relation between response requirement and reinforcer value for this child is required.

18. Reinforcement Dependent

Immediate and continuous reinforcement for correct responses is one of the most powerful tools for establishing new instructional and educational stimulus control. However, another behavioral principle, intermittent reinforcement, suggests that in order to maintain this control, less reinforcement systematically provided is more effective (Ferster & Skinner, 1957). For example, in teaching a child to first learn to tact a car, the most effective reinforcement schedule is continuous reinforcement (CRF). That is, each successive approximation that is closer to the target response "car" should be reinforced. Once the child can consistently tact car, the reinforcement schedule should be gradually moved to an intermittent schedule where the tact "car" is reinforced on an average of every 3 or 4 responses. This is called a variable ratio schedule and begins to teach the child that every tact of a car will not result in obtaining a reinforcer such as food or praise from an adult. The benefit of this procedure is that it develops "persistence" by teaching the child how to behave and learn in conditions where reinforcement is not a constant (i.e., the "real world"). Another problem associated with reinforcement delivery is that children may be dependent on consumable and tangible reinforcers, and fail to make the transition to other forms of reinforcement such as social and verbal reinforcement.

The shift to intermittent reinforcement and away from consumable and tangible reinforcers is an essential component of a behavioral intervention program. The failure to program for this progression can result in reinforcer dependency and the quick loss of skills when they are not reinforced each time, or are not reinforced with consumable or tangible items. This failure competes with the eventual goal of transferring acquired skills to the natural environment and to the natural contingencies that maintain behavioral repertoires for typically developing children, or in a less restrictive classroom setting.

Scoring Criteria

Give the child a score of 0 on the Barriers Assessment if he has no problem with moving to intermittent reinforcement or to social and verbal reinforcers. Give the child a score of 1 if he prefers consumables and tangibles, but is reinforced by praise and attention, although he may show some reluctance to go without these preferred items as reinforcers, but eventually does so and continues to learn new skills. Give the child a score of 2 if he is reluctant to go without the preferred reinforcers and learning is much slower without them; however, he will work on intermittent schedules (e.g., token systems) and shows consistent skill growth.

Give the child a score of 3 if it is difficult to work with the child without using frequently delivered consumable and tangible reinforcement (e.g., every 3 or 4 responses). The child may be quick to emit negative behaviors or attempt to avoid or escape adult demands and instructional tasks. Give the child a score of 4 if it takes an extensive amount of consumable and tangible reinforcers to establish a single skill, and that level of reinforcement is necessary to maintain that skill. If the child's score on this Barriers Assessment is a 1, his progress should be monitored, and there should be an increased focus on pairing social praise with the delivery of other reinforcers. If the child scores a 2 to 4, a further analysis of the types of reinforcement used and the delivery schedule is required.

19. Self-Stimulation

Many children with developmental disabilities, especially those with autism, exhibit some form of self-stimulation or stereotypic behaviors (colloquially termed "stims"). These can include flapping, rocking, humming, flicking objects, picking lint, lining up objects, tearing paper, staring at shapes, corners, patterns, letters, or numbers, and so on. These behaviors are often difficult to reduce or eliminate because the reinforcement is in the behavior itself, that is, the behavior may be entertaining or fun for the person to emit. In behavioral terminology, this effect is called automatic reinforcement. Many behaviors have reinforcing properties and don't require outside or contrived reinforcers to maintain them. These effects can also be easily observed in typical child and adult behaviors. For example, an infant's babbling is reinforced by the sounds that he produces. Adults may hum or sing a certain song and find they can't stop the behavior, despite specific efforts to do so. Some adults with Aspergers Syndrome have reported that the stims reduce anxiety. A similar effect can be observed when professional speakers or actors pace back and forth before going on stage.

The reinforcement obtained from self-stimulation is often not contingent on any specific behavior or demands. In a sense, it is free reinforcement. Thus, it may be no surprise why these behaviors become strong for some children, especially those who have weak verbal and social repertoires. For many children the stims are relatively harmless, but for others the reinforcing value is so powerful that typical reinforcers have a very low value, and the stim behaviors compete with other activities and the development of stimulus and instructional control, and as a result disrupt learning.

Scoring Criteria

Give the child a score of 0 on the Barriers Assessment if he does not engage in self-stimulatory or repetitive behaviors that are out of the ordinary. Give the child a score of 1 if he does engage in some self-stimulation, but it is not too problematic (e.g., finger tapping) and doesn't seem to compete with learning or other activities. Give the child a score of 2 if he engages in a relatively high rate of self-stimulation, and he may emit several different types (e.g., flipping objects in front of the eyes and staring at patterns). Also, the reinforcement from stim behavior may compete with or reduce the value of other reinforcers. However, the child may still learn new material and be able to demonstrate some degree of control over the behavior (e.g., he will stop flapping if told to do so).

Give the child a score of 3 if he engages in a high rate of self-stimulation that does compete with learning and social interactions, and he will not stop, or only stop briefly, with verbal reprimands. Give the child a score of 4 if he almost constantly engages in some form of self-stimulation, and other reinforcers are weak. Also, his learning is very disrupted by these behaviors, and his skill acquisition is slow. If the child's score on this Barriers Assessment is a 1, the behaviors should be monitored, but there probably is no cause for concern at this point. If the child scores a 2 to 4, a further analysis of the specific function of the self-stimulation is required.

20. Articulation Problems

Many children experience articulation problems, but some are quite severe and often an augmentative communication (AC) system such as sign language or PECS (Frost & Bondy, 2002) is necessary. Often AC can be of great help in teaching language skills, reducing negative behaviors, and promoting improvements in articulation. Note that speech and language are two different things (they are close to the distinction between form and function presented in Chapter 1). A child can emit perfectly articulated words (speech), but may not be able to use them appropriately (language), or vice versa. Any child with significant articulation problems should be referred to a speech and language pathologist.

Scoring Criteria

Give the child a score of 0 on the Barriers Assessment if most adults can understand his existing vocal behavior. Even if the child only has a small vocabulary of words, but his words can be understood, give him this score. Give the child a score of 1 if he demonstrates some difficulty pronouncing certain words, but usually can be understood with the vocabulary that he has, and his articulation continues to improve. Give the child a score of 2 if he has difficulty being understood by strangers, despite showing mostly Level 2 Milestones.

Give the child a score of 3 if he has very limited vocal skills and demonstrates a wide variety of articulation errors. Give the child a score of 4 if he is non-vocal, or has completely unintelligible speech, despite other elevated milestone scores. If the child's score on this Barriers Assessment is a 1, his progress should be monitored, but there probably is no cause for concern at this point. If the child scores a 2 to 4, he should be referred to a speech and language pathologist for a complete evaluation and potential intervention program, and a behavior analysts should conduct a further functional analysis of the problem.

21. Obsessive-Compulsive Behavior

Some children with developmental disabilities, especially those with autism, may demonstrate strong obsessions over particular aspects of the environment, such as clothing, textures, routines, patterns, etc. These obsessions become a more serious problem if they compete with establishing instructional and educational stimulus control by weakening other MOs and the related reinforcers. Obsessions are often not much different from stims, but they can take odd forms and be very disruptive. For example, some children will insist that the exact same route be driven home each day after school. A left turn instead of the typical right turn will evoke a strong and immediate tantrum. Other children will only wear certain clothing (e.g., red sweatpants) and attempts to put any other clothing on them may evoke tantrums and even aggressive and self-injurious behaviors. The causes of these obsessive behaviors are quite complicated, but they are learned behaviors that are usually related to a history of reinforcement. They also may be related to the aversive nature of certain types of sensory stimuli (see barrier number 24), such as scratchy material.

Scoring Criteria

Give the child a score of 0 on the Barriers Assessment if he does not demonstrate any obsessive-compulsive behaviors that impede learning. Give the child a score of 1 if he demonstrates some minor obsessions, but they are easily overcome and don't interfere with learning. These obsessions may be interpreted as "stubbornness," but the issues and the behaviors are often the same (e.g., insists on having the lights off in a room). Give the child a score of 2 if he has several different obsessions, and emits mild negative behaviors when they are not met but he will usually comply with not being allowed to complete the obsessive behaviors, and will participate in the learning tasks without further disruption. For example, if the child is not allowed to circle around a chair before sitting down, he will emit a short tantrum, but will eventually sit down without circling and will participate in the work task.

Give the child a score of 3 if he emits several different obsessions or a few very strong ones, and if they are disrupted he engages in immediate and strong negative behaviors that impede learning. He is usually very reluctant to participate in tasks or activities without completing the obsession. Give the child a score of 4 if his obsessions are consistent and strong, and are the major focus of each day. If the obsessions are not allowed, his negative behaviors may be severe and learning is regularly disrupted. The obsessions are a constant battle for all involved with the child and consume a significant amount of time. If the child's score on this Barriers Assessment is a 1, his behaviors should be closely monitored, and even perhaps provide a further analysis and begin an intervention at this point, as obsessions tend to grow. If the child scores a 2 to 4, a further analysis of the obsessive behaviors is required.

22. Hyperactivity

Some children with developmental disabilities may also be diagnosed with attention-deficit/ hyperactivity disorder (AD/HD). These children may exhibit a wide range of behaviors involving high rates of motor behavior such as running around, climbing on things, fidgeting, difficulty playing quietly, and frequently seems to be "on the go." They may also have difficulty attending to academic work, completing daily chores and self-help skills, or engaging in other tasks that involve bringing something to completion. These behavior patterns usually affect learning, language, and social development, especially for children who are also diagnosed with autism. The causes of hyperactive behavior, like the causes of autism, tend to be attributed to a variety of variables consisting of a blend of genetic, prenatal, and environmental factors. It is often difficult to identify which of many possible variables is the cause for any given individual. The most common treatment is a combination of medication and behavioral intervention, although substantial controversy can be found in the literature on what is most effective for these children.

Scoring Criteria

Give the child a score of 0 on the Barriers Assessment if he is not excessively hyperactive compared to his typically developing peers, and he attends to most tasks and activities without difficulty. Give the child a score of 1 if he occasionally emits hyperactive behavior or fails to attend to ongoing activities or events, but these behaviors are not disruptive to learning or daily living. The child will easily calm down, or with some minor prompting attend to the task at hand. Give the child a score of 2 if he moves around the environment frequently (and is clearly more active than his peers), seems restless, and has difficulty attending to tasks, especially tasks that are hard (although he may have no trouble attending to enjoyable activities such as TV or video games). Also, give him a score of 2 if the hyperactive and inattentive behaviors are interfering with learning.

Give the child a score of 3 if it is often difficult to control his hyperactive behavior. He may not wait in lines, sit calmly, or stay on task longer than a couple of minutes, and requires frequent prompting to attend, sit still, and complete an activity. Give the child a score of 4 if he is constantly "on the go," and his hyperactive behavior is the major focus of each day. He may be fidgety, impulsive, and climbs or jumps on furniture, talks excessively, and is generally difficult to manage or to keep engaged in any academic or social activity. If the child's score on this Barriers Assessment is a 1, his progress should be monitored, but there probably is no cause for concern at this point. If the child scores a 2 to 4, a further analysis of his hyperactive behavior and inattention is required.

23. Failure to Make Eye Contact or Attend to People

Typically developing infants and toddlers learn to communicate with others long before they begin to emit words. Much of their early communication involves making eye contact to get the attention of others (a mand), followed by gesturing, or distal point and reach behavior (also usually a mand). Eye contact precedes the beginning of most social exchanges in that the speaker and listener both acknowledge each other. Even a brief glance or gaze allows a speaker to be assured that he has the attention of a listener. However, some children with developmental disabilities, especially those with autism, do not make eye contact with other people. Also, they may not look at other people in the same way that typically developing children look at each other or at adults.

There are a variety of different reasons why making eye contact can be a valuable skill, most are related to the fact that a significant amount of information can be found in another person's eyes and face. But this information is only valuable if the child can act or react in some meaningful way. The child's tendency to make eye contact may depend on the context. Children will often look at an adult's eyes when manding for things because of a history of reinforcement. The child may get the adult's attention by using eye contact (a mand), and use a gaze to direct attention to the desired item (another mand). However, the same child may overtly avoid eye contact in social, academic, or other demand situations, even though they may make eye contact to mand.

If a child fails to acquire mands in general, this reduces the value of eye contact, and thus the natural contingencies that shape eye contact may be ineffective. If a child does mand, but does not make eye contact while manding, Carbone et al. (2013) have demonstrated the use of an extinction procedure for those who mand without eye contact. The extinction can evoke a variety of responses, one of which is often eye contact. The differential reinforcement of this eye contact when accompanied with the original mand can increase the frequency of eye contact while manding.

Scoring Criteria

Give the child a score of 0 on the Barriers Assessment if he makes age-appropriate eye contact with others, and appropriately attends to people. Give the child a score of 1 if adults begin to notice that the child is not making eye contact in a manner similar to that of typically developing children. Give the child a score of 2 if he does not make frequent eye contact, or attends to faces and people in a manner similar to that of typically developing children. Give the child a score of 3 if he makes no eye contact while manding and it is difficult to get him to make eye contact under most circumstances. Give the child a score of 4 if he almost never makes eye contact and he avoids looking at faces and people. If the child's score on this Barriers Assessment is a 1, his progress should be monitored, and it might be prudent to begin some intervention. If the child scores a 2 to 4, a further analysis of why eye contact in not occurring is required.

24. Sensory Defensiveness

Some children with developmental disabilities, especially those with autism, might be hypersensitive to various types of sensory stimulation. Sensitivity to sounds is probably the most common. A child may frequently put his hands over his ears, sometimes given only the slightest increase in auditory stimuli. Others are affected by tactile stimuli, such as clothing texture or liquids or other substances on the hands. In both auditory and tactile sensitivity the actual stimulation to the sensory system may function as an aversive motivator (MO), and any behavior that terminates the sensation is evoked (e.g., covering the ears, removing the scratchy clothing, or rubbing the hands) and be automatically reinforced. Sensitivity to visual stimuli also occurs, as might smells and tastes; however, these three may be related to a variety of other variables. For example, visual stimuli aversions may be more closely related to demands (e.g., a child puts his hands over his eyes when asked to complete a task). Taste aversions may be related to feeding issues. Auditory and tactile sensitivity are subject to these other variables as well, which is why an analysis of an individual child is necessary to sort out exactly what source of control is affecting that child.

Scoring Criteria

Give the child a score of 0 on the Barriers Assessment if he does not have any problems related to sensory stimuli. Give the child a score of 1 if adults begin to notice that sensitivity to various sensory stimuli is different from that of other children. For example, the child may grimace when certain sounds occur, or complain about the volume on the television. Give the child a score of 2 if certain sensory stimulation predictably affect the child (e.g., long sleeve shirts or glue on his hands), but the defensiveness is mild and does not usually interfere with learning activities. Give the child a score of 3 if he frequently reacts to specific sensory stimuli with avoidance behavior, such as hands over ears or closing his eyes. He may also become agitated, especially if the aversive stimulation is not removed. It may be quite difficult to work with the child in this state. Give the child a score of 4 if he consistently reacts to specific sensory stimuli with more severe negative behavior such as tantrums and aggression. If the child's score on this Barriers Assessment is a 1, his progress should be monitored, but an analysis may be valuable at this point since there is some chance the sensitivity will become greater (especially if it gets reinforced). If the child scores a 2 to 4, a further analysis of sensory defensiveness is required.

Summary

Learning and language barriers can be responsible for a number of problems experienced by children with autism or other developmental disabilities. The Barriers Assessment provides a way to identify which ones might be causing a specific problem for a child. Many children demonstrate multiple barriers, or a combination of barriers. Once a barrier has been identified, it is essential that a more detailed functional (or descriptive) analysis of the problem be conducted. There are many potential causes for the various learning and language problems (e.g., inadvertent reinforcement, curriculum design, wrong source of control is established), and the only way to develop an effective intervention program is to determine which cause is affecting the target child. It is also important to be aware of any medical problems such as illnesses, seizures, sleep disorders, or gastrointestinal disorders. Following the behavioral analysis of the barrier, an individualized intervention program needs to be designed and implemented by a qualified professional. As is usually the case with most behavioral interventions, the program then should be carefully monitored and adjusted on a regular basis.

CHAPTER 7

The Transition Assessment Scoring Instructions

The VB-MAPP Transition Assessment is designed to provide an objective evaluation of a child's overall skills and existing learning capabilities. There are 18 measurable areas identified on the Transition Assessment that collectively can help educators and parents make decisions and set priorities. The decision to move a child to a different placement or different type of educational format must be determined by the child's Individualized Education Program (IEP) team. The Transition Assessment simply provides the team with quantifiable information relevant to that decision.

It is often difficult to determine what educational setting and instructional format may best suit an individual child. A common goal for many educators and parents of children with special needs is transitioning a child from a more intensive program to that of a regular educational setting, whether through integration (part-time placement) or inclusion (full-time placement). However, it is not uncommon to base transition decisions on personal beliefs, a movement, emotion, or economics, rather then on what type of educational setting and instructional format will be of the best value to the child. That is, one in which he will truly learn the best, rather than just be managed or kept busy. Transition problems can also be observed in the opposite direction as well, where a child is held in a 1:1 or intensive teaching program too long, when in fact he could benefit from the learning and social opportunities characteristic of a less restrictive setting.

The range of placement options available to an individual child varies across school districts. There are often a variety of choices within a large public school setting, but the breath of a special education program is usually dependent on the size of the district and resources available. Some districts may also make use of private programs and agencies that provide services. The choices for placement vary along a continuum of what is commonly identified as "restrictiveness." A highly restrictive setting—such as in-home, one-on-one intervention—requires extensive resources. In contrast, fewer resources are necessary for a child who can learn in an inclusion setting. The general goal, and intent of special education law, is to place a child in the least restrictive educational setting, where he will make the most meaningful and measurable progress. The choices may include, in-home programs, special day classrooms, classrooms specifically designed for children with autism, private schools, learning handicapped classrooms, communicatively handicapped classrooms, pre-kindergarten classrooms, regular education classrooms with support, and full inclusion in a regular education classroom. The availability of these or similar classrooms vary across individual school districts.

Guidelines for Conducting the Transition Assessment

There are three general categories in the Transition Assessment (Table 7-1). The first category (numbers 1-6) covers the child's language skills, social skills, academic independence, and the existence of potential learning and language barriers, all of which will affect learning in a less restrictive environment. The second category (numbers 7-12) covers the child's specific leaning patterns, and the third category (numbers 13-18) covers self-help, spontaneity, and independence. Some of the areas assessed in the Transition Assessment are covered in other sections of the VB-MAPP, but they also fit within the context of transition (e.g., group skills, generalization). Thus, rather than refer the reader back and forth to these sections, they are repeated in this component of the VB-MAPP.

Table 7-1
VB-MAPP skills related to transition to a less restrictive educational environment.

Transition Category 1: VB-MAPP Scores and Academic Independence

Overall VB-MAPP Milestones score

Overall VB-MAPP Barriers score

VB-MAPP Barriers score on negative behaviors and instructional control

VB-MAPP scores on classroom routines and group skills

VB-MAPP scores on social behavior and social play

Independent work on academic tasks

Transition Category 2: Learning Patterns

Generalization

Variation of reinforcers

Rate of skill acquisition

Retention of new skills

Natural environment learning

Transfer to new verbal operants

Transition Category 3: Self-help, spontaneity, and self-direction

Adaptability to change

Spontaneous behaviors

Independent play skills

General self-help skills

Toileting skills

Eating skills

The first category will yield the most significant content regarding the language, social, and behavioral domains, as well as academic independence. The second category provides information about the child's ability to learn new skills outside of an intensive teaching format. Generally, these first two categories are inversely related: if a child requires less intensive teaching, it is likely that his skills are higher and stronger. If intensive and structured teaching is necessary to move a child forward, the progress is likely to be slower and require a higher teacher-to-student ratio.

The third category, while very important, should not bear as directly on placement, but often it does (e.g., self-help). For example, while independent toileting is important in a typical first grade class, if a child with special needs has the language, social, and academic abilities to learn in a first grade class, the inability to independently use the toilet should not prevent him from participating in that classroom. On the other hand, a child who can independently use the toilet, but does not have the skills that are commensurate with the other children, may not benefit from the content and teaching format used in that room, and may even loose skills. Each child's situation and needs are unique, and it is up to the IEP team to determine what is in the best interest of the individual child. No individual item or score on this scale is a determining factor. The transition assessment is simply a tool that can provide a team with information that may help in the placement process, and in monitoring the child's progress in that placement. For more information on transition and related issues visit www.wrightslaw.com.

Scoring the Transition Assessment

Scores should be marked on the Transition Assessment Forms found in the VB-MAPP Protocol (pp. 30-34). High scores are desireable, while low scores indicate areas that need work. The forms contain boxes for four administrations, but the assessment can be administered any number of times. The first assessment can serve as a baseline measure at the beginning of an intervention program, and can help to provide direction for skills to build and strengthen. The Transition Assessment can also be used as a guide to help determine immediate placement. Additional administrations can occur as part of the annual IEP review, or when placement is an issue for a child. The first 2 of the18 measures on the Transition Assessment are for overall scores on the VB-MAPP Milestones Assessment and the VB-MAPP Barriers Assessment. There are several subsections of these assessments that are measured a second time because of their significance for placement in a less restrictive setting (e.g., behavior problems, group responding, social skills, and generalization).

The assessor should rate the child's behaviors on a 1 to 5 Likert-type scale, based on the criteria identified in each section of the scoring forms in the VB-MAPP Protocol, and then transfer the scores to the Transition Scoring Form (see Figure 7-1). Some of the data are scores from other sections of the VB-MAPP Assessment, while others call for more of a subjective evaluation of the child. It may be of value to have multiple people who are familiar with the child participate in the scoring of these subjective areas for reliability and agreement purposes. There are some items that a score of zero can be given on the Transition Assessment (e.g., "spontaneous behavior" where a child has absolutely no spontaneous behaviors). For items like this one, not giving a "1" would be equal to a zero (leave that item on the form blank). However, some items can't have a zero like the total score on the VB-MAPP milestones (1 = 0-25).

Figure 7-1

A sample Transition Scoring Form.

VB-MAPP Transition Scoring Form

Child's name:	Isabella
Date of birth:	3-27-03
Age at testing:	**1** 5 yrs. **2** **3** **4**

Key:	Score	Date	Color	Tester
1ST TEST:	53	5-03-08		MS
2ND TEST:				
3RD TEST:				
4TH TEST:				

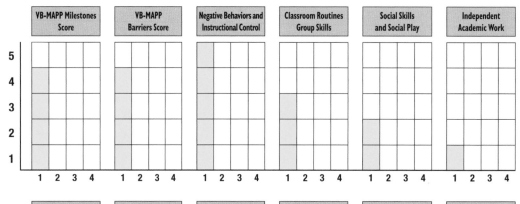

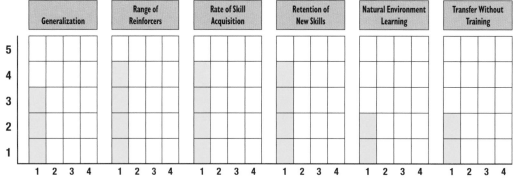

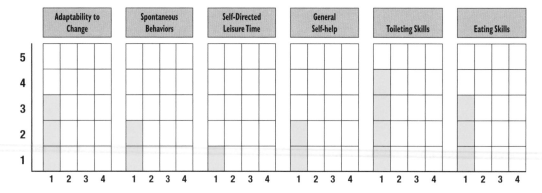

Transition Category 1: VB-MAPP Scores and Academic Independence

1. Overall VB-MAPP Milestones Assessment Score

Perhaps one of the most significant problems related to a successful transition to a less restrictive environment for a child is being placed in a classroom where the daily verbal content is beyond his comprehension level. The placement may be of some value (e.g., offering social modeling and peer interaction), but if the child's skills are significantly below those of the other children in the classroom, it is unlikely that he will be able to access the curriculum content and learn along with the other children. Thus, valuable educational time and possibly skills may be lost. The overall score on the VB-MAPP Milestones Assessment can provide a foundation for making decisions regarding placement. While all children with special needs can benefit from regular contact and integration with typically developing peers, the issue is to determine what are the educational priorities for an individual child and which teaching format and educational setting can deliver an intervention program that meets those priorities.

Scoring Criteria and Placement Suggestions

If a child's overall scores on the VB-MAPP Milestones Assessment primarily fall in Level 1, he is still in need of an intensive and specialized intervention program. This program can be in-home, in a specialized classroom, or a combination of both; it should also be the focus of his prime learning time (usually in the morning or after a nap for young children). Peer interaction, while important, may not be a major priority at this time, but could occur later in the day and in less formal activities (e.g., play dates, parks, and after school pre-schools for younger children). For more specific information on curriculum placement for a child who scores primarily in Level 1, see Chapter 8. As stated before, it is up to the IEP team to determine what is in the best interest of the child.

If the child's overall VB-MAPP scores fall primarily in Level 2, it shows that the child has acquired a basic repertoire of mands, tacts, and listener skills, and may be acquiring new skills rapidly. This child may begin to benefit from more group teaching, age-appropriate natural environment teaching (e.g., arts and crafts, games, music, and other common activities), and a greater focus on interaction with more verbal peers. However, the bulk of the instructional time (and the prime time) for a Level 2 child should still be in a high-ratio intensive teaching format. There are a number of specific language and social skills that the child still needs (e.g., prepositions, adjectives, intraverbals, and social and play skills), and while some of these skills may be acquired in a less restrictive setting, structured teaching may produce them faster and more thoroughly. For more specific information on curriculum placement for a child who scores primarily in Level 2, see Chapter 9.

If the child's overall VB-MAPP scores fall primarily in Level 3, this child has not only acquired many basic verbal and social skills, but also may be demonstrating some advanced mand, tact, and intraverbals skills. The child's ability to ask WH questions (mands), answer those questions (intraverbals), and spontaneously comment on the physical features of his environment constitutes significant milestones that demonstrate that the child has the linguistic foundation for a more advanced academic and social placement in a less restrictive setting. For more specific information on placement for a child who scores primarily in Level 3, see Chapter 10.

2. Overall VB-MAPP Barriers Assessment Score

The Barriers Assessment is designed to identify language and learning barriers that impede skill acquisition (see Chapter 6). These barriers need to be reduced or removed and often constitute a major part of the child's daily intervention program (e.g., prompt dependency, behavior problems, self-stimulation, hyperactive behavior, and non-compliance). Often, it is these barriers that constitute the biggest obstacle for a child's transition to a less restrictive educational setting.

Scoring Criteria and Placement Suggestions

A high score on the overall Barriers Assessment (31 to 96) suggests that the child is experiencing several barriers and needs a program that is designed to focus on reducing or removing them. That program is likely to be more restrictive due to the types of interventions necessary. For example, if a child has failed to acquire an intraverbal repertoire despite having acquired hundreds of tacts and listener skills, a carefully designed intraverbal program is necessary. Teaching intraverbal behavior is often quite difficult and requires a high teacher-to-student ratio, staff with specialized skills, careful teaching procedures, and close monitoring because the probability of developing rote intraverbals is often quite high. A lower score on the Barriers Assessment (30 or less) suggests a less restrictive placement may be successful, depending on the specific barriers. For example, significant negative behaviors often limit options and thus an additional measure for these barriers is provided below (behavior problems and instructional control issues are scored twice in the Transition Assessment).

3. VB-MAPP Barriers Assessment Score on Negative Behaviors and Instructional Control

Behavior problems such as screaming, aggression, property destruction, and refusing to participate in activities will seriously limit a child's access to less restrictive settings. These behaviors make it very difficult to teach a child, and may constitute safety issues for the child as well as others in the classroom. Teachers may not be trained in the appropriate behavior management techniques needed to analyze and change severe behavior problems and may not have the support available. Also, an integrated classroom setting may not be conducive to changing the behavior, and for a variety of reasons may exacerbate the behavior problem. For example, if a child is required to sit in a morning circle, but does not want to and starts tantruming, the common practice is to remove him from the circle (usually followed by one-on-one aide time) so the teacher and other children can proceed with their educational program. However, the target child's negative behavior gets reinforced (by removal of demand), and the tantrum is likely to occur again under similar circumstances. The alternative intervention of leaving him in the circle (not removing the demand) may be clinically correct, but may prevent the teacher from instructing the other children. There can be many potential causes for negative behavior in a less restrictive setting, and these must be analyzed and ameliorated as part of the placement process. Placement too soon, or without the necessary trained support, can jeopardize future placement.

Scoring Criteria and Placement Suggestions

The scores from the negative behaviors and instructional control subsections of the VB-MAPP Barriers Assessment can be used to scale the child's abilities in these areas as they relate to transition. The scores from these subsections of the Barriers Assessment should be converted to match the others on the Transition Assessment. For example, if a child receives a combined total score of 6 points on the negative behaviors and instructional control area of the VB-MAPP Barriers Assessment, he would be given a score of 1 on the Transition Assessment. The complete criteria for the 5 levels are contained in the VB-MAPP Transition Assessment Protocol scoring forms. The assessor should use these scores for conversion.

If a child scores a 1 or 2 on the negative behaviors and instructional control section of the VB-MAPP Transition Assessment, placement in a less restrictive classroom may be difficult, unsafe, and unproductive. A child who demonstrates this level on negative behaviors would benefit from a carefully designed behavior intervention program that is implemented by trained classroom staff in a setting where they can focus on the reduction of these behaviors. If the child scores a 3 on the Transition Assessment, then it is less likely that the negative behaviors will regularly disrupt the educational process and more options become available for placement. A score of 4 or 5 suggests that negative behaviors should not be an issue in deciding placement.

4. VB-MAPP Milestones Assessment Score on Classroom Routines and Group Skills

A major component of moving along the continuum of least restrictive settings is the child's ability to follow classroom routines and learn in a group-teaching format. If a child requires extensive prompting and reinforcement to transition and participate in daily classroom activities, then more teacher resources are necessary. Regarding group responding, early learners whose scores fall primarily in Level 1 and early Level 2 of the VB-MAPP Milestones Assessment may learn best with a 1:1 or 1:2 teacher-to-student ratio. A high ratio is required because of the need to implement careful teaching procedures involving prompting, fading, shaping, and rich schedules of reinforcement that often require small steps and numerous teaching trials. The number of trials necessary to move the child forward cannot easily be provided in a larger ratio. However, as the child's skills progress to where, for example, less prompting and fading are necessary and new skill acquisition occurs in relatively fewer teaching trials, there are several advantages of moving away from exclusive reliance on a 1:1 or 1:2 teaching model. These issues are described in detail in Chapter 8 in the sections on placement as it relates to classroom routines and group skills.

Scoring Criteria and Placement Suggestions

The scores on the Classroom Routines and Group Skills subsections of the VB-MAPP Milestones Assessment can be used to scale the child's abilities in these areas as they relate to transition. The scores from these subsections of the Milestones Assessment should be converted to match the others on the Transition Assessment. For example, if a child receives a total score of 3 points on the classroom routines and group skills area of the VB-MAPP Milestones Assessment, he would be given a score of 2 on the Transition Assessment (note that these 3 points can come from any item on the classroom routines and group skills subsection, that is, they do not need to be restricted to just items 1, 2, and 3). The complete conversion criteria for the 5 levels of the Transition Assessment are contained in the Protocol scoring forms.

If a child receives a score of 1 or 2 points on the classroom routines and group skills section of the VB-MAPP Milestones Assessment, placement in a less restrictive classroom may be difficult and not productive. A high score on this measure, such as a 4 or 5, would suggest that the child follows classroom routines and is able to learn in a group teaching format, which is a major component of the progression to less restrictive settings.

5. VB-MAPP Milestones Assessment Score on Social Behavior and Social Play

There are many opportunities for developing social skills in a classroom setting. Many of these opportunities are not available in an in-home program. Given that social behavior and social play constitute one of the defining hallmarks of autism, a setting that involves a carefully designed social skills program with peers can be quite beneficial for a child. However, the degree to which an individual child can benefit from a given setting—without significant costs to the other parts of his program—varies and must be carefully evaluated by his IEP team.

There are many factors that must be considered when transitioning children to different educational environments. Often, one setting will not meet all of the child's needs. Many schools offer a variety of options, such as partial integration with other classrooms or combinations of in-home and school based programs, but each school district is different and has different resources and options available. For example, many small rural school districts do not have a range of classrooms that serve children with special needs and transportation to other districts is prohibitive. Thus, a child's social needs must be weighed along with language, behavioral, academic, and other skill needs identified in the various VB-MAPP Assessments.

Finding the right balance for a child is often complicated. In general, the goal is to find a setting where the child's existing social skills are not at the top or the bottom of the range of skills of the other children in the classroom. Each extreme may have little social value to the child. For example, if a child who does not imitate peers, mand to peers, intraverbally respond to peers, etc., is placed in a classroom of peers who have these skills, the target child may become socially isolated. While the child's absence of some social behaviors may not be obvious to their peers (e.g., sympathy, offering assistance), other children will certainly notice more obvious social behaviors that are clearly inappropriate to them, such as high rates of self-stimulation, removing clothing, or excessive and loud interruption. These types of behaviors can be damaging to the child's social status with his peers. On the other hand, if a child who is interested in peers, mands to peers, and initiates interactions is placed in a classroom where the peers don't respond to his mands or initiations, this placement may also be of little social value to the child.

Scoring Criteria and Placement Suggestions

The points from the Milestones Assessment should be converted according to the criteria provided on the scoring forms in the VB-MAPP Protocol. A child who scores a 1 or 2 on the social skills Transition Assessment and has weak verbal skills (e.g., his overall VB-MAPP skills fall primarily in Level 1) may be better served in a more restrictive setting that provides the intensive teaching format previously described for Level 1. A placement for a child who scores a 3 on the social skills Transition Assessment and has overall VB-MAPP scores primarily in Level 2 would likely benefit more from a setting that is less restrictive and provides some partial integration into a classroom of typically developing peers (e.g., lunch, music, recess, and physical education). If the child scores a 4 or 5 on the social skills Transition Assessment and has overall VB-MAPP scores primarily in Level 3, placement in a classroom with peers who are verbal and social would be beneficial—the teaching format can also be less intensive than that necessary for those who score in Level 1 and Level 2. Children on all three levels who have ASD would most likely continue to benefit from more formal and direct social skills training as well. For more specific information on placement regarding social skills, the reader is referred to the relevant placement sections on the three levels of social behavior and social play found in Chapters 8, 9, and 10.

6. Works Independently on Academic Tasks

A major component of a less restrictive classroom is independent academic work, such as completing worksheets, participating in small group projects, and silent reading. During these periods a child is expected to participate in a specified activity or complete an assigned worksheet without teacher prompting to stay on task, or to stop engaging in disruptive behavior. For example, a common activity for a first grade classroom is 3 or 4 small group stations where 4 or 5 children sit at a table and complete writing sheets that contain sample letters and words that are to be copied. The children are usually given their sheet and told to start the assignment. The teacher may go around the room and spend a minute or two with each child, expecting that the other children in the class will continue their work without a teacher standing over their shoulder, or prompting them to work or keep their hands to themselves. In order for a child with special needs to be successful in this type of teaching format, he must be able to independently engage in the assigned activity and wait for attention or assistance. These independent activities increasingly become a daily component of many classrooms, thus they appear in Category 1 of the Transition Assessment. If a child is unable to do independent work, he may require a one-on-one aide during this period. Although a one-to-one aide may be helpful, if steps are not taken to prepair the student for thinner schedules of reinforcement while remaining on task for longer periods of time, it may move the child backwards in terms of a least restrictive setting and placement appropriateness.

Scoring Criteria and Placement Suggestions

Give the child a score of 1 to 5 on independent academic work based on the criteria provided on the Transition Assessment Form. For example, if the child is able to work independently for at least 30 seconds with only 1 adult prompt to stay on task, he should be given a score of 1. If the child can stay on task for 5 minutes without any adult prompts, give him a score of 4. If a child receives a score of 1 on the assessment, he is still in need of independence training, which will require a high teacher-to-student ratio. For this child, integration activities might be restricted to time periods other than independent work activities (e.g., reading stories, sensory motor). If the child scores a 4 or 5, it suggests that he may do well in a classroom that contains independent academic activities (which ultimately occurs in all regular education classrooms).

Summary of Category 1 Scores

The six areas from Category 1 represent perhaps the most significant aspects to consider for transitioning to a less restrictive setting. The information obtained from the assessment of these areas should be used in conjunction with the other areas in the Transition Assessment, along with any other evaluations of the child by qualified professionals (e.g., speech and language reports or psychological reports). There is no fixed score on this assessment or no criteria for transition since there are a multitude of variables involved. The decision to transition a child is always made by his IEP team, and is based on their knowledge of the child and the available resources.

Transition Category 2: Learning Patterns

7. Generalization of Skills Across Time, Settings, Behaviors, Materials, and People

The process of generalization allows for learning to accelerate rapidly. Initially, many children with language delays must be directly taught each skill, often with the careful arrangement of prompts, fading techniques, and the differential reinforcement of slightly improved responding. Eventually, it often takes only a few trials to acquire a new behavior, and new behaviors begin to occur with little or no training. One of the ways this happens is through the process of generalization. Skinner (1953) noted, "In reinforcing one operant we often produce a noticeable increase in the strength of another. Training in one area of skilled behavior may improve performance in another" (p. 94). Stokes and Baer (1977) further elaborated on several aspects of generalization and have provided a framework for its clinical application.

Basically, there are two major types of generalization: stimulus generalization and response generalization. In stimulus generalization a child may learn a response under the control of one specific stimulus (e.g., the tact "shoe" for his own shoe), and then without further training tacts a novel stimulus that is in the same stimulus class (e.g., tacts his brother's shoe without training). There are several circumstances where stimulus generalization occurs. Stokes and Baer (1977) describe how a trained response may occur at different times, in different settings, with different people, and with different materials, all without further training. The second type of generalization is response generalization. Here, a child may learn one response under the control of one stimulus (e.g., tacts a family pet as "dog"), then without formal training emits a different but appropriate response under that same stimulus (e.g., he also tacts the family dog by her name, "Maggie"). These two types of generalization should be occurring at all levels of the intervention program and across all skill areas (e.g., a child should be able to use a different toilet when toilet trained).

Scoring Criteria and Placement Suggestions

Give the child a score of 1 to 5 on generalization based on the criteria provided in the Transition Assessment Protocol. For example, if the child only generalizes to other people, but not easily to other materials, give him a score of 1. Give the child a score of 5 if he easily and frequently demonstrates both stimulus and response generalization. The ability to easily generalize is a significant milestone in learning, and allows for the transition to a less restrictive setting because the need for multiple training trials, prompts, fading, and the careful reinforcement of each skill becomes far less frequent. Thus, a child is in a better position to learn in a lower teacher-to-student ratio, where the teacher simply does not have time to implement the careful teaching procedures necessary at the early stage of learning.

8. Range of Items and Events that Function as Reinforcers

The most powerful teaching tool available for developing language, learning, and social skills for children with autism or other developmental disabilities is reinforcement. Fortunately, there are over 75 years of accumulated research, applications, and training materials on reinforcement available from the field of Behavior Analysis. One aspect of reinforcement is the variation of items and events that function as reinforcement for a particular individual. A problem for many children with language delays, especially those with autism, is a limited range of reinforcers. Generally, the first types of items and events that function as reinforcement for all children are those related to the innate biological drives (unconditioned motivating operations), such as hunger, thirst, physical contact, warmth, and the removal of pain. The initial technological application to treatment of disabilities that has arisen from this fact was the successful use of food, drinks, and physical contact as reinforcers to shape specific skills in individuals previously thought to be incapable of learning (e.g., Fuller, 1949). Other early reinforcers that are often effective for many individuals are toys, manipulatives, cause-and-effect items, visual movement, and so on. These types of reinforcers also have a long history of successful use in teaching individuals with developmental disabilities (e.g., Meyerson, Michael, Mowrer, Osgood, & Staats, 1963; Wolf, Risley, & Mees, 1964), as well as with typically developing children (e.g., Bijou & Sturges, 1959; Staats, Staats, Schutz, & Wolf, 1962).

Unfortunately, many individuals are never moved beyond reliance on frequent delivery of edible or tangible reinforcers. A goal of an intervention program should be to fade out the reliance on these types of reinforcers and move toward social, automatic (i.e., intrinsic), and other forms of age-appropriate reinforcers. These are the types of reinforcers experienced by typically developing children, and are more likely to occur in a less restrictive classroom. The purpose of the current measure is to assess the range of the target child's reinforcers.

Scoring Criteria and Placement Suggestions

Give the child a score of 1 on the Transition Assessment if the items and activities that function as reinforcement must occur frequently, and are mostly limited to unlearned (innate) reinforcers. Items 2 through 4 show a movement toward a wider variety of reinforcers that are social, age appro priate, peer delivered, change often, and are delivered less frequently. Reinforcers also become automatic in that no one needs to formally deliver them, rather many reinforcers experienced by individuals are intrinsic in that they are contained in the behavior itself, that is, it is fun to emit the behavior (e.g., a child likes the picture that he just drew, or enjoys the hunt in finding the next number in a dot-to-dot work sheet). Give the child a score of 5 if he is easily reinforced by social praise; verbal information; and age-appropriate games, toys, and activities and these reinforcers are widely varied and change frequently (e.g., mands, "What's that? I want to try." upon seeing a new item).

The ability to be reinforced by a wide range of social and age-appropriate consequences, some of which are automatic, or can be intermittent, plays a major role in transitioning a child to a less restrictive setting. A child who is affected by a wide range of reinforcers will not only be more likely to learn more, but the tendency to satiate on any one reinforcer or group of reinforcers will be lower. Also, most classrooms that approach the format of regular education do not make use of frequent edible, tangible, or manipulative reinforcers. Rather, teachers rely on other forms of reinforcement such as social praise, grades, and automatic reinforcers. If a child is dependent on edible and tangible reinforcers, or a rich schedule of reinforcers (e.g., requires lots of attention), it will be more difficult to integrate that child into a less restrictive setting, especially if the other children in the class are not receiving those types of reinforcers.

9. Rate of Acquisition of New Skills

The number of training trials that it takes to acquire a new skill is a common measure in behavioral research, often referred to a "trials to criteria" (e.g., Cooper, et al., 2007; Sundberg & Sundberg, 1990). For example, when two teaching procedures are compared to each other, the target skills are balanced out (e.g., teaching a group of 5 different nouns), and one condition might involve imitative prompts while the other condition involves intraverbal prompts. The researcher then records the number of training trials that it takes to reach the target criteria for each of the two different teaching procedures. The visual display of the data will often quickly reveal that one procedure is better than another in teaching a new skill. Thus, the number of teacher trials (and hence the amount of teacher time) that it takes to teach a child new skills can be used as a measure of progression towards a less restrictive educational format. Initially, it may take a hundred trials to teach a child a new tact, but as the child becomes a more proficient learner, the number of trials required for learning new tacts might drop to one or two.

Scoring Criteria and Placement Suggestions

Give the child a score of 1 on the Transition Assessment if he requires several days or weeks of training sessions that may contain hundreds of trials to acquire a new response, but he eventually does so. The scores between 2 and 4 demonstrate a gradual progression toward fewer and fewer training trials necessary to acquire new skills. Give the child a score of 5 if he acquires new skills in only a few training trials. As a child acquires skills more rapidly, the complexity and range of the skills can be increased, and other skills that support successful integration can be developed.

10. Retention of New Skills

A child's ability to retain new skills is an essential component of learning. If the child constantly requires re-training on previously acquired skills, a further analysis of the curriculum and teaching procedures is warranted. Re-teaching may be frequently required because the skills taught are out of developmental, linguistic, or academic sequence (e.g., teaching adjectives before the child has a solid repertoire of nouns), or the target skill was never truly acquired to begin with (e.g., tacting noun-verb combinations with subtle prompts, or from 2D stimuli), or the skill was taught out of any functional context. These are among the most common causes of failure to retain skills, all of which are preventable with a better curriculum sequence and more careful teaching practices. This problem can be seen at all academic levels. For example, an elementary student who cannot retain math facts may not have the basic prerequisite skills for those facts, or the teaching procedures may have involved some inadvertent prompting that resulted in the student being given credit for a repertoire that never broke free from the prompts.

Additional causes for "forgetting" a skill (a common human phenomenon) may be that the skill was not functional to the person to begin with (e.g., learning trigonometry), or the skill was not practiced or generalized enough to maintain it (e.g., hitting a golf ball). An early measure of retention is that the child is able to continue to provide a correct response to a task after a short amount of time has passed. For example, if a child was taught to tact "wagon" in a session and ended that session with several correct responses, could he still correctly tact the wagon after a 60 minute period without prompting?

Scoring Criteria and Placement Suggestions

Give the child a score of 1 on the Transition Assessment if he is successful with this short time delay. The scores 2 through 4 involve a gradual increase in the time delay between training and testing, and include maintenance trials that may be necessary to keep the skill strong. Number 4 is a measure of retention without maintenance trials. Give the child a score of 5 if he consistently maintains a new skill after long periods of time (e.g., 1 week) without maintenance trials (the skills have become a more permanent component of his behavioral repertoire). If a child is able to retain skills for long periods of time and without maintenance trials, he is likely to gain more from a less restrictive setting that may not provide frequent maintenance trials.

11. Learning from the Natural Environment

The phrase "natural environment" has multiple meanings in its relation to teaching and learning. One common use of the phrase involves a description of events occurring outside of a formal teaching arrangement. This use of "natural environment" often refers to events related to a child's day-to-day activities (arts and crafts, eating, social play, recess, car rides, etc.). "Natural" is often used as a contrast with the word "structured." However, learning can and should occur in both discrete trial training (structured teaching) and in the child's natural environment. A second use of the phrase "natural environment" is in relation to learning that involves situations where changes in behavior occur without the direct arrangement of contingencies by a teacher, parent, or other individual. The phrase "natural consequences" refers to this meaning where, for example, failing to attend to a closing door results in getting one's fingers pinched, and these naturally occurring negative consequences may make one more attentive next time. Or, blowing correctly on a soapy wand produces bubbles, but blowing too hard makes the bubbles quickly pop, and not blowing hard enough will not produce any bubbles at all. The perfect amount of breath to blow bubbles is shaped by the naturally occurring consequences. The two meanings are not mutually exclusive in that programmed contingencies can occur in both a natural and a contrived setting, and non-programmed (or automatic) contingencies can occur in a natural or contrived setting. Both of these meanings of "natural environment" are relevant to a child's learning.

Much of the early learning for many children with autism or other developmental disabilities requires structured teaching and careful programming provided by skilled teachers and parents. However, learning usually becomes easier and children begin to acquire new skills without the careful arrangement of prompts and reinforcement, or intensive intervention, thereby increasing the chances of success in a less restrictive setting. Formal instruction is, of course, still necessary, but often new skills begin to emerge and are maintained without direct training. It was previously suggested that generalization was one way that these new skills are strengthened, but another way is learning from events and consequence that occur naturally in a child's day-to-day contact with a social world, without the arrangement of programmed contingencies. For example, many children learn new skills by the observation of others performing that skill (termed "observational learning"). One child may pour sand over a spinning wheel and gain enjoyment watching the wheel spin. Another child then imitates the behavior with his sand and wheel and also gains enjoyment. This new behavior occurs without adult intervention of prompts and reinforcement, but rather through observing the peer, with the reinforcement automatically provided by the spinning wheel. Once skills such as imitation are established (as in structured teaching) they are best maintained by the functional use of the skill and their natural consequences.

Scoring Criteria and Placement Suggestions

Give the child a score of 1 on the VB-MAPP Transition Assessment if he has demonstrated at least two new skills that were acquired in the natural environment without the formal programming of antecedents and consequences. Generally, motor behaviors are the easiest to acquire without formal training. Children learn to imitate the behavior of others in play and social activities without much training. Verbal behaviors are more complex to learn without formal training, but certainly children do begin to learn them in this manner. Give the child a score of 2 through 4 depending on frequency and complexity of new skills that are acquired without formal or structured teaching. Give the child a score of 5 if he easily and frequently learns new skills in a natural environment setting.

12. Demonstrates Transfer Between the Verbal Operants Without Training

There is a solid body of behavioral research that demonstrates that learning one type of verbal behavior (e.g., a tact) does not guarantee transfer to other types of verbal behavior (e.g., a mand) (e.g., Hall & Sundberg, 1987; Lamarre & Holland, 1985; Sigafoos, Doss, & Reichle, 1989; Twyman, 1996; Watkins, Pack-Teixeira, & Howard, 1989). There is also a body of research that shows learning listener skills does not automatically produce transfer to speaker skills (e.g., Guess & Baer, 1973; Lee, 1981). Thus, supporting Skinner's (1957) basic premise that language is composed of several functionally independent repertoires (for more detailed reviews of the research on the distinction between the verbal operants see Oah & Dickenson, 1989 and Sautter & LeBlanc, 2006).

However, it has been pointed out that this separation of skills is most prominent in early language acquisition and eventually a transfer between the verbal operants does automatically occur (e.g., Hall & Sundberg, 1987; Skinner, 1957). For example, once a child has a solid mand and tact repertoire, leaning a new tact (e.g., pinwheel) may result in the transfer of the response to mand conditions without additional training (e.g., later, as a function of an MO for the pinwheel the child mands "pinwheel" despite not having a single mand training trial on pinwheel). This effect is termed the "transfer of control among the verbal skills," and represents a significant milestone in language acquisition. Many language-training programs designed for children with autism and other developmental disabilities make extensive use of transfer procedures designed to establish new skills that are based on existing skills (e.g., Greer & Ross, 2007; Sundberg, 1980; Sundberg & Partington, 1998). The goal of these procedures is to achieve untrained transfer between the language skills.

Scoring Criteria and Placement Suggestions

Give the child a score of 1 on the Transition Assessment if he demonstrates transfer from one skill to another (e.g., echoic to mand) for two new verbal responses with two or less transfer training trials (e.g., it only takes two echoic prompts to learn a new mand). The scores between 2 and 4 represent a progression towards more frequent transfers with less training and with an increasing complexity of verbal skills, such as mands that involve prepositions that were initially trained as a tact. Give the child a score of 5 if transfer between the verbal skills occurs daily and reliably, and involves more advanced parts of speech (i.e., adjectives, prepositions, or adverbs) and intraverbal behavior (e.g., after a child visits the doctor's office, without any specific training, he is able to tell someone what he did at the doctor's office). When transfer among the verbal skills begins to consistently occur, the amount of specific teaching time that a child requires in order to acquire new skills begins to decrease; thus, increasing the child's probability of learning in a less restrictive education setting where the intense intensive transfer teaching procedures are not provided.

Summary of Category 2 Scores

The six areas from Category 2 provide important information regarding how a child learns new skills. These measures collectively can provide guidance regarding the teaching resources that are necessary to ensure that the child learns and retains new material. A child who scores high in all of these areas is easier to teach and has a better chance of keeping up with a more advanced curriculum, especially with a curriculum that has a looser teaching format that may not involve multiple teaching trials, prompts, prompt fading, and high levels of tangible reinforcement.

Transition Category 3: Self-help, Spontaneity, and Self-Direction

13. Adaptability to Change

Many individuals with developmental disabilities, especially those with autism, have difficulty handling changes in routines or planned activities. However, day-to-day life for most families and classrooms is full of unplanned events. For example, a typical classroom may have a fire drill in the middle of a fun activity, an impromptu assembly may be announced, or recess might not start the exact minute the bell rings. At home a family may decide it's a nice day to go on a picnic, a relative stops by, or a planned activity must be canceled. A child's inability to be flexible may cause the family members, classroom teachers, aides, and even fellow classmates to "walk on eggshells" around the child, especially if there is the pending threat of severe or embarrassing tantrums, or other negative behavior associated with a change in routine. This way of handling the problem usually results in it getting worse, because the negative behaviors often get reinforced when early signs of distress on the part of the child are followed by a return to the routine. Although some of the child's resistance to change may initially be from fear and anxiety—and the adult should certainly be sensitive to this—if the child is often placated, the behaviors could become worse. Also, the appropriate skills and emotional coping behaviors that comprise being adaptable to change may never be acquired.

The child may also verbally perseverate on a change in routine and have difficulty getting back on task. The ability to accept change is another factor to consider in a move to a less restrictive environment. The probability of unexpected changes increases significantly as classrooms move away from highly structured teaching and high teacher-to-student ratios. A child must be able to quickly adapt to the constantly changing nature of many of these classrooms.

Scoring Criteria and Placement Suggestion

Give the child a score of 1 on the Transition Assessment if he is able to adapt to some changes with verbal preparation and careful pre-planning, but he generally demonstrates negative behavior when unpredictable changes occur, and a substantial amount of effort goes into keeping these unpredictable changes at a minimum. The scores between 2 and 4 demonstrate a progression towards improved adaptability to change in terms of a reduction of negative behavior and the reduction in the amount of preparation necessary to make changes. Additional measures of adaptability can include the number of different changes and unplanned disruptions that are tolerated, the immediacy of the change, and the nature of the competing events during the change (i.e., engaged in a fun activity versus a work activity). Give the child a score of 5 if he easily adapts to changes and disruptions in routines and activities and rarely emits any negative behavior when these changes occur. A score of 4 or 5 would demonstrate that the child is potentially able to adapt to the unpredicted events that may occur in a less restrictive setting.

14. Spontaneous Behaviors

Spontaneity is a relative term that is actually quite complicated when applied to language acquisition. That is, there are many degrees of spontaneity and they apply differently to different behavioral repertoires and situations. The American Heritage Dictionary's first-listed definition of "spontaneous" is, "Happening or arising without apparent external cause; self-generated." The word "spontaneous" is an adjective that modifies the word "behavior;" it describes a property of the behavior that is emitted, and on the surface the definition suggests that there are no antecedents that cause the behavior. If this is true, it presents a problem if the goal is to teach spontaneous behavior. What are the variables that evoke spontaneous behavior? When is spontaneity appropriate and when is it inappropriate? How does one know when they have established this important repertoire for a language-delayed individual? How is this behavior measured?

It is beyond the scope of the current treatment of this topic to answer all of these questions. However, an important word in the dictionary definition of spontaneous is "apparent." A suggestion will be made that there are antecedents that evoke spontaneous behavior; however, they often are quite subtle or private (i.e., "self-generated"). But a hierarchy of antecedents that identifies the degree of spontaneity can be helpful in determining a specific individual's existing spontaneous repertoire and its comparison to his typically developing peers. One way to look at spontaneity is in contrast to what is called being "prompt bound," and by identifying a continuum of additional prompts that might be necessary to evoke a particular skill.

A common problem faced by many children with language delays, especially those with autism, is that the language and social skills they have acquired are prompt bound. That is, the target behaviors do not occur without some additional antecedent variable (a prompt). For example, a child may have learned to say "open" to gain access to a container of crayons, but only does so if an adult prompts with the phrase "What do you want?" The failure to be spontaneous (i.e., free from prompting) can be observed in all 16 areas assessed on the Milestones Assessment. A spontaneous tact, for example, would be one where there is no adult verbal prompt to tact. Rather, the physical world alone (the nonverbal S^D) evokes the tact, as in a child saying "Spiderman" as a tact of a poster on a movie store wall without an adult saying, "Who's that?" Making such comments about naturally occurring things in the environment is a part of making conversation. The initiation of social interaction may not occur because the social behavior is prompt bound by extraneous verbal prompts. Without prompts to respond, the target behaviors do not occur (for more detail on being prompt bound, see the Barriers Assessment in Chapter 6). Any skill can become prompt bound, and fail to occur spontaneously because the skill is never freed from the extraneous (and often subtle) control by prompts. A well-meaning one-on-one aide often defeats the purpose of progression to a less restrictive setting by excessively providing prompts.

Scoring Criteria and Placement Suggestions

Give the child a score of 1 on the Transition Assessment if he emits some behaviors without prompts, but most of his language and social interactions must be prompted. The scores between 2 and 4 demonstrate a progression towards more spontaneous behavior as measured by less prompting, and a wider range of behaviors (the 16 skill areas) that occur spontaneously. Give the child a score of 5 if he emits strong and frequent spontaneous behaviors across all 16 areas of the VB-MAPP Milestones Assessment. A score of 4 or 5 would suggest that the lack of spontaneous responding is not a problem for the child and add to the collection of information supporting his ability to learn in a less restrictive setting.

15. Self-Directed Play and Leisure Skills

Most children have little difficulty independently entertaining themselves. After all, play is (by definition) fun. It's behavior that is automatically reinforcing and usually occurs without adult prompting or reinforcement. Children do, of course, "get bored" when the available choices of play and leisure activities are limited, or of less value than adult attention. Perhaps surprisingly, self-directed play and leisure behaviors are a component of most educational settings. There are many times in a classroom where there is non-directed time, such as recess, adult clean-up after snack and lunch, silent reading time, or during classroom disruptions (e.g., visitors, meetings). Even some elements of a structured teaching session with a 1:2 teacher-to-student ratio may involve working a few minutes with one child, then a few minutes with the other child. The hardest part of this arrangement is finding "downtime" activities for the child who is not receiving direct adult attention. For some children, self-direction is not a problem, but for some children with special needs, especially those with autism, self-direction in relation to play and leisure time may be difficult. This is especially a problem for children who engage in a high rate of self-stimulatory behavior, which competes with more acceptable age-appropriate play and leisure activities that would be expected in a less restrictive classroom.

Scoring Criteria and Placement Suggestions

The scores from the VB-MAPP Milestones Assessment section on independent play can be used as a measure of a child's ability to self-direct his play and leisure time. Give the child a score of 1 on the Transition Assessment if his total score on the independent play area is at least 3. The scores between 2 and 4 on the Transition Assessment Form measure a child's progression toward the ability to independently engage in play and leisure activities, and the child's ability to engage in these activities without the adult directing the activity. This progression is measured by the occurrence of a variety of behaviors identified on the VB-MAPP Milestones and Task Analysis Assessments. Some of the activities include playground play, assembling and playing with toys, drawing, arts and crafts, sports, games, engaging in imaginary play, helping with daily activities, and other age-appropriate activities. Give the child a score of 5 on the Transition Assessment if he scores at least 14 on the independent play area of the VB-MAPP Milestones Assessment.

If a child scores a 1 or 2 on this part of the Transition Assessment and must be prompted to entertain himself, or engage in some form of play or leisure activities, then a further analysis and intervention may be necessary. A more restrictive setting consisting of a higher teacher-to-student ratio might be of more value. A higher score of 4 or 5 would suggest that the child is able to engage in a number of self-directed activities, and this ability will be of value in supporting his success in a less restrictive academic setting.

16. General Self-help Skills

The last three transition areas (16-18) involve the child's ability to independently care for himself. There are several aspects of learning self-help skills that can be assessed independently of the actual skills themselves. The first aspect is motivation (MOs): Is the child self-motivated to care for himself (e.g., he wants to put on his shoes by himself)? The second aspect is self-initiation: Does the child care for himself without prompts (e.g., is he motivated to put on his shoes and initiates doing so)? The third aspect is attempting approximations to self-help skills: Does the child try to care for himself (e.g., tries to independently put on his shoes by himself)? The fourth aspect asks whether the self-help skills are generalized: Do the self-help skills occur in different settings, with different materials, and with different people (e.g., the child uses the self-help skills he has learned at home in a school setting)? The final aspect asks whether a child engages in negative behaviors when adults provide the care (e.g., the child hits an adult trying to brush his teeth).

When these five areas are combined with the specific steps in teaching self-help skills, an overall assessment of the child's skill levels and the potential intervention needs can be revealed. The larger goal is not just that the child "knows" the skills on a self-help list, but rather that the child uses those skills in a functional way. Expectations regarding the child's level of self-help should be developmentally appropriate (e.g., typically developing four-year olds may not independently wash their hands before eating).

In regard to the specific skills, in addition to toileting and eating (covered below in 17 and 18), children need to be able to at least approximate washing their hands, dressing themselves, brushing their teeth, blowing their nose, and removing minor aversives (e.g., removing layered clothing because they are too hot). These areas are important considerations for transition to a less restrictive setting, because if a child is unable to provide basic care for himself, an adult must do it, which requires a higher teacher-to-student ratio and consumes instructional time. If the child's learning is fast and requires little intensive teaching, then it is less of a problem. However, these skills should be established in a setting where they can be taught, rather than managed, preferably in the child's home environment prior to transition.

Scoring Criteria and Placement Suggestions

Give the child a score of 1 on the Transition Assessment if he has no independent self-help, but usually does not engage in negative behaviors when adults provide personal care. For example, when an adult is washing the child's face, he does not scream and pull away from the adult or engage in other negative behavior that is related to getting out of the face washing. The scores between 2 and 4 demonstrate a progression towards more independent and successful self-help as measured by the progression from physical prompts to verbal prompts, more attempts to independently approximate to the task (e.g., does some face washing by himself), and self-initiating and partial success for some tasks (e.g., gets his coat without prompts and tries to put it on, sometimes successfully). Give the child a score of 5 if he is motivated to perform some self-help tasks (e.g., wants the mud off his hands), initiates and attempts approximations to performing the tasks (e.g., goes to the sink and turns on the water), and generalizes (e.g., will wash his hands when he gets paint on them and at a different sink in a different classroom). A score of 4 or 5 would indicate that the child is potentially able to learn to care for himself in a less restrictive setting, and additional resources would be minimal.

17. Toileting Skills

"Is he potty trained?" That is often the first questions asked by teachers when transitioning children to a less restrictive setting. This concern is due to the fact that additional time requirements are placed on a classroom teacher for a child who must be diapered and changed or taught toileting skills. Often, toileting is a major component of the decision to provide a one-on-one aide in a less restrictive setting. Thus, toileting is an important consideration for transition, and should be targeted while the child is still in a setting that has a higher teacher-to-student ratio, and with staff who have toilet training experience. All the issues presented above in the section titled "General self-help skills" are relevant to toileting (e.g., motivation, initiation, generalization). The current scale measures the child's specific level of toileting skills.

Scoring Criteria and Placement Suggestions

Give the child a score of 1 on the Transition Assessment if he demonstrates toilet training readiness (e.g., dry periods, sits still for 2 minutes, shows some indication that he has to urinate or defecate), but still wears a diaper. The scores between 2 and 4 demonstrate a progression towards more independent and successful toileting, and learning the toileting routines (e.g., un-dressing, wiping, re-dressing, flushing, washing, and drying hands). These scores also reflect the emergence of both bladder and bowel control and elimination on the toilet. Give the child a score of 5 if he initiates or mands to use the bathroom, and independently completes the age-appropriate steps of the toileting routine. A score of 4 or 5 would indicate that the child's toileting skills are well established, and toileting issues shouldn't affect transition decisions.

18. Eating Skills

Independent eating skills allow a child to participate in the lunch settings with typically developing peers with minimum supervision (this also depends on the existence of any behavior problems, such as running from the group). Lunchtime is often a time when staff members take their breaks (typically a mandatory component of employment), and there are fewer resources available. If a child requires extensive adult prompting and reinforcement to eat, it will be a variable to consider for his placement into a less restrictive setting. As with toileting, the general self-help skills described in transition area 16 above apply to eating (i.e., motivation, initiation, generalization).

Scoring Criteria and Placement Suggestions

For eating skills, give the child a score of 1 on the Transition Assessment if he can eat some things independently—usually highly desired finger foods (e.g., cookies)—but usually requires physical prompting to eat. The scores between 2 and 4 demonstrate a progression towards more independent eating as indicated by the progression from physical prompts to verbal prompts, the need for fewer prompts, the use of a spoon, independently getting his own lunch box, opening up items from his lunch box, and cleaning up his own mess. Give the child a score of 5 if he independently gets and opens his own food items, eats without prompts, uses utensils, and cleans up with just a few prompts for the whole group. A score of 4 or 5 would indicate that the child's independent eating skills are well established, and eating problems shouldn't affect transition decisions.

Summary of Catagory 3 Scores

A child who can care for himself, at least to some degree, and is adaptable to daily routine changes and requires less one-on-one teacher and aide time has a higher probability of success in a less restrictive setting. These independent skills are important in that they allow a teacher to focus on the more important language, academic, and social skills, as well as other age-appropriate activities. While self-help issues may not be as important as basic language skills, for example, they still can have an impact on the child's probability of success in a less restrictive setting.

Interpreting the VB-MAPP Transition Assessment

The results from the three categories of the Transition Assessment should be weighed differently. Category 1 is the most important because it addresses the primary issues in transition consisting of the child's language, social, and academic levels; the presence or absence of language and learning barriers; and the child's ability to learn in a group teaching format and complete independent academic work. Category 2 is clearly important, and often is the reason why scores may be high or low in Category 1. This category contains measures of the child's patterns of learning, such as the rate of acquisition, generalization, retention, and learning from the natural environment. If Category 2 scores are high, it is likely that Category 1 scores are high, if they are low then Category 1 scores are probably also low, and more intervention is necessary for the child to acquire new skills. Finally, Category 3 contains measures of self-help, adaptability to changes in routines, and self-direction in everyday activities. These skills play a roll in functioning in a less restrictive setting, but are not as critical as those in Categories 1 and 2.

The decision to transition a child to a less restrictive setting is the sole responsibility of the child's IEP team. The general goal is to base the decision on the child's ability to learn and make meaningful progress in the chosen setting. The purpose of the Transition Assessment is to provide those making decisions with data about the child that might assist in the process. As a result, there are no formal criteria provided in this assessment for transition. However, as a general statement, if a child's scores on the Transition Assessment are primarily in the range of 0 to 2, then it is likely that the child will benefit most from a classroom that provides a high teacher-to-student ratio, individualized and intense teaching sessions, careful use of behavioral methodology and performance measurement (i.e., data collection), regular supervision and monitoring by a qualified professional, and formal training for the child's parents or caretakers. If a child's scores fall mostly in the 4 to 5 range, then it is likely that the child would benefit from a classroom that has a lower teacher-to-student ratio, and uses a teaching format closer to that used for typically developing children, but still uses behavioral methodology and performance measurement, as well as providing parent and caretaker training. There are many possible steps between these two ends of the least restrictive continuum, but again, that placement decision is up to the IEP team, with the focus on the child's ability to make meaningful gains.

CHAPTER 8

Interpreting the Level 1 Assessment: Curriculum Placement and Writing IEP Goals

The results of the Milestones Assessment, the Barriers Assessment (Chapter 6), and the Transition Assessment (Chapter 7) provide a comprehensive overview of a child and can be used to design an individualized intervention program. These three assessments identify what skills a child needs to acquire, and what language and learning barriers need to be reduced or removed in order to move the child forward. The VB-MAPP Supporting Skills list contained in the Protocol (pp. 38-72) can also provide further information about the many additional skills that can be incorporated into a daily program. Although the Supporting Skills list is not designed to be a formal assessment tool because of its size (approximately 500 skills), it can be used to identify skills that contribute to the development of a more complete intervention program. The Task Analysis list, also contained in the Protocol (pp. 38-72), can provide earlier steps towards meeting each milestone.

The next three chapters will describe how to read a VB-MAPP Milestones Assessment profile, and how to determine placement within a verbal behavior intervention program. The basic components of a verbal behavior program can be found in any number of available texts and book chapters (e.g., Barbera, 2002; Greer & Ross, 2008; Schramm, 2011; Sundberg, 2007; Sundberg & Partington, 1998; Vargas, 2009). The current chapter focuses on a child whose scores fall primarily in Level 1 of the Milestones Assessment. Following several general points about a Level 1 program, each milestone will be presented with specific recommendations for the next step after meeting that milestone.

How to Interpret the Overall VB-MAPP Milestones Assessment Results

The first step in reading a VB-MAPP Milestones profile is to identify the general level of the child. A child who scores primarily in the Level 1 area will require an intervention program quite different from a child whose scores fall primarily in Level 2 or Level 3. Many children may show specific strengths and weaknesses, and may score points in multiple levels. However, a child could be identified as primarily scoring in Level 1, Level 2, or Level 3. Since each level is designed to correspond with an approximate linguistic and developmental age, certain skills, targets, and teaching styles may be more effective with particular levels (e.g., intensive 1:1 teaching strategies versus natural environment and group teaching strategies). In addition, major programming issues may be of more concern at certain levels, such as whether to use augmentative and alternative communication (AAC) for children scoring in Level 1, or the nature and degree of the integration program for children scoring in Level 2, or the specific focus of an academic program for children scoring in Level 3.

The second step in reading a VB-MAPP profile is to analyze the scores in each of the relevant domains and their relation to the child's performance in other areas. The assessor should look at the strengths and weaknesses, and determine if there are particular strengths in one area that can be of special benefit to a child, or weaknesses that need to be addressed. For example, if a child with limited language skills demonstrates a strong motor imitation repertoire, but has relatively weak echoic skills, a sign language program may provide the child with a head start for language development. The third step is to look for balance across all of the domains for each level. The Milestones Assessment is designed to be able to quickly read a profile by looking for a general balance of one repertoire in relation to another. Efforts were made to identify, for example, how many mands, tacts, and LDs an average typically developing 2-year-old child might have, and the milestones reflect that average. A child is out of balance if he has, for example, a hundred LDs but only a few tacts, and thus tacting should be a bigger focus of the program in order to bring the child into balance.

A sample VB-MAPP for a child scoring primarily in Level 1 is presented in Figure 8-1. This sample shows a common profile for many young children with language delays. Charlie is a 3-year-old child who is showing elevated echoic skills, but does not have any mands, tacts, or LDs, and his play and social skills are weak. For this child, an intervention program should obviously begin immediately. The initial focus should be on using the echoic repertoire to establish mands by using the transfer of control procedures described in Sundberg and Partington (1998). It could be predicted that this child will quickly acquire manding because of the strength of his echoic repertoire. However, the specific rate of mand acquisition would be dependent on the strength of the child's motivation and the skill level of the adult trainer. For example, if the child really likes Elmo and can echo an approximation to the word "Elmo," and the trainer is skilled in the basic echoic-to-mand transfer procedure, the transfer to manding may only take a few minutes (Sundberg, 1980). Once a couple of mands are established, tact and listener training should begin (of course each individual child may progress at different rates and programming decisions should be based on an analysis conducted by a qualified person).

Interpreting the VB-MAPP for a Child Scoring in Level 1

In general, if a child scores primarily in the Level 1 area, the focus of the intervention should be on establishing the following six basic language and related skills: mands, echoics, motor imitation, LDs, tacts, and visual perceptual and matching skills. Play and social skills are also important and should be a major part of the intervention, as well as increasing spontaneous vocalizations. It is important to note that there are a variety of other skills that a child may need to learn, such as fine motor, gross motor, self-help, and toileting skills, and if appropriate these should be added to the overall intervention program.

The teaching style for a child scoring in Level 1 may be more of an intensive teaching format that involves a high number of teaching trials with carefully arranged contingencies (i.e., prompting, fading, careful shaping, transfer of stimulus control, use of strong MOs, reinforcement, etc.), and careful measurement of progress. However, for some children, a more loose teaching strategy such as natural environment training may also be effective, but the learning goals remain the same. Ultimately, a combination of both teaching strategies will be necessary (Sundberg & Partington, 1999).

Writing IEP Goals

IEP goals should identify primarily learning, language, and social milestones that have a 1-year time frame and are consistent with the child's learning history. Projecting appropriate goals for one year is often difficult. The overall scores on the VB-MAPP Milestones and Barriers Assessment can provide some guidance as to the child's ability to acquire new skills, and these data can help to suggest specific numbers for the IEP. In addition to the milestones and barriers goals, there may be other goals that are appropriate, such as those relating to special services such

Figure 8-1
Sample VB-MAPP for a child whose scores fall primarily in Level 1.

Child's name:	Charlie
Date of birth:	7-12-05
Age at testing:	**1** 3 yrs. **2** **3** **4**

Key:	Score	Date	Color	Tester
1ST TEST:	20	7-15-08		MS
2ND TEST:				
3RD TEST:				
4TH TEST:				

LEVEL 3

	Mand	Tact	Listener	VP/MTS	Play	Social	Reading	Writing	LRFFC	IV	Group	Linguistics	Math

LEVEL 2

	Mand	Tact	Listener	VP/MTS	Play	Social	Imitation	Echoic	LRFFC	IV	Group	Linguistics

LEVEL 1

	Mand	Tact	Listener	VP/MTS	Play	Social	Imitation	Echoic	Vocal

as speech, occupational therapy, and adaptive physical education. Some skills, while needing further development, may not warrant an IEP goal such as imitation or echoic skills. These skills can be incorporated into other activities such as self-help, arts and crafts, group activities, music, games, or playground activities. If a particular skill is a problem for a child, it certainly can and should be targeted for intervention. If goals are met during the course of a year, the program should naturally progress to more advanced skills as suggested by the VB-MAPP. The need to reassemble a full IEP team for such changes would be dependent on the nature and composition of each child's IEP team. In general, the total number of goals for 1 year should be limited to around 12 to 18; while there are exceptions, it's best to not have too many or too few goals.

Table 8-1 contains a list of possible IEP goals for a child whose profile looks similar to Charlie's Profile (Figure 8-1). In addition to these goals, there are a variety of other skills and activities that can strengthen a child's early verbal repertoires (but need not be identified as IEP goals). A review of the tasks from the VB-MAPP Supporting Skills list can provide some possible suggestions for specific targets that may be of value in designing a daily intervention program for an individual child. The goals in Table 8-1 are only generic suggestions. The actual objectives used for an individual child should be tailored specifically for that child, and based on the recommendations of the child's IEP team. When determining goals, the IEP team might consider some of the points about "targets" suggested by Cooper et al. (2007, pp. 55-69).

Table 8-1
Sample IEP goals for a child whose scores fall primarily in Level 1.

1. Charlie will emit 10 different mands without echoic prompts in the presence or absence of the desired item or activity (verbal prompts are okay such as, "What do you want?").

2. Charlie will spontaneously emit (without a verbal prompt such as, "What do you want?") an average of 50 or more different mands per day (objects can be present).

3. Charlie will tact 50 items.

4. Charlie will tact 10 actions.

5. Charlie will identify 50 items in a messy array of at least 8.

6. Charlie will perform 20 specific actions on command.

7. Charlie will match 100 non-identical objects or pictures in an array of at least 10 comparison stimuli.

8. Charlie will imitate 25 two-component actions.

9. Charlie will echo 50 vowel-consonant combinations of 2 syllables or more, or full words during testing.

10. Charlie will spontaneously construct, assemble, or set up toys or other play items that come with several different parts (even combining different sets), and engage in independent play with these items for 5 minutes.

11. Charlie will spontaneously follow or imitate the motor behavior of peers 10 times per day.

12. Charlie will spontaneously mand to peers 5 times per day.

Special Considerations for a Child Whose Scores Fall Primarily in Level 1

Intensity of Intervention

There are a variety of issues that must be addressed for a child who may be just beginning an intervention program. A child whose scores fall in Level 1 is in need of an intensive and direct language and social skills intervention program. The word "intensive" suggests that training should occur daily in an organized and planned fashion, with clear targets, and best-practice behavioral and educational intervention procedures (e.g., Cooper, et al., 2007; Maurice, Green, & Luce, 1996). The number of formal teaching hours should be substantial, such as 25 hours per week of a school program, with follow-up and generalization provided by the parents and others throughout the child's day. That is, language and social skills intervention is 24/7, and should be conducted in all environments, and by all the individuals who interact with the child, especially the family members. The number of hours is neither as important as what is accomplished during those hours, nor as important as having the most accurate analysis of the individual child's needs.

Discrete Trial Training (DTT) and Natural Environment Training (NET)

A language intervention program for a child with autism or other intellectual disabilities should include both DTT (structured teaching sessions, usually conducted at a table or on the floor) and NET (teaching skills during the child's day-to-day activities) (Sundberg & Partington, 1999). However, the degree of these general teaching formats may vary depending on the child's skill level, and other needs such as those that relate to barriers (e.g., behavior problems or non-compliance). A child whose scores are primarily in Level 1 will almost certainly need a structured and formal intensive teaching format (DTT) that involves the careful teaching strategies derived from applied behavior analysis (e.g., Cooper et al., 2007). This same child, however, could also benefit from training in the natural environment (e.g., mand training when MOs are occurring, such as in play settings, during mealtime and other daily routines, or in the community).

It is unlikely that all of the child's educational needs can be met in either a DTT or NET setting. Thus, the right balance is essential, with usually the best arrangement being an intensive DTT component primarily conducted in the classroom or in an in-home program (with NET components still included), and the NET component primarily conducted in the home and community (with DTT components still included). However, regardless of the specific setting, once a child acquires a skill in a structured teaching arrangement it is important to provide opportunities to practice and generalize that skill in the context of the child's naturally occurring daily activities (e.g., snack time, dressing, social play). While a mixture of both strategies in both environments is highly suggested, the classroom or in-home teaching environment may be more conducive to DTT if the staff have the formal training to implement the intensive teaching strategies, and the necessary supervision to guide the overall program. The home environment may be more conducive to the looser teaching strategies of NET, and allow parents to take advantage of the potentially wide range of MOs and S^{D}s that occur in a child's natural setting versus those that occur in structured teaching settings.

Augmentative and Alternative Communication

Skinner (1957) made it clear that verbal behavior can occur with a variety of response forms. We communicate with each other in a number of different ways, such as speech, gestures, body posture, visual stimuli, and written words. For a child with autism or other developmental disabilities, speech is the most desired response form and every effort should be made to use it as the target response. However, under many circumstances, a child can receive a jump-start to more effective verbal behavior by using sign language, icons, or even in some cases written words (primarily for a child who is identified as "hyperlexic," for whom reading is easy and fun). However, there is a fair amount of disagreement among speech pathologists, classroom teachers, and other professionals regarding which form of augmentative communication might be of best value to a child with language delays. The results of a child's VB-MAPP can help to provide some guidance in this area.

Specifically, a child's scores on the echoic, motor imitation, and matching-to-sample (MTS) areas of the VB-MAPP Milestones Assessment Levels 1 and 2 can provide important information regarding the selection of a response form. If a child scores 3 or higher on the echoic area of the Milestones Assessment, regardless of his score in the other two areas, speech should be initially tried as a response form using the mand training and pairing procedures described in Sundberg and Partington (1998). If a child scores higher than 3 on the echoic, the probability of transferring these vocal responses to mands and tacts is high, but completely dependent on the skills of the staff and parents to implement the specific training procedures. Even if a child scores a 1 or 2 on the echoic evaluation, the mand and pairing procedures should be tried first before moving to sign language or icons. Lovaas (1977) has long been a strong advocate of focusing on speech before types of augmentative communication are used, and this author shares that view.

If mand training using speech as a response form is unsuccessful after a serious and well-designed attempt that correctly utilizes behavioral analysis and verbal behavior techniques, then a look at alternative response forms would be warranted. At this point, the decision needs to be made as to which type of response form would be most appropriate for an individual child. The choices are primarily sign language (Sundberg, 1980) or an icon system such as PECS (Frost & Bondy, 2002), and in rare cases (at this early level) written words. The child's milestones scores on the imitation and MTS areas can provide some direction. If the child's scores are significantly higher in one of these areas, but not the other, a direction is suggested. For example, if a child scores 5 or higher on the VP/MTS (he can do picture matching), but scores 1 or less on imitation, then perhaps an icon system might help develop some early manding more quickly. On the other hand, if imitation is stronger than matching-to-sample as indicated by a score of 2 or more on imitation and 4 or less on VP/MTS (matching is not assessed until item 5 on the VB-MAPP), then sign language should be tried. It may be that if one system is tried first (after carefully following the guidelines for that system), and the results are unsatisfactory for a specific child, the other system may work better, and thus it is reasonable to try that AAC system.

If the matching and imitation skills are close to equal, then sign language should be used because of its linguistic parallel to speech and many other long-term advantages (for more detail on this issue see Schafer, 1993; Sundberg, 1993b; Sundberg & Partington, 1998; Sundberg & Sundberg, 1990; Tincani, 2004). In addition, while PECS can be of great value in generating an early form of manding (Charlop-Christy, Carpenter, Le, LeBlanc, & Kellet, 2002; Frost & Bondy, 2002), tact and intraverbal behaviors are more difficult to establish with an icon system. Specifically, "tacting" with icons involves showing an object (e.g., a shoe) to a child, and then the child selects an icon of that object (e.g., a picture of a shoe). However, this is more parsimoniously classified as matching-to-sample than it is as tacting. Likewise, an intraverbal with icons where, for example, the adult says, "What do you wear?" and the child selects an icon of a shirt, is more parsimoniously classified as a listener behavior (LRFFC), not as an intraverbal. If icon training results in the emergence of vocal behavior, which is often the case with any of the types of AC, then the child emitting a vocal response solves the tact and intraverbal issue. Also, for some children, it is not uncommon to start with speech, make some progress, but add sign language at a later date to improve articulation, and also speed up the acquisition of mands and tacts.

Summary

There are several elements of an effective intervention program for a child with autism or other intellectual disabilities. The first is an accurate assessment of the child's language and learning skills and the barriers that might be blocking further gains. Once these baseline measures have been obtained, an intervention program needs to be designed and implemented by a qualified professional. Decisions need to be made regarding many aspects of the program, such as the daily schedule of activities, the possible use of AAC, teaching format and style, data collection and measurement, and the curriculum progression. Hands-on staff need formal training and regular supervision by a formally trained behavior analyst (or equally qualified professional) in order to implement and keep the intervention program current and effective. And finally, parents need to be involved, trained, and provided with on-going support.

Interpreting the Scores for the Level 1 Milestones and Suggested IEP Goals

An analysis of a child's performance in each domain, and its relation to his scores on other domains and the Barriers Assessment, can provide specific direction for an individualized intervention program. For example, if a child has no mands or no tacts, the immediate focus may be just on establishing a beginning mand repertoire and delaying tact training until a couple of mands are established. Or, if a child scores high on the tact, but low on listener skills, he may also have elevated scores on several of the language barriers such as scanning, conditional discriminations, and response requirements that weaken the MO. Intervention on these barriers along with the specific target skill can help to ensure that appropriate repertoires are established.

The following sections contain more specific placement suggestions. Each Level 1 Milestone is presented (including "0" scores where the child did not get any points on the milestone measure) along with various considerations as to how specific scores in one domain may be related to scores in other areas, and scores on the barriers as well. Suggestions are made as to what direction and focus the intervention program might take given that a child has met a particular milestone (e.g., Mand 2-M is met; "What's next?"). The general goal is to establish all of the domains in a balanced manner, while reducing barriers. A list of possible IEP goals to select from are presented after each skill level. As previously stated, these goals are only generic suggestions. The actual objectives used for an individual child should be tailored specifically for that child, and based on the recommendations of the child's IEP team.

MAND – LEVEL I

MAND 0-M	Zero score

If a child fails to receive any points on the mand scale, then significant efforts are necessary to establish this important linguistic skill. In general, specific forms of reinforcement need to be identified along with the relevant MOs (i.e., what makes these items valuable). Next, a target response form needs to be selected (vocal, signs, or icons), and the basic transfer procedures involving prompting, fading, and differential reinforcement need to be implemented (e.g., Hall & Sundberg, 1987; Sundberg & Partington, 1998; Sweeney-Kerwin, Carbone, O'Brien, Zecchin, & Janecky, 2007). The decision to use augmentative communication may involve a number of factors and the reader is referred to the previous section for more information on that topic. This child may also have elevated scores on several of the barrier measures, such as response requirements that weaken the motivators, instructional control, behavior problems, or weak MOs in general. Part of the intervention program will need to address these problems as well, but the overall program should be based on a more careful and detailed individual analysis of this child by a qualified professional.

MAND 1-M	Emits 2 words, signs, or icon selections, but may require echoic, imitative, or other prompts, but no physical prompts (e.g., *cracker, book*).

If a child is able to mand but requires echoic, imitative, or pointing prompts, this can be a significant step for him. The main focus should be on fading out these prompts, as well as working on increasing the number of different mands. At this point it is better to increase the number of single word mands rather than attempting to put the mand in a sentence (e.g., adding "I want…"). In addition, avoid the temptation to teach general words (e.g., more, please, mine, yes) and focus on words for specific items or activities (e.g., milk, ball, push), and words that are more likely to be used frequently in the child's natural environment. A variety of additional activities for this level, and the upcoming levels, can be found in the VB-MAPP Mand Supporting Skills list contained in the Protocol.

MAND 2-M	Emits 4 different mands without prompts (except, *What do you want?*) the desired item can be present (e.g., *music, Slinky, ball*).

If a child is able to emit 4 different mands without echoic, imitative, or pointing prompts, this represents the beginnings of an early functional mand repertoire. At this point in mand training, the desired item can be present and efforts to get manding to occur in the absence of the desired item should be minimal. Much of a typical child's early manding is multiply controlled by both MOs and nonverbal stimuli (the desired item is present). The primary goal is to eliminate the prompts that give away the response form (physical, echoic, and imitative prompts) or intraverbal prompts of the response form (i.e., saying the spoken word for children who are using sign language). The attempt to fade out the desired item too quickly may result in an impaired mand repertoire for some children. The focus going forward should be on (1) generalization of the mands to different people, places, materials, and verbal prompts to mand, (2) increasing the frequency of daily manding, (3) increasing the number of different mands, and (4) getting some mands to occur without verbal prompts such as, "What do you want?" In addition, training on tacts and LDs should be occurring along wtih training on the other domains (unless there are some specific barriers that suggest otherwise).

MAND 3-M	**Generalizes 6 mands across 2 people, 2 settings, and 2 different examples of a reinforcer (e.g., mands *bubbles* from mom and dad, inside and outside, a red bottle and a blue bottle).**

Generalization might occur quickly for some children, but slower for others; however, it is a very important component of linguistic development, thus a milestone. The failure to generalize is a common barrier for many children, and early manding is often a good place to begin formal generalization training. The focus for a child beginning to show some generalization should be on (1) increasing the frequency of daily manding, (2) more of an effort to get mands to occur spontaneously, (3) more complex types of generalization, and (4) increasing the number of different mands. Generalization training for the other domains should be provided as well.

MAND 4-M	**Spontaneously emits (no verbal prompts) 5 mands — the desired item can be present.**

Spontaneous mands at this point would be those that occur without a verbal prompt from an adult; however, the desired item can be present. This is a powerful type of verbal behavior. Once a child begins to emit this type of manding, the rate of mands often increases due to the natural reinforcement occurring when the MO is the strongest (i.e., the child has verbal behavior that allows him access to reinforcers when they are most desired). The focus now should be on increasing the number of different mands, while continuing to encourage spontaneous, generalized, and frequent manding. In addition, a more intensive tact and LD program should be implemented.

MAND 5-M	**Emits 10 different mands without prompts (except, *What do you want?*) — the desired item can be present (e.g., *apple, swing, car, juice*).**

A child who now has a variety of mands that are generalized, spontaneous, and occurring frequently should begin to learn to mand for some items that are not present. It is also important to ensure that the other skills such as tacts and LDs are also growing in a manner commensurate with the mand (i.e., the child should have approximately 10 tacts and 20 LDs).

Suggested IEP Goals for Mand Level 1 (select only 1 or 2 goals and modify them as appropriate for the individual child).

- The child will emit at least 5 different mands with verbal prompts (e.g., "What do you want?"), but without physical, echoic, or imitative prompts.

- The child will emit at least 10 different mands with verbal prompts (e.g., "What do you want?"), but without echoic, imitative, or intraverbal prompts (for signers).

- The child will spontaneously emit at least 2 different mands per day for desired items and activities.

- The child will spontaneously emit an average of 10 or more **different** mands per day (objects can be present).

- The child will spontaneously emit an average of 100 or more **total** mands per day (objects can be present).

- The child will mand for at least 25 different desired items that are missing without prompts (other than a verbal prompt such as "What do you need?").

TACT – LEVEL 1

TACT 0-M	Zero score

If a child fails to receive any points on the tact scale, tact training should be part of his immediate intervention program. However, if the child also fails to score any points on the mand, then it is possible that tact training should be delayed until a couple of mands are established. If the child scores a 2 or above on the imitation or echoic scale, then it is possible that careful use of the transfer of stimulus control procedures described in Sundberg and Partington (1998) could be effective for this child. This child may also have elevated scores on several of the barrier measures, such as instructional control, behavior problems, or response requirements that weaken the motivators. As always, an individual child analysis is necessary to determine the specific components of a child's intervention program.

TACT 1-M	Tacts 2 items with echoic or imitative prompts (e.g., people, pets, characters, or favorite objects).

If a child is able to tact 2 items with echoic or imitative (for those using sign language) prompts during testing, a major focus should be on fading out the echoic or imitative prompt, as well as increasing the number of tacts, with an initial focus on 3D objects that are reinforcing or familiar to the child. A variety of additional activities for this level, and the upcoming levels can be found in the VB-MAPP Tact Supporting Skills list.

TACT 2-M	Tacts any 4 items without echoic or imitative prompts (e.g., people, pets, characters, or other objects).

A child who scores a 2 is showing the beginnings of a basic tact repertoire and should be receiving intensive tact training daily (as well as training on the other relevant domains). Tact training should be conducted in a variety of environments, including both home and school programs, as well as in intensive teaching settings and in the natural environment. Efforts should begin to promote generalization across people, settings, times of day, carrier phrases, tones of voice, etc. In addition, generalization across different examples of specific items should begin, as should tacting involving both pictures and objects.

TACT 3-M	Tacts 6 non-reinforcing items (e.g., *shoe, hat, spoon, car, cup, bed*).

A score of 3 demonstrates that the child has an early tact repertoire that is breaking free from motivation as a source of control. The focus should now be on (1) increasing the size of tact repertoire, (2) generalizing the tact repertoire to a wider variety of examples of specific items (e.g., tacting 3 different dogs as "dog"), and (3) fading out the verbal "What is that?" prompt on occasion to promote spontaneous tacting. At this point, the child should be receiving hundreds of tact trials every day. In addition, it is important to include LD training on the same words acquired as tacts.

TACT 4-M	Spontaneously tacts (no verbal prompts) 2 different items.

Many children with language delays have difficulty reaching this milestone. Often, this is because of a long history of tacts that are partly controlled by an adult's verbal prompt to tact, and the delivery of contrived reinforcers. However, if a child can tact a couple of items without verbal prompts, this type of tacting should be further strengthened, but with caution because at a certain point excessive unprompted tacting becomes inappropriate.

TACT 5-M	Tacts 10 items (e.g., common objects, people, body parts, or pictures).

A child who reaches this milestone should have an intensive tacting program that focuses on (1) increasing the size of the tact repertoire, (2) generalization to a wider variety of stimuli, (3) fluency activities, (4) spontaneity, and (5) beginning to tact a few actions. As before, tacting should occur frequently throughout each day with a focus on growth and generalization. It is also important to make sure the LDs are progressing at a rate commensurate with tacting. In general, new tacts and LDs should be introduced and taught at the same time (although there are exceptions for some children). In addition, it is important to continue to work on balancing the skills across all Level 1 domains, and to reduce any existing barriers.

Suggested IEP Goals for Tact Level 1 (select only 1 or 2 goals and modify them as appropriate for the individual child).

- The child will tact at least 10 items (people, objects, or pictures) reliably on command.
- The child will spontaneously tact (no verbal prompts) at least 10 different items in a day.
- The child will tact at least 20 items (people, objects, body parts, or pictures) reliably on command.
- The child will tact at least 50 items.
- The child will tact at least 20 actions.
- The child will tact at least 50 two-component noun-verb (or verb-noun) relations.
- The child will spontaneously tact items an average of 5 times per hour.

LISTENER RESPONDING – LEVEL I

LISTENER 0-M	Zero score

If a child fails to receive any points on the listener scale, listener training should be part of his immediate intervention program. The intervention strategy for a child who does not attend to speech should involve procedures that make speech sounds conditioned reinforcers (Sundberg & Partington, 1998) and discriminative stimuli (S^{D}s). For example, pairing words with strong forms of reinforcement can often make sounds reinforcing, and reinforcement of attending to speech sounds can establish them as S^{D}s for looking.

LISTENER 1-M	Attends to a speaker's voice by making eye contact with the speaker 5 times.

Once a child begins to attend to speech sounds, the next task is to get different responses under the control of different sounds. This, of course, is the main activity of standard LD training (also identified as receptive labeling). The focus for this child might be to just get him to attend to his own name, or the name of a favorite person, pet, or character (e.g., "There's Big Bird!"). A variety of additional activities for developing listener skills can be found in the VB-MAPP Listener Supporting Skills list.

LISTENER 2-M	Responds to hearing his own name 5 times (e.g., looks at the speaker).

The focus for a child who does attend to his own name and perhaps a few other verbal stimuli is to increase the number of LDs that he is able to make. Again, procedures that establish attending to favorite items should be the focus of the intervention at this point. This child may also be ready for more intensive listener training, perhaps beginning with LDs that involve only two stimuli in an array (e.g., responding to, "Where's Cookie Monster?" when shown Cookie Monster and a cat). It may also be appropriate to begin some training on listener skills involving actions (e.g., "show me clapping").

LISTENER 3-M	Looks at, touches, or points to the correct family member, pet, or other reinforcer when presented in an array of 2, for 5 different reinforcers (e.g., *Where's Elmo? Where's mommy?*).

Reaching this milestone means a child has begun to differentially respond to verbal stimuli as demonstrated by identifying specific items during testing. The focus should now be on (1) increasing the number of items the child is able to identify as a listener, (2) begin generalization to different people, settings, and materials, etc., (3) beginning work on emitting specific motor actions on command, and (4) increasing the number of items in a visual array. Also, these same words should be developed as tacts, and perhaps mands.

LISTENER 4-M	Performs 4 different motor actions on command without a visual prompt (e.g., *Can you jump? Show me clapping*).

A score at this level suggests that listener training should become a significant part of the child's daily intervention program, along with mands, tacts, and social behavior. The other skills are clearly important, but not as critical as these four skills are for a child whose scores begin to reach the top of Level 1. At this point in the intervention program the focus for listener training should be on (1) increasing the number of items the child is able to identify as a listener, (2) increasing the number of items in a visual array—more extensive use of pictures and the use of picture books, (3) an increased effort to generalize to different materials, (4) an increase in training on actions, and (5) more LD training in the natural environment and in the context of social games and social interaction.

LISTENER 5-M	Selects the correct item from an array of 4, for 20 different objects or pictures (e.g., *Show me cat. Touch shoe*).

The average typically developing 18-month-old child has a well-established listener repertoire. He can respond to dozens of words and is learning to respond to new words almost daily. He has learned that spoken words relate to physical objects and actions in his environment. A child with language delays who scores at this level should be receiving intensive training on advancing these important listener skills. The focus is a continuation of that described above (Milestones 1-4), but also on teaching the child to identify a few body parts, and providing more natural and social environment listener training. In addition, as previously stated, it is important to work on balancing out the skills in each domain (i.e., focus on teaching the missing skills), as well as reducing the barriers.

Suggested IEP Goals for Listener Responding Level 1 (select only 1 or 2 goals and modify them as appropriate for the individual child).

- The child will look at, or point to, at least 10 family members, pets, or reinforcers when named by an adult.

- The child will emit at least 4 motor actions on command.

- The child will respond to verbal reprimands such as "no," "hot," or "stop," an average of 2 times per day.

- The child will select, point to, or differentially look at a total of at least 25 objects, pictures, people, or body parts when named by an adult.

- The child will identify at least 50 items in a messy array of at least 8 that contains at least 3 similar stimuli.

- The child will perform at least 20 specific actions on command.

- The child will emit at least 100 two-component noun-verb (or verb-noun) responses on command.

VISUAL PERCEPTUAL SKILLS AND MATCHING-TO-SAMPLE (VP-MTS) – LEVEL 1

VP-MTS 0-M	Zero Score

If a child fails to receive any points on the VP-MTS scale, his vision should be checked. If his visual system is okay, try highly reinforcing items and move them around in front of the child (including stim-toys if they are valuable at that moment), and differentially reinforce tracking the item by giving him the reinforcer he tracks.

VP-MTS 1-M	Visually tracks moving stimuli for 2 seconds, 5 times.

Once a child begins to track items, procedures that involve reaching and grabbing a static or moving item can help to establish eye-hand coordination. Training may be more successful if reinforcing items are used, and the adult starts with small steps (e.g., easy to grab at first). Much of this type of interaction should be in the natural environment and in a play or game format. A variety of additional activities for this level and the upcoming levels can be found in the VB-MAPP VP-MTS Supporting Skills list.

VP-MTS 2-M	Grasps small objects with thumb and index finger (pincer grasp), 5 times.

A child who can successfully grab small items should be given lots of opportunities to play with a variety of manipulatives. Also, a wide variation of items can be used (e.g., small clumps of Play Doh, cotton balls, beans, or small reinforcing toys). The goals are to strengthen eye-hand coordination, strengthen fine motor skills, and establish early play skills.

VP-MTS 3-M	Visually attends to a toy or book for 30 seconds (not a self-stim item).

When a child begins to attend to specific material for a period of time, many perceptual behaviors are occurring. This type of attending can help tacting and listener skills later on and should be reinforced. The focus at this point should be on manipulating objects to achieve a specific outcome (e.g., squeezing a toy to make a noise, trying to put shapes in shape ball).

VP-MTS 4-M	Places 3 items in a container, stacks 3 blocks, or places 3 rings on a peg for 2 of these or similar activities.

A child who reaches this milestone is demonstrating some good visual perceptual skills and should be provided with opportunities to engage in manipulating objects and cause-and-effect activities. These should be conducted in a play format in the child's natural environment, with more complex skills being differentially reinforced. Also, more systematic matching-to-sample activities should begin in the form of in-set puzzles, 3D games and toys, matching characters, and any other reinforcing items that match. The child should be provided with a wide variety of matching opportunities and materials and be differentially reinforced for more advanced forms of matching.

VP-MTS 5-M	Matches any 10 identical items (e.g., inset puzzles, toys, objects, or pictures).

The child is now demonstrating the ability to manipulate and attend to stimuli, match identical objects, and produce cause-and-effect in his world. The focus at this point should be to increase the complexity of the visual activities by (1) increasing the opportunities to match-to-sample, (2) increase the size of the comparison array, (3) play matching games in the natural environment (e.g., placing the spoons in the utensil drawer with the other spoons), and (4) gradually begin to introduce matching non-identical items (e.g., different sizes or colors of dogs). These activities will also advance listener discriminations, and later LRFFC skills, because the ability to carefully scan a comparison array is the same for all three skills, but the easiest way to teach scanning an array is with matching-to-sample.

Suggested IEP Goals for Visual Perceptual Skills and Matching-to-Sample Level 1 (select only 1 or 2 goals and modify them as appropriate for the individual child).

* The child will place items in a container or form ball, stack blocks, or place rings on peg totaling at least 10 different visual motor activities.

* The child will match at least 10 identical objects or pictures to the corresponding object or picture in an array of at least 3 items.

* The child will complete at least 10 different inset puzzles.

* The child will match at least 100 identical objects or pictures in a messy array of at least 10.

* The child will match at least 100 non-identical objects or pictures in a messy array of at least 10.

* The child will sort similar colors and shapes for 10 different colors or shapes.

INDEPENDENT PLAY – LEVEL 1

PLAY 0-M	Zero score

If a child fails to receive any points on the independent play scale, efforts should begin immediately to create interest in objects and actions. Since much of "play" consists of emitting behavior that is automatically reinforcing (Vaughan & Michael, 1982), efforts should be focused on developing this type of natural reinforcement for a child. The intervention procedures should involve pairing and creating MOs to increase the value of items and actions as forms of reinforcement, and differentially reinforcing successive approximations to play behavior. Ultimately, the contrived differential reinforcement needs to be reduced, allowing naturally (automatically) reinforcing play behaviors to develop.

PLAY 1-M	Manipulates and explores objects for 1 minute (e.g., looks at a toy, turns it over, presses buttons).

Once the child begins to show interest in playing with objects, the frequency of this behavior needs to be increased. Toys that make noise, have specific textures, bright colors, unique smells, produce sounds, or movement may be the most interesting for the child. When "play" behavior does occur, adults should reinforce the behavior (using attention, smiles, and praise). Also, efforts should begin to make actions reinforcing by using pairing and creating motivation (e.g., spinning in an office chair). A variety of additional activities for this level and the upcoming levels can be found in the VB-MAPP Play Supporting Skills list.

PLAY 2-M	Shows variation in play by independently interacting with 5 different items (e.g., plays with rings, then a ball, then a block).

A child who scores a 2 on the play assessment is beginning to demonstrate that engaging in particular behaviors can have naturally occurring consequences. The focus at this point should be on increasing the frequency of these behaviors, by providing opportunities to play with fun objects and actions, as well as reinforcement for doing so. In addition, the child should be provided with many opportunities to experience toys that produce specific effects (e.g., pop-up toys, musical books, horns).

PLAY 3-M	Demonstrates generalization by engaging in exploratory movement and playing with the toys in a novel environment for 2 minutes (e.g., in a new playroom).

A child who scores a 3 on the play scale is demonstrating a strong interest in playing with things, and this behavior should automatically maintain itself. Play behaviors are excellent for developing a number of important components of future learning, such as fine motor skills, visual perceptual skills, creative behaviors, new forms of reinforcement, and establishing stimulus control (e.g., a certain pop-up toy must be twisted to operate it, and eventually the toy evokes a specific twisting movement). Again, it is important to provide frequent opportunities for this behavior. The adult should also introduce novel items in order to maintain interest, pair reinforcers with these activities, and provide reinforcement in the form of praise and social attention. Play skills may develop more quickly for some children then skills in the other domains of Level 1. Thus, it is important to make sure that training is provided in a balanced manner for all skills in Level 1.

PLAY 4-M	**Independently engages in movement play for 2 minutes (e.g., swinging, dancing, rocking, jumping, climbing).**

Movement is an important form of play for children. Much of early social play (discussed in the social section of the VB-MAPP) involves movement. A strong interest in independent movement can facilitate social games and opportunities to mand for movement. For example, if a child likes going around on a merry-go-round, it will be easier to play with another child who also likes to go around. At this point, novelty and variation can keep play behavior entertaining (automatically reinforcing). The child should be provided with many opportunities to experience cause-and-effect events such as a jack-in-the-box, air coming out of a balloon, a ball going down a ramp, or sand pouring into a spinning wheel. Also, it is not uncommon for typical children in this developmental age range to play with a toy for only a few seconds or minutes, and then move on to other toys. If something is no longer fun for the child, then it is no longer "play."

PLAY 5-M	**Independently engages in cause-and-effect play for 2 minutes (e.g., dumping containers, playing with pop-up toys, pulling toys, etc.).**

A child who obtains a score of 5 on the independent play scale is well on his way to benefit from the learning opportunities associated with play. The focus on play should now be on increasing the complexity of the play and the amount of time playing with a particular toy, or engaging in a particular activity. Toys that have multiple parts and need to be assembled may become of interest to a child at this point. This type of play can develop important skills such as learning temporal relations and predicting what will happen next.

Suggested IEP Goals for Independent Play Level 1 (select only 1 or 2 goals and modify them as appropriate for the individual child).

- The child will spontaneously engage in cause-and-effect play, such as pushing buttons to makes sounds, stacking and knocking over blocks, pushing things, pulling things, etc., for a total of at least 2 minutes.

- The child will spontaneously demonstrate the use of toys or objects according to their function, such as looking at and turning the pages of a book, holding a telephone to the ear, cradling a doll, brushing hair with a brush, etc., at least 10 times a day.

- The child will spontaneously engage in physical play like riding a tricycle, kicking a ball, pulling a wagon, running, jumping, climbing on play structures, sliding, swinging, etc., 10 times a day.

- The child will spontaneously engage in object play involving a sandbox, bean or rice tray, buckets and shovels, toys, or puzzles for at least 5 minutes.

SOCIAL BEHAVIOR AND SOCIAL PLAY – LEVEL 1

SOCIAL 0-M	Zero score

If a child fails to score any points on the social skills scale, a trained behavior analyst should conduct a functional analysis of the potential causes of the child's behavior. Children are generally quite social, even many children with the diagnosis of autism. However, there could be variables that make interaction with other people aversive, or not reinforcing. Once a cause is identified, intervention can begin. Possible procedures might consist of attempts to make other people conditioned reinforcers by using pairing, increased reinforcement delivery, mand training, capturing and creating MOs, and the reduction of the use of aversive control (Sundberg & Partington, 1998).

SOCIAL 1-M	Makes eye contact as a type of mand 5 times.

It is a good sign that a child makes eye contact to mand (e.g., gain attention). If the sight of familiar people functions as reinforcement for a child, this suggests that people are conditioned reinforcers, which is important because a major component of social behavior involves the fact that a child likes to be close to other people. If people are aversive, any stimuli associated with them can also become aversive, such as their voices or smell. If a child is showing limited interest in other people, increase the systematic use of reinforcement and pairing procedures, and reduce any possible aversive variables that might be affecting the child (e.g., the volume or tone of an adult's voice might be aversive to a child). A variety of additional activities for this level, and the upcoming levels can be found in the VB-MAPP Social Skills Supporting list.

SOCIAL 2-M	Indicates that he wants to be held or physically played with 2 times (e.g., climbs up on his mom's lap).

A child who scores at this level is showing some social interaction, although he may not emit any social verbal behavior, or interact with peers. Goals for a child at this level should include manding for adult social and physical interaction (e.g., "tickle," "up," "peek-a-boo," "spin"), attending to peers, tolerating physical proximity to peers, and imitating peers.

SOCIAL 3-M	Spontaneously makes eye contact with other children 5 times.

Some children will socially interact with adults, but not socially interact with peers (peers might be aversive for a number of possible reasons). If a child makes eye contact with peers, but does not approach or interact with peers, procedures to make peers conditioned reinforcers and not aversive should be implemented. Many of these procedures are the same procedures suggested above for adults (e.g., pairing, mand training, prompting interactions). The goal at this point is not verbal interaction with peers, but more physical proximity (parallel play), and possibly imitative behavior.

SOCIAL 4-M	Spontaneously engages in parallel play near other children for a total of 2 minutes (e.g., sits in the sandbox near other children).

Engaging in parallel play is perhaps one of the most significant milestones for early social development. If a child is spontaneously approaching other children playing by them (e.g., play involving a sandbox, water table, fort, play structure), or playing his own game near other children, the next step is to focus on establishing specific peer interactions and peer stimulus control over the child's behavior. That is, a child emits a behavior because the peer emits a behavior. Three simple forms of stimulus control at this point consist of motor imitation (e.g., pouring sand in a similar fashion of a peer), echoic behavior (e.g., repeating the vocal behavior of a peer), and chasing or following a peer. Procedures for prompting and reinforcing these behaviors should be the focus of the intervention at this point. Once these skills begin to occur, it is important to focus on fading out adult prompts, and adult delivered consequences. The reinforcement for social interaction should ultimately be either automatic reinforcement, or peer-mediated reinforcement.

SOCIAL 5-M	Spontaneously follows peers or imitates their motor behavior 2 times (e.g., follows a peer into a playhouse).

If a child scores a 5 on this measure of social skills, the focus should now be on teaching the child to initiate interactions with peers. Nonverbal interactions are usually easier for children to initiate than verbal interactions. Play, group, and outside activities provide a good opportunity to prompt a child to initiate a nonverbal interaction with a peer (toy exchange, toy operation, handing things to each other, physical play, or roughhousing). Social games (e.g., hide and seek, Ring Around the Rosie) also are good vehicles for teaching children to initiate social interactions. The first types of verbal initiations are usually mands or mand-tact combinations (e.g., "Ice cream truck!"). Procedures to teach these mands involve giving the reinforcers that are valuable to the target child to the peer, and prompting the target child to mand to the peer.

Suggested IEP Goals for Social Behavior and Social Play Level 1 (select only 1 or 2 goals and modify them as appropriate for the individual child).

- The child will spontaneously follow or imitate the motor behavior of a peer at least 10 times per day.

- The child will spontaneously mand to a peer at least 10 times per day.

- The child will spontaneously mand for others to attend to the same stimulus that he is attending to at least 5 times per day.

- The child will emit appropriate listener behavior when a peer is speaking at least 10 times per day.

- The child will spontaneously echo peers at least 10 times per day.

- The child will spontaneously respond to the mands of peers 10 times per day.

MOTOR IMITATION – LEVEL I

IMITATION 0-M	**Zero score**

If a child fails to receive any points on the imitation scale, efforts should begin immediately to teach this skill. The ability to observe and imitate others is the foundation for many skills (e.g., play, social, self-help). The child should be directly taught to imitate others using physical prompts, fading, and reinforcement. Procedures and more detailed intervention strategies for a child who does not imitate can be found in Leaf & McEachin (1998) and Lovaas (2003).

IMITATION 1-M	**Imitates 2 gross motor movements when prompted with, *Do this* (e.g., clapping, raising arms).**

For many children the ability to imitate 2 motor behaviors can be a significant step. If motor imitation is substantially weaker than the other areas, a more intensive effort should be made on teaching the child to imitate the behavior of others using behaviors and activities that the child might enjoy (e.g., jumping, dancing). If the child's scores on the other Level 1 areas are about equal, then imitation training should be conducted on a daily basis along with the other skills. If the child cannot emit any echoic behavior (scores 0 or 1 on the echoic assessment), but can imitate some motor movements, it is possible that the child could benefit from using sign language as a way to develop early mands or tacts (see the teaching procedures for early mand training with sign language in Sundberg & Partington, 1998). A variety of additional activities for this level and the upcoming levels can be found in the VB-MAPP Motor Imitation Supporting Skills list.

IMITATION 2-M	**Imitates 4 gross motor movements when prompted with, *Do this*.**

Early learners may demonstrate strengths in the imitation area faster than other areas due to the availability of physical prompting procedures, and often naturally reinforcing aspects of imitation. For example, playing peek-a-boo may be fun for a child, and the child may begin to cover his own eyes as part imitation, but also possibly as a mand to continue the game. Imitation training with and without objects should be a major focus of the daily intervention program. The focus of the intervention at this point should be on increasing the number of imitative behaviors, generalization to other people and settings, etc., and teaching imitation with objects. A child who scores a 2 on the imitation scale and 0 or 1 on the echoic scale may immediately benefit from mand training with sign language.

IMITATION 3-M	**Imitates 8 motor movements, 2 of which involve objects (e.g., shaking a maraca, tapping sticks together).**

Often, most of the imitative behaviors for a child who scores a 3 on this section of the VB-MAPP are gross motor movements (e.g., clapping, tapping a table, putting his arms up, beating a drum with a drum stick). At this point, these skills should be further strengthened, but gradually more fine motor movements such as wiggling the fingers (as in the sign for "tickle") should be introduced. One of the primary goals of imitation training is to establish a "generalized imitation repertoire." That is, the child should ultimately be able to imitate new behaviors on the first trial. Other primary goals include imitation without prompts, spontaneous imitation, and imitation of peers. Teaching imitation skills can also improve play and social skills, as well as attention and eye contact.

IMITATION 4-M	**Spontaneously imitates the motor behaviors of others on 5 occasions.**

The ability to spontaneously imitate the behaviors of others will be of great value to a child. For example, a child can solve the problem of not knowing what to do by following others (e.g., what door to go into, how to use a particular toy). A child who scores at this level is beginning to demonstrate the basic foundations of an imitative repertoire. If this skill is balanced with the other skills on Level 1, it should continue to be a daily focus of the intervention. If the skill is well below the other areas, then more intensive training should be provided. If the skill is stronger than the others (this is more common), it should be used to help teach other skills. For example, using imitation to develop mands and tacts through sign language. It is also possible that motor imitation training can facilitate echoic development by teaching the child to specifically control and emit motor sequences of behavior.

IMITATION 5-M	**Imitates 20 motor movements of any type (e.g., fine motor, gross motor, imitation with objects).**

A child who scores at this level is probably beginning to show the early signs of a "generalized imitative repertoire." If this score is equal to the others, then moving on to functional forms of imitation (e.g., toy play, self-help, social play), two-component imitations (e.g., clapping and jumping) and two-step imitative behavior chains (e.g., getting a tissue, and then wiping his nose) would be appropriate. Also, reinforcement should be provided for spontaneous and peer imitation. Some children may enter an intervention program with a score of 5 on imitation, and a score of 0-1 on the echoic, mand, and tact sections of the VB-MAPP Level 1. These children are excellent candidates for a sign language program.

Suggested IEP Goals for Motor Imitation Level 1 (select only 1 or 2 goals and modify them as appropriate for the individual child).

- The child will imitate at least 8 motor movements, plus 6 actions involving objects, on command.

- The child will imitate 25 or more motor movements of any type, on command.

- The child will imitate 25 two-step chains of motor behavior.

- The child will imitate at least 25 two-component functional actions.

- The child will spontaneously imitate adults or peers 10 times in one day.

ECHOIC (EESA) SUBTEST – LEVEL 1

ECHOIC 0-M	Zero score

If a child fails to emit a single echoic response during testing, efforts should begin immediately on developing this important skill. An intervention strategy for a child who does not echo can be found in Sundberg and Partington (1998). A major component of this intervention strategy involves pairing procedures, mand training, and the use of augmentative communication, as well as a variety of other techniques (Drash, High, & Tutor, 1999; Sundberg, Michael, Partington, & Sundberg, 1996; Yoon & Bennett, 2000).

ECHOIC 1-M	Scores at least 2 on the EESA subtest.

The ability to echoically emit even 2 sounds during testing can be of great benefit to a child who scores 0 on the mand and tact scales. These echoic behaviors can often be transferred to mand conditions by using strong motivators, reinforcers, and the transfer of control procedures described in Sundberg and Partington (1998). For a child at this level echoic training should be a major part of the daily intervention, and should make use of the many different ways to strengthen echoic skills.

ECHOIC 2-M	Scores at least 5 on the EESA subtest.

If a child scores a 2 on the echoic subtest, he is beginning to demonstrate control of his vocal musculature. A major focus of the intervention program should be on increasing the number of different echoic responses and the daily frequency of emitting echoic behavior. As previously mentioned, any echoic response can be used to develop a mand. This transfer to motivation and echoic control can have dramatic effects for some children. It is recommended that speech as a response form be attempted for a child who has only a few echoics, before considering augmentative communication.

ECHOIC 3-M	Scores at least 10 on the EESA subtest.

If the child obtains a score of 3 on the echoic section and this score is in balance with the others scores on the VB-MAPP Level 1, then echoic training should be a regular part of the daily intervention program. If the score of 3 is substantially lower than the other scores, then more extensive intervention would be warranted. If this score is higher than the scores on mands and tacts, then an intensive focus on using the child's existing echoic skills to teach mands and tacts would be beneficial, along with continued echoic training.

ECHOIC 4-M	Scores at least 15 on the EESA subtest.

A score of 4 on the EESA suggests that the child has an early foundation for echoic development, as well as the potential for transferring echoics to mands and tacts. Also, echoic behavior can also be used to increase spontaneous vocalizations and provide opportunities to shape better articulation. However, a more thorough speech evaluation by a speech pathologist should provide some specific direction for a child's echoic and articulation skills at this point.

ECHOIC 5-M	Scores at least 25 on the EESA subtest (at least 20 from group 1).

A score of 5 on the EESA demonstrates a strong echoic repertoire for an early learner. This score should be approximately balanced with the child's other scores, that is, most scores should be at the top of Level 1 or beginning to break into Level 2. If this is the case, then training should continue in an equally balanced manner. If a child scores higher on the echoic assessment than on the mand and tact assessment, then an increase in the frequency of mand and tact training is warranted (but don't slow down echoic training). If the score of 5 on the echoic scale is lower than the other scores, then an increased effort to improve echoic behavior is warranted.

Suggested IEP Goals for Echoic Level 1 (select only 1 goal and modify it as appropriate for the individual child).

- The child will echo at least 5 vowels, diphthongs, or consonants on command.

- The child will echo at least 10 vowels, diphthongs, or consonants on command.

- The child will echo at least 25 vowel-consonant combinations on command.

- The child will echo at least 50 vowel-consonant combinations of 2 syllables or more, or full words on command.

SPONTANEOUS VOCAL BEHAVIOR – LEVEL 1

VOCAL 0-M	Zero score

A typically developing child may vocalize thousands of times a day without adult prompting. This vocal play has a significant effect on strengthening vocal muscles and allows for the ultimate development of echoic behavior. If a child does not emit any, or very few speech sounds during the day, efforts should begin immediately to increase the frequency of vocal output. The goal is to strengthen the child's vocal muscles in order to increase the probability of achieving echoic control over vocal behavior. An intervention strategy for a child who does not emit much vocal behavior should consist of a multi-pronged approach involving a variety of procedures that may increase vocal behavior. Some of the possible procedures that may increase a child's vocal output are (1) pairing, (2) use of a mand frame with vocal behavior, (3) standard echoic trials, (4), direct reinforcement of any vocalization, (5) use of augmentative communication, (6) motor imitation training, and (7) echoic trials in the context of objects and actions.

VOCAL 1-M	Spontaneously emits an average of 5 sounds each hour.

A child who is making a few sounds per hour can benefit from the above procedures as well. In addition to increasing the frequency of sounds, the adults should also focus on increasing the variations of the sounds produced, as well as the same sound with varied intonation, pitch, volume, and prosody. The focus at this point is to make vocalizing fun for the child and automatically reinforcing. The pairing and manding procedures can help to establish automatic consequences for babbling (i.e., the child likes to hear his voice). Achieving this effect for vocal play is significant because the behavior can be maintained without adult mediated consequences, much in the same way that infant babbling is maintained. This effect can self-strengthen the vocal muscles and increase the chances of obtaining echoic control over vocal behavior, which is a significant milestone in language development.

VOCAL 2-M	Spontaneously emits 5 different sounds, averaging 10 total sounds each hour.

A child who scores at this level may also have some echoic behavior, and continued efforts to increase vocal output are important. The adults may adjust their reinforcement schedule at this point to focus more on the production of novel sounds and blends, varied intonations, and so on.

VOCAL 3-M	Spontaneously emits 10 different sounds with varying intonations, averaging 25 total sounds each hour.

At this point vocal production may not be that much of an issue for a child. The adults should continue to focus on providing differential reinforcement for novelty, but now adults should reinforce attempts to produce blended sounds and approximations to whole words. Adults may not understand these "words," but they should be acknowledged and reinforced.

VOCAL 4-M	Spontaneously emits 5 different whole word approximations.

If the child is babbling frequently and beginning to emit whole words, a formal intervention program on vocal output will probably not be necessary. Most likely the automatic consequence of vocal output are having the desired effect. The focus regarding vocal output should shift to bringing these sounds under echoic, mand, and tact control, and improving articulation.

VOCAL 5-M	Spontaneously vocalizes 15 whole words or phrases with appropriate intonation and rhythm.

If the child is babbling more frequently, and beginning to emit phrases and more varied whole words with varied intonation, this is usually the last step before babbling "naturally" transfers to mands and tacts.

Suggested IEP Goals for Spontaneous Vocal Behavior Level 1 (select only 1 goal and modify it as appropriate for the individual child).

- The child will spontaneously emit at least 10 different sounds, averaging at least 30 total sounds each hour.

- The child will spontaneously demonstrate varied intonation, volume, and prosody with the same sounds at least 5 times in a day.

- The child will spontaneously vocalize word approximations that include mulitsyllabic utterances on at least 10 occasions in a day.

CHAPTER 9

Interpreting the Level 2 Assessment: Curriculum Placement and Writing IEP Goals

A child whose scores are entering Level 2 of the VB-MAPP is still an early learner, but is beginning to show some solid learning and language skills. The focus of the intervention program at this point should be on systematically expanding those skills in a variety of ways. The following general targets should form the core of the language intervention program: (1) expanding the size and scope of the mand, tact, and listener repertoires (by teaching more nouns, verbs, adjectives, etc.), (2) developing two- and three-component verbal and nonverbal antecedents and responses (i.e., sentences), (3) beginning LRFFC training, (4) beginning intraverbal training, (5) developing social and verbal interactions with peers, (6) developing group and classrooms skills, and (7) learning in less restrictive settings (e.g., natural environment, group settings, play, arts and crafts).

There are, of course, several other skills and areas that should comprise a total program (e.g., fine motor, gross motor, independence, self-help, toileting, and the reduction of any language and learning barriers), but more advanced language and social skills will be dependent on the core skills identified in Level 2 of the VB-MAPP. The teaching style should still primarily consist of an intensive teaching format with careful use of basic behavioral procedures. However, elements of less structured teaching and natural environment training (NET) should be gradually increased.

The specific aspects of a child's IEP and intervention program will depend on an analysis of all the child's VB-MAPP Milestones and Barriers scores. The assessor should analyze the scores in each of the domains and their relation to the child's performance in other domains. Are the mand, tact, and LD scores fairly close to each other (balanced), or is one significantly higher than another? The assessor should identify the strengths and weaknesses of the skills, and determine if there are particular strengths in one area that can be of special benefit to a child, or weaknesses that need to be a larger part of the intervention program. For example, a child may have a strong tact repertoire, but a limited mand repertoire. The tacts can be used to develop and balance out the mand repertoire. A sample VB-MAPP for a child scoring primarily in Level 2 is presented in Figure 9-1. This sample shows a common profile for many young children with autism or other intellectual disabilities. Christy is a 4-year-old girl who is showing beginning mand, tact, and listener repertoires along with elevated echoic, imitation, and matching skills. Her LRFFC and intraverbal skills are emerging, but her play and social skills are relatively weak.

At 4 years of age, Christy's language skills are significantly below her typically developing peers. She is in need of an intensive intervention program that focuses on the seven areas identified in the first paragraph of this chapter. In addition, an analysis of any existing learning and language barriers will be of value in designing a specific intervention program. Table 9-1 contains a list of possible IEP goals for a child whose VB-MAPP Milestones profile looks similar to Christy's. The skills identified in the VB-MAPP Supporting Skills list may provide additional suggestions for targets that may be of value in designing a daily intervention program for Christy (but not necessarily used as IEP goals).

Figure 9-1

Sample VB-MAPP Milestones Assessment for a child scoring in Level 2.

VB-MAPP Milestones Master Scoring Form

Key:	Score	Date	Color	Tester
1ST TEST:	53	7/01/08		MS
2ND TEST:				
3RD TEST:				
4TH TEST:				

Child's name:	Christy
Date of birth:	6/08/04
Age at testing:	**1** 4 yrs. **2** **3** **4**

LEVEL 3

LEVEL 2

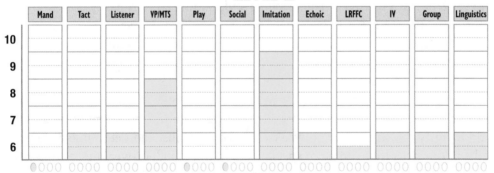

LEVEL 1

Table 9-1

Sample IEP goals for a child whose scores fall primarily in early Level 2.

1. Christy will mand for 50 different missing items with only verbal prompts (e.g., "What do you need?").

2. Christy will spontaneously mand for other individuals to emit 10 different specific actions in a play setting, game, or other natural environment setting.

3. Christy will tact and LD 250 different items.

4. Christy will tact and LD 25 different actions.

5. Christy will tact and LD 200 two-component noun-verb (or verb-noun) combinations.

6. Christy will select or point to 10 different colors or shapes in an array that contains 5 different colors or shapes.

7. Christy will match 200 non-identical objects or pictures in an array that contains 10 items, with 3 similar items in the array.

8. Christy will select the correct item from a messy array that contains 10 items, given 200 different fill-in or WH questions involving the function, features, or class of items (LRFFC).

9. Christy will be able to correctly answer 200 different fill-in and WH questions involving nouns and verbs (intraverbal).

10. Christy will respond to mands from peers 10 times per day.

11. Christy will independently construct, assemble, or set up toys, or other play items that come with several different parts (even combining different sets), and engage in independent play with these items for 5 minutes.

12. Christy will spontaneously engage in physical play, such as riding a bike, kicking a ball, pulling a wagon, running, jumping, climbing on play structures, sliding, swinging, etc., for a 10-minute period.

13. Christy will attend to peers or teachers in a group setting for 50% of the intervals sampled in a 10-minute group period.

Special Considerations for a Child Whose Scores Fall Primarily in Level 2

The VB-MAPP Milestone scores along with the Placement Program and IEP Goals presented in this chapter can help to identify specific curriculum needs for an individual child. However, since every child is unique it is important to also consider several other variables, such as the child's learning barriers, history of learning (e.g., rate of acquisition of new skills), educational setting, family support, and available resources. It is also important to ensure that a qualified professional who is knowledgeable in behavior analysis and Skinner's analysis of verbal behavior regularly monitors the program. As language becomes more complex, there are many potential pitfalls that can be avoided by using the conceptual tools provided by behavior analysis. For example, many children with autism or other developmental disabilities are susceptible to rote learning; however, a poorly sequenced curriculum is often responsible for this problem, such as the common practice of teaching adjectives, pronouns, prepositions, or intraverbal skills too early in an intervention program. If a child does not have the basic supporting verbal skills for these more advanced components of verbal behavior, the probability of rote responding is high.

An intervention program for a child scoring in Level 2 is much more complicated than a Level 1 program in several ways. For example, in Level 1 the primary goals are straightforward. The child must learn the basic mand, tact, LD, imitative, echoic, and matching repertoires, as well as some beginning play and social skills. The teaching procedures are relatively clear, and supported by an abundant body of basic and applied research (e.g., Brady, Saunders, & Spradlin, 1994; Sautter & LeBlanc, 2006). Many children move rapidly through Level 1 targets, but often stagnate and fail to move past the milestones of Level 2. This learning plateau is common for many children, as demonstrated by the sizeable number of children who fail to acquire a functional intraverbal repertoire, advanced manding, or meaningful social behavior.

The move beyond nouns and verbs and basic mands and tacts quickly becomes complicated (e.g., noun-verb combinations, LRFFC, intraverbals, and verbal and nonverbal social interaction). Staff must be able to implement several advanced procedures such as taking known tacts and LDs and moving them to LRFFC and intraverbal frames, contriving and capturing motivation in order to move manding beyond consumable and tangible reinforcers, and arranging for teaching situations where a child must attend to more than one target stimulus and emit more than one response (e.g., sentences). In addition, teaching needs to include procedures for generalization, spontaneity, transfer between the verbal operants, social and verbal interaction with peers, and the use of newly acquired skills in a functional and meaningful way in the child's day-to-day natural environment. There are often several paths to the same goal, but many more potential barriers, pitfalls, and linguistic traps that must be removed or, better yet, avoided. The placement suggestions for each milestone and the general IEP goals are designed to provide a curriculum progression (a "road map") that can help guide the program designer through the challenges she may face in the journey toward establishing an effective verbal and social repertoire for a child.

Intensity of Intervention and Teaching Format

A child whose scores fall in Level 2 is still in need of an intensive and carefully designed language and social skills intervention program. The number of formal teaching hours should be similar to that recommended for Level 1 children (i.e., 25 hours a week of a school program, with follow-up and generalization provided by the parents and others throughout the child's days, evenings, weekends, and vacations). Language and social skills intervention is still 24/7, and teaching should be provided by all the individuals who interact with the child, especially family members. The number of hours is neither as important as what is accomplished during those hours, nor as important as having the most accurate analysis of the individual child's needs.

Discrete Trial Training (DTT) and Natural Environment Training (NET)

A Level 2 child will still benefit from an intensive and formal teaching arrangement, but there should be an increased focus on generalization and the functional use of the acquired skills in the natural (non-tabletop) environment. It remains important to seek a balance between DTT and NET training, since both provide unique contributions to learning, and both play a critical role in language and social development. There are many natural environment teaching opportunities and activities that can be of greater value to a child scoring in Level 2, such as arts and crafts, facilitated play, community outings, social games, and other common preschool and elementary school activities. However, teaching in these settings requires skillful teachers who understand what the linguistic and behavioral goals are for the child, and how to achieve them in this looser teaching format.

Integration and Socialization

From the very beginning of an intervention program, there should be a focus on integration and social interaction with peers. However, this focus should become a bigger part of the intervention program as the child begins to acquire more advanced verbal and behavioral skills. Social behavior is complicated, and the reader is referred to the relevant VB-MAPP Milestones, the Placement Program, and the Supporting Skills list for curriculum guidelines and teaching activities. In addition, there are many excellent resources available for determining appropriate integration levels, and for teaching social and play skills to children with autism or other developmental disabilities (e.g., Attwood, 1998; Baker, 2003; Bellini, 2006; Krempa & McKinnon, 2005; Leaf & McEachin, 1999; Leaf, Taubman, & McEachin, 2008; Taubaum, Leaf, & McEachin, 2011; Taylor & Jasper, 2001; Weiss & Harris, 2001; Wolfberg, 1999).

Summary

Language skills grow very rapidly for typically developing children between the ages of 2 and 3, and it is common for many children with autism or other intellectual disabilities to miss out on this "language explosion." The VB-MAPP is designed to guide professionals and parents through these different phases of language and social development (e.g., basic skills, mands for information, intraverbal skills, multiple responses, spontaneity, social behavior). It is important to be consistent with typical language and social development as much as possible, and to maintain the view that advanced skills are based on a solid foundation of prerequisite skills. The temptation to move too quickly through an intervention program, or neglect a careful analysis of the appropriate sources of control for verbal behaviors, can produce unwanted barriers and learning problems that must eventually be addressed in order to move the child into Level 3 language and social skills.

Interpreting the Scores for the Level 2 Milestones and Suggested IEP Goals

The analysis of a child's performance on each milestone, and its relation to his scores on other parts of the VB-MAPP assessment, can provide specific direction for the intervention program. For example, if a child has a strong tact repertoire, but weak listener skills, then a more intensive effort on listener skills would be warranted. Or, if there are several barriers affecting mand development, then those barriers need to be reduced or removed before progressing much further with tacts and LDs. The following section contains general placement suggestions for children who score at each milestone. All the Level 2 Milestones are presented, along with various considerations as to how specific scores on one skill area may be related to the scores on other areas, and the scores on the Barriers Assessment. A list of possible IEP goals will be presented after each skill area. These goals are only generic suggestions. The actual objectives used for an individual child should be tailored specifically for that child, and based on the recommendations of the child's IEP team.

MAND – LEVEL 2

MAND 6-M	Mands for 20 different missing items without prompts (except, e.g., *What do you need?*) (e.g., mands for paper when given a crayon).

If a child scores at this level, then he is demonstrating the valuable ability to mand for items that are not present. This represents a significant milestone for a developing mand repertoire. These skills should be expanded on, and generalized to different people and materials, while being worked into as many natural environment settings as possible. In addition, spontaneous responses that occur without a verbal prompt such as, "What do you need?" should be differentially reinforced. The next step should involve teaching the child to mand for actions. Some children may already mand for some actions if the MO is strong (e.g., "push" while on a swing). Training should now include adult actions needed to complete a specific chain of behavior (similar to manding for objects). For example, if a child is making an art project and can't get the glue to come out, he should hand the glue to the adult and mand "squeeze," or "help." It is important to note that the mand is totally dependent on the existence of an MO for a particular item or activity.

Teachers and parents need to be able to identify if and when a child's MO for something is strong in order to conduct mand training (see Carbone, 2013; Hall & Sundberg, 1987; Sundberg, 1993a, 2004, 2013 for more detail on capturing and contriving motivation). MOs can vary greatly in strength, and occur in all environments, especially a child's natural environment (as opposed to a formal teaching session); thus mand training is 24/7, and all those involved with the child need to be "on the same page." It is not uncommon to see a mand repertoire lag behind tact and LD repertoires for children with autism or other intellectual disabilities. There are a number of causes of this, but often it is due to the complexities of capturing and contriving MOs, and the fact that presenting discrete S^Ds is easier to do in structured teaching. Mand training needs to be conducted in all environments, and when the MO is at strength. Additional activities for teaching mands that would be appropriate for a child scoring at this level can be found in the corresponding sections of VB-MAPP Mand Supporting Skills list.

MAND 7-M	**Mands for others to emit 5 different actions needed to enjoy a desired activity (e.g., *open* to get outside, *push* when on a swing).**

A child who is learning to mand for nouns and verbs should be encouraged to do so frequently and spontaneously. Typically, the natural consequences will take over (the specific reinforcement inherent in the mand) and little should be necessary to maintain this skill. The focus should now be on increasing the size of the mand repertoire by capturing and creating new motivating opportunities. The natural environment and typical play and social activities are excellent for teaching new mands. In fact, it may be very difficult and forced to teach this type of manding in formal discrete training arrangements. In addition, mands that contain both a noun and a verb or other parts of speech should be prompted (or required) and reinforced (e.g., "push me," "more juice," "light on").

MAND 8-M	**Emits 5 different mands that contain 2 or more words (not including *I want*) (e.g., *Go fast. My turn. Pour juice.*).**

Around two years of age most typically developing children emit mands containing two (or more) words. At this point in a language intervention program the focus should be on generalization, spontaneity, and increasing the variation and frequency of manding. Beginning mands for information such as, "What's that?" and, "Where's mommy?" should also be introduced, as well as mands for other parts of speech such as pronouns (e.g., "my shoes"), adjectives (e.g., "big cookie"), and adverbs (e.g., "go fast"). Other mand activities can include mands to remove aversives (e.g., "stop it") and mands involving "yes" and "no." Mands that contain gestures should also be reinforced, such as the child holding his palms up and open when manding for information (e.g., "Where's mommy?"), or emitting an outstretched arm along with "Stop!" Mands are dependent on a child's existing MO. If there is no MO currently at strength for a particular item, activity, or piece of information, mand training cannot be correctly conducted and the probability of developing an impaired mand becomes high.

MAND 9-M	**Spontaneously emits 15 different mands (e.g., *Let's play. Open. I want book.*).**

There are many components of an effective mand repertoire. A child who reaches the current milestone in mand development should be demonstrating (1) prompt-free manding, (2) a large variety of different mands, (3) a high frequency of daily manding, (4) a generalized mand repertoire (including stimulus, response, and MO generalization), (5) mands that contain 2 or more words, (6) mands for missing items, (7) mands for reinforcers other than consumables and manipulatives (e.g., verbs, adjectives, information), (8) persistence in manding (resistant to extinction), and (9) manding to peers. All of these skills should continue to be developed in a natural and functional way, with a focus on developing new mands by providing the child with a variety of new motivational items, activities and opportunities. Also, it is important to begin to teach mands for information, to "politely" remove aversives, and to foster mands that are acquired without direct training.

MAND 10-M	**Emits 10 new mands without specific mand training (e.g., spontaneously says *Where kitty go?* without formal mand training).**

Adults rarely need to formally teach typically developing children to mand. Sometimes intervention is more about reducing the frequency of manding, or emitting more "polite" mands. The goal for a child with autism or other language delays is to establish a basic mand repertoire that will functionally allow the child to control the behavior of others with verbal behavior. The specific reinforcement of the mand will do that, and once it does, the mand can often develop further without intensive intervention. Also, as previously mentioned, the natural environment becomes the best teaching arrangement for further mand development. The primary focus at this point should be on manding for verbal information. This type of manding often presents problems for some children with autism because they are not strongly reinforced by verbal information. If that is the case, then procedures to contrive information as valuable reinforcers may be necessary (e.g., Endicott & Higbee, 2007; Lechago, Carr, Grow, Love, & Almason, 2010; Sundberg, Loeb, Hale, & Eigenheer, 2002). Additional mand training activities can include the differential reinforcement of novel mands, mands containing different parts of speech, and mands that contain three or more words.

Suggested IEP Goals for Mand: Level 2 (select only 1 or 2 goals and modify them as appropriate for the individual child).

- The child will spontaneously mand in a natural environment setting for at least 25 different items.

- The child will spontaneously mand for other individuals to emit at least 3 different specific actions in a play setting, game, or the natural environment an average of 5 times a day.

- The child will spontaneously mand at least 50 times per day with at least 3 words in a sentence.

- The child will spontaneously mand for information at least 25 times a day with at least 3 different WH questions or question words (e.g., "what," where," "who," "when," "can," "do," "is").

- The child will spontaneously mand at least 25 times a day with at least 8 different adjectives or prepositions (at least two of each) with an average of 3 words per sentence.

- The child will spontaneously mand at least 25 times a day with at least 8 different pronouns or adverbs.

TACT – LEVEL 2

TACT 6-M	Tacts 25 items when asked, *What's that?* (e.g., *book, shoe, car, dog, hat*).

A score at this level demonstrates that the child has acquired the basic ability to tact nouns. The focus should now be on increasing and strengthening this repertoire in a variety of ways. Perhaps most important is vigilant generalization to new people, items, contexts, etc. For example, a child who can tact "dog," should be provided with opportunities to tact the many different types of dogs, so that the response doesn't accidentally come under the control of an irrelevant feature of a dog such as its color or its tail.

The size of the tact repertoire should also be the target of the intervention program. Typically, tact training for nouns can be conducted most efficiently in an intensive teaching format. Training in the natural environment is also valuable, but at this early tact level, tabletop training can allow for more careful use of correction procedures, prompting, fading, differential reinforcement, interspersal techniques ("mixed VB"), and other aspects of behavioral teaching procedures. It is also important to include training trials on LD types of tasks as well. In most cases with nouns, it is best to teach both the tact and LD skills simultaneously (Petursdottir & Carr, 2011; Sundberg & Partington, 1998). In addition, training on tacting verbs should be included in the daily intervention program. Adults should avoid the temptation to formally teach tacts for other parts of speech such as adjectives, pronouns, prepositions, adverbs, etc. The majority of a typical child's verbal behavior at this level consists of nouns and verbs, and lots of mands (as well as echoic and imitative behaviors). Additional activities that would be appropriate for a child scoring at this level can be found in the corresponding sections of the VB-MAPP Tact Supporting Skills list.

TACT 7-M	Generalizes tacts across 3 examples of 50 items, tested or from a list of known generalizations (e.g., tacts 3 different cars).

Typically, by this stage in language development, a child should be able to acquire a new tact every couple of days. New items to tact can come from contact with stimuli in the home or community, books, videos, preschool and classroom settings, novel stimuli, and other age appropriate material. Use these opportunities to conduct tact trials, but be careful not to overdo tact training, or make it too drill like. Make it fun and seem as little as possible like a formal discrete trial or a drill. There should be an increased focus on tacts of nouns and verbs, and other responses involving more than one word (e.g., responses that contain carrier phrases like "there's a...").

TACT 8-M	Tacts 10 actions when asked, for example, *What am I doing?* (e.g., *jumping, sleeping, eating*).

The ability to tact different types of movement is a significant milestone for all children. The focus at this point (as with nouns) is to expand and strengthen the repertoire with new verbs and more extensive opportunities to generalize known verbs. This type of training can perhaps best be conducted in the natural environment, since there is a greater potential for a wider variety of movement than would be possible at a tabletop setting. Additional tacting activities might consist of tacts of auditory stimuli; tacts involving the other sensory stimuli; tacts from books, scenes, and the natural environment; and tacts of body parts, people, and other common stimuli. Spontaneous tacting of any type should also be reinforced, as well as any tact that contains two or more words. A beginning focus on multiple noun tacting (e.g., "dog and cat"), and verb-noun (and noun-verb) tacting (e.g., "spinning top," "mom cooking") would also be appropriate.

TACT 9-M	Tacts 50 two-component verb-noun or noun-verb combinations tested or from a list of known two-component tacts (e.g., *washing face, Joe swinging, baby sleeping*).

A child who can tact nouns and verbs as one response (forming longer sentences) is ready to begin more formal training on adjectives, pronouns, and other modifiers (depending on the child's general learning and retention pattern). As previously suggested, it is generally best to teach LD responses at the same time that tacts are taught. Thus, it is important to ensure that the child is able to emit correct noun-verb, adjective, and pronoun LD responses as well (however, as language becomes more complex there are many skills where LDs are easier to acquire than tacts, such as the pronouns "your" and "my"). These same responses should also occur, if appropriate, as a mand. Spontaneous tacts, and any tacts (including generalized tacts) that occur without direct training, should be reinforced.

TACT 10-M	Tacts a total of 200 nouns and/or verbs (or other parts of speech) tested or from an accumulated list of known tacts.

Once the tact repertoire reaches this size, it is important to make sure that it is in balance with the other verbal skills (actually, this should be checked all along the way). It is not uncommon to see children who can tact hundreds of items, actions, and properties, but have weak or absent mand and intraverbal repertoires. As far as further development of the tact repertoire, there should be a continued focus on increasing the vocabulary size, promoting generalization, fluency, and the functional use of the skills in natural environment. Additional tacting activities can consist of beginning to tact the function of items (e.g., "things you draw with," "eat with," "jump on"), tacts of classes (e.g., "animals," "clothing," "toys"), and tacts of specific features of items (e.g., "wings," "wheels," "tails"). Tacting locations and tacts involving "yes" and "no" would also be appropriate at this time.

Suggested IEP Goals for Tact: Level 2 (select only 1 or 2 goals and modify them as appropriate for the individual child).

- The child will tact at least 50 two-component noun-verb (or verb-noun) combinations.

- The child will spontaneously tact items an average of 5 times per hour.

- The child will tact a total of at least 150 nouns and/or verbs (or other parts of speech).

- The child will tact at least 5 different colors and 5 different shapes.

- The child will tact 20 different adjectives.

- The child will tact 6 different prepositions.

- The child will tact at least 50 three-component nonverbal combinations (e.g., adjective-noun-verb, subject-verb-noun, etc.).

LISTENER RESPONDING – LEVEL 2

LISTENER 6-M	Selects the correct item from a messy array of 6, for 40 different objects or pictures (e.g., *Find cat. Touch ball.*).

A score at this level demonstrates that the child has acquired the ability to discriminate among specific items when asked to do so. The focus now should be on increasing and strengthening this repertoire in a variety of ways. In addition to increasing the number of items that a child can identify, there should be a significant focus on generalization and making these listener skills functional for the child. Listener discriminations (LDs) should occur in a variety of contexts, with different adults, and with different materials. It is important to move into natural environment settings as soon as possible. Make LDs fun by incorporating them into age-appropriate games and activities, arts and crafts, and other naturally occurring events in a child's day. Try not to make them look like a structured discrete trial (even though they still are discrete trials). For example, when making cookies in the kitchen the adult should ask the child to hand her a spoon from an array of other utensils on the counter. The array should also become more complex by using more stimuli, scenes, the natural environment, and stimuli that look similar by color, class, shapes, etc. Additional listener skills can be found in the VB-MAPP Listener Supporting Skills list.

LISTENER 7-M	**Generalizes listener discriminations (LDs) in a messy array of 8, for 3 different examples of 50 items (e.g., the child can find 3 examples of a train).**

At this point the focus should be on expanding the size of the LD repertoire along with a greater focus on two-component stimuli and responses, especially those involving nouns and verbs. The goal is to move away from single S^{D}s and single responses as soon as possible, because most verbal behavior involves multiple stimuli and multiple responses. However, single stimuli presentations may still be required for new discriminations. In addition, a continued focus on LDs in the child's natural environment is usually quite beneficial, as well as in other age-appropriate activities such as games, stories, art and crafts, music, and playground activities. More verbs should be incorporated into the LD training program as the child progresses. The easiest way to establish an understanding of verbs as a listener is for the child to perform simple motor actions on command.

LISTENER 8-M	**Performs 10 specific motor actions on command (e. g., *Show me clapping. Can you hop?*).**

A child's ability to engage in specific motor actions given just verbal instructions is a significant developmental milestone. Once a child can emit these specified actions, the focus shuold be on expanding and strengthening the repertoire by generalizing the skills, increasing the number of skills, identifying the actions of others, increasing the complexity of the actions, and moving the skills to naturally occurring events in the child's day-to-day life. For example, during a facilitated play session, ask the child to "rock the doll" in the cradle. Avoid the temptation to teach verbs using pictures. Successful LDs of verbs involves teaching a child to discriminate among moving stimuli (verbs), not static stimuli (nouns). For example, while on a playground ask the child, "Which girl is jumping?" Pictures are always static, but they can be used later as a form of generalization, but in early training it is often the case that an impaired LD verb repertoire is being established with this procedure. At this point it is also important to begin to increase the verbal instruction to a two-component verbal stimulus and a two-component nonverbal response. Usually, the simplest form of this task is to teach the child to select two target items (noun-noun) on command (e.g., "Give me shoe and book"). The next step is usually to teach the child to perform a specified action with a specified object (verb-noun) on command (e.g., "Show me the monkey jumping").

LISTENER 9-M	**Follows 50 two-component noun-verb and/or verb-noun instructions (e.g., *Show me the baby sleeping. Push the swing.*).**

At this point the intervention program can begin to focus more on other parts of speech, such as adjectives involving colors (e.g., red, blue, yellow) and shapes (e.g., circle, square, heart). Also, once verbs and nouns are firmly established in two-component tasks (there eventually should be hundreds of these), the other parts of speech can be used in two- and three-component tasks. Again, teaching and generalizing in the natural environment is a significant part of listener training. Often, a formal discrete trial training environment contains aversive variables, such as being cornered at a table, that might not be present in the natural environment, and generalization may not occur without the elimination of these additional variables.

LISTENER 10-M	Selects the correct item in a book, picture scene, or natural environment when named, for 250 items (tested or from an accumulated list of known words).

Once the LD repertoire reaches this size, as with the tact, it is important to make sure that it is in balance with the other verbal skills. Mand, tact, intraverbal, and LRFFC skills should also be close to a score of 10 on those respective sections of the VB-MAPP. If not, the focus should shift somewhat to strengthen the other skills. As far as further development of the listener repertoire, there should be a continued focus on increasing the vocabulary size, teaching the other parts of speech (i.e., adjectives, pronouns, prepositions), and promoting generalization, fluency, and the functional use of the skills in the natural environment. Additional listener activities can consist of beginning to discriminate among the function of items (e.g., "cut with," "climb on") classes of items (e.g., animals, clothes, toys), and specific features of items (e.g., tails, legs, wheels).

Suggested IEP Goals for Listener Responding: Level 2 (select only 1 or 2 goals and modify them as appropriate for the individual child).

- The child will perform at least 20 specific actions on command.
- The child will LD 25 different actions in the natural environment.
- The child will emit at least 100 two-component noun-verb (or verb-noun) responses on command.
- The child will go to 10 different natural settings and retrieve or point to at least 5 different items from each setting (50 total tasks).
- The child will select or point to 10 different colors or shapes from a large array containing similar items.
- The child will select or point to 20 different adjectives from a large array containing similar items.
- The child will select or point to 6 different prepositions from a large array containing similar comparisons.
- The child will select or point to at least 50 three-component nonverbal combinations (e.g., adjective-noun-verb, subject-verb-noun, etc.).
- The child will select or point to at least 250 items in a book, picture scene, or natural environment.

LEVEL 2

VISUAL PERCEPTUAL SKILLS AND MATCHING-TO-SAMPLE (VP-MTS) – LEVEL 2

VP-MTS 6-M	Matches identical objects or pictures in a messy array of 6, for 25 items.

Many important intellectual and linguistic skills can be established through matching-to-sample training. One of those skills is the ability to look carefully for items in a visual field. Initially, this visual field might consist of a few pictures or objects on a table, but eventually the target visual field is the natural environment or representations of that environment in videos, picture scenes, or books. The simplest way to develop visual scanning skills is when the child has a visual sample to match with the target item in the natural array. Eventually, the sample stimulus will not be there and the child might be asked to find the same target item in the same natural array, but under the control of a verbal (i.e., LDs and LRFFCs) rather than a visual stimulus. Thus, not only can matching-to-sample teach a child that things go together and how to sort and categorize things, but how to look for and find things when they are not right in front of the child.

A child who meets the current milestone is demonstrating the ability to visually associate physical items in his environment. This is an important skill that will be of value to the child in many ways as he develops. The focus now should be on increasing the number of items matched and increasing the array size and complexity. One important goal of VP-MTS training is to teach a child to scan, or look carefully at the physical (nonverbal) world. One way to do this is to begin to use arrays that contain similar stimuli (e.g., matching a spoon to a spoon in an array that also contains a knife and a fork). Also, training should begin to include matching non-identical items such as different colors and types of socks, cars, and shoes. Additional VP-MTS skills for all the following levels can be found in the VB-MAPP VP-MTS Supporting Skills list.

VP-MTS 7-M	Matches similar colors and shapes for 10 different colors or shapes given models (e.g., given red, blue, and green bowls and a pile of red, blue, and green bears the child matches the items by color).

Matching colors and shapes is often one of the first ways that children demonstrate the ability to group items together. Children eventually learn that animals, toys, vehicles, and foods go together in a variety of ways, and these other categories should now be added to the training program in the form of identical matching to sample, and then later non-identical matching to sample. In addition, matching 2D items (pictures) to 3D items (objects) in large arrays containing similar stimuli (the items all look alike in some way) and matching associated items, should become part of the VP-MTS training program. There are a variety of natural environment and play activities that can develop this repertoire, such as play sets, puzzles, games, assembly of toys and structures, and arts and crafts activities.

VP-MTS 8-M	Matches identical objects or pictures in a messy array of 8 containing 3 similar stimuli, for 25 items (e.g., matches a dog to a dog in an array that also contains a cat, pig, and pony).

A child's ability to discriminate among similar stimuli demonstrates good scanning skills. These will be the same skills that will be part of more advanced LD and LRFFC tasks. It is best to firmly establish the scanning repertoire with easier tasks like those of identical MTS, then non-identical matching, association matching, and 2D to 3D matching. Errors at this level are a good predictor of potential problems with LD and LRFFC tasks, both of which require visual scanning. The ultimate goal is to establish a "generalized MTS repertoire." That is, a child should be able to find the closest match to any sample he is presented on the first trial.

VP-MTS 9-M	Matches non-identical objects or non-identical pictures in a messy array of 10, for 25 items (e.g., matches a Ford truck to a Toyota truck).

At this point the child should have a well-established MTS repertoire and the focus should move to more MTS in books, scenes, and the natural environment, as well as to more 2D to 3D matching. The child should not be too far from a generalized matching repertoire. The array at this point should be complex and contain multiple similar stimuli.

VP-MTS 10-M	Matches non-identical objects (3D) to pictures (2D) and/or vice versa, in a messy array of 10 containing 3 similar stimuli, for 25 items.

The focus should now be on the expansion and generalization of matching skills, and the transfer of these skills to the listener repertoires. There are several ways to expand the repertoire, such as by increasing the non-identical aspects of the sample and comparison stimuli, by asking for multiple comparisons, and by making the array more difficult by increasing the size and number of similar stimuli in the array. For example, if the child can find the hammer on a table after being shown a picture of a hammer, the task can be made more difficult by showing a silhouette (instead of a picture) of a hammer, and moving the real hammer to a messy toolbox that contains a number of different tools. This specific task allows the child to carry the sample stimulus with him in that he can hold the picture and has it when he reaches the toolbox. Eventually, the picture can be removed and the S^D is transferred to a verbal S^D such as, "Can you help me find a hammer?" (an LD task now). This is clearly a more complicated task. However, if the child can scan a complex array in the natural environment, and efforts are made to carefully transfer the visual stimulus (the picture sample) to a verbal stimulus (the word "hammer"), the probability of success with this harder task increases.

Suggested IEP Goals for Visual Perceptual Skills and Matching-to-Sample: Level 2 (select only 1 or 2 goals and modify them as appropriate for the individual child).

- The child will match at least 200 non-identical objects or pictures in an array of least 10 with at least 3 similar stimuli in the array.

- The child will match at least 25 different items that are associated to each other.

- The child will match at least 200 non-identical objects to pictures (or vice versa) in an array of at least 10, with at least 4 similar stimuli in the array.

- The child will complete 50 different block designs, parquetry, shape puzzles, or similar tasks that contain at least 6 different items.

- The child will continue 25 different patterns or sequences that have at least three different components.

- The child will match 100 identical or non-identical items to the corresponding items in a scene from a picture or book, or in the natural environment.

INDEPENDENT PLAY – LEVEL 2

PLAY 6-M	Searches for a missing or corresponding toy or part of a set for 5 items or sets (e.g., a puzzle piece, a ball for a drop-in toy, a bottle for a baby doll).

When a child begins to search for missing items without adult prompts, this demonstrates that MOs are a source of control for play, and finding the desired items will be automatically reinforcing. Thus, this behavior should occur in the absence of adult prompting and contrived reinforcement (i.e., "independent play"). However, it still will be important to provide direct prompting and modeling of play activities, as well as reinforcement to further strengthen these and other play behaviors. At this point, novelty and variation of toys and activities can keep play behavior entertaining (automatically reinforcing). Verbal interactions can be facilitated through play. When a child is at ease and having fun they are more likely to spontaneously vocalize. The child should be provided with opportunities to experience cause-and-effect events such as a jack-in-the-box, air coming out of a balloon, blowing a pinwheel, or a ball going down a ramp. These activities provide opportunities for shared exploration. It is not uncommon for typical children in this developmental age range to play with a toy for only a few seconds or minutes, and then move on to other toys. Additional activities that would be appropriate for a child scoring at this level can be found in the corresponding sections of VB-MAPP Independent Play Supporting Skills list.

PLAY 7-M	Independently demonstrates the use of toys or objects according to their function for 5 items (e.g., placing a train on a track, pulling a wagon, holding a telephone to the ear).

The focus at this point should be on increasing the frequency and variation of play behaviors by providing opportunities to come in contact with different objects and actions. Modeling can be used to demonstrate how to operate a toy for a child, then prompt the child to independently manipulate the toy on his own, and providing social reinforcement when he does so. The reinforcement can be as simple as just sitting with a child, making eye contact, smiling, laughing, and providing attention and approval. While the ultimate goal is to establish play as initiated by the child, and automatically reinforcing to the child, direct modeling, prompting, and reinforcement may still be necessary for many children. The child should also be provided with opportunities to come in contact with toys and sets of toys that involve different parts (e.g., blocks, pegs, Mr. Potato Head, Little People sets, barn yard animal sets). "Play" can involve any object or activity and it will also be of value to break play free from just "toys" (e.g., a blanket made into a tent, a shoe as a telephone, socks worn as gloves, rolling oranges and apples down a ramp).

PLAY 8-M	Plays with everyday items in creative ways 2 times (e.g., uses a bowl as a drum or a box as an imaginary car).

Typically developing children often seem to spend their entire day playing. The range of different play activities is wide, although a child may have several favorite activities. As previously mentioned, these play activities help to develop a number of important behavioral skills such as imitation, fine and gross motor control, part-to-whole completion, visual discriminations, and problem solving. Many forms of play may begin to emerge that do not involve standard toys, but rather common items used in a variety of different ways that are entertaining to the child. Children with autism often have difficulty enjoying these forms of creative play, thus it is especially important to foster them early. Variation is important, so the same item could be used in many ways (e.g., use the spoon as a drum stick or to feed a doll), or one activity could involve a variety of items (e.g., use a pencil, a ladle, or Lincoln Log roof board as a drum stick). The goal is to teach the child how to have fun with things and that these things need not always be commercial toys. Also, focusing on variation and pretend play may provide a preventive measure against the development of ritualistic and stereotypic play.

PLAY 9-M	Independently engages in play on structures and playground equipment for a total of 5 minutes (e.g., going down a slide, swinging).

Physical play is important in many ways for a child. In addition to the health benefits, a significant part of early childhood social behavior involves physical play activities such as those on a playground, pool, or activity center (e.g., fast food play structures). It will be of social value to a child if he can complete some of these activities first as independent play. For example, if a group of other children are crawling in and out of a tunnel at a fast food restaurant and the target child cannot crawl through a tunnel, or is afraid to, he will miss the possible social interaction of following or playing with the other children. If the child had previously mastered this play skill, he is more likely to be able to participate in impromptu social games that occur in such settings. As with many play skills, it may be necessary to demonstrate or physically guide the child, then gradually fade adult prompts and reinforcement.

PLAY 10-M	Assembles toys that have multiple parts for 5 different sets of materials (e.g., Mr. Potato Head, Little People sets, Cooties bugs, Kid K'Nex).

The length of time spent in a single activity generally increases as children grow. Their interests change, and things such as seeing a completed toy set (e.g., The Little People pool party) or having all the parts in place (e.g., Mr. Potato Head's arms, legs, ears, eyes, and hat on), become stronger reinforcers. These play activities foster many important skills such as persistence, attending to a task, matching-to-sample, imitation, fine motor skills, and eye-hand coordination. As with physical play, these skills can also be valuable for social interaction. In a sense, the child with good play skills "brings something to the social setting." For example, if the target child knows how to assemble a train set, that skill may be of social value if a peer cannot complete the set, or has weaker skills and can benefit from the target child's abilities. Play involving assembly may initially require more adult prompting, modeling, and reinforcement than physical play, but again the goal is to move to independence.

Suggested IEP Goals for Independent Play: Level 2 (select only 1 or 2 goals and modify them as appropriate for the individual child).

- The child will spontaneously engage in pretend and imaginary play, (sometimes with accompanying verbal behavior), role-playing, and acting out daily routines, movies, TV shows, or favorite activities at least 10 times in a one-week period.

- The child will engage in arts and crafts type activities such as coloring, drawing, painting, cutting, pasting, taping, stringing beads, play doh, etc., for at least 5 minutes.

- The child will repeat a gross motor play behavior to obtain a better effect for 5 activities.

- The child will assemble toys that have multiple parts for 10 different sets of materials.

SOCIAL BEHAVIOR AND SOCIAL PLAY – LEVEL 2

SOCIAL 6-M	Initiates a physical interaction with a peer 2 times (e.g., a push in a wagon, hand holding, Ring Around the Rosy).

A child who attends to peers, imitates peers, and wants to interact with peers, but does not have the necessary verbal skills, may engage in negative behavior as a form of social interaction. It is important at this point in social development to place a focus on teaching simple verbal interactions between the target child and peers. Successful interactions with peers can also decrease the likelihood of social anxiety and withdrawal. The most functional type of early verbal behavior between children is manding. Tacts and intraverbals are important, but are more complex and come later. The child must learn four types of mand-related behaviors, two as a speaker and two as a listener. As a speaker the child needs to learn to (1) mand to a peer to obtain a reinforcer (e.g., a second person on a teeter-totter), and (2) mand to a peer to remove an aversive (e.g., not taking turns on a swing). As a listener a child must learn to (3) respond to the mands of a peer to deliver a reinforcer (e.g., get on the teeter-totter), and (4) respond to the mand of a peer to remove an aversive (e.g., get off the swing). These are complicated behaviors because they, like all mands, are controlled by motivational variables and may be complicated to identify and control. Even more complex is teaching a child to emit the socially correct behavior when the MO is strong (e.g., not to hit to get a turn on the swing, or to passively surrender a reinforcer to a peer).

The easiest of these four different mand relations to teach a child is to mand for a desirable item from a peer. This often must be taught in a contrived situation, but can be easily accomplished using a manding to peers procedure. It is important when teaching this behavior to fade out adult prompting (e.g., "Ask Joe for the gummy bear") and reinforcement (e.g., "Nice sharing!"), because the goal is for the social behavior to come under the antecedent and consequential control of the peer, not the adult. Spontaneous manding to peers will be difficult to achieve if adults continue to control the social contingencies. Additional activities that may further develop other aspects of social behavior can be found in the corresponding sections of VB-MAPP Social Behavior and Social Play Supporting Skills list.

SOCIAL 7-M	Spontaneously mands to peers 5 times (e.g., *My turn. Push me. Look! Come on.*).

Once spontaneous manding to peers for desirable reinforcers begins to occur, the other three types of mands can be developed. Responding to a peer's mand can be easy for some children, but quite difficult for others. The task is to teach the child to attend to the peer's mand (e.g., "pull me") and emit a nonverbal response to that mand (e.g., pulling the peer in a wagon) without adult prompting. This behavioral repertoire is more complicated than it might seem. The target child may not want to pull the peer, understand the peer's mand, know how to pull the peer, be focused on getting the wagon himself, or be focused on some other activity. Training may be slower than teaching a target child to mand to the peer because the target child gets something from it, which is not always the case when he responds to the mands of others (e.g., even adults often fail to reinforce those who respond to their mands). Manding to remove aversives and responding to a peer's mand to stop a behavior, or return an item, are also more complicated, but are essential components of effective social interaction. Much of what is identified as "turn taking" and "sharing" involve these basic elements of the mand, as well as other skills identified in the VB-MAPP Social Behavior and Social Play Supporting Skills list. Play contexts provide opportunities to teach these types of mands and promote other aspects of social behavior. Encouraging and facilitating sustained play with peers will provide opportunities for social development.

SOCIAL 8-M	Engages in sustained social play with peers for 3 minutes without adult prompts or reinforcement (e.g., cooperatively setting up a play set, water play).

If the target child is now spontaneously engaging in cooperative social play that involves imitation and echoic behavior, as well as manding and perhaps some tacting, there can be an increased focus on responding to peer mands, turn taking, sharing, and beginning intraverbal behavior. Also, aspects of creative and imaginative play can be introduced allowing the child to move beyond concrete play. The child's increased ability to engage in social play with fewer adult prompts may indicate a readiness for "play dates" that may provide social interaction with peers in a looser and more natural environment. More complex social skills may still need to be established in a more structured environment.

SOCIAL 9-M	Spontaneously responds to the mands from peers 5 times (e.g., *Pull me in the wagon. I want the train.*).

Once a child is manding to a peer and responding to the peer's mands, other more complex verbal and nonverbal interactions may naturally develop. Much of what is called "friendship" involves the delivery of reinforcers (including attention) and the removal of aversives. Manding can do this. Once a peer becomes a conditioned reinforcer, imitating his behavior becomes fun for the child and new behaviors are learned this way. Wanting to be with other children can be a fragile process, and even many typically developing children have trouble with successful social interaction because of the many complicated variables involved (i.e., the complex verbal, nonverbal, and listener skills that form the basis of effective social interaction). If a child is successful at manding for reinforcers from peers, this increases the probability that the target child will "invite" the peer to join an activity, hang out with him, or cooperate in some other social game or interaction. Specific teaching procedures to prompt and reinforce a target child to include other children in activities can be valuable in starting this important social process.

SOCIAL 10-M	Spontaneously mands to peers to participate in games, social play, etc., 2 times (e.g., *Come on you guys. Let's dig a hole.*).

This milestone represents a significant step for most children with autism or other developmental disabilities. It demonstrates that the necessary motivating variables for social interaction are operative, and are effective in evoking behaviors that can lead to further emotional and social development. Verbal behavior is an essential component of social behavior, and any opportunity to encourage children to verbally interact during social play should be taken. Once children are imitating and manding to each other, additional types of verbal interactions can be developed through social play. Narrating play activities is a type of tacting, but it may have mand and intraverbal elements as well; it is thus a complicated form of behavior that will only begin to emerge at this point, but should nevertheless be encouraged. For example, a child says, "I'm shooting webs from my hand like Spiderman" (a type of tact, but also a mand for attention). The second child may respond "Me too. Look out!" (an intraverbal and a mand). Thus, this forms the beginning of verbal exchanges on a single topic, and represents a very healthy type of social behavior. The more time that the target child spends in verbal and nonverbal interaction with peers, the higher the probability that social behavior will become more comfortable and productive for the child. A focus on cooperation to achieve a result, sharing responsibilities, turn taking, and verbal interactions using mands for information and intraverbal responses between children, will be an important component of the program at this point.

Suggested IEP Goals for Social Behavior and Social Play: Level 2 (select only 1 or 2 goals and modify them as appropriate for the individual child).

- The child will spontaneously mand to peers at least 25 times per day.

- The child will spontaneously respond to the mands from peers 25 times in a single day.

- The child will engage in cooperative, constructive, or physical play activities with peers lasting at least 5 minutes.

- The child will spontaneously mand to peers using questions, directions, instructions, etc. (e.g., "What's that?" "Where is your lunch?" "Come on, get your bike") at least an average of 25 times per day.

- The child will take turns and share reinforcers with peers without prompts at least 5 times in a day.

MOTOR IMITATION – LEVEL 2

IMITATION 6-M	Imitates 10 actions that require selecting a specific object from an array (e.g., selects a drumstick from an array also containing a horn and a bell, and imitates an adult's drumming).

A child who scores at this level is learning to imitate the behavior of others, but this skill may be under the multiple control of adult verbal prompts such as "do this." The formal teaching of imitation skills can have several valuable payoffs for a child. For example, imitation helps teach a child to attend to the behavior of others (a major deficit for many children with autism), and can become a powerful vehicle for teaching new behaviors such as play, self-help, group responding, general compliance, and social skills. Imitation can also strengthen fine and gross motor skills, as well as promote physical fitness. The goal at this point is to encourage spontaneous imitation and imitation of others in the child's natural play and social (group) contexts. In addition, adults should focus on increasing the number of different imitative behaviors, as well as teaching more complex imitation with objects (e.g., building a block house, tooth brushing, putting on a shoe), and functional imitation in the child's day-to-day natural environment. Motor imitation along with vocal imitation (echoic) should be encouraged as well (e.g., pretending to be sleeping and snoring, pretending to be driving a car and saying "beep-beep"). A variety of additional activities for this level and the upcoming levels can be found in the VB-MAPP Imitation Supporting Skills list.

IMITATION 7-M	Imitates 20 different fine motor actions when prompted, *Do this* (e.g., wiggling fingers, pinching, making a fist, making a butterfly).

The ability to imitate small motor movements will help set the stage for the development of a number of skills such as self-help, eating, drawing, writing, connecting things, assembling things, etc. Eventually, imitation begins to occur spontaneously and frequently, and as it does, it should become less of a formal target of the daily intervention program (as in intensive discrete trial training). For many children, acting like others becomes automatically reinforcing. In fact, the establishment of automatic reinforcement is one of the primary goals in developing both motor and vocal imitation. The reinforcers that maintain echoic and imitative behavior should gradually shift from contrived (extrinsic) reinforcers to natural and automatic (intrinsic) reinforcers, like in typical child development. Initially children may need to be taught to imitate others, but eventually children imitate others because the behavior itself automatically produces reinforcers. This becomes very obvious when children spontaneously imitate adults (e.g., talking on a phone, brushing their own hair, or putting a doll in a crib). It is fun to act like mom or dad, sound like a movie or TV character, or follow peers. Imitation also often results in natural or non-contrived reinforcers in play or social activities, such as when a "thumbs up" evokes a reciprocal "thumbs up" and reinforcement occurs from the other person. Many of these imitative skills can be further developed in a natural environment with age-appropriate activities, such as interactive songs and games that promote motor imitation (e.g., Head, Shoulders, Knees and Toes; The Hokey Pokey). The goal at this point should be to fade out verbal prompts, increase the complexity of the behaviors, and focus more on imitation in the natural environment.

IMITATION 8-M	**Imitates 10 different three-component sequences of actions when prompted, *Do this* (e.g., clapping, jumping, touching toes; pick up a doll, place her in a crib, and rock the crib).**

Once a child has learned to attend to the behavior of others and copy their behavior, many elements of teaching become easier. For example, if an adult says to a child, "I'll show you how to do it," and then demonstrates putting seeds in a bird feeder, and without special training the child is able to put seeds in the bird feeder, this ability to imitate opens up new learning opportunities. The focus of the intervention at this point should be to increase the variety of imitative activities, establish longer chains of imitative behavior that are developmentally appropriate, and continue to promote imitation in a functional and natural context (e.g., making things, art projects, self-help activities, pretend play, fitness activities).

IMITATION 9-M	**Spontaneously imitates 5 functional skills in the natural environment (e.g., eating with a spoon, putting on a coat, removing shoes).**

A child who spontaneously imitates the behavior of others in the natural environment has achieved one of the most significant milestones in the acquisition of imitation skills. The child can begin to learn new behaviors and complete tasks simply by watching how other people do it (observational learning). This is also a good indicator that the child can learn in a less restrictive environment. The focus at this point should be to make sure this behavior gets reinforced, and to provide opportunities to copy additional functional behaviors, with the general goal being to develop a generalized imitative repertoire.

IMITATION 10-M	**Imitates (or attempts to with approximations) any novel motor action modeled by an adult with and without objects (i.e., a "generalized imitative repertoire").**

Motor imitation, echoing, matching-to-sample, and copying written words are all skills that ultimately should become a "generalized repertoire." That is, a child can copy any new action, sound, gesture, or word without further training. Once a child has learned to imitate others, novel imitative behaviors can often occur on the first trial, thus a generalized repertoire is exhibited. The child has learned how to imitate. This repertoire can be very functional for any individual. A child who has reached this skill level will be in a much better position for integration in less restrictive academic settings. Imitation skills will continue to be quite helpful in academic, social, recreational, and community activities. In the home setting, imitation can be a valuable tool for building self-help skills and teaching simple daily living skills (e.g., setting the table, putting things away, feeding the dog, dressing). At this point in the verbal behavior curriculum, further IEP goals on motor imitation may not be necessary, but functional imitation should be incorporated into the child's daily activities.

Suggested IEP Goals for Motor Imitation: Level 2 (select only 1 or 2 goals and modify them as appropriate for the individual child).

- The child will imitate 5 novel actions in a 15-second fluency test.

- The child will imitate at least 25 three-step sequences of activities.

- The child will spontaneously imitate others in order to produce a matching outcome in a non-structured pretend activity, play setting, or other natural environment setting, for at least 5 different activities.

- The child will imitate any new movement on the first trial for 25 movements (a generalized imitative repertoire).

ECHOIC (EESA) SUBTEST – LEVEL 2

ECHOIC 6-M	Scores at least 50 on the EESA subtest (at least 20 from Group 2).

A score at this level demonstrates that a child is able to control his vocal muscles on command. The focus should be on increasing the strength of this skill by socially reinforcing spontaneous vocalizations and focusing on more multisyllabic echoic responses. The adult may be most successful teaching echoic skills in a play context (pairing sounds with reinforcers). Or, it may be also helpful to present visual cues to give some basis for the echoic response (e.g., show the child a ball while attempting to improve the echoic "ball"). The goal is also to improve articulation, and ultimately transfer known echoics to mands, tacts, and intraverbals.

ECHOIC 7-M	Scores at least 60 on the EESA subtest.

For a child scoring at this level, formal echoic training would become less of a specific target for intervention. Rather, it should be incorporated into all other verbal activities (e.g., mand and tact training should involve the differential reinforcement of better vocal approximations). However, it is likely that a child at this level would continue to benefit from formal speech therapy that might target specific articulation development.

ECHOIC 8-M	Scores at least 70 on the EESA subtest.

The echoic repertoire should now be quite functional for a child. That is, a new mand or tact can be acquired faster because the child is quickly able to learn to echo a new word, and the new word then is transferred to establish a new mand or tact. Specific articulation errors should continue to be addressed by a speech therapist.

ECHOIC 9-M	Scores at least 80 on the EESA subtest.

The child should be reaching a generalized echoic repertoire, that is, he should be able to echoically approximate most novel words. The focus should be to continue to gently shape better response forms.

ECHOIC 10-M	Scores at least 90 on the EESA subtest (at least 10 from Groups 4 and 5).

This score represents the target goal for the echoic repertoire: a "generalized repertoire" where a child can provide a close approximation for almost any word or short phrase. The developmental age at this point is approximately 30 months. Most children at this age emit words and phrases that are sometimes difficult for strangers to understand, but daily practice shapes better articulation. It may be useful to consider every session, or language interaction, as an opportunity to improve a child's articulation.

Suggested IEP Goals for Echoic: Level 2 (select only 1 goal and modify it as appropriate for the individual child).

- The child will echo at least 50 vowel-consonant combinations of 2 syllables or more, or two-word phrases on command.

- The child will echo at least 100 vowel-consonant combinations of 3 syllables or more on command.

LISTENER RESPONDING BY FUNCTION, FEATURE, AND CLASS (LRFFC) – LEVEL 2

LRFFC 6-M	Selects 5 different foods or drinks when each are presented in an array of 5 (along with 4 non-food or non-drink items) and asked the verbal fill-ins *you eat...* and *you drink....*

There are two major values of conducting LRFFC training. One is to develop more advanced listener skills, which can be accomplished in a variety of ways through LRFFC, and the second is to facilitate the development of intraverbal behavior. For a child who scores at this level on LRFFC, the focus of the LRFFC intervention program should be on listener skills, rather than on intraverbal skills (this will come a little later). A goal of LRFFC listener training is to teach a child to correctly respond to increasingly more complex verbal stimuli in a systematic way.

The first level of complexity beyond standard listener discrimination (LD) training is that LRFFC skills are based in part on the premise that people frequently refer to items and events in the environment without directly naming them, but rather by describing them in one way or another. The classification of this description as the function, feature, and class is only a rough distinction (there certainly are other ways of describing things and events), but it does provide a general guideline for assessment and training. Another way that verbal stimuli become more complex is that there are more parts to the verbal statement (e.g., "Find an animal that lives in the water and on land"). And a third way is that the content becomes increasingly complex (e.g., everyday clothing versus the parts of a motor). These increasing levels of complexity are incorporated into the assessment program.

Foods and drinks are identified as the first milestone in LRFFC assessment because of the powerful motivation often associated with these items, and a child's frequent exposure to the words "eat" and "drink." Other less motivating classifications typically don't occur until later in verbal development. The next step for a child who can select foods and drinks without an adult naming them, but identifying them by their class, is to move to fill-in statements that involve verbs or functions and common nouns. In order to be successful at this task it is imperative that the child already be able to identify the verbs and nouns (as tacts and LDs), as well as verb-noun (or noun-verb) combinations. For example, if a child cannot tact and LD an object spinning, it will be hard for him to learn (in a non-rote manner) to select a top in an LRFFC task (when asked, "you spin a...."). For some children with strong LD repertoires and weak tact repertoires, they may be successful at these types of LRFFC tasks, but it is important to not let the listener repertoire get too far ahead of the speaker repertoire. Thus, the focus of the intervention at this point should be on teaching the child to identify the items that they already know as tacts and LDs, but under the control of different and more complex verbal stimuli. A variety of specific activities and a sequence for more advanced skills can be found in the VB-MAPP LRFFC Supporting Skills list.

LRFFC 7-M	Selects the correct item from an array of 8, for 25 different LRFFC fill-in statements of any type (e.g., *You sit on a...*).

A child who scores at this level is just beginning to develop more advanced listener skills. The focus at this point should be to (1) expand the repertoire by introducing new fill-in LRFFC relations (shoot for several hundred), (2) gradually move to the WH-question format, (3) generalize known items to variations of the items, (4) generalize to different people, (5) use new carrier phrases, (6) use different tones of voice, volume, prosody, etc., and (7) increase the size of the array. Perhaps most importantly, LRFFC training can teach a child to attend more carefully to complex verbal stimuli, a skill that will be very important for later intraverbal development.

New items can continue to be introduced with fill-in statements, but they should be moved to WH questions as soon as possible, or to more natural statements that a child is likely to encounter (fill-ins do not occur much in natural discourse, and should be considered a prompt that needs to be faded at some point). For example, instead of saying, "You ride in a..." now say in a child friendly and playful voice, "Hey Ryan, what are we going to ride in?" (with perhaps an emphasis on "ride in" as a step in the fading process). LRFFC provides an excellent opportunity to develop verbal stimulus control, and can be a fun procedure to run in the natural environment. Known relations should be incorporated into play and social activities, group instruction, arts and crafts, and other classroom and home activities. Other WH questions such as "where," "which," and "who" can also be introduced at this point. Again, these tasks can begin with a few trials in a fill-in format, then quickly moved to the WH-question format.

LRFFC 8-M	Selects the correct item from an array of 10 (or from a book), for 25 different verb-noun LRFFC *what, which,* or *who* questions (e.g., *What do you ride? Which one barks? Who can hop?*).

As a child acquires new tacts and LD responses, these should be immediately moved into LRFFC tasks. Generalization remains an important element of LRFFC development and should be a part of training everyday. It is important at this point to begin working on developing verbal stimulus classes where different verbal S^Ds evoke the selection of the same item (e.g., "What do you ride?" "What has wheels?"). And the array should begin to move to scenes, books, and the natural environment.

LRFFC 9-M	Selects an item given 3 different verbal statements about each item when independently presented (e.g., *Find an animal. What barks? What has paws?*) for 25 items.

The ability to select a specific item given different statements about that item is important for many reasons and training should continue from here in a variety of ways. The teaching procedure known as multiple exemplar training where several different examples and non-examples of stimuli and responses are combined helps to establish concepts, advanced discriminations, and exclusion of incorrect or rote responses. For example, when a picture of a fire truck is presented in an array, a child should be able to select that fire truck given a wide variety of statements (e.g., "Find a red vehicle." "What does a fireman drive?" "What is used to put out fires?"), but not select the fire truck when given other statements (e.g., "What flies in the air," "What floats on the water?"). It is important that this skill is established across a variety of items and activities (e.g., animals, people, toys, clothing) to ensure that verbal stimulus and response generalization is occurring. Also, LRFFC nicely sets the stage for intraverbal development as described below.

Previously, it was suggested that the second value of LRFFC was that it could facilitate intraverbal behavior. That's because the verbal stimulus in the LRFFC trial can be almost exactly the same verbal stimulus found in an intraverbal relation. For example, if the verbal stimulus in an LRFFC trial is, "What do you draw with?" and the child touches a crayon, this exact same verbal stimulus can occur in the intraverbal where instead of touching a crayon (a nonverbal response) the child says the word "crayon" (a verbal response). Many children will begin to spontaneously tact the target nonverbal stimulus in the array during an LRFFC trial. When this begins to happen, it is an excellent indicator that the child is ready for more extensive intraverbal training, and the LRFFC to intraverbal transfer procedure is likely to be effective. Specific LRFFC skills to work on at this point include selecting multiple members of a class (multiple exemplar training), fluency activities (timed responding with a focus on rapid responses), making more use of books and the natural environment, and moving into adjective-noun multiple component verbal stimuli.

LRFFC 10-M	Spontaneously tacts the item on 50% of the LRFFC trials (e.g., says *dog* given the verbal statement *find an animal,* and a visual array containing a picture of a dog).

A child who reaches this milestone is ready for more intensive intraverbal training. Regarding LRFFC development, the array and the verbal stimuli should continue to become more complex. The array should begin to contain stimuli that are similar by any one of several ways such as shape, color, size, function, class, or texture. The task is to begin to make it harder for the child to find the target item (like the "Where's Waldo" game). This activity strengthens attention and visual scanning, which plays a significant role in many aspects of human behavior (e.g., social behavior, sports, self-help, and vocational skills). The verbal stimuli should begin to contain more multiple parts, such as providing things with two or three features or functions that distinguish one choice from another. For example, "Find a big animal that likes the water," versus "Find a little animal that likes the water."

Skills relating to the past and future can also be developed in an LRFFC format. For example, if a child saw a fire truck at school earlier, an LRFFC task could consist of presenting an array containing a fire truck and the question, "What did you see at school today?" Sequencing skills can also be developed in a similar manner. For example, an LRFFC trial can consist of presenting an array containing a towel and the verbal stimulus, "After you take a bath what do you need?" Finally, there should be a continued focus on generalization training in the natural environment; the introduction of new topics; and making the trials fun, natural, and relevant to the child.

Suggested IEP Goals for Listener Responding by Function, Feature, and Class (LRFFC): Level 2 (select only 1 or 2 goals and modify them as appropriate for the individual child).

- The child will select the correct item from an array of at least 8 given 25 different song fill-ins, animal sounds, or eat and drink classifications.

- The child will select the correct item from an array of at least 8 given 50 different noun-noun associations, verb-noun associations, and verb-noun WH questions.

- The child will select the correct item from an array of at least 8 given 100 different fill-in or WH questions involving the function, feature, or class of the items.

- The child will select the correct item from an array of at least 10 and with similar stimuli given 200 different fill-in or WH questions involving the function, feature, or class of items.

- The child will select 10 correct items in a one-minute period from an array of at least 8 and with similar stimuli.

INTRAVERBAL – LEVEL 2

INTRAVERBAL 6-M	Completes 10 different fill-in-the-blank phrases of any type (e.g., song fill-ins, social games and fun fill-ins, animal or object sounds).

A child who scores at this level is beginning to demonstrate some early intraverbal behavior, but the behavior may not be very functional for the child. However, a primary purpose for developing this type of early and simple verbal stimulus control is to begin the process of breaking verbal responding free from echoic and tact sources of control. Verbal stimulus control is extremely complex, and often the tendency is to begin this type of language training with verbal stimuli that are far too difficult for a child (e.g., "What do you like to play?" "What did you do today at school?"). Fill-in-the-blank phrases are usually much easier than WH questions, and can more successfully teach a child to discriminate among the thousands of verbal stimuli he may encounter every day. The immediate goal for a child scoring at this level is to expand the variation of the verbal stimuli and the intraverbal responses emitted by the child. Training should occur daily with formal training sessions, as well as training in the natural environment, in an effort to provide a child with frequent opportunities to learn this extremely important skill. Additional activities that may further develop the intraverbal repertoire can be found in the corresponding sections of VB-MAPP Intraverbal Supporting Skills list.

INTRAVERBAL 7-M	Provides first name when asked, *What is your name?*

This intraverbal is often considered a significant milestone for a child and usually occurs around 2 years of age. Make sure the child does not call everybody by the same name. Once a child can provide his own name, other names should be added, and should be part tact at first (e.g., conduct training in the presence of a sister and with the verbal fill-in "Your sister's name is...," then fade the presence of the sister). However, the main focus of the intraverbal program at this point should be on verb-noun and noun-noun fill-ins, and some WH questions.

INTRAVERBAL 8-M	Completes 25 different fill-in-the-blank phrases (not including songs) (e.g., *You eat... You sleep in a... Shoes and...*).

Once a child is successfully responding to a variety of verbal discriminative stimuli in a fill-in format, procedures should be implemented to transfer stimulus control to a WH-question format. For example, if a child can respond "car" following the verbal stimulus, "You ride in a...," the next step is to change the phrasing to a WH question as in, "What do you ride in?" The correct response is still "car," but now the response occurs under a slightly different, but more functional verbal stimulus. That is, the child is more likely to encounter WH questions in his natural environment, but fill-ins are initially easier to acquire. The fill-in format can still be a valuable tool for introducing new intraverbal relations. Following the successful acquisition of answers to several "what" questions, it may also be possible to begin to introduce training on a few "where" and "who" questions. Generalization training to different people, different tones of voice, different settings, etc., should also be occurring. These activities and the others suggested in the Supporting Skills list at this level should also now become a more significant part of a child's daily language intervention program.

INTRAVERBAL 9-M	Answers 25 different *what* questions (e.g., *What do you like to eat?*).

A child at this level is now demonstrating a solid beginning intraverbal repertoire and the focus should be on expansion and generalization. Expansion should consist of intensive intraverbal training activities that take known mands and tacts and bring them under verbal stimulus control. For example, if a child can tact and LD a shovel, and the action of digging and engaging in digging behavior, it may now be appropriate to teach the intraverbal, "What do you dig with?" or, "What do you do with a shovel?" Generalization should occur in the form of both stimulus and response generalization. For stimulus generalization, it is important that the child be able to emit the same verbal response under a variety of different verbal stimuli. For example, if the child can respond "shovel" to the verbal stimulus, "What do you dig with?" then training might occur with other verbal stimuli that might also evoke the response "shovel," such as, "What do we need to make a hole here?" or, "We need a bucket and a...."

Intraverbal response generalization consists of teaching the child to emit a variety of verbal responses to the same verbal stimulus. For example, if the child can respond, "shovel" to the verbal stimulus, "What do you dig with?" training should occur on expanding the response class (e.g., "What else can you dig with?") to other things that you could dig with such as a "spoon," "pick," "stick," "backhoe," etc. There are several procedures that can promote generalization, such as multiple exemplar training within the LRFFC to intraverbal transfer procedure, or natural environment play such as digging a hole with a spoon.

INTRAVERBAL 10-M	Answers 25 different *who* or *where* questions (e.g., *Who is your friend? Where is your pillow?*).

By this time in a language intervention program a child should be easily acquiring new mands and tacts, and intraverbal training should become more of a major focus of the program. In some respects, it may be thought of as "using the words" that a child already has, but in a variety of different contexts. It happens that many of those contexts are verbal, and transfer may require formal training. For example, a child may be able to mand and tact "barn" and "cow," but not be able to verbally state that "a cow lives in a barn," or that "a cow gives us milk," or that there are other animals that live in a barn, etc. Intraverbal training can develop these skills so a child is able to talk about things and events even though those things and events may not be physically present. At this point in the intraverbal program there can be more of a focus on two-component questions where one word might change the meaning of the next (called "verbal conditional discriminations"). For example "Can you name a hot food?" versus "Can you name a cold food?" While the word "food" is the same in each question, the words "hot" and "cold" change the correct answer, and require that the child attend more carefully to the individual components of a sentence (for more detail see Axe, 2008; Eikeseth & Smith, 2013; Ingvarsson & Duy, 2011; Sundberg & Sundberg, 2011). In addition to these activities, training on "what" questions involving the function of things would also be appropriate at this time (e.g., "What do you do with a hose?").

Suggested IEP Goals for Intraverbal: Level 2 (select only 1 or 2 goals and modify them as appropriate for the individual child).

- The child will intraverbally respond to 25 different song fill-in-the-blanks, animal sounds, or fun fill-in verbal stimuli.

- The child will be able to provide correct verbal responses to 100 different fill-in-the-blank questions involving nouns and verbs.

- The child will be able to correctly answer 100 different "what" questions involving nouns and verbs.

- The child will be able to correctly provide the function or class for 100 nouns, and provide the noun given 100 functions or classes.

- The child will be able to correctly answer 50 different "where" questions.

- The child will be able to correctly answer 25 different "who" questions.

- The child will be able to correctly answer at least 3 different questions about 25 different objects shown to him.

- The child will identify 25 different classes when given at least three members of that class.

CLASSROOM ROUTINES AND GROUP SKILLS – LEVEL 2

GROUP 6-M	Sits at a group snack or lunch table without negative behavior for 3 minutes.

Children with special needs who first enter a preschool or elementary school setting may be quite uncomfortable with large groups of unfamiliar children and adults in one room. Also, a formal classroom routine and structure may be novel. A common pattern for many children new to a school setting is to cry (sometimes demonstrating separation anxiety), or in some other way express unhappiness with the new setting (e.g., standing by the door, tantruming, aggression, property destruction, or self-injurious behavior). For these children, providing reinforcement the minute the child is appropriate, pairing (comfort), opportunities to mand (if possible), stimulating activities, and lowered demands typically reduces the emotional or negative behavior. Generally, by the end of the first week or two most children are more comfortable in the new setting. Some children don't demonstrate any separation problems, and immediately begin exploring the new environment, interacting with interesting toys, and sometimes even the other children. However, they still may not sit for an extended period of time (3-5 minutes) and respond when told to do so. Any given child can fall between these two ends of the continuum, but the goal for all children with special needs is to not only be comfortable in the classroom, but to learn in that setting.

All classrooms differ, but most operate with some kind of formal structure such as snack or lunchtime, group time, stations, activity centers, toileting, recess, and formal teaching sessions. Some children are able to immediately comply with classroom routines, but others may have difficulty giving up their freedom. These are often children who may have elevated scores on the barriers assessment, specifically instructional control and/or behavior problems. For some children, this may be a significant problem and a more thorough descriptive or functional analysis may be warranted along with a formal behavior intervention program. It is not uncommon for children with special needs to resist any imposed structure (e.g., bedtime, car seats, sit down meals, table activities, or any type of confinement). However, if a child is able to sit for 3 minutes at a snack table, but maybe not much longer, or not at a work station, group setting, or table task, the focus should be on establishing instructional control, including reinforcement of longer periods of staying in a seat. Demand should be kept low, the activities at the table or in the group should be fun, and contingent reinforcement for sitting carefully and systematically provided, while demand and amount of sitting time is gradually increased. The goal at this point is primarily establishing instructional control and compliance with classroom routines. If adults do not have instructional control of a child, teaching new skills will be difficult. Additional activities that may further develop these skills can be found in the VB-MAPP Classroom Routines and Group Supporting Skills list.

GROUP 7-M	Puts away personal items, lines up, and comes to a table with only 1 verbal prompt.

Classroom routines can help to establish a number of important skills such as imitating peers (e.g., lining up when the other children line up), following group instructions (e.g., "Everybody line up."), self-help skills (e.g., using a napkin), reducing prompt dependency, and independence. Once a child begins to comply with everyday classroom routines with minimal prompting, the focus can shift to other skills. For example, transitions from one activity to another are important, but initially may be difficult for some children because they may not have a history of going to a specific activity on command. In addition, transitions may require that a child give up a reinforcing activity (e.g., recess) for a less desirable one (e.g., tabletop tasks), or the child may become distracted transitioning between activities, and these contingencies must compete with the verbal instruction or independent transitioning. A focus at this point in classroom routines is to continue to reduce direct adult prompting (e.g., "Ryan, get your lunch."), transitioning with minimal prompting and negative behavior, and sitting in a group activities for longer periods of time, without attempting to leave, or emit other undesirable behaviors.

GROUP 8-M	Transitions between classroom activities with no more than 1 gestural or verbal prompt.

Once a child is able to follow the basic classroom routines and move from one activity to another without much adult prompting, the focus can shift more to learning specific skills in a group-teaching format. A major goal for any child is to acquire the skills to move to a less restrictive teaching format. While many children benefit significantly from a 1:1 teacher-to-student ratio, there comes a point where this instructional format throughout the whole day may not be in the best interest of the child. Perhaps the most obvious problem is that the adult acquires strong stimulus control over a child due to a long history of careful stimulus presentation and reinforcement delivery (even if several adults are involved, due to its very arrangement and success, the 1:1 format establishes strong stimulus control).

The child's success within a 1:1 format may initially make it difficult for learning to respond in more typical adult-to-child social and educational ratios. These more typical situations may not involve ongoing prompts, errorless teaching, or careful reinforcement delivery. In addition, an over reliance on a 1:1 adult-child instruction format may hinder peer interactions because of the strong reinforcement history established with adults, and the lack of experience interacting with other children in a group. There are a variety of other potential problems associated with relying solely on a 1:1 teaching ratio, such as generalization, prompt and other forms of dependence, establishing new conditioned reinforcers, accepting change and variation, as well as difficulty with supervision and curriculum progression. While clearly many children need and greatly benefit from 1:1 instruction at a certain point in an educational and social program, group instruction can be quite valuable.

Therefore, it is suggested that the focus at this point should be on developing a child's ability to learn within a group-teaching format. This activity should be part of the child's daily program, while not necessarily giving up the 1:1 or 1:2 instructional format, but by including direct training of age-appropriate social rules and social activities as part of the child's program. At this point the goal is to get the child to stay seated in a group format (3 or more children) and not engage in negative behaviors. Eventually, attending to the teacher and the material, as well as emitting appropriate verbal and nonverbal responses should also become target behaviors. Early group activities may have the feel of "entertaining" the child (e.g., arts and crafts, music, puppet shows, games) rather than teaching the child, but learning to sit in a group format is a critical skill that often must be taught, and is a prerequisite to learning more advanced skills in this educational format.

GROUP 9-M	Sits in a small group for 5 minutes without disruptive behavior or attempting to leave the group.

Once a child will sit in a group without disruptive behaviors the focus can now be on increasing the time attending to the teacher and materials presented in the group, and responding to the teacher's questions and instructions. Initially, the trials presented to the child in a group setting should come from the list of known responses (i.e., known tacts, LDs, intraverbals). The main goal at this point is simply to get the child to respond to the teacher in the group format, rather than teach new verbal or nonverbal behaviors. Sitting, attending, and responding should be reinforced at a level appropriate for the individual child. For some children there may be additional target behaviors, such as not touching the other children or grabbing their material (e.g., "quiet hands"), not talking or getting up out of turn, sharing items with others, appropriate use of the materials, and attending to peers when appropriate.

GROUP 10-M	Sits in a small group for 10 minutes, attends to the teacher or material for 50% of the period, and responds to 5 of a teacher's S^{D}s.

If the child will easily respond to known tasks in a group format, attend to the teacher and materials, and emit little or no disruptive behaviors, then begin to target the acquisition of new verbal and nonverbal behaviors. Many morning circle groups contain a variety of short activities or topics, and may also follow a general theme of the day or week (e.g., holidays, caterpillars and butterflies, winter, farm animals). New tacts and LDs can be targeted for acquisition in the group format using the same basic prompt, fading, transfer, and reinforcement procedures used in 1:1 instruction. In addition, the instruction format should begin to include "group S^{D}s" where the teacher's questions and instructions do not include an individual child's name or any clear indication that a specific child should respond (e.g., "Who can tell me..." "Does anyone know..." "Everybody..."). This will begin to teach the child to attend to these types of verbal stimuli, which are very different than the types of indirect adult prompts that are inherent in a 1:1 format (e.g., saying the child's name, sitting directly in front of the child, conducting all trials for one child, mild aversive control in the form of confinement or tone of voice, or similar daily teaching patterns, etc.). It may also be appropriate at this point to begin to increase the size of the group, which will naturally reduce the amount of prompts given to one child.

There are many variations of group instruction formats that are common to preschools and elementary classrooms. "Stations" or "centers" involve small groups that might focus on a particular activity or component of a particular theme. Children rotate through the different activities in small groups of 3 or 4 each, while the instructional assistants or teachers stay at a particular station. For example, if the theme is fish, one station may contain an arts and crafts activity that involves cutting out and pasting fish. This activity can easily include new mands, tacts, intraverbals, and imitative behaviors. In addition, there can be a focus on reinforcing independent work and/or peer interactions. A second station may involve reading a book about fish (e.g., Dr. Seuss's *One Fish Two Fish Red Fish Blue Fish*). New verbal and nonverbal behaviors can also be taught in the group format with this material. A third station may involve a fishing game where children can use a magnetic fishing pole to catch fish in a pond. This presents lots of opportunities for verbal behavior, imitation, peer interactions, sharing, matching-to-sample, etc., set in a fun and age-appropriate instructional format. Finally, a closing large group circle may contain intraverbal questions about the three different stations.

Suggested IEP Goals for Classroom Routines and Group Skills: Level 2 (select only 1 or 2 goals and modify them as appropriate for the individual child).

- The child will put away personal items, line up, and come to a table with only 1 verbal prompt.

- The child will sit in a small group for 10 minutes, attend to the teacher or material for 50% of the period, and respond to 5 teacher S^Ds.

- The child will transition between classroom activities with no more than 1 gestural and/or 1 verbal prompt.

- The child will respond to 5 different group instructions or questions without direct prompts in a group of 3 or more children.

- The child will use the toilet and wash his hands with only verbal prompts.

LINGUISTIC STRUCTURE – LEVEL 2

LINGUISTICS 6-M	The child's articulation of 10 tacts can be understood by familiar adults who cannot see the item tacted.

Articulation is typically the clearest under echoic control due to the matching relation between the verbal stimulus and the verbal response. However, once that match is unavailable (i.e., as in the mand, tact, and intraverbal) the quality of the articulation deteriorates for many early learners, and it often becomes difficult for listeners to understand what a child is saying. The current milestone is designed to be an early indicator of the quality of the child's articulation in the absence of an echoic prompt, as well as when the listener is out of contact with the item tacted. It is usually much harder to understand a word emitted by an early learner if one cannot see (or hear, touch, etc.) the referent, but this is the direction that a verbal repertoire must head in order for it to be of functional value for a child. This effect is easy to observe with an adult who can echo a language he does not know very well and be very close to the words of the language, but when the echoic prompt is gone, he may be a long way from the proper pronunciation.

The ability for adults to understand a small set of tacts emitted by a child is a significant milestone for many children, but a further analysis of the individual child may be important for taking the next step (also see the section on articulation barriers). Avoid adding new words too quickly, especially those that rhyme with each other, contain alliteration, or difficult blends (a similar case can be made for the child learning sign language). It is common for the words to become increasingly more difficult to understand if new vocabulary words are added too fast. This is perhaps why the tact-test presented in this milestone should be an ongoing activity for the early learner who is having difficulty with articulation. In addition, the expertise of a speech and language pathologist can help keep vocal development on track. It is important to keep in mind the long process that is involved in the vocal development of typically developing children. Articulation practice begins with cooing and babbling (3-4 months of life), and continues on for several years. And despite the hundreds of thousands of "practice" sounds, words, and phrases emitted by most children over the first few years of life, it is still often hard for strangers to understand the articulation of many 3-year-old children. Additional activities that may further develop a child's linguistic structure repertoire can be found in the VB-MAPP Linguistic Structure Supporting Skills list.

LINGUISTICS 7-M	**Has a total listener vocabulary of 100 words (e.g., *Touch nose. Jump. Find keys.*).**

Vocabulary size is perhaps the most common linguistic measure of language development. Typically, the size of the listener repertoire (traditionally referred to as receptive language) grows faster than the speaker repertoire (traditionally referred to as expressive language). However, this general pattern can be quite deceptive. It certainly is not a rule that a child must be able to emit a listener response before learning a tact response (Petursdottir & Carr, 2011). In fact, some children acquire tacts first, and still fail to acquire listener discriminations. However, at this early stage, both skills should be developed simultaneously. If a child scores high on LDs, but low on tacts, there should be an increased focus on tact development, and vice versa. It is important to keep these two repertoires fairly close together in vocabulary size. The mistake is to consider listener skills to be cognitively similar to speaker skills. They are best viewed as separate behavioral repertoires, and a child should be able to demonstrate both. The focus for a child who meets the current milestone, and is demonstrating balance with the other skills, would be to continue to increase the complexity of the LD skills, along with the related tact skills, as described in the listener and tact sections of this VB-MAPP Guide.

LINGUISTICS 8-M	**Emits 10 different 2-word utterances per day of any type except echoic (e.g., mand, tact).**

Another common measure of linguistic development is the Mean Length of Utterance (MLU). Typically, this measure considers the number of independent morphemes ("individual utterances with meaning") that a child emits in one phrase or sentence. Carrier phrases that occur "without meaning" (i.e., no separate antecedent source of control) such as "I want..." or "It's a..." do not count for these purposes as individual utterances. The importance of this measure is that it shows that a child's verbal behavior is beginning to be controlled by multiple variables such as an object and its movement, color, shape, etc. In general a 2-year-old child demonstrates an MLU of 2, a 3-year-old child an MLU of 3, but beyond the age of 3, MLUs can vary tremendously. Note that MLUs also vary between each of the verbal operants. For example, a mand for a 3-year-old child might contain just one or two words (e.g., "Go fast"), while an intraverbal for the same child may contain dozens of individual responses chained together (e.g., a story about a princess). The goal is to continue to increase the MLU, and this can be accomplished in a variety of ways. The most common procedures involve prompting, fading, chaining, and differential reinforcement of increasingly more complex responses.

LINGUISTICS 9-M	**Emits functional prosody (i.e., rhythm, stress, intonation) on 5 occasions in one day (e.g., puts emphasis or stress on certain words such as *It's MINE!*).**

There are a variety of ways that a single word can be emitted in order to have special effects on a listener. Skinner identifies this behavior as an example of autoclitic behavior (Skinner, 1957, ch. 12). Autoclitics consist of additional verbal responses that a speaker emits that modify in some way other words that the speaker emits. Thus, autoclitic behavior consists of verbal behavior about the speaker's own verbal behavior. For example, a child may say, "Don't take that," or a child might scream, "DON'T TAKE THAT!" The scream reveals an emotional state (an MO) and is an autoclitic mand of strength that accompanies the primary mand in order to have a special effect on the listener (e.g., I mean REALLY don't take that). Prosody often involves these additional autoclitic responses and typically occurs without any special training. That is, once the primary mands, tact, and intraverbals are learned, children are differentially shaped into adding secondary autoclitics to what they say, due to their special effects on listeners (for more detail on the autoclitic see Peterson, 1978).

LINGUISTICS 10-M	**Has a total speaker vocabulary of 300 words (all verbal operants, except echoic).**

A typically developing child has acquired several hundred verbal responses by 30 months of age. A child who scores at this level of linguistic development in the VB-MAPP should be acquiring new vocabulary words in each of the verbal operants on a daily basis. Again, the measure of vocabulary size is important, but it is common in linguistics not to distinguish between the different verbal operants when using this measure. However, individual vocabulary words can be mands, tacts, or intraverbals, and the ability to emit certain words as one verbal operant does not guarantee that those words will occur in another verbal operant. This makes the reliance on vocabulary size as a primary measure of language development somewhat deceptive and often misleading. For example, a child may be able to mand for bounce, but cannot tact bounce; or a child may be able to intraverbally say "farm," when singing the Old MacDonald song, but cannot tact a farm.

Suggested IEP Goals for Linguistic Structure: Level 2 (select only 1 or 2 goals and modify them as appropriate for the individual child).

- The child will emit at least 25 different two-word utterances per day.

- The child will be able to correctly use the plural form for 25 nouns.

- The child will correctly emit the appropriate tense marker for past and future at least 20 times a day.

- The child will emit phrases and sentences that contain an average of 3 words.

- The child will correctly respond to at least 10 different negation questions and situations as a listener, tacter, or intraverbal responder (at least 2 from each category).

CHAPTER 10

Interpreting the Level 3 Assessment: Curriculum Placement and Writing IEP Goals

Once a child begins to reach the milestones presented in Level 3, he is demonstrating a solid foundation of skills that will allow for more advanced language, social, and academic instruction. Level 3 begins at the developmental equivalent of about 30 months of age, and by that time most typically developing children have acquired hundreds of mands, tacts, and listener responses and easily learn new words on a daily basis. Mands are spontaneous, frequent, and clearly controlled by the child's personal motivators, especially MOs that relate to verbal information (i.e., asking questions). These mands are constantly changing and very little formal training is necessary to develop new mands, in fact the problem at this age is often that a child has too many mands ("the terrible two's"). Echoic and imitation skills are well established, which makes teaching new words and skills easier. The visual perceptual and matching skills demonstrate more abstract thinking and are beginning to help pave the way for a variety of social and academic skills. Intraverbal skills are growing rapidly and daily, and will soon reach thousands of intraverbal connections. Social interactions with adults and peers are a cornerstone of each day and regularly contribute to the development of a wide variety of new skills.

The specific aspects of a child's IEP and intervention program will depend on an analysis of the child's overall VB-MAPP scores (including the barriers). The assessor should analyze the scores in each of the domains and their relation to the child's performance in other domains. Are the mand, tact, and LD scores close to each other (balanced), or is one significantly higher than another? The assessor should identify the strengths and weaknesses of the skills, and determine if there are particular strengths in one area that can be of special benefit to a child, or weaknesses that need to be a larger part of the intervention program. For example, a child may have a strong LRFFC repertoire, but a limited intraverbal repertoire. The LRFFC skills can be used to develop and balance out the intraverbal repertoire.

In general, the focus of the intervention at this point should be on (1) expanding the content of what the child talks about by teaching new mands, tacts, and LD responses, (2) expanding the sentence size by teaching the child how to modify basic nouns and verbs with adjectives, prepositions, pronouns, adverbs, and so on, (3) developing more complex mands, such as mands for information and mands involving the different parts of speech, (4) teaching intraverbal behavior (e.g., how to talk about things and events that are not present), (5) learning to use these verbal skills in socially appropriate ways, (6) increasing the frequency and complexity of peer play and other social interactions, (7) expanding the child's ability to learn in a group teaching format, (8) movement toward a less restrictive educational setting, and (9) developing beginning academic skills. In addition to these targets, there are several other skills that a child might need to comprise a more complete program, such as self-help, fine and gross motor, independence, leisure, safety, and the reduction of any significant behavior problems or other language and learning barriers.

A sample VB-MAPP for a child scoring primarily in Level 3 is presented in Figure 10-1. Jacob is a 4-year-old child who is showing strong tact and listener skills; has well established echoic, imitation, and matching skills; and some beginning academic skills. However, his mand and intraverbal repertoires

Figure 10-1

Sample VB-MAPP Milestones Assessment for a child scoring in Level 3.

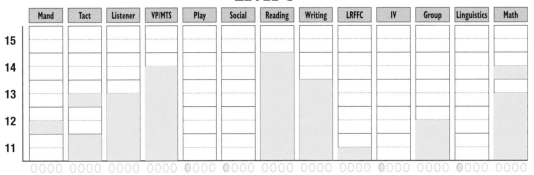

VB-MAPP Milestones Master Scoring Form

Child's name:	Jacob			
Date of birth:	2/28/04			
Age at testing:	**1** 4 yrs.	**2**	**3**	**4**

Key:	Score	Date	Color	Tester
1ST TEST:	115	4/2/08		MS
2ND TEST:				
3RD TEST:				
4TH TEST:				

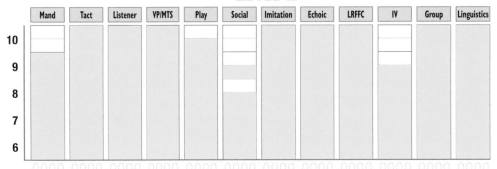

LEVEL 3

Mand | Tact | Listener | VP/MTS | Play | Social | Reading | Writing | LRFFC | IV | Group | Linguistics | Math

LEVEL 2

Mand | Tact | Listener | VP/MTS | Play | Social | Imitation | Echoic | LRFFC | IV | Group | Linguistics

LEVEL 1

Mand | Tact | Listener | VP/MTS | Play | Social | Imitation | Echoic | Vocal are relatively weak, as are his social and play skills. At 4 years of age, Jacob's reading, writing, and math skills are not far behind, but his language (mand and intraverbal) and social skills are well below his typically developing peers. He is in need of an intervention program that focuses on several of the 9 different skill areas identified above. In addition, an analysis of any existing language and learning barriers will be of value in designing a specific intervention program. Table 10-1 contains a list of possible IEP goals for a child whose VB-MAPP profile looks similar to Jacob's. The further breakdown of the steps between the milestones contained in the VB-MAPP Supporting Skills list and the skills identified in the Transition Assessment may provide additional suggestions for specific goals that may be of value in designing a daily intervention program for Jacob.

Table 10-1
Sample IEP goals for a child scoring primarily in early Level 3.

1. Jacob will spontaneously mand for information at least 50 times a day with at least 4 different question words (e.g., what, where, who, which, can, do, will, or is).

2. Jacob will tact specific aspects of at least 25 different items when given at least 4 randomly rotating verbal questions about the items (e.g., "What is this?" "Where do you find this?" "What do you do with this?").

3. Jacob will complete or continue 25 patterns or sequences with at least three parts.

4. Jacob will select the correct item from a messy array of 10 items for 500 WH questions involving the function, features, or class (LRFFC) for at least 100 different items.

5. Jacob will be able to answer 2 questions about a story after being read a short passage from a story or a book for 50 different passages.

6. Jacob will be able to answer 500 different intraverbal questions.

7. Jacob will engage in cooperative, constructive, or physical play activities with peers lasting at least 10 minutes.

8. Jacob will take turns and share reinforcers with peers without prompts at least 10 times in a day.

9. Jacob will spontaneously emit at least 4 verbal exchanges with a peer an average of 15 times per day (reciprocal interactions and beginning conversations).

10. Jacob will copy all 26 upper and lowercase letters legibly.

11. Jacob will read and identify as a listener at least 25 written words.

12. Jacob will match number to quantity and quantity to number for the numbers 1-10.

13. Jacob will sit in a 20-minute group session involving 5 children without disruptive behaviors, and answer 10 intraverbal questions.

14. Jacob will emit 50 different noun and verb phrases containing at least 3 words with 2 modifiers (e.g., adjectives, prepositions, pronouns, or adverbs).

Special Considerations for a Child Whose Scores Fall Primarily in Level 3

The VB-MAPP scores and the placement guide presented in this chapter can help to identify specific curriculum needs for an individual child. However, since every child is unique, it is important to also consider several other variables such as the child's strengths and weaknesses, learning barriers, history of learning (e.g., rate of acquisition of new skills), educational setting, and available resources. It is also important that the program be regularly monitored by a qualified professional who is knowledgeable in behavior analysis and the application of Skinner's analysis of verbal behavior. As language becomes more complex, there are many potential pitfalls that can be avoided or mitigated by using the conceptual tools provided by Skinner. For example, many children at Level 3 have difficulty with complex mands and intraverbal behavior. These language skills are hard to acquire because the antecedents for mands and intraverbals (motivating operations and complex verbal stimuli, respectively) become increasingly complicated, and are quite susceptible to producing a wide variety of impaired repertoires. These weaknesses can in turn affect the development of social behavior because mands and intraverbals form the core of verbal social interaction.

A child whose scores fall in Level 3 has acquired a number of important language skills and has demonstrated the ability to learn new content. However, a child at this level often presents many unique challenges to the program designer because the high level of skills may mask significant linguistic, social, and behavioral deficits. These must be identified and ameliorated in order to continue to move a child forward.

Teaching Format

It is common to identify "intensity" in terms of number of hours, number of training trials, the teaching format, and the teacher-to-student ratio. A child whose scores fall in Level 3 is still in need of an intensive intervention, but not in the same way that a Level 1 or Level 2 child might need an intensive intervention. It remains important to seek a balance between DTT and NET training, since both provide unique contributions to learning and both play a critical role in language and social development. A carefully designed intervention program is still necessary, but 1:1 and 1:2 tabletop instructions may become less of a focus. This teaching format may now be used more for academic skills, independent work, generalization, expansion of known skills, and other developmentally appropriate tasks, while the natural environment and group-teaching formats can be used for developing other important language and social skills. For example, many of the motivators that need to be in place for developing advanced mands cannot be easily captured or contrived in a formal tabletop teaching session. These types of antecedents often occur in other environments, such as during social play, arts and crafts, group activities, recess, the community, or home, etc., but it still requires careful teaching procedures to establish the targeted skills. It is usually a mistake to assume that children will simply learn advanced manding (as well as intraverbal and social behavior) by placement in a program that follows these teaching formats, but does not employ the sophisticated teaching procedures necessary to establish and maintain these skills.

Integration and Socialization

Integration is an important aspect of the intervention program for children scoring in Level 3, and given the absence of severe behavior problems, should become a bigger part of their educational day. A child at this level has many strong basic verbal skills, but may benefit from peer models to further develop his social, mand, and intraverbal skills. Also, he is now in a better position to benefit from the teaching format and curriculum characteristic of a less restrictive classroom placement. The reader is referred to the Transition Assessment presented in Chapter 7 for more specific information about a child's readiness for transition to a less restrictive educational environment.

Summary

Level 3 of the VB-MAPP involves a wide range of complex language, learning, and social skills. Language grows rapidly in typically developing children between the ages of 30 and 48 months. For example, there are mands for information, elaborate descriptions of events, more appropriate use of adjectives, prepositions, pronouns, and adverbs, interest in peer interactions, creative play, increased independence, and beginning academics. The curriculum becomes more complex at this point and requires a different approach to its delivery than might have been essential in Level 1 and Level 2 instruction. The focus becomes more about using existing vocabulary words in a variety of ways and contexts, such as moving tact and LD skills into complex mands, intraverbals, and LRFFC relations, transitioning to less restrictive and natural settings, and placing a larger emphasis on areas such as social interactions, independence, emotional regulation, and problem solving. Behavioral procedures are still essential, but even more challenging is keeping up with the curriculum demands at this level. The following placement content is designed to help the reader through these advanced levels of social and verbal behavior.

Interpreting the Scores for the Level 3 Milestones and Suggested IEP Goals

Each of the Level 3 Milestones are presented followed by suggestions and considerations for a child who has met that specific milestone. The format for interpreting the assessment is the same as that used for Level 1 and Level 2.

MAND – LEVEL 3

MAND 11-M	Spontaneously mands for different verbal information using a WH question or question word 5 times (e.g., *What's your name? Where do I go?*).

The ability to mand for information has significant effects on a child's developing verbal repertoire. Typically developing children experience a "language explosion" between 2 and 3 years of age. It is common to attribute this verbal development to the child's high frequency of asking questions (e.g., Brown, Cazden, & Bellugi, 1969). Once a child begins asking for different information, it is important to reinforce this behavior, as well as to use this opportunity to expand the response beyond the original question (Hart & Risley, 1975, 1995). For example, if a child asks, "Who is that?" when a plumber comes to the door, the adult's response, "He is a plumber who is here to fix the drain," can be followed by a discussion about what a plumber does, how water gets into the house, how the drain might have become plugged-up, demonstrations of water going through pipes, and watching the plumber work, etc. After the plumber leaves further intraverbal discussions are possible.

These language expansion opportunities are excellent activities for developing intraverbal and other related behaviors, and they exemplify how a single MO ("curiosity" about the man coming to the door) can lead to the development of more advanced verbal behavior. These MOs, often occurring in a child's natural environment, should be captured as often as possible and used for the further development of a child's language skills. It also demonstrates what can be referred to as a "verbal module" where a particular topic (e.g., a plumber) can provide a context for mand, tact, intraverbal, and listener training on a thematically related topic. When there is an MO at strength for that topic the procedures can become much more effective. These types of exchanges should become a daily part of the child's program. It is also important to monitor the emergence of new barriers, such as verbal perseveration (e.g., excessive discussions about plumbers). Additional activities for developing a mand repertoire can be found in the corresponding sections of the VB-MAPP Mand Supporting Skills list.

MAND 12-M	Politely mands to stop an undesirable activity, or remove any aversive **MO** under 5 different circumstances (e.g., *Please stop pushing me. No thank you. Excuse me, can you move?*).

One distinction among the different types of motivation is between wanting certain things or events and **NOT** wanting certain things and events (mands to remove aversives). Typically developing children often quickly learn the power of "No!" as a mand. This mand often causes problems for parents and generally would not be recommended as an early mand to teach children who have minimal mands. Rather, it is recommended that learning to mand for desired items be the initial focus of an early intervention program, but at some point learning to mand to remove aversive events is a major part of a mand repertoire. Once this skill is acquired it should be monitored carefully because of the complexity of the repertoire and "emotional" variables involved. For example, when a child is experiencing an aversive motivator (e.g., another child takes a toy) the probability of negative behavior is high and the probability of appropriate behavior is often low. An effective mand repertoire is part of the solution, but also there are emotional variables that are often more complicated to control (e.g., anger).

Teaching sharing, cooperation, turn taking, and general tolerance of others is an essential part of the child's social success. However, without an acceptable mand to remove an aversive, it will be difficult to decrease negative behavior that serves the same function. Once a child has a beginning repertoire of these mands, expansion and generalization to novel aversive situations becomes quite important, as do the other parts of controlling emotions (e.g., self-control). It may also be useful to teach the child appropriate gestures that often go along with mands to remove aversives such as shaking the head "no," or wiggling a finger. Like with many of the positive MOs described previously, most of the aversive MOs are going to be occurring in the child's natural environment and the focus of the intervention program needs to be there.

MAND 13-M	Mands with 10 different adjectives, prepositions, or adverbs (e.g., *My crayon is broken. Don't take it out. Go fast.*).

A child should be able to mand for anything he can tact if there is motivation for that item, action, or modifier of the item or action (e.g., "Lift me up in the tree"). Once a child's mands move beyond nouns and verbs and he begins to emit prepositions, adjectives, pronouns, and adverbs as mands, the natural contingencies (specific reinforcement) should maintain manding. At this stage in mand development many of a child's mands may be for social interactions (e.g., "Let's play dress up."), attention to their own intraverbal behavior (e.g., "I want to tell the story."), mands to engage others in a variety of activities (e.g., games, play, and help with problems), and more complex mands for information (e.g., "when," "how," and "why"). These types of mands should be encouraged and intermittently reinforced, to develop verbal persistence.

MAND 14-M	Gives directions, instructions, or explanations as to how to do something or how to participate in an activity 5 times (e.g., *You put the glue on first, then stick it. You sit here while I get a book*).

Telling other people what to do can provide a powerful form of reinforcement for many children. Mands have such a unique consequence that usually little is necessary to maintain them. If anything, the focus may be on teaching the child to be more independent and on reducing these types of mands as some children become too "bossy." As children grow, mands should always be changing because MOs change during a child's development. For example, mands for others to attend to the content of a child's intraverbal behavior (i.e., what he is talking about) becomes more important to the child as his intraverbal behavior becomes more complex. For example, when a child tells his parents about a problem he had with another child, he may be manding for sympathy, help, suggestions, advise, etc., and it is important that the adult attends to the details of his problem (e.g., "What do I do?"). It is also important to monitor this to ensure that MOs are actually the source of control for manding (watch out for rote mands).

MAND **15-M**	Mands for others to attend to his own intraverbal behavior 5 times (e.g., *Listen to me... I'll tell you... Here's what happened... I'm telling the story...*).

At this point the child should be demonstrating a mand repertoire commensurate with that of a typically developing 4-year-old child. Most 4-year-old children have quite a sophisticated mand repertoire, but that doesn't mean mand training is finished. Children and adults often have difficulty expressing their "needs and emotions." However, if a child reaches this level of manding the foundation is established for working with the motivational issues, emotions, and internal events that will be a significant part of growing into adolescence and adulthood.

Suggested IEP Goals for Mand Level 3 (select only 1 or 2 goals and modify them as appropriate for the individual child).

- The child will spontaneously mand in the natural environment for information at least 50 times a day with at least 4 different question words (e.g., "what," "where," "who," "which," "when," "why," "how," "can," "do," "will," "is").

- The child will spontaneously mand for others to attend to his story, verbal description of events, or other intraverbal behavior at least 10 times a day.

- The child will spontaneously mand at least 25 times a day by telling others how to do things, put things together, take turns, follow directions, or participate in an activity, etc.

TACT – LEVEL 3

TACT **11-M**	Tacts the color, shape, and function of 5 objects (15 trials) when each object and question is presented in a mixed order (e.g., *What color is the refrigerator? What shape is the valentine? What do you do with the ball?*) (This is part tact and part intraverbal).

The ability to correctly respond to tasks that involve both complex verbal stimuli and complex nonverbal stimuli presented in a random order prepares a child for many of the linguistic complexities he will face in future learning. In day-to-day discourse it is common to talk about things that are present in a variety of different ways. Some of the ways that things are talked about make certain aspects of the physical world more salient, and a child must learn to attend to both verbal and nonverbal stimuli simultaneously in order to verbally respond correctly. Connecting the multiple words that people say with the multiple things and events that they talk about in the immediate environment constitutes a conditional discrimination where one stimulus changes the effects of another stimulus. For example, while reading a Curious George story to a child, an adult might ask the child, "What color is George's hat?" In order for the child to correctly respond, he must attend to George and the color of his hat and tact that color. If the verbal stimulus is changed to, "What shape is George's hat?" he must now tact the shape of the hat, rather than its color. The words "color" and "shape" change what aspects of the hat that the child should attend to. These words demonstrate intraverbal control, and the nonverbal stimuli related to the actual shape and color of the hat demonstrates tact control (e.g., the word "color" along with the actual color controls "black" and the word "shape" along with the actual shape controls "round"). Thus, this type of verbal behavior is part intraverbal and part tact (i.e., it is multiply controlled), and it is quite common in more advanced verbal interactions (Michael et al., 2011; Sundberg & Sundberg, 2011).

This part-tact and part-intraverbal arrangement can become quite complicated. What if the picture contains three different characters with three different hats, holding three different boxes that all have different shapes and different colors? The words "color," "shape," "hat," "box," "George," "Fred," etc., must all have stimulus control, but stimulus control over what? It depends on what is on the page that the child is looking at in the book. The word "color" should evoke attending to the color of the next noun spoken (rather than its shape). The word "hat" should evoke attending to the hat (rather than the shirt or the box), and the word "George" should evoke attending to George (rather than Fred). This combination of verbal and nonverbal stimuli could easily result in dozens of correct responses to the exact same picture. The true test of this skill is the ability to respond to these arrangements when the verbal and nonverbal stimuli are presented in a mixed order (e.g., "What color are George's shoes?" "What shape is Fred's box?"). This is important because these mixed conditions more closely resemble the conditions that a child will face in his day-to-day social and academic environment.

A child who scores at this level of tacting should have opportunities to make these types of discriminations in a wide variety of contexts, especially those occurring in the natural environment and during age-appropriate activities (i.e., generalization and functional use). For example, arts and crafts, games, outings, social events, etc., can all provide constantly changing nonverbal stimuli and should be accompanied by constantly changing verbal stimuli. This activity can help offset the strong tendency to become a rote responder (a common barrier for many children with autism at this point in language development). It is suggested that these skills become strong at the noun, verb, function, shape, and color level before other modifiers such as adjectives, prepositions, pronouns, and adverbs are added to the language curriculum. However, these individual tacts (e.g., "in," "on," "big," "little," "fast," "slow") should become the focus (i.e., teaching the discrimination between "big" and "little" comparisons in a formal teaching arrangement). Additional activities that would be appropriate for a child scoring at this level can be found in the corresponding sections of the VB-MAPP Tact Supporting Skills list.

Tact 12-M	Tacts 4 different prepositions (e.g., *in, out, on, under*) and 4 pronouns (e.g., *I, you, me, mine*).

The ability to tact the spatial relation between objects (prepositions) demonstrates a complex type of nonverbal stimulus control not demonstrated by typically developing children until around 3 to 4 years of age. The use of pronouns as substitutes for nouns also demonstrates a complex type of stimulus control and occurs around the same age as prepositions (the listener discrimination for these skills usually occurs at an earlier age). As with all newly acquired verbal skills, there should be a focus on generalization and the functional use of the skills in a wide variety of daily activities. Once the individual discriminations are acquired, they can be inserted into more complex discriminations such as those described in Tact Level 3-11. For example, once a child learns to tact "in" and "out," they can be asked intraverbal-tact questions in the visual context of a farm such as, "What animal is on the fence?" "Where is the cow?" "Which animal is on the barn?" "Where is the chicken?" (Note that these procedures can first be conducted in an LD or an LRFFC format.)

Tact 13-M	Tacts 4 different adjectives, excluding colors and shapes (e.g., *big, little, long, short*) and 4 adverbs (e.g., *fast, slow, quietly, gently*).

Tacting relative adjectives requires that the child be able to discriminate among the different properties of objects when those properties are compared to each other. For example, "a big truck" is only big when it is compared to a smaller truck. That previously big truck will become the smaller truck if it is compared to an even bigger truck. These are hard discriminations for young children to make. Adverbs are also complex because they usually modify an action in some way. Both adjectives and adverbs are generally dependent on an existing noun and verb repertoire respectively, which is why most typically developing children have a well-established noun and verb repertoire before they acquire and appropriately use adjectives and adverbs. Once a child learns various adjectives and adverbs they should be inserted into a variety of noun and verb phrases that involve different verbal and nonverbal contexts in order to establish generalization and the functional use of these descriptors. In addition, different adjectives and adverbs should be gradually added to formal teaching sessions, as well as incorporated into natural environment contexts and more complex tasks.

TACT 14-M	Tacts with complete sentences containing 4 or more words, 20 times.

Ultimately, tacts should contain both noun phrases and verb phrases connected by conjunctions, articles, and other parts of speech. Once a child begins to emit longer response forms (phrases and sentences) the natural contingencies involved in day-to-day verbal behavior will help to shape better syntactical and grammatical construction (i.e., the process of automatic reinforcement—sounding like others plays a major role in the shaping of a child's syntactical and grammatical skills; see Palmer, 1996). At this point in language development, a child should be acquiring an average of 1-3 new tacts a day, thus it is important to provide the child with opportunities to come in contact with novel nonverbal stimuli (e.g., reading stories and looking at books, and community outings).

TACT 15-M	Has a tact vocabulary of 1000 words (nouns, verbs, adjectives, etc.), tested or from an accumulated list of known tacts.

By 4 years of age most typically developing children have a total speaking vocabulary of 1200 to 2000 words. Many of these different words are tacts, but the highest frequency of the words emitted by 4-year-old children is usually intraverbal. Much of their intraverbal behavior, however, is dependent on their tacts. That is, children talk about things that they can tact. For example, if a child goes to a novel event such as a Renaissance Faire and watches a jousting match, and learns to tact the knights, shields, swords, jousting poles, etc., he is then in a better position to tell others about what he saw. Thus, tacting is often viewed as a major cornerstone in language development. However, as is the theme in Skinner's analysis, a complete verbal repertoire requires that the response acquired as a tact also be available to the speaker as a mand and an intraverbal, given the appropriate antecedent variables. Procedures to move known tacts to intraverbal and mand conditions should be ongoing, but intraverbal activities may become a bigger focus as a child more quickly and easily acquires new tacts. Also, the tact repertoire may involve thousands of relations, but the intraverbal repertoire should ultimately contain hundreds of thousands of relations.

Suggested IEP Goals for Tact Level 3 (select only 1 or 2 goals and modify them as appropriate for the individual child).

- The child will tact 20 different adjectives (excluding colors and shapes) and 10 adverbs in both a formal and a natural setting.

- The child will tact with complete sentences containing 4 or more words 20 times per day.

- The child will tact specific aspects of at least 25 different items when given 4 randomly rotating verbal questions about each item (e.g., "What is this?" "Where do you find this?" "What do you do with this?").

- The child will tact 4 different emotions occurring within his body.

- The child will tact 5 common social situations.

- The child will tact a total of at least 1000 nonverbal stimuli (includes all nouns, verbs, adjectives, etc.).

LISTENER RESPONDING – LEVEL 3

LISTENER 11-M	Selects items by color and shape from an array of 6 similar stimuli, for 4 colors and 4 shapes (e.g., *Find the red car. Find the square cracker.*).

The ability to discriminate among colors and shapes from an array of choices is a language milestone that can be found on many developmental charts. However, there are several different verbal and nonverbal repertoires that involve colors and shapes (e.g., tacts, mands, intraverbals), and credit for "knowing colors" or "knowing shapes" should not be given to a child who simply can touch a specific color or shape when asked to do so. A theme for the whole VB-MAPP assessment is that the same word can occur in all the verbal and nonverbal operants, and in increasingly complex arrangements. Demonstration of one skill at one level does not guarantee that the child has learned the other skills. For example, a child may be able to touch red when given an array of three different colored blocks, but errors may occur when asked to touch the red shirt while given an array containing a red shirt, red car, blue shirt, blue hat, red ball, and a green shirt. Obviously, this is a harder task (two-component), but one might be surprised when it is stated that a child "knows colors" and "knows shapes" but fails this test. One explanation for this error is that most adjectives modify nouns and the learner must be able to abstract (Skinner, 1957) a particular property (adjective) of an item regardless of the specific item (noun). Adjectives are of less (or little) value without their noun-modifying function. When adjectives, like colors and shapes, are taught as single responses (without abstraction from a noun) it becomes more like a noun than an adjective.

Once a child is able to successfully abstract color and shape (often the easiest of adjectives) from objects, multiple opportunities for generalization and functional use should be provided. For example, when getting dressed in the morning a parent might say to her child, "How about wearing the red socks today?" "Can you get the red socks?" Adding new adjectives should also be the focus of the intervention (e.g., broken, dirty, striped, silly, or noisy), but they should be introduced along with a variety of nouns (multiple exemplar training). Other parts of speech should also be included in formal listener training, such as prepositions, pronouns, and adverbs. It is important to keep in mind that these other parts of speech are also considered modifiers of nouns and verbs, thus they should be taught in conjunction with a variety of nouns and verbs. For example, in teaching prepositions the child should be asked to place a variety of items on and under a variety of surfaces. Additional activities for teaching listener skills can be found in the corresponding sections of the VB-MAPP Listener Discrimination Supporting Skills list.

LISTENER 12-M	Follows 2 instructions involving 6 different prepositions (e.g., *Stand behind the chair.*) and 4 different pronouns (e.g., *Touch my ear.*).

A child who reaches this milestone is demonstrating the ability to attend to multiple complex stimuli and emit multiple responses. It is important to ensure that these skills are not specific to certain objects, locations, people, etc. For example, a child may learn to stand behind a chair when asked to do so, but it may have more to do with the setting and the chair (the source of the stimulus control), than the word "behind." Learning the concept of "behind" as a listener involves multiple variables. As with all the milestones, they are only makers along the road, they are not the end of the road. One should be able to place any item behind any other item (e.g., "Put the cow behind the fence."), or perform an action behind an item (e.g., "Bounce the ball behind the garage."). In addition, the child must be able to discriminate "behind" from other locations (e.g., next to, in front of, near, or far) with the same items and actions. This is where generalization, functional use, multiple exemplar training, expansion, and other behavioral procedures are essential for reaching the goal of establishing a verbal repertoire that matches that of typically developing peers, and these extended activities should be the focus of the intervention for the further development of these listener skills.

Pronouns involve many of the same complexities as prepositions. While it is an important milestone, the ability to touch one person's nose versus the child's own nose—given "touch your nose," versus "touch my nose"—does not ensure the child has acquired the concept of "yours" and "mine." Possession is not a simple concept, and like the preposition "behind" it requires more than just a few simple demonstrations. Again, generalization, functional use, multiple exemplar training, etc., can help to firmly establish listener repertoires regarding pronouns. However, typically developing children continue to have difficulty with pronouns well after 4 years of age.

LISTENER 13-M	**Selects items from an array of similar stimuli based on 4 pairs of relative adjectives (e.g., *big-little, long-short*) and demonstrates actions based on 4 pairs of relative adverbs (e.g., *quiet-loud, fast-slow*).**

Relative adjectives and adverbs present special challenges for most young learners. Once a child reaches this milestone all the issues and suggestions presented above now apply to this type of listener skill. However, there are additional complexities in these types of modifiers. For example, an item that is long is only long when compared to other items. A straw might be first identified as long when compared to a shorter straw, but when the straw that was first identified as long is compared to another straw that is longer than the first straw, it now becomes the short straw. This listener discrimination involves a comparison response and can be quite difficult. Adverbs present similar problems. For example, what is smooth is relative to the properties of other movement. A "smooth ride" is contrasted with a "rough ride." As with all the noun and verb modifiers, it is important to ensure that the modifier reflects the correct source of stimulus control. If not, rote responding will result. The focus of the continued intervention on these skills is the same as in Level 3-12 above (e.g., generalization, function, and expansion).

LISTENER 14-M	**Follows 3-step directions for 10 different directions (e.g., *Get your coat, hang it up, and sit down.*).**

Responding to three-component verbal instructions is a common developmental milestone that appears on many developmental charts between 3 and 5 years of age. This skill in not so easy because all three instructions are presented before any behavior is emitted, and no individual behavior is immediately preceded by the relevant individual verbal stimulus. For example, if an adult says, "Wash your hands, get your coat, and wait by the door," not only are all three of these instructions presented together, but the first instruction is followed by two additional instructions, thus a child might have a tendency to go to the door first because that was the last instruction he heard. The second instruction, "Get your coat," may not be effective either because that verbal stimulus must function as an S^D **after** the hands are washed. How can it be an S^D when it may have occurred 1 to 2 minutes earlier? In order to respond correctly, the child may need some kind of bridging prompt like a self-echoic prompt (repeating the instruction to himself) (Esch, Mchoney, Kestner, LaLonde, & Asch, 2013; Lowenkron, 1998). The focus of the intervention at this point is to first ensure that there are no extraneous variables responsible for a correct response (e.g., the child always emits that chain of behavior after snack). Next, as described above, generalization, functional use, multiple exemplar training, etc., can ensure that the child is truly acquiring the right repertoire.

LISTENER 15-M	**Has a total listener repertoire of 1200 words (nouns, verbs, adjectives, etc.), tested or from an accumulated list of known words.**

The size of a child's listener vocabulary is a common marker in language development. The reported size of the vocabulary varies tremendously on most developmental charts (as do the specific numbers identified for most skills), but the range for a typically developing 4-year-old child appears to be between 2000 and 4000 words. The current assessment uses the measure of only 1200 words in part for ease of assessment, but also because many of the words that children understand at this age are abstract and hard to measure (e.g., believe, sure, maybe, hope, and worry). A child who reaches this milestone should be learning new listener words at an average rate of 2-4 words per day without much formal instruction (one trial learning). The focus at this point in a formal intervention program might be advancing the content along the lines of age appropriate material, LRFFC activities, functional use of listener skills, and listening to peers.

Suggested IEP Goals for Listener Behavior Level 3 (select only 1 or 2 goals and modify them as appropriate for the individual child).

- The child will discriminate as a listener among at least 100 four-component nonverbal combinations (e.g., subject-verb-adjective-noun; subject-verb-preposition-noun).

- The child will discriminate as a listener among 20 different adjectives (excluding colors and shapes) and 10 adverbs.

- The child will discriminate as a listener among 5 common social situations and 5 emotional states.

- The child will discriminate as a listener among a total of at least 1000 words (includes all nouns, verbs, and adjectives, etc.).

VISUAL PERCEPTUAL SKILLS AND MATCHING-TO-SAMPLE (VP-MTS) – LEVEL 3

VP-MTS 11-M	**Spontaneously matches any part of an arts and crafts activity to another person's sample 2 times (e.g., a peer colors a balloon red and the child copies the peer's red color for his balloon).**

Children constantly learn through the behaviors and teachings of others in many ways. A strong matching repertoire is one of these ways. A child can benefit by copying the results of other's behavior, especially when others produce a higher quality product (e.g., a better drawing of a barn). Hopefully, this matching activity will allow the child to produce a better product independently in the future. At this point in the intervention program, the focus should begin to shift to other more abstract forms of visual perceptual and matching skills such as block designs, complex puzzles, and natural environment and age-appropriate matching. In addition, other visual perceptual skills such as coloring, drawing, cutting, and various sports and outside games can further strengthen these skills. Additional activities that can develop visual perceptual and matching skills can be found in the corresponding sections of the VB-MAPP VP-MTS Supporting Skills list.

VP-MTS 12-M	Demonstrates generalized non-identical matching in a messy array of 10 with 3 similar stimuli, for 25 items (i.e., matches new items on the first trial).

This skill represents a significant milestone in the development of a matching repertoire. Once a child can match any novel item on the first trial he is demonstrating a "generalized repertoire." This usually suggests that formal training on picture and object matching is no longer necessary. The focus should continue to move in the direction of more abstract types of matching tasks.

VP-MTS 13-M	Completes 20 different block designs, parquetry, shape puzzles, or similar tasks with at least 8 different pieces.

Block designs and shape puzzles such as parquetry puzzles are actually a type of matching-to-sample, but involve more abstract stimuli. These tasks move the child beyond matching by the content of an item, to matching by abstract features (e.g., shape, color, or pattern). The focus at this point should be on patterns and sequences such as placing things in order of start-to-finish, part-to-whole, first-to-last, and other types of seriation tasks. Another important skill that would be appropriate at this time is learning to sort and group items that are members of a specific category, such as animals, clothing, furniture, or vehicles. At first this task can be accomplished with a model (e.g., put out one member of each category), but eventually the child should be able to sort items into categories without a model.

VP-MTS 14-M	Sorts 5 items from 5 different categories without a model (e.g., animals, clothing, furniture).

Sorting items by categories is a common milestone found on many developmental charts. This skill demonstrates the child's ability to not only identify an item, but also to identify the class to which that item belongs. Children often learn to sort reinforcing items much earlier in development (e.g., their toys from other items), but sorting categorically without a model is a much more complex skill. Once a child reaches this milestone, there should be a focus on generalization and expansion, as well as more extensive activities involving sequences and patterns.

VP-MTS 15-M	Continues 20 three-step patterns, sequences, or seriation tasks (e.g., star, triangle, heart, star, triangle...).

Many IQ tests use these types of tasks to help assess "cognitive ability." What they measure is a child's ability to visually discriminate complex patterns and emit behavior that is controlled by some aspect of those patterns. More complex patterns require more complex visual discriminations. Thus, such tasks can separate out various levels of intellectual performance. For example, a pattern consisting of ABCABC... should evoke "ABC;" however, this conditional discrimination is difficult for most typically developing children until about 3 to 4 years of age. Thus, the results for a child with language delays can help to identify an intellectual level as compared that of a typically developing child (thus, one of the values of standardized IQ testing). For a child who reaches this milestone, a continued focus on more complex patterns, designs, sequences, etc., would be valuable to the child in that such activities teach more careful visual discrimination skills, many of which will be essential components of later language and academic skills (e.g., math, reading, spelling, and sequencing intraverbal stories).

Suggested IEP Goals for Visual Perceptual Skills and Matching-to-Sample Level 3 (select only 1 or 2 goals and modify them as appropriate for the individual child).

- The child will complete 100 different block designs, parquetry, shape puzzles, or similar tasks that contain at least 8 different items.

- The child will continue 25 different patterns or sequences that have at least three different components.

- The child will match 300 identical or non-identical items to the corresponding items in a scene from a picture or book, or in the natural environment.

- The child will sort at least 5 related items from 10 different categories without a sample.

- The child will complete or continue 25 patterns or sequences with at least three parts.

INDEPENDENT PLAY – LEVEL 3

PLAY 11-M	Spontaneously engages in pretend or imaginary play on 5 occasions (e.g., dressing up, a pretend party with stuffed animals, pretends to cook).

Some children with autism or other developmental disabilities have difficulty reaching this point in play development. Often, the impasse is due to the inability of the child to move beyond concrete events, or due to the failure of this type of play to function as reinforcement for the child. Among the many advantages of reaching this milestone is an increase in the child's creativity and language. Children who engage in pretend play typically act out and vocalize their own scripts, whether they pretend to serve food or have a battle with action figures, children tend to vocalize, use gestures, and become very imaginative during pretend play. This skill can be quite valuable for participating and maintaining successful social play with peers. A simple activity such as pretending to have a tea party can involve many different skills from other sections of the VB-MAPP, such as listener behavior (e.g., "Can you pour some tea?"), mands (e.g., "Please pass the sugar."), tacts (e.g., "Your tea is good."), imitation (e.g., "I'll show you how to pour the tea."), intraverbal (e.g., "Would you like something to eat with your tea?"), and so on. Once a peer becomes involved in the pretend play, social interactions become inherent in the activities.

At this point in the development of play skills the adult should encourage age-appropriate pretend play activities with various props and scripts. Pretend play can also set the stage for "behavioral rehearsal" of everyday events such as social situations, or events that the child might otherwise find stressful (e.g., going to the doctor). Additional activities that would be appropriate for a child scoring at this level can be found in the corresponding sections of the VB-MAPP Independent Play Supporting Skills list.

PLAY 12-M	Repeats a gross motor play behavior to obtain a better effect for 2 activities (e.g., throwing a ball in a basket, swinging a bat at a T-ball, foot stomping to launch a rocket, pumping a swing).

A major theme in the current analysis of play development is that the child's behavior and the outcome of that behavior provides automatic reinforcement (not delivered by an adult) for the child. One effect of automatic reinforcement is that it shapes behavior in an extremely efficient manner, often much better than contrived reinforcers (Palmer, 1996; Skinner, 1957). A child who reaches the current milestone is demonstrating that his play behavior is being automatically shaped by its consequences. The barrier for some children is that hitting a ball further or making a successful basketball shot may not be a reinforcer for them, which is why contrived reinforcers are often necessary to reach this point. An analogy could be made to learning to read. Contrived reinforcers and careful teaching are necessary to teach a child the basics of reading in order for him to eventually be automatically reinforced by reading an entertaining book (e.g., Harry Potter). At this point in the intervention, contrived reinforcement may still be necessary for new activities (just like with typically developing children), and the child should be provided with opportunities to try a variety of physical activities. Like other types of independent play (e.g., pretend play), these gross motor and sports skills are a natural component of social play (e.g., throwing and catching a ball, chasing and playing tag, or jumping rope).

PLAY 13-M	Independently engages in arts and crafts type activities for 5 minutes (e.g., drawing, coloring, painting, cutting, pasting).

Children learn to focus on activities they enjoy long before they focus on those imposed on them by adults. Arts and crafts provide a wide range of opportunities to teach children new skills such as attending to a task, independence, fine motor skills, and task completion. These activities are a significant component of most preschool and early elementary school programs. If a child will work independently on an activity for 5 minutes, it suggests that automatic reinforcement is at work. Contrived reinforcement is still important, and prompts can still be used with new activities. However, when reinforcing the child's behavior while engaging in arts and crafts activities, it is best to reinforce the child's on-task behavior (e.g., "You are so good at coloring") as much as their final product. Variation and generalization continue to be important, as they are in all learning. There are many excellent arts and crafts project books and an endless list of suggestions and materials available on the Internet. Arts and crafts activities can tie into other group, language, and academic activities. Completed projects also provide opportunities for intraverbal behavior later in the day.

PLAY 14-M	Independently engages in sustained play activities for 10 minutes without adult prompts or reinforcement (e.g., playing with an Etch-A-Sketch, playing dress-up).

A child who reaches this milestone is demonstrating a number of important skills and has acquired a repertoire that will be of great benefit to him as he grows. It is virtually impossible for an adult to constantly provide attention to a child, especially if there are siblings or classmates involved. The failure to develop independent play and leisure skills for a child is often directly related to negative (attention seeking) behaviors. In order to further develop this independence it is important to do it gradually, and have toys available that can be played with solo. A child does not suddenly start playing independently for 10 minutes, it may have started with 10 seconds and gradually increased with time. It is also important to make sure that the independent play milestones are in balance with the social play milestones.

PLAY 15-M	Independently draws or writes in pre-academic activity books for 5 minutes (e.g., dot-to-dot, matching games, mazes, tracing letters and numbers).

Independence is a significant component of moving to a less restrictive educational environment. While this skill may initially develop with toys, games, and fun activities, ultimately it may move to other age-appropriate and more academic oriented activities, which can be of value to the child. Once the child begins to demonstrate enjoyment in completing independent academic materials, the probability of success in a typical classroom increases. However, independent play activities that are age appropriate will be the most socially beneficial and will prepare the child to engage in social play with peers.

Suggested IEP Goals for Independent Play: Level 3 (select only 1 or 2 goals and modify them as appropriate for the individual child).

- Independently engages in arts and crafts type activities for 15 minutes (e.g., drawing, coloring, painting, cutting, or pasting).

- Independently engages in sustained play activities for 15 minutes without adult prompts or reinforcement (e.g., playing with an Etch-A-Sketch or playing dress-up, etc.).

- Independently draws or writes in pre-academic activity books for 10 minutes (e.g., dot-to-dot, matching games, mazes, or tracing letters and numbers).

SOCIAL BEHAVIOR AND SOCIAL PLAY – LEVEL 3

SOCIAL 11-M	Spontaneously cooperates with a peer to accomplish a specific outcome 5 times (e.g., one child holds a bucket while the other pours in water).

Children often develop prosocial relationships with other children because they discover that under many circumstances they need other children ("Two heads are better than one" as the adage goes). Meeting the current milestone suggests that the child is beginning to come in contact with the benefits of cooperating with other children. However, as with all the milestones, they are simply markers on the way to a greater goal. There is much more work to be done to firmly establish a child's skills in social cooperation. Social cooperation is not just one set of skills, or one collection of behaviors, but covers a wide variety of many different arrangements of social contingences. Along with needing two people to accomplish a desired goal, there are many other skills and activities where cooperation constitutes a core component, such as turn taking, sharing, problem solving, games, team activities, sports, leadership, delay of self-gratification, and restraint from negative behaviors in social play. It may be necessary to formally teach social skills using role-playing but once the basic skills are acquired the child should be provided with supervised opportunities to transfer these skills to interactions with peers.

It often takes years for typically developing children to acquire effective cooperative and social skills. For a child who reaches the current milestone, the focus should be on providing daily opportunities to generalize and expand prosocial behaviors. Additional activities that would be appropriate for a child scoring at this level can be found in the corresponding sections of the VB-MAPP Social Behavior and Social Play Supporting Skills list. In addition, there are a number of programs available for teaching cooperative social behaviors, as well as other supporting social play behaviors, to children with autism and other developmental disabilites (e.g., Attwood, 1998; Baker, 2003; Bellini, 2006; Krempa & McKinnon, 2005; Leaf & McEachin, 1999; Taubman et al., 2011; Taylor & Jasper, 2001; Weiss & Harris, 2001; Wolfberg, 1999).

SOCIAL 12-M	Spontaneously mands to peers with a WH question 5 times (e.g., *Where are you going? What's that? Who are you being?*).

In order to mand to a peer for information there must be an MO at strength for obtaining some specific verbal information from the peer. It is important to ensure that the MO is the source of control for the question (i.e., the child really wants to know the answer to the specific question). Once a child begins to demonstrate this type of manding to peers, often the natural consequences will maintain and expand the behavior. That is, getting specific verbal information from peers, such as the location of a toy or how it works, will naturally reinforce question asking, and may lead to asking other questions. The focus of the intervention at this point should be to encourage the expansion of question asking to a variety of motivators that might be related to other types of questions (e.g., "who," "what," "where," "when," "which," "why," "how," "can," "do," "will"). Generalization to new situations, new peers, new settings, and new social contexts is also an important component of the development of a solid manding for information repertoire.

There is another feature of this type of mand that plays a critical role in social development. A significant component of a "conversation" consists of manding for information. For example, one child might ask another child "What video game do you have?" The second child might then intraverbally respond to the question with "Mario," which in turn creates a new MO for more information and evokes "Which Mario?' which evokes "Mario 3," and so. Conversations may also consist of many other forms of verbal and nonverbal behavior (echoics, tacts, LDs, LRFFCs, eye contact, gestures, etc.), but mands and intraverbals serve as the cornerstones of most conversations. Thus, it is important at this time to also focus on teaching a child to intraverbally respond to the mands from peers, and on teaching responses that sound natural and typical to their peers. Fluency training can help in the success of this particular skill. The child needs to be able to respond fairly quickly to the verbal statements made by peers. Children are often on the go and may not wait around for a response from the target child.

SOCIAL 13-M	Intraverbally responds to 5 different questions or statements from peers (e.g., verbally responds to *What do you want to play?*).

Intraverbal behavior with peers is a major social and linguistic milestone. Many important skills come together with this seemingly simple task. Consider that two of the most significant diagnostic criteria for autism consist of language delays and social impairment. Within the domain of language skills, intraverbal skills tend to be the biggest challenge for children with autism (as well as those with other intellectual disabilities). It is common for many children with autism to acquire rudimentary intraverbal responses that are rote, out of context, or in other ways quite different from the types of intraverbal behavior acquired by typically developing peers. For a child who has acquired a successful intraverbal repertoire, the transfer to verbal stimuli presented by peers addresses the second component of the current milestone. Peers often emit unpredictable verbal stimuli, which often differ drastically from the standard intraverbal tasks presented by an adult. In addition, the peer's verbal stimuli are usually emitted with different words in different contexts; and with different syntax, grammar, prosody, etc. When a child has successfully responded intraverbally to these types of verbal stimuli, one of the hardest steps in generalization has occurred. The focus of the intervention at this point is to continue to generalize and expand these repertoires by providing varied contexts and opportunities for intraverbal responding to peers. Often, a peer with more advanced manding and intraverbal skills can be a key component for further intraverbal development.

SOCIAL 14-M	Engages in pretend social play activities with peers for 5 minutes without adult prompts (e.g., dress up play, acting out videos, playing house).

Children are imaginative, and pretend play with peers is an important part of learning, and entertainment. Unfortunately, many children with language delays have difficulty breaking free from structured routines and concrete activities. Thus, adults should foster creative activities (as previously stated) because once a child reaches the current milestone, the natural contingencies related to such behavior can develop forms of verbal and social interaction that would be virtually impossible to teach in a formal structured teaching session. Contact with peers who demonstrate this type of play behavior should be fostered. Even if the target child is not the "inventor" or leader of the game, or if the child is not verbal during the game, the primary goal at this point is simply participation in the game or activity. This type of play often results in the child learning without direct adult teaching, and helps to develop play and social concepts by listening, observing, and imitating. As participation increases, reinforcement should be provided for individual creative behaviors, verbal behaviors, extensions, generalization (e.g., to other peers or siblings), or other targets that involve unscripted, creative, and imaginative social behaviors. Like many social and play behaviors, the ultimate reinforcement should come from the activity itself and the peers, not the adults.

SOCIAL 15-M	Engages in 4 verbal exchanges on 1 topic with peers for 5 topics (e.g., the children go back and forth talking about making a creek in a sandbox).

If a child can maintain a verbal conversation on a single topic with a peer, it demonstrates that he can clearly benefit from regular social and academic contact with verbal peers. This level of social-verbal behavior involves many important skills, such as giving and accepting information and direction, staying on a topic, being attuned to the interest of others, allowing others to take a turn, and acknowledging the verbal behavior of others, including through eye contact. Once a child reaches this level of social interaction it shows that many of the previous milestones and individual tasks have successfully come together. The reinforcement for this social behavior should come almost entirely from the peers and other naturally occurring reinforcers. This type of reinforcement and social contact can develop and shape prosocial repertoires in a manner that formal instruction cannot. However, the child may still benefit from some on-going social skills training, especially during the teen years (Attwood, 1998).

Suggested IEP Goals for Social Behavior and Social Play: Level 3 (select only 1 or 2 goals and modify them as appropriate for the individual child).

- The child will engage in cooperative, constructive, or physical play activities with peers lasting at least 15 minutes.

- The child will spontaneously mand to peers using questions, directions, instructions, etc. (e.g., "What's that?" "Where is your lunch?" "Come on, get your bike") an average of 20 times per day.

- The child will take turns and share reinforcers with peers without prompts at least 10 times in a day.

- The child will spontaneously emit at least 4 verbal exchanges with a peer an average of 10 times per day (reciprocal interactions and beginning conversations).

- The child will intraverbally respond to questions from peers at least 20 times per day.

- The child will verbally identify the activities or emotions of peers at least once per day.

- The child will participate in 10 age-appropriate games with peers.

READING – LEVEL 3

READING 11-M	Attends to a book when a story is being read to him for 75% of the time.

Once a child begins to show interest in books and stories several activities can begin to promote reading. Pointing to words can teach the child that the story comes from the words, not the pictures. Adding expression to the words and making the story come alive can increase interest. Also, having the child follow along by making echoic responses while the adult points to words and reads can help to establish the words as S^{D}s. Some children will begin to "pretend to read" by looking at the pictures and words and tell the story. For example, while looking at the *Goodnight Moon* book the child tells the story even though it does not correspond with the written print. These behaviors should be reinforced, and adults and others should read with the child as often as possible.

Learning the names and sounds of individual letters is usually the next step. Often, a beginning step for children is singing the ABC song or completing ABC inset puzzles. There are at least eight different repertoires in early letter identification: (1) matching (MTS) letters to each other, (2) matching (MTS) uppercase letters to lowercase letters and vice versa, (3) selecting (LD) a specific letter given the letter name, (4) selecting (LD) a specific letter given the letter sound, (5) providing the name (tact) of a printed letter (this could also involve intraverbal control as in "What letter is this?" versus "What sound does this letter make?"), (6) providing the sound (tact) of a printed letter (also part IV), (7) providing the letter name given only the sound (IV), and (8) providing the sound the letter makes given only the letter name (IV). Eventually, the child will need all of these skills for both uppercase and lowercase letters, but usually letter names come before letter sounds. In addition, some children will begin to recognize (tact and LD) whole words, and often those words are of special interest to the child (related to personal MOs) or frequently associated with a specific visual stimuli. Additional activities for teaching reading can be found in the corresponding sections of the VB-MAPP Reading Supporting Skills list.

READING 12-M	Selects (LDs) the correct uppercase letter from an array of 5 letters, for 10 different letters.

The ability to select a specific letter from a group of other letters demonstrates good visual discrimination skills, because the stimuli in an array of all letters look very similar. These skills play an important role in reading and the focus should be on learning the rest of the letters, generalization to different fonts and contexts, finding letters in whole words, tacting letters, and moving into lowercases and the sounds of letters. Letter games can also help to develop letter identification skills (e.g., letter matching games). A child may begin to recognize (LD) his own name and perhaps the name of other important people or characters. Additional activities at this point can include beginning to match whole words to corresponding pictures, playing with rhyming words, and guessing what letter a word starts with. Adults should also continue to read to the child often, and reinforce the child for his attempts to read.

READING 13-M	Tacts 10 uppercase letters on command.

As the child learns to name specific letters, it becomes important to teach him that the letters also make certain sounds (and also that the same letter can make different sounds). That is where the intraverbal part of the task will be of value. For example, when shown the letter B and asked,

"Can you name this letter?" the child should say "b." When shown the same letter and asked, "What sound does this letter make?" the child should say "ba." The primary task is to establish intraverbal discrimination and control between the word "name" and "sound." Many of the activities described above should be continued with a focus on whole words and moving from left to right in naming letters and looking at words.

READING 14-M	**Reads his own name.**

This is a common milestone found in many developmental charts. The child should also be able to select his own name from an array of other names, and some children will be able to spell and write their own names at this point.

READING 15-M	**Matches 5 words to the corresponding pictures or items in an array of 5, and vice versa (e.g., matches the written word *bird* to a picture of a bird).**

At this point the child should know the names of all the letters in the alphabet and many of the sounds. The focus should move to whole words and reading comprehension. A simple form of comprehension is matching words to pictures. This can be done in a game format and teaches the child how the two correspond. Other comprehension activities can include showing a child an action word and have the child perform that action (e.g., jump or clap, etc.). There are also many commercially available reading programs that could now benefit the child as well as computer programs that can teach reading (e.g., www.headsprout.com).

Suggested IEP Goals for Reading: Level 3 (select only 1 or 2 goals and modify them as appropriate for the individual child).

- The child will tact and identify as a listener all 26 uppercase and lowercase letters.

- The child will provide the sounds made by at least 20 letters when asked to do so, and select at least 20 letters when given the sound.

- The child will read and identify as a listener at least 25 written words.

- The child will match at least 25 words to the corresponding pictures and vice versa.

WRITING – LEVEL 3

WRITING 11-M	**Imitates 5 different writing actions modeled by an adult using a writing instrument and writing surface.**

Early writing skills usually begin with the enjoyment (i.e., automatic reinforcement) of seeing a cause-and-effect relation between moving a writing instrument and a mark on some type of writing surface (e.g., paper, whiteboard, or Magna Doddle). After scribbling, an early milestone in learning to write is the ability to control the writing instrument in order to imitate specific configurations (e.g., circles, vertical lines, horizontal lines, or curved lines). Modeling, prompting, and reinforcement can be powerful teaching tools to develop this skill. The goal at this point is to further improve the child's fine motor ability to control the writing instrument in order to make smaller and more specific writing movements. Coloring, tracing, and following patterns provide excellent opportunities for the automatic shaping of writing skills. Additional activities for teaching writing can be found in the corresponding sections of the VB-MAPP Writing Supporting Skills list.

WRITING 12-M	**Independently traces within ¼ inch of the lines of 5 different geometrical shapes (e.g., circle, square, triangle, rectangle, star).**

The ability to trace shapes is an important step towards learning to write letters and numbers. By this point the child should be demonstrating an appropriate grip and control of a variety of writing instruments (e.g., crayons, pencils, markers, chalk, paint brushes, or a Magna-Doodle wand), and may help establish hand dominance. Prompts and reinforcement can be used to teach more careful tracing, as well as age-appropriate entertaining and fun material that keeps a child's interest. Gradually the child should be introduced to tracing letters and numbers, often beginning with his own name. It is important to note that learning to write legibly often requires thousands of practice trials over several years for typically developing children. Thus, for a child scoring at this level, he should be provided with daily opportunities to engage in writing activities.

WRITING 13-M	**Copies 10 letters or numbers legibly.**

Once a child reaches this milestone the focus should be on copying easy uppercase and lowercase letters and introducing some simple whole words. The child should also be working on copying numbers as suggested in the related early math skills found in the VB-MAPP Writing Supporting Skills list. A continued emphasis on other drawing and writing activities can be of value. For example, drawing simple pictures such as a stick person, house, tree, ball, or car can be fun, and help to further improve fine motor skills, as well as independent play and leisure skills.

WRITING 14-M	**Legibly spells and writes his own name without copying.**

A common milestone on many assessments is a child's ability to write his name on command. This skill is important because it demonstrates a number of advanced skills that come together in one task. The tasks not only involve writing and fine motor skills, but sequencing, start-to-finish ability, spelling, independence, and intraverbal behavior (i.e., the verbal prompt, "Write your name," should not only evoke saying his name, but also spelling his name). The focus at this point should be to move towards copying whole words that are fun for the child (e.g., the names of favorite characters), and writing and drawing games such as dot-to-dot, mazes, and other paper and pencil activities. In addition, drawing and painting pictures can be fun, involve social interactions, and be of great value to the child.

WRITING 15-M	**Copies all 26 uppercase and lowercase letters legibly.**

As the child's writing improves, a focus on producing smaller letters and staying within established writing lines is the next step. Additional activities can now include writing letters and small words from dictation, as well as writing uppercase letters (given lowercase letters) and vice versa. A child who reaches this milestone is usually ready for the standard writing curriculum found in many pre-kindergarten and kindergarten programs.

Suggested IEP Goals for Writing: Level 3 (select only 1 or 2 goals and modify them as appropriate for the individual child).

- The child will independently trace within 1/4 inch of the lines for 6 different geometrical shapes.

- The child will trace within 1/8 inch of 10 uppercase and lowercase letters of any size.

- The child will trace within 1/8 inch of 30 upper or lowercase letters that are less than 1 inch in size.

- The child will copy numbers 1-20 legibly.

- The child will copy all 26 uppercase and lowercase letters legibly.

- The child will legibly write his own name without copying it.

LISTENER RESPONDING BY FUNCTION, FEATURE, AND CLASS (LRFFC) – LEVEL 3

LRFFC 11-M	Selects the correct item from an array of 10 that contains 3 similar stimuli (e.g., similar color, shape, or class, but they are the wrong choices), for 25 different WH-question LRFFC tasks.

A child who scores at this level is demonstrating a strong LRFFC repertoire, and the focus should be on more complex arrays from books and pictures that contain similar stimuli, complex scenes, stories, sequences, social events, or new places, etc. Pictures books and computerized devices can offer a wealth of visual stimuli to use in training, often significantly more than is available in the child's natural environment. However, the natural environment should continue to play a major role in LRFFC activities, but training should be conducted in a manner that does not make trials look or feel like structured training. The verbal stimuli should continue to increase in complexity by including more adjectives that require the child to attend to the properties of items more carefully. Asking the child to "find a big animal" requires the child to attend to both the size and the class of all the options in an array, and make multiple discriminations for a single selection response (e.g., selecting an elephant). As always, it is important to ensure that the components of these skills are already strong in the child's repertoire before they are combined in this manner (i.e., he can at least LD "big" and "little," and emit correct LRFFC tasks involving "animals"). Additional activities to further strengthen the LRFFC repertoire can be found in the VB-MAPP LRFFC Supporting Skills list.

LRFFC 12-M	Selects items from a book based on 2 verbal components: either a feature (e.g., color), function (e.g., draw with) or class (e.g., clothing) for 25 LRFFC tasks (e.g., *Do you see a brown animal? Can you find some clothing with buttons?*).

The verbal stimuli used in LRFFC tasks should now involve multiple components that contain a mixture of nouns, verbs, adjectives, prepositions, pronouns, adverbs, features, functions, or classes. LRFFC training can help to teach the child to attend to each part of a sentence (i.e., make verbal conditional discriminations where one word changes the meaning of the next). Also, the arrays used should now be almost exclusively from scenes, books, computerized devices, or the natural environment (except for teaching new complex discriminations such as WH rotation questions). Not only will this training strengthen a child's listener skills, but it provides a foundation for eventual intraverbal skills where a child is able to, for example, talk about a story from a book well after the book has been put away. At this point in LRFFC training an increased focus on moving LRFFC activities to intraverbal trials would be appropriate and of great value to a child. Basically, the LRFFC activities can be used to provide content, or things that a child can talk about later in conversations and social interactions.

LRFFC 13-M	Selects items from a page in a book or in the natural environment based on 3 verbal components (e.g., verb, adjective, preposition, pronoun), for 25 WH-question LRFFC tasks (e.g., *Which fruit grows on trees?*).

At this point a child should be an accomplished listener who can successfully attend to complex auditory verbal stimuli, make conditional discriminations within a spoken sentence, and act upon that information. These are advanced skills that are very valuable to a young child who may soon enter an educational system that is filled with such complexities. While LRFFC activities are important, the focus on them as a formal listener training activity should be gradually replaced by using LRFFC for more intensive intraverbal training. LRFFC activities of some types will always occur, but what becomes more important is that a child be able to talk about events and activities when those events and activities are no longer present, and that's intraverbal behavior. LRFFC trials can be a good step toward developing verbal conditional discriminations and teaching intraverbal behavior, and at this point they should occur in a child's natural environment, as opposed to tabletop tasks. For example, reading stories to children while looking at the scenes in books or events on computerized devices and asking the child WH questions about those scenes and events in an LRFFC format is a valuable language development activity.

LRFFC 14-M	Selects the correct items from a book or the natural environment given 4 different rotating LRFFC questions about a single topic (*Where does the cow live? What does the cow eat? Who milks the cow?*) for 25 different topics.

A variety of complex discriminations can be taught to a child within an LRFFC format, and this teaching strategy can still be used for a number of important language skills. For example, the concept of negation can be taught by using LRFFC. "Not" is difficult because this verbal stimulus must override a stronger verbal stimulus that has already been well established. The verbal part of the following LRFFC task, "Which one is not an animal?" contains the verbal stimulus "animal" and the array contains pictures of animals. The child will come to this task with a strong relation between the word "animal" and the pictures of animals. The word "not" requires that the child ignore this strong relation and form a completely opposite stimulus-response relation, and to the child this is a counterintuitive relation. This complex conditional discrimination requires special training, and that is why most typically developing children only begin to acquire a generalized negation repertoire around 4 years of age. LRFFC training can help to develop this skill. Other negation words should also be introduced such as "isn't," "can't," "don't," and "won't," etc.

LRFFC 15-M	Demonstrates 1000 different LRFFC responses, tested or obtained from an accumulated list of known responses.

A child who has reached this level in the LRFFC program should be well prepared for these kinds of tasks in a less restrictive educational setting.

Suggested IEP Goals for LRFFC: Level 3 (select only 1 or 2 goals and modify them as appropriate for the individual child).

- The child will select the correct item from a scene or the natural environment given 500 different WH questions involving the function, features, or class of items.

- The child will select the correct item from an array of at least 10 or a scene given 200 different 4-component WH questions containing adjectives, prepositions, nouns, pronouns, or verbs, involving the function, features, or class of items.

- The child will select multiple items from an array of at least 10 given one instruction that contains words prompting multiple items such as "all," "two," "three," or "both."

- The child will select the correct item from a scene, computerized device, or the natural environment given 1000 different WH questions involving the function, features, or class of items.

INTRAVERBAL – LEVEL 3

INTRAVERBAL 11-M	**Spontaneously emits 20 intraverbal comments (can be part mand) (e.g., Dad says *I'm going to the car*, and the child spontaneously says *I want to go for a ride!*).**

Of all the different verbal operants presented in this program, the intraverbal repertoire presents the greatest challenge for developing verbal skills that match those of typically developing peers. One important milestone in this road to intraverbal proficiency is spontaneous intraverbal behavior that is relevant to naturally occurring events in the child's life, and not prompted by additional adult behavior. A child who reaches this milestone will usually begin to acquire new intraverbal relations at a rapid pace, due to the functional nature of the repertoire. Specifically, effective intraverbal behavior usually gets reinforced in the natural environment.

The focus for the child should now be on expanding the complexity of intraverbal stimuli and intraverbal responses. There is no single way to accomplish this, and thus a variety of teaching strategies and activities that contribute to intraverbal development are recommended (see the VB-MAPP Intraverbal Supporting Skills list). Two important elements of increasing complexity consist of teaching the child to (1) respond to verbal stimuli that have multiple components, and (2) emit responses that have multiple components. For example, a verbal stimulus that has multiple components would be a WH question that contains nouns, verbs, and adjectives, etc., such as, "What color is a fire truck?" Technically, these involve verbal conditional discriminations (VC^{D}s) where one word changes the meaning of the next word, and thus changes the correct answer (Michael et al., 2011; Sundberg & Sundberg, 2011). If the example had been, "Who drives a fire truck?" the response "fireman" rather than the response "red" would have been correct. This level of verbal discrimination is often difficult for children with language delays and must be taught carefully, and in a reasonable order of increasing complexity. The other element of increasing the complexity of intraverbal behavior involves establishing more complex response forms, that is, longer and more detailed sentences. The verbal responses children make should begin to contain combinations of nouns, verbs, and adjectives, etc. The potential combinations of intraverbal stimuli and responses will ultimately reach well into the thousands, and tens of thousands. Keep in mind that a significant component of the K-12 educational system is focused on developing intraverbal behavior (although usually not called that).

INTRAVERBAL 12-M	Demonstrates 300 different intraverbal responses, tested or obtained from an accumulated list of known intraverbals.

Once a child's verbal behavior is clearly under verbal stimulus control, and occurs outside of a discrete trial teaching format and without adult prompting, the focus should be on more rapid expansion of the intraverbal content. The sources for new intraverbal content are endless. The day-to-day activities in a child's life provide numerous topics to talk about. Books, stories, videos, and other forms of entertainment can also provide a rich source of verbal stimuli that can be used to develop intraverbal behavior. The important element is that an adult uses these opportunities to prompt and expand intraverbal responding. Some of the techniques of incidental teaching (Hart & Risley, 1975) can be effective in getting children to talk more about things and events in their world. In general, at this point in the language intervention program there should be a significant focus on intraverbal behavior, more so than on acquiring new tacts or LDs. While these skills are important, a verbal repertoire that contains mostly tacts and LDs is highly restrictive in social and academic settings. While tacts and LDs are important foundations, functionally it would seem odd to walk around tacting things, and touching things upon hearing words. Much of a child's language at this point in development involves talking about activities and things, rather than just naming them, or receptively identifying them.

INTRAVERBAL 13-M	Answers 2 questions after being read short passages (15+ words) from books, for 25 passages (e.g., *Who blew the house down?*).

The ability to attend to stories and respond to questions about the story is a common milestone that appears on many developmental charts. This is because the task involves several important linguistic skills, such as attending to verbal stimuli, comprehension, recall, and expansion of novel verbal content. In addition, as previously mentioned, books, computerized devices and stories are powerful vehicles for introducing new intraverbal content. Again, intraverbal development is a monumental task that involves many different components of teaching and parenting. Of the suggestions for development on the VB-MAPP Intraverbal Supporting Skills list, two warrant a special emphasis: stimulus generalization and response generalization. These two forms of generalization have been discussed previously, but it is critical to stress the importance of monitoring this development in children with language delays, especially those with autism. The intraverbal repertoire is highly susceptible to becoming rote. Even many typically developing individuals have defective intraverbal behavior in that they talk about the same topic in the same manner frequently. Intraverbal behavior must be flexible and generalized. Encourage generalization at every step of the way. A large intraverbal repertoire is of little value to a child if it is non-functional, rigid, not generalized, or prompt bound. Careful and vigilant stimulus and response generalization training is the key to avoiding this problem.

INTRAVERBAL 14-M	Describes 25 different events, videos, stories, etc. with 8+ words (e.g., *Tell me what happened...The big monster scared everybody and they all ran in the house*).

Between 3 and 4 years of age typically developing children begin to tell long stories about events that are important to them. It is often hard to stop them from talking. Often, this behavior is partly a mand for attention; nonetheless, the core verbal behavior constitutes intraverbal relations and is a major milestone in verbal development. The behavior typically occurs in the absence of tact variables (e.g., the event that occurred is no longer present), and is free from echoic or other prompts. It also has a major social element to it that is quite important for development. Another important milestone is the ability to accurately answer multiple questions about a single topic. The questions may contain several components and require that the child attend carefully to each component. This skill provides the foundation for much of the academic training that a child might soon encounter. There are far too many intraverbal activities to list at this point. A child should be engaging in 100s, if not 1000s, of intraverbal interactions per day. A single story of a 3½ or 4-year-old child may contain 100s of intraverbal connections.

INTRAVERBAL 15-M	**Answers 4 different rotating WH questions about a single topic for 10 topics (e.g., *Who takes you to school? Where do you go to school? What do you take to school?*).**

Intraverbal behavior constitutes the core of social and academic behavior, and plays a significant role in almost all aspects of human development. A child who reaches this milestone is better prepared to gain from standard educational methods. Intraverbal development is an on-going activity, much different from mand and tact development. While all individuals continue to acquire new mands and tacts, there is somewhat of a limited number of these verbal relations relevant to a specific individual, relative to the potential number of different intraverbal relations. A typical adult has an intraverbal repertoire consisting of hundreds of thousands of intraverbal connections. Just reading the daily newspapers can evoke thousands of intraverbal responses. Thus, once a basic intraverbal repertoire is established for a child, it is important to continue to provide the child with new content, generalization opportunities, and increasingly complex stimuli while encouraging increasingly complex responses. Again, this is the primary focus of a K-12 educational system and early intraverbal training can provide a child with the prerequisite skills to learn from this system.

Suggested IEP Goals for Intraverbal: Level 3 (select only 1 or 2 goals and modify them as appropriate for the individual child).

- The child will be able to correctly answer at least 4 different questions about 50 different objects shown to him.

- The child will be able to describe 50 different events, videos, stories, etc., with at least 8 words.

- The child will be able to answer 250 different intraverbal yes-no questions.

- The child will be able to answer 1000 different intraverbal questions.

- The child will be able to answer 3 questions about a story after being read 50 different short passages from a book.

- The child will be able to answer 4 different WH questions about a single topic for 25 topics (e.g., "Who takes you to school?" "Where do you go to school?" "What do you take to school?").

- The child will be able to complete 25 different verbal sequences.

- The child will be able to identify 25 activities that happened in the past or will happen in the future.

- The child will engage in at least 5 different short "conversations" with others consisting of at least three verbal and nonverbal (LD) exchanges.

CLASSROOM ROUTINES AND GROUP SKILLS – LEVEL 3

GROUP 11-M	Uses the toilet and washes hands with only verbal prompts.

Toileting is a major part of all preschool programs. Once a child is able to independently eliminate on the toilet, even with verbal prompts, it becomes less of a focus and frees up more teaching time. In addition, it increases the child's probability of acceptance and success in a less restrictive setting where toileting skills are expected for all children (e.g., a kindergarten classroom). Additional activities for teaching classroom routines and group skills can be found in the corresponding sections of the VB-MAPP Classroom Routines and Group Skills Supporting Skills list.

GROUP 12-M	Responds to 5 different group instructions or questions without direct prompts in a group of 3 or more children (e.g., *Everybody stand up. Does anyone have a red shirt on?*).

The majority of educational systems are based on group instruction. The transition for a child who has primarily been in a high-ratio structured teaching arrangement to a group-teaching format may be difficult. A child must learn to respond without direct prompts such as stating the child's name, sitting directly in front of the child, using a discrete trial tone of voice, or presenting clear S^Ds for the individual child to respond to specific teacher task. Also reinforcers for responding are different in a group format, in that rarely are consumable or tangible reinforcers used. At some point a child must learn to attend to a teacher without being told to attend, or given a tangible reinforcer for doing so. In addition, much can be gained from peers in a group setting, including social interaction and learning in a peer-based natural environment. Group responding is an essential component of moving to a less restrictive educational and social environment. Once a child is able to sit in a group, not engage in negative behavior, attend to a teacher, and respond to "group S^Ds," the focus can shift to more independent work activities and learning new skills in the group instruction format.

GROUP 13-M	Works independently for 5 minutes in a group, and stays on task for 50% of the period.

A common element of many preschool and elementary classrooms is independent group-work stations or centers. Children are often given language or academic worksheets, art projects, or fine motor tasks, and are expected to complete the tasks without disruptive behavior; and carry on with little adult prompting or direct reinforcement. These independent skills should continue to be fostered by providing the child with a range of activities, both leisure and academic. Working independently without disruptive behavior is a major component of being successful in a less restrictive academic setting.

GROUP 14-M	Acquires 2 new behaviors during a 15-minute group-teaching format involving 5 or more children.

Learning new language and academic skills in a group-teaching format is a significant milestone for many children. Many of the preschool and elementary programs at this level contain a theme of the day, or in some way introduce new material each day. Once a child begins to learn a new tact, LD, or intraverbal responses in this group-teaching format, additional academic, language, and social options become available. As previously mentioned, an important element of a group format is that the S^{D}s and MOs to respond to specific adult or teacher instruction or other verbal or nonverbal information are very different. This format can help to promote learning in the natural environment and in a variety of educational settings where the discrete format is not present (e.g., field trips, casual daily activities, peers, and educational videos). As the child becomes more proficient with group skills, the verbal content can be systematically increased to include more intraverbal responding, which is more characteristic of higher-level groups (e.g., "Who can tell me what happened to the seed we planted?").

GROUP 15-M	**Sits in a 20-minute group session involving 5 children without disruptive behaviors, and answers 5 intraverbal questions.**

At this point a majority of the child's instruction should occur in a group-teaching format, regardless of chronological age. While certainly some 1:1 and small group activities can benefit the child, much in the same way a tutor might for a typically developing child, a child who scores at this level has demonstrated he can learn in this significantly less restrictive and potentially more beneficial educational format.

Suggested IEP Goals for Classroom Routines and Group Skills: Level 3 (select only 1 or 2 goals and modify them as appropriate for the individual child).

- The child will work independently for 15 minutes in a group setting, and stay on task for 75% of the period.

- The child will respond to 10 different group instructions or questions without direct prompts in a group of 5 or more children (e.g., "Everybody stand up." "Does anyone have a blue shirt on?").

- The child will acquire 1 new behavior a day in a 25-minute group-teaching format involving 5 or more children.

- The child will sit in a 20-minute group session involving 5 children without disruptive behaviors, and answer 10 intraverbal questions.

LINGUISTIC STRUCTURE – LEVEL 3

LINGUISTICS 11-M	**Emits noun inflections by combining 10 root nouns with suffixes for plurals (e.g., *dog vs. dogs*) and 10 root nouns with suffixes for possessions (e.g., *dog's collar vs. cat's collar*).**

Nouns and verbs provide the foundation for linguistic structure. Nouns and verbs can be modified and combined in an almost infinite number of ways. Thus, prior to providing intensive teaching on words that modify a noun or verb (e.g., adjectives, prepositions, pronouns, adverbs, affixes), or words that combine nouns and verbs (e.g., conjunctions, disjunctions, articles, or affixes) it is essential that a child have a solid noun and verb repertoire. Inflections are one way that root words can be modified, and a child's correct emission of inflections represents a significant linguistic milestone. An inflectional affix "conveys grammatical information" about the root word (usually a noun or verb) to the listener.

Nouns (and pronouns) have two types of inflectional markers: number and possession. A noun like "dog" can be inflected by an additional response that identifies how many dogs (number) and aspects of ownership or possession. In lay terms, is there more than one dog present, and what is "owned" by the dog(s)? In an analysis of a tact of plurality, for example, there are two nonverbal antecedent S^Ds, the dog and the number of dogs. The response "dog" is controlled by the type of animal seen, and the suffix "s" (or "grammatical tag") is controlled by the nonverbal S^D of more than one dog. Thus, this type of verbal behavior represents a complex tact containing two separate antecedents and two separate responses (i.e., each response has a separate source of antecedent control). Plural and possession inflections occur in all verbal operants and listener skills (i.e., echoics, mands, tacts, intraverbals, LD, and LRFFC).

Once a child is successfully emitting at least some plurals and possession tags correctly, it is important to make sure these verbal skills are generalized to a variety of nonverbal stimuli. For example, if a child can tact plurality for animals and toys, they may get credit for this milestone, but eventually it is essential that the child be able to tact plurality for any collection of nouns presented (e.g., spoons, books, and trees), and eventually use the correct emission of irregular plurals (e.g., geese, people, and feet). In addition, as mentioned above, teaching plurality for mands, tacts, and LDs is also essential. For example, in intraverbal plurality the verbal stimulus, "What do you wear on your feet?" should eventually evoke "shoes," not "shoe." This example of plurality demonstrates how traditional structural linguistics and Skinner's verbal behavior analysis each offer essential components of language assessment and intervention for children with language delays (i.e., form and function). Additional activities for developing various aspects of more complex grammatical skills can be found in the corresponding sections of the VB-MAPP Linguistic Structure Supporting Skills list.

LINGUISTICS 12-M	Emits verb inflections by combining 10 root verbs with affixes for regular past tense (e.g., *played*) and 10 root verbs with affixes for future tense (e.g., *will play*).

Verbs can also be modified in a variety of ways, for example, by adding adverbs that tell where and how an action should be carried out (e.g., "hide quick"). Verbs can also be modified with inflections that provide time markers for when an action was carried out. There are three basic (or "simple") time markers: past, present, and future. An important milestone in linguistic development is the appropriate emission of these time markers with verbs. Most typically developing children acquire these inflections, along with many other grammatical conventions, without formal training, but rather through the process of automatic reinforcement and automatic shaping (Palmer, 1996). However, it is common for children with language delays to require formal instruction in order to correctly inflect verbs with time markers. Once a child is able to pass the current milestone the same issues described above for noun inflection are relevant. Specifically, there should be a focus on generalization and functional use of the inflection in all the different verbal operant and listener repertoires. In addition, verbs also have irregular forms (e.g., run and ran, break and broken, stand and stood) that often must be directly taught.

LINGUISTICS 13-M	Emits 10 different noun phrases containing at least 3 words with 2 modifiers (e.g., adjectives, prepositions, pronouns) (e.g., *He's my puppet. I want chocolate ice cream.*).

Noun phrases consist of a noun as the head of a larger grouping of other words. These words modify the noun in any of a number of ways. The most common modifiers are those that describe a property of the noun (adjective), the location of the noun in relation to other nouns (prepositions), or words that take the place of nouns (pronouns). Other modifiers (e.g., determiners) may limit a noun, such as articles (e.g., a, and, the) and demonstratives (e.g., this, that, these, and those). There are many additional modifiers in most languages and far more detailed classification systems (e.g., predeterminers and post determiners), but a description of them goes beyond the scope of this assessment and placement system.

As previously mentioned, a common measure in linguistics is the Mean Length of Utterance (MLU), which generally consist of the average number of morphemes ("utterances with a specific meaning or grammatical function") in a phrase or sentence. In contrast, this linguistic structure milestone focuses on whole words rather than individual morphemes in order to ensure that the major modifiers (adjectives, prepositions, etc.) are properly included in a noun phrase. Any individual noun phrase may actually contain 5-10, or more, individual morphemes. If a child's utterance appropriately contain two or more of the major modifies, the focus is again on generalization and use of the skills in the other language repertoires (i.e., mand, tact, LD). In addition, there should be a focus on the expansion of the utterance to include more modifiers and eventually connecting the noun phrase to a verb phrase (Linguistic Structure Level 3-15-M).

LINGUISTICS 14-M	**Emits 10 different verb phrases containing at least 3 words with 2 modifiers (e.g., adverbs, prepositions, pronouns) (e.g., *Push me hard. Go up the steps.*).**

Verb phrases consist of a verb as the head of a larger grouping of other words. And like the additional words in a noun phrase, these words modify the headword in any of a number of ways. Verbs can be subdivided into intransitive (they stand alone and don't require modifiers, for example, "smile"), transitive (they require a following noun phrase, for example, "He threw...") and linking (they connect a subject to the description of that subject, for example, "The dog is barking."). All of these types of verbs can include modifies (they tell the listener something more about the main action) such as adverbs, prepositions, and pronouns. Once a child reaches this milestone the focus is on generalization, expansion, variation, and use in all the elementary operants and listener skills. The next step is to focus on connecting noun and verb phrases to form complete grammatical sentence.

LINGUISTICS 15-M	**Combines noun and verb phrases to produce 10 different syntactically correct clauses or sentences containing at least 5 words (e.g., *The dog licked my face.*).**

Sentences can be made up of individual words, clauses, or connections between two or more clauses. Typically a sentence contains both a noun and verb phrase. A child who reaches this linguistic milestone across all the verbal operants and listener skills is usually one who can benefit from a less restrictive educational setting such as that provided in a regular education classroom.

Suggested IEP Goals for Linguistic Structure: Level 3 (select only 1 or 2 goals and modify them as appropriate for the individual child).

- The child will demonstrate a mean-length-of-utterance (MLU) of 4 words, and most sentences are in the correct word order.

- The child will emit 50 different noun phrases containing at least 3 words with 2 modifiers (e.g., adjectives, prepositions, pronouns).

- The child will emit 50 different verb phrases containing at least 3 words with 2 modifiers (e.g., adverbs, prepositions, pronouns).

- The child will combine noun and verb phrases to produce 10 different syntactically correct clauses or sentences containing at least 5 words.

MATH – LEVEL 3

MATH 11-M	Identifies as a listener the numbers 1-5 in an array of 5 different numbers.

A child's ability to understand numbers constitutes the foundation of mathematics. Children are often able to identify numbers sooner than letters because of the immediate importance of numbers to them versus letters. For example, 1 versus 2 gummy bears has a significance that A versus B does not. The ability to select a specific number from a group of other numbers demonstrates good visual discrimination skills, because the stimuli in an array of all numbers look similar. Tacting numbers can also be taught at about the same time as LDs, and at this point moving on to numbers past 5 would also be appropriate. Additional activities that are important at this early level consist of generalization to different fonts, colors, shapes, and styles of numbers, matching numbers to each other, and practicing rote counting and filling-in missing numbers (e.g., "1, 2..."). There are a variety of number games and songs that also can be of value such as "1, 2, 3 get you!" "1 potato, 2 potato..." "5 little monkeys jumping on a bed...." Additional activities for teaching math skills can be found in the corresponding sections of the VB-MAPP Math Supporting Skills list.

MATH 12-M	Tacts the numbers 1-5.

Once a child can consistently identify the numbers 1-5 (and they are generalized) the focus can shift to counting out items with one-to-one correspondence (e.g., "How many?"), tacts and LDs for the numbers 6-10, and rote counting beyond 10. In addition, a variety of other math related activities should be incorporated into the time allocated for math. These activities include simple measurement (e.g., big and little), simple geometry (e.g., circle, square, triangle), spatial sense (i.e., prepositions), patterns (e.g., clap, stomp, clap, stomp), and classification (e.g., sorting). Several of these skills are contained in other sections of the VB-MAPP.

MATH 13-M	Counts out 1-5 items from a larger set of items with 1 to 1 correspondence (e.g., *Give me 4 cars. Now give me 2 cars*).

Counting out objects with one-to-one correspondence is a major milestone in the development of number skills. It demonstrates the child's ability to put previously rote counting into a purely functional context. Counting out a specific number from a larger set of items is important (otherwise the child just stops counting when the items are gone), as is enumeration (emphasis on the final number), both of which demonstrate true correspondence of the spoken number to the quantity counted. At this point there should be an increased focus on the other aspects of math described above. A variety of functional math activities can help a child learn the many skills related to math. For example, measurement skills can be further developed by pouring water in and out of containers and working on full and empty, or noises can be presented as loud and quiet. Patterns can become more complex and locations such as first and last, top and bottom, near and far, and time markers (yesterday, today, and tomorrow) can also be introduced.

MATH 14-M	Identifies as a listener 8 different comparisons involving measurement (e.g., *show me more or less, big or little, long or short, full or empty, loud or quiet*).

Many of the comparison skills are identified as pre-math skills and some kindergarten math programs start with these concepts. Children acquire these skills at widely varying ages, often due to the amount of specific instruction they receive as they are growing up. At this point in math instruction, continued work is necessary on learning the various aspect of numbers such as matching a specific quantity of items to a specific number and vice versa (e.g., give the child 6 cars and ask him to select the written number that matches the quantity of cars). These types of activities are common for independent work sheets and activities found in many pre-kindergarten math books.

MATH 15-M	Correctly matches a written number to a quantity and a quantity to a written number for the numbers 1-5 (e.g., matches the number 3 to a picture of 3 trucks).

Once a child meets this milestone, and demonstrates the pre-math skills contained in Math Level 3-13-M, he is usually ready for beginning simple addition. Other math related skills that might be appropriate for a child at this level are time concepts (e.g., morning, evening, yesterday today, and tomorrow), money concepts (penny, nickel, and dime), ordering size and position (e.g., ranking little to big, first to last), and the use of measurement tools (e.g., scales and rulers) may be appropriate. There are a variety of commercially available materials for developing these early math skills, and once a child reaches this level, he most likely will benefit from the standard curriculum provided by many regular education programs.

Suggested IEP Goals for Math: Level 3 (select only 1 or 2 goals and modify them as appropriate for the individual child).

- The child will rote count up to 30.

- The child will tact and identify as a listener the numbers 1-10.

- The child will demonstrate 1:1 correspondence in counting to 10.

- The child will match number-to-quantity, and quantity-to-number for 1-10.

- The child will correctly respond to listener tasks involving 10 different math concepts, such as more and less, big and little, long and short, first and last, or near and far, etc.

Conclusion

Applied behavior analysis has had a significant impact on the treatment of individuals with autism or other intellectual disabilities over the past 50 years. The current program suggests that further gains are possible by making systematic use of B. F. Skinner's conceptual analysis of verbal behavior, along with typical developmental milestones as the basic framework for assessment and intervention programs. The VB-MAPP brings together these different areas of study in a set of measurable and quantifiable assessments that identify a child's learning, language, and social needs. The results of the assessments, along with the VB-MAPP Placement program, can help guide the development of an individualized intervention program and allow a child to achieve his maximum potential.

REFERENCES

Andresen, J. T. (1990). Skinner and Chomsky thirty years later. *Historiographia Linguistica, 17,* 145-165.

Attwood, T. (1998). *Asperger's Syndrome: A guide for parents and professionals.* Philadelphia: Jessica Kingsley Publishers.

Axe, J. B. (2008). Conditional discrimination in the intraverbal relation: A review and recommendations for future research. *The Analysis of Verbal Behavior, 24,* 159–174.

Baker, J. S. (2003). *Social skills training for children and adolescents with Asperger Syndrome and social communication problems.* Shawnee Mission, KS: Autism Asperger Publishing.

Barbera, M. L. (2007). *The verbal behavior approach.* London: Jessica Kingsley Publishers.

Barnes, C. S., Mellor, J. R., & Rehfeldt, R. A. (2014). Implementing the *Verbal behavior milestones assessment and placement program (VB-MAPP)*: Teaching assessment techniques. *The Analysis of Verbal Behavior.* doi: 10.1007/s40616-013-0004-5

Barry, A. K. (1998). *English grammar: Language as human behavior.* Upper Saddle River, NJ: Prentice-Hall.

Bellini, S. (2006). *Building social relationships.* Shawnee Mission, KS: Autism Asperger Publishing.

Bijou, S. W., & Baer, D. M. (1961). *Child development I: A systematic and empirical theory.* Englewood Cliffs, NJ: Prentice-Hall.

Bijou, S. W., & Baer, D. M. (1965). *Child development II: Universal stage of infancy.* Englewood Cliffs, NJ: Prentice-Hall.

Bijou, S. W., & Baer, D. M. (1967). *Child development III: Readings in the experimental analysis.* Englewood Cliffs, NJ: Prentice-Hall.

Bijou, S. W., & Ghezzi, P M. (1999). The behavioral interference theory of autistic behavior in young children (pp. 33-43). In P. M. Ghezzi, W. L. Williams, & J. E. Carr (Eds.), *Autism: Behavior analytic perspectives.* Reno, NV: Context Press.

Bijou, S. W., & Sturges, P. T. (1959). Positive reinforcers for experimental studies with children-consumables and manipulatives. *Child Development, 30,* 151-170.

Brady, N. C., Saunders, K. J., & Spradlin, J. E. (1994). A conceptual analysis of request teaching procedures for individuals with severely limited verbal repertoires. *The Analysis of Verbal Behavior, 12,* 43-54.

Brazelton, T. B., & Sparrow, J. D. (2006). *Touchpoints.* Cambridge, MA: Da Capo Books.

Brown, R., Cazden, C., & Bellugi, U. (1969). The child's grammar from I to III. In J. P. Hill (Ed.), *The 1967 symposium on child psychology* (pp. 28-73). Minneapolis, MN: University of Minnesota Press.

Carbone, V. J. (2013). The establishing operation and teaching verbal behavior. *The Analysis of Verbal Behavior, 29,* 45-49.

Carbone, V. J., Morgenstern, B., Zecchin-Tirri, G., & Kolberg, L. (2008). The role of the reflexive conditioned motivating operation (CMO-R) during discrete trial instruction of children with autism. *Journal of Early and Intensive Behavioral Intervention, 4,* 658-680.

Carbone, V. J., O'Brien, L., Sweeney-Kerwin, E. J., & Albert, K. M. (2013). Teaching eye contact to children with autism: A conceptual analysis and single case study. *Education and Treatment of Children, 36,* 139-159.

Carr, E. G., & Durand, V. M. (1985). Reducing behavior problems through functional communication training. *Journal of Applied Behavior Analysis, 18,* 111-126.

Catania, A. C. (1972). Chomsky's formal analysis of natural languages: A behavioral translation. *Behaviorism, 1,* 1-15.

Catania, A. C. (1998). *Learning* (4th ed.). Upper Saddle River, NJ: Prentice-Hall.

Charlop-Christy, M., Carpenter, M. L., Le, L., LeBlanc, L. A., & Kellet, K. (2002). Using the picture exchange communication system (PECS) with children with autism: Assessment of PECS acquisition, speech, social-communicative behavior, and problem behavior. *Journal of Applied Behavior Analysis, 35*, 213-231.

Cooper, J. O., Heron, T. E., & Heward, W. L. (2007). *Applied behavior analysis* (2nd ed.). Upper Saddle River, NJ: Merrill/Prentice-Hall.

Dipuglia, A., & Miklos, M. (2014, May). Instructing functional verbal behavior in the public schools: Recent outcomes from the PaTTAN autism initiative. Paper presented at the 40th Annual Convention of the Association for Behavior Analysis International, Chicago, IL.

Drash, P. W., & Tutor, R. M. (2004). An analysis of autism as a contingency-shaped disorder of verbal behavior. *The Analysis of Verbal Behavior, 20*, 5-23.

Drash, P. W., High, R. L., & Tutor, R. M. (1999). Using mand training to establish an echoic repertoire in young children with autism. *The Analysis of Verbal Behavior, 16*, 29-44.

Eikeseth, S., & Smith, D. P. (2013). An analysis of verbal stimulus control in intraverbal behavior: Implications for practice and applied research. *The Analysis of Verbal Behavior, 29*, 125-135.

Endicott, K., & Higbee, T. S. (2007). Contriving motivating operations to evoke mands for information in preschoolers with autism. *Research in Autism Spectrum Disorders, 1*, 210-217.

Esch, B. E., LaLonde, K. B., & Esch, J. W. (2010). Speech and language assessment: A verbal behavior analysis. *The Journal of Speech-Language Pathology and Applied Behavior Analysis, 5*, 166-191.

Esch, J. W., Mahoney, A. M., Kestner, K. M., LaLonde, K. B., & Esch, B. E., (2013). Echoic and self-echoic responses in children. *The Analysis of Verbal Behavior, 29*, 117-123.

Ferster, C. B., & Skinner, B. F. (1957). *Schedules of reinforcement.* New York: Appleton-Century-Crofts.

Foxx, R. M. (1982). Decreasing behaviors of persons with severe retardation and autism. Champlaign, IL: Research Press.

Frost, L., & Bondy, A. (2002). *The picture exchange communication system (PECS) training manual* (2nd ed.) Newark, DE: Pyramid Products, Inc.

Fuller, P. (1949). Operant conditioning of a vegetative organism. *American Journal of Psychology, 62*, 587-590.

Grannan, L., & Rehfeldt, R. A. (2012). Emergent intraverbal responses via tact and match-to-sample instruction. *Journal of Applied Behavior Analysis, 45*, 601-605.

Greer, R. D., & Ross, D. E. (2007). *Verbal behavior analysis.* Boston: Allyn and Bacon.

Guess, D., & Baer, D. M. (1973). An analysis of individual differences in generalization between receptive and productive language in retarded children. *Journal of Applied Behavior Analysis, 8*, 411-420.

Guess, D., Sailor, W. S., & Baer, D. M. (1976). *A functional speech and language program for the severely retarded.* Lawrence, KS: H & H Enterprises.

Gunby, K. V., Carr, J. E., & LeBlanc, L. A. (2010). Teaching abduction-prevention skills to children with autism. *Journal of Applied Behavior Analysis, 43*, 107-112.

Hall, G. A., & Sundberg, M. L. (1987). Teaching mands by manipulating conditioned establishing operations. *The Analysis of Verbal Behavior, 5*, 41-53.

Halle, J. W., Marshall, A. M., & Spradlin, J. E. (1979). Time delay: A technique to increase language use and facilitate generalization in retarded children. *Journal of Applied Behavior Analysis, 8*, 411-420.

Hart B., & Risley T. R. (1975). Incidental teaching of language in the preschool. *Journal of Applied Behavior Analysis, 8*, 411-420.

Hart, B., & Risley, T. R. (1995). *Meaningful differences in the everyday experience of young American children.* Baltimore, MD: Brookes.

Hedge, H. M. (2010). Language and grammar: A behavioral analysis. *The Journal of Speech-Language Pathology and Applied Behavior Analysis, 5*, 90-213.

Ingvarsson, E. T., & Duy, D. L. (2011). Further evaluation of prompting tactics for establishing intraverbal responding in children with autism. *The Analysis of Verbal Behavior, 27*, 75-93.

Iwata, B.A., Dorsey, M. F., Slifer, K. J., Bauman, K. E., & Richman, G. S. (1994). Toward a functional analysis of self-injury. *Journal of Applied Behavior Analysis, 27*, 197-209. (Reprinted from *Analysis and Intervention in Developmental Disabilities, 2*, 3-20, 1982.)

Kaitlin G., Causin, K. G., Albert, K. M., Carbone, V. J., & Sweeney-Kerwin, E. J. (2013). The role of joint control in teaching listener responding to children with autism and other developmental disabilities. *Research in Autism Spectrum Disorders, 7*, 997-1011.

Kent, L. (1974). *Language acquisition program for the retarded or multiply impaired.* Champaign, IL: Research Press.

Koegel, R. L., & Koegel, L. K. (1995). *Teaching children with autism: Strategies for initiating positive interactions and improving learning opportunities.* Baltimore: Brooks.

Krantz, P. J., & McClannahan, L. E. (1993). Teaching children with autism to initiate with peers: The effects of script fading. *The Journal of Applied Behavior Analysis, 26*, 121-132.

Krempa, J., & McKinnon, K. (2005). *Social skills solutions.* New York: DRL Books.

Lamarre, J., & Holland, J. G. (1985). The functional independence of mands and tacts. *Journal of the Experimental Analysis of Behavior, 43*, 5-19.

Leaf, R., & McEachin, J. (1998). *A work in progress.* New York: DRL Books.

Leaf, R., Taubman, M., & McEachin, J. (2008). *It's time for school.* New York: DRL Books.

Lechago, S. A., Carr, J. E., Grow, J. R., Love, J. R., & Almason, S. M. (2010). Mands for information generalize across establishing operations. *Journal of Applied Behavior Analysis, 43*, 381–395.

Lee, V. L. (1981). Prepositional phrases spoken and heard. *Journal of the Experimental Analysis of Behavior, 35*, 227-242.

Lepper, T. A., Petursdottir, A. I., & Esch, B. A.

(2013). Effects of operant discrimination training on the vocalizations of nonverbal children with autism. J*ournal of Applied Behavior Analysis, 46*, 656–661.

Lorah, E., Tincani, M., Dodge, J., Gilroy, S., Hickey, A., & Hantula, D. (2013). Evaluating picture exchange and the iPad as a speech generating device to teach communication to young children with autism. *Journal of Developmental and Physical Disabilities, 25*, 637-649.

Lovaas, O. I. (1977). *The autistic child: Language development through behavior modification.* New York: Irvington.

Lovaas, O. I. (2003). *Teaching individuals with developmental delays.* Austin, TX: Pro-ed.

Lowenkron, B. (1998). Some logical functions of joint control. *Journal of the Experimental Analysis of Behavior, 69*, 327–354.

Malott, R. W., & Trojan, E. A. (2008). *Principles of behavior* (6th ed.). Upper Saddle River, NJ: Prentice Hall.

Martin, G., & Pear, J. (2003). *Behavior modification: What is it and how to do it* (7th ed.). Upper Saddle River, NJ: Prentice-Hall.

Maurice, C., Green, G., & Luce, S.C. (1996). *Behavior interventions for young children with autism.* Austin, TX: Pro-ed.

Meyerson, L., Michael, J., Mowrer, O. H., Osgood, C. E., & Staats, A. W. (1963). Learning, behavior and rehabilitation. In L. Loftquist (Ed.), *Psychological research in rehabilitation.* Washington: American Psychological Association.

Michael, J. (1982a). Distinguishing between discriminative and motivational functions of stimuli. *Journal of the Experimental Analysis of Behavior, 37, 149-155.*

Michael, J. (1982b). Skinner's elementary verbal relations: Some new categories. *The Analysis of Verbal Behavior, 1*, 1-4.

Michael, J. (1984). Verbal behavior. *Journal of the Experimental Analysis of Behavior, 42*, 363-376.

Michael, J. (1988). Establishing operations and the mand. *The Analysis of Verbal Behavior, 6*, 3-9.

Michael, J. (2004). *Concepts and principles of behavior analysis* (rev. ed.). (2nd ed.). Kalamazoo, MI: Association for Behavior Analysis.

Michael, J. (2007). Motivating operations. In J. O. Cooper, T. E. Heron, & W. L. Heward, (Eds.), *Applied behavior analysis* (2 nd ed.) (pp. 374-391). Upper Saddle River, NJ: Merrill/Prentice Hall.

Michael, J., Palmer, D. C., & Sundberg, M. L. (2011). The multiple control of verbal behavior. *The Analysis of Verbal Behavior*, 27, 3–22.

Miguel, C. F. (2013). Jack Michael's motivation. *The Analysis of Verbal Behavior*, 29, 3-11.

Miltenberger, R. (2004). *Behavior modification: Principles and procedures* (3rd ed.). Belmont, CA: Wadsworth/Thomson Learning.

Morris, E. K., Smith, N. G., & Altus, D. E. (2005). B. F. Skinner's contributions to applied behavior analysis. *The Behavior Analyst*, 28, 99-131.

Neef, N. A., & Peterson, S. M. (2007). Functional behavior assessment. In J. O. Cooper, T. E. Heron, & W. L. Heward (Eds.), *Applied behavior analysis* (2 nd ed.) (pp. 499-524). Upper Saddle River, NJ: Merrill/Prentice Hall.

Novak, G. (1996). *Developmental psychology: Dynamical systems and behavior analysis.* Reno, NV: Context Press.

Oah, S., & Dickinson, A. M. (1989). A review of empirical studies of verbal behavior. *The Analysis of Verbal Behavior, 7,* 53-68.

Palmer, D. C. (1996). Achieving parity: The role of automatic reinforcement. *Journal of The Experimental Analysis of Behavior, 65,* 289-290.

Partington, J. W., & Sundberg, M. L. (1998). *The assessment of basic language and learning skills (The ABLLS).* Pleasant Hill, CA: Behavior Analysts, Inc.

Peterson, N. (1978). *An introduction to verbal behavior.* Grand Rapids, MI: Behavior Associates, Inc.

Petursdottir, A. I., & Carr, J. E. (2011). A review of recommendations for sequencing receptive and expressive language instruction. J*ournal of Applied Behavior Analysis, 46,* 859-876.

Sautter, R. A., & LeBlanc, L. A. (2006). Empirical applications of Skinner's analysis of verbal behavior with humans. *The Analysis of Verbal Behavior, 22,* 35-48.

Schlinger, H. D., Jr. (1995). *A behavior analytic view of child development.* New York: Plenum Press.

Schlinger, H. D., Jr. (2008). The long goodbye: Why B.F. Skinner's *Verbal Behavior* is alive and well on the 50th anniversary of its publication. *The Psychological Record, 58,* 329-337.

Schramm, R. (2006). *Educate toward recovery: Turning the tables on autism.* Germany: Knospe-ABA.

Shafer, E. (1993). Teaching topography-based and stimulus selection-based verbal behavior to developmentally disabled individuals: Some considerations. *The Analysis of Verbal Behavior, 11,* 117-133.

Sidman, M., & Tailby, W. (1982). Conditional discrimination vs. matching-to-sample: An expansion of the testing paradigm. *Journal of the Experimental Analysis of Behavior, 37,* 5-22.

Sigafoos, J., Doss, S., & Reichle, J. (1989). Developing mand and tact repertoires with persons with severe developmental disabilities with graphic symbols. *Research in Developmental Disabilities, 11,* 165-176.

Skinner, B. F. (1953). *Science and human behavior.* New York: Free Press.

Skinner, B. F. (1957). *Verbal behavior.* New York: Appleton-Century-Crofts.

Spradlin, J. E. (1963). Assessment of speech and language of retarded children: The Parsons language sample. *Journal of Speech and Hearing Disorders Monograph, 10,* 8-31.

Spradlin, J. E., Cotter, V. W., & Baxley, N. (1973). Establishing a conditional discrimination without training: A study of transfer with retarded adolescents. *American Journal of Mental Deficiency, 77,* 556-566.

Staats, A. W., Staats, C. K., Schutz, R. E., & Wolf, M. (1962). The conditioning of textual responses using "extrinsic" reinforcers. *Journal of the Experimental Analysis of Behavior, 5,* 33-40.

Stokes, T. F., & Baer, D. M. (1977). An implicit technology of generalization. *Journal of Applied Behavior Analysis, 10, 349-367.*

Sundberg, C. T., Hall, G., & Elia, J. (2014, May). Assessing outcomes of intensive ABA/verbal behavior therapy for children with autism using the VB-MAPP. Paper presented at the 40th Annual Convention of the Association for Behavior Analysis International, Chicago, IL.

Sundberg, C. T., & Sundberg, M. L. (1990). Comparing topography-based verbal behavior with stimulus selection-based verbal behavior. *The Analysis of Verbal Behavior, 8, 31-41.*

Sundberg, M. L. (1980). *Developing a verbal repertoire using sign language and Skinner's analysis of verbal behavior.* Unpublished doctoral dissertation, Western Michigan University.

Sundberg, M. L. (1983). Language. In J. L. Matson, & S. E. Breuning (Eds.), *Assessing the mentally retarded* (pp. 285-310). New York: Grune & Stratton.

Sundberg, M. L. (1987). *Teaching language to the developmentally disabled.* Prince George, BC: College of New Caledonia Press.

Sundberg, M. L. (1990). *Teaching verbal behavior to the developmentally disabled.* Pleasant Hill, CA: Behavior Analysts, Inc.

Sundberg, M. L. (1993a). The application of establishing operations. *The Behavior Analyst, 16, 211-214.*

Sundberg, M. L. (1993b). Selecting a response form for nonverbal persons: Facilitated communication, pointing systems, or sign language? *The Analysis of Verbal Behavior, 11, 99-116.*

Sundberg, M. L. (2004). A behavioral analysis of motivation and its relation to mand training. In L. W. Williams (Ed.), *Developmental disabilities: Etiology, assessment, intervention, and integration* (pp. 199-220). Reno NV: Context Press.

Sundberg, M. L. (2007). Verbal behavior. In J. O. Cooper, T. E. Heron, & W. L. Heward (Eds.), *Applied behavior analysis* (2nd ed.) (pp. 526-547). Upper Saddle River, NJ: Merrill/Prentice Hall.

Sundberg, M. L. (2013). Thirty points about motivation from Skinner's book *Verbal behavior. The Analysis of Verbal Behavior, 27, 13–40.*

Sundberg, M. L., Loeb, M., Hale, L., & Eigenheer, P. (2002). Contriving establishing operations to teach mands for information. *The Analysis of Verbal Behavior, 18, 14-28.*

Sundberg, M. L., & Michael, J. (2001). The benefits of Skinner's analysis of verbal behavior for children with autism. *Behavior Modification, 25, 698-724.*

Sundberg, M. L., Michael, J., Partington, J. W., & Sundberg, C. A. (1996). The role of automatic reinforcement in early language acquisition. *The Analysis of Verbal Behavior, 13, 21-37.*

Sundberg, M. L., Ray, D. A., Braam, S. E., Stafford, M. W., Reuber, T. M., & Braam, C. A. (1979). A manual for the use of B. F. Skinner's analysis of verbal behavior for language assessment and programming. *Western Michigan University Behavioral Monograph #9* Kalamazoo, MI.

Sundberg, M. L., & Partington, J. W. (1998). *Teaching language to children with autism or other developmental disabilities.* Concord, CA: AVB Press.

Sundberg M. L., & Partington, J. W. (1999). The need for both discrete trial training and natural environment training for children with autism. In P. M. Ghezzi, W. L. Williams, & J. E. Carr (Eds.), *Autism: Behavior analytic perspectives* (139-156). Reno, NV: Context Press.

Sundberg, M. L., San Juan, B., Dawdy, M., & Arguelles, M. (1990). The acquisition of tacts, mands, and intraverbals by individuals with traumatic brain injury. *The Analysis of Verbal Behavior, 8, 83-99.*

Sundberg, M. L., & Sundberg, C. A. (2011). Intraverbal behavior and verbal conditional discriminations in typically developing children and children with autism. *The Analysis of Verbal Behavior, 27, 23–43.*

Sweeney-Kerwin, E. J., Carbone, V. J., O'Brien, L., Zecchin, G., & Janecky, M. N. (2007). Transferring control of the mand to motivating operations in children with autism. *The Analysis of Verbal Behavior, 23*, 89-102.

Taubman, M., Leaf, R., & McEachin, J. (2011). *Crafting connections: Contemporary applied behavior analysis for enriching the social lives of persons with autism spectrum disorder*. New York: DRL Books.

Taylor, B. A., & Jasper, S. (2001). Teaching programs to increase peer interactions. In C. Maurice, G. Green, & R. M. Foxx (Eds.), *Making a difference* (pp. 97-162). Austin, TX: Pro Ed.

Tincani, M. (2004). Comparing picture exchange communication system (PECS) and sign language training for children with autism. *Focus on Autism and Other Developmental Disabilities, 19*, 162-173.

Touchette, P. E. (1971). Transfer of stimulus control: Measuring the moment of transfer. *Journal of the Experimental Analysis of Behavior, 15*, 347-354.

Twyman, J. S. (1996). The functional independence of impure mands and tacts of abstract stimulus properties. *The Analysis of Verbal Behavior, 13*, 1-19.

Vandbakk, M., Arntzen, E., Gisnaas, A., Antonsen, V., & Gundhus, T. (2012). Effect of training different classes of verbal behavior to decrease aberrant verbal behavior. *The Analysis of Verbal Behavior, 28*, 137-144.

Vargas, J. S. (2009). *Behavior analysis for effective teaching*. New York: Routledge/ Taylor & Francis Group.

Vaughan, M. E., & Michael, J. L. (1982). Automatic reinforcement: An important but ignored concept. *Behaviorism, 10*, 217-227.

Watkins, C. L., Pack-Teixteira, L., & Howard, J. S. (1989). Teaching intraverbal behavior to severely retarded children. *The Analysis of Verbal Behavior, 7*, 69-81.

Watts, A. C., Wilder, D. A., Gregory, M. K., Leon, Y., & Ditzian, K. (2013). The effects of rules on differential reinforcement of other behavior. *Journal of Applied Behavior Analysis, 46*, 680-684.

Weiss, M. J., & Harris, S. L. (2001). Teaching social skills to people with autism. *Behavior Modification, 25*, 785-802.

Wolf, M. M., Risley T. R., & Mees H. (1964). Applications of operant conditioning procedures to the behavior problems of an autistic child. *Behavior Research and Therapy, 1*, 305-312.

Wolfberg, P. J. (1999). *Play and imaginative behavior in children with autism*. New York: Teachers College Press.

Yoon, S., & Bennett, G. M. (2000). Effects of a stimulus-stimulus pairing procedure on conditioning vocal sounds as reinforcers. *The Analysis of Verbal Behavior, 17*, 75-88.